M000233817

REVISED EDITION

## Month-By-Month™
### WHAT TO DO EACH MONTH TO HAVE A BEAUTIFUL GARDEN ALL YEAR

# GARDENING
# GEORGIA
## IN

Copyright © 2001, Revised and Additional Content Copyright © 2006 Walter Reeves and Erica Glasener

All Rights Reserved. No part of this book may be reproduced or transmitted in any form or by any means, electronic or mechanical, including photocopying, recording, or by any information storage and retrieval system, without permission in writing from the publisher.

Published by Cool Springs Press
101 Forrest Crossing Boulevard
Franklin, Tennessee, 37064

Reeves, Walter.
    Month-by-month gardening in Georgia : what to do each month to have a
    beautiful garden all year / Walter Reeves & Erica Glasener. – Rev. ed.
        p. cm.
    Includes bibliographical references and index.
    ISBN-10: 1-59186-251-5 (pbk.)
    ISBN-13: 978-1-59186-251-2
    1. Gardening–Georgia. I. Glasener, Erica. II. Title.
SB453.2.G4R44 2006
635.09758–dc22

                                        2006026338

First Printing Revised Edition 2006

Printed in the United States
10 9 8 7 6 5 4 3

Managing Editor: Billie Brownell
Designer: James Duncan, James Duncan Creative
Production Design: S.E. Anderson

Visit Cool Springs Press website at **www.coolspringspress.net**

## PHOTOGRAPHY AND ILLUSTRATION CREDITS

On the Cover: Pink dogwood, © Lee Anne White, Lee Anne White Photography

Page 7 (bottom of page): verbena, © Dency Kane

All illustrations Copyright © by Bill Kersey, Kersey Design

Copyright © all photographs:

Thomas Eltzroth: pages 14 (impatiens border, bottom of page); 53; 64; 76 (peach, top of page); 90; 92; 98; 104 (fescue lawn, bottom of page & zoysia close-up, top of page); 122; 133 (aster, top of page); 164 (rose, top of page); 172; 178; 180; 188 (loropetalum, top of page); 209; 217 (apple trees underplanted with annuals, bottom of page); 228; 245; 246 (morning glory, top of page); 254; 256; 261; 263; 268; 270; 273; 276

Neil Soderstrom: pages 36; 63; 66; 73; 84; 103; 141; 142; 144; 148; 152; 158; 166; 171; 176; 198; 212; 226; 236; 264; 275;

Jerry Pavia: pages 7 (rhododendron, top of page); 14 (zinnias, top of page); 26; 32; 38; 44 (drumstick allium, top of page & iris path, bottom of page); 60; 160; 163 (climbing roses, bottom of page); 206;

Liz Ball and Rick Ray: pages 68; 76 (harvest bench, bottom of page); 130; 133 (heuchera, bottom of page); 188 (azalea landscape, bottom of page); 216; 238; 242; 256; 267;

Lorenzo Gunn: page 217 (magnolia, top of page)

Andre Viette: page 246 (clematis, bottom of page)

REVISED EDITION

# Month-By-Month™
### WHAT TO DO EACH MONTH TO HAVE A BEAUTIFUL GARDEN ALL YEAR

# GARDENING in GEORGIA

## WALTER REEVES AND
## ERICA GLASENER

COOL
SPRINGS
PRESS

Franklin, Tennessee

# DEDICATION

To my wife, Sandi, my gardening partner forever.
—W. R.

To my Nana, who loved nature and beauty, and whose art continues to inspire me.
—E. L. G.

# ACKNOWLEDGEMENTS

We are grateful for the research and information provided by the dedicated
county agents, specialists and Master Gardeners who tirelessly serve the citizens of this
state through The University of Georgia Cooperative Extension Service.
Erica especially thanks Daryl and her family for their loving support.

# CONTENTS

# BASIC HORTICULTURAL PRACTICES

Are you instantly skilled at whatever you try to do? Of course not! You practiced long and hard in your parents' car before you were ready to hit the highway. Professional athletes spend their youth mastering the basics of their sport in order to rise to the top of the sports world. Great cooks don't become great by making macaroni and cheese from a box.

Successful gardeners don't become one without experience. Maybe in the past they started a few annuals, planted some seeds, pruned a bush, or dug weeds from their lawn. Each completed task gave them confidence to try another. Many say they learned the most from their failures, not from their achievements.

Some folks are convinced their thumbs can never be as green as their neighbors'. They look at a beautiful bed of flowers, a pristine lawn, or a neat landscape and persuade themselves that others have some secret they can never share.

In truth, all they lack is experience. A basketball player will practice his jumpshot thousands of times. Some shots will go in; some will bounce off the rim; some will fly over the backboard. Still the ballplayer practices, confident that eventually his successes will outnumber his failures.

To be a good gardener, you have to start somewhere. If you were lucky enough to have a parent or neighbor who taught you the basics, GREAT . . . but you still have lots to learn! If you grew up in a tenth-floor apartment and have never planted a plant, GREAT . . . you can learn the basics without having to get rid of any misconceptions.

Every gardener needs to know the basics. What follows are some of the skills and techniques you should know in order to grow as you garden.

## TESTING YOUR SOIL

Plants need adequate nutrients in order to grow properly. They receive the nutrients from the soil and from the fertilizer you add. In order to know how much fertilizer to add, your soil should be tested at least every two years. (See pages 7 and 8, Testing the Soil.)

Good gardeners notice when they have different soil types in different areas of their landscape. It is possible that you have the same soil throughout. It might be a dark brown, sandy loam; a gray, sticky clay; or common Georgia red clay. If earth grading was done before your home was built, perhaps the front yard is one soil type and the backyard is another.

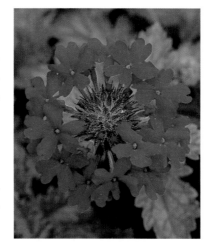

Separate samples of soil should be collected from each of your soil types. After you have tested the soil, you can decide how to fertilize each area properly.

## TESTING THE SOIL

1. Use a clean trowel and bucket. In each area with different soil, take ten plugs (deep, hearty scoops) of soil. A plug should be four to six inches

# BASIC HORTICULTURAL PRACTICES

deep so that soil from the plant root zone will be tested, not the soil on top of the ground. Place the plugs in the bucket.

2. When ten plugs have been collected from an area, mix them together in the bucket. Remove stones, grass, worms, and other materials. Scoop out approximately two 8-ounce cups of soil—this is a representative sample of all the soil in a particular area.

Repeat steps 1 and 2 for each different type of soil in your landscape.

3. Test the soil.

**Using a Commercial Kit:** Purchase a soil-testing kit from a garden center and read the directions carefully. If you do not understand them, ask a garden center employee or a gardening friend to explain them. Most kits require that you add chemicals to a small sample of soil and water, and to wait for a color change. Once the color has developed, it can be compared to a color chart, giving you an estimate of the nutrients available for your plants. Commercial kits are generally easy to use, but the results might not be as accurate as you would like. It takes a sharp eye to compare colors, a task made more difficult by the orange hue of Georgia red clay.

**Using a Laboratory:** The most convenient soil-testing laboratory is usually the University of Georgia Soils Laboratory. Look in the phone book under the government listings for your county, under either "Cooperative Extension Service" or "University of Georgia." Your County Extension office can give you details on how to bring a soil sample to them. There is a nominal charge, in the range of $8 to $12, for each sample. The University of Georgia Soils Laboratory will test your soil and send you a written report on the nutrients it contains. The acidity (pH) of the soil will be noted. Fertilizer recommendations are included, along with the amount of lime your soil needs. A single composite sample of soil can be tested for five different plants that might be grow-

ing in that soil type in your landscape. In other words, if you are growing flowers, fescue, azaleas, and a maple tree in your front yard, specify that your soil should be tested, and recommendations given, for each. The single laboratory charge includes up to five individual tests.

4. Interpret the results: The most important soil-test result is the acidity (pH) of the soil. Add the recommended amount of lime to your soil before worrying about fertilizers. The commercial kits will make general recommendations for the amount of fertilizer to use, but the laboratory will recommend specific amounts. Don't worry if you cannot find the exact fertilizer analysis mentioned in a soil-test result. If 10-10-10 fertilizer is recommended, either 8-8-8 or 13-13-13 can be substituted as long as you use a bit more or a bit less, respectively, than the recommended amount of 10-10-10.

## UNDERSTANDING THE NUMBERS ON A FERTILIZER BAG

There are three major nutrients needed by a plant: Nitrogen (N), Phosphorus (P), and Potassium (K). The numbers on a container of fertilizer denote the percentages of N, P, and K inside. For example, a bag of 24-4-8 has 24 percent Nitrogen, 4 percent Phosphorus, and 8 percent Potassium. Thirty-six percent of the bag's content is plant food; the rest is an inert filler, like clay. Nitrogen, phosphorus, and potassium are called *macro*nutrients because plants need them in significant amounts.

1. *What does nitrogen do?*

Nitrogen promotes the growth of roots, stems, and leaves. An appropriate supply of nitrogen gives plants healthy dark-green foliage. Too much nitrogen can cause growth to be too rapid, causing the plant to grow tall and fall over. Excess nitrogen can also delay or prevent flower and fruit formation.

2. *What does phosphorus do?*

- Plants store energy in their seeds, roots, and bark, and they need adequate phosphorus in order to flower. Phosphorus is essential for flower, fruit, and seed production. Plants lacking sufficient phosphorus usually have purplish leaves, petioles, and stems. They grow slowly and mature very late.

3. *What does potassium do?*

Potassium is important for the manufacturing of carbohydrates (sugar and starch) by plants. When sufficient potassium is available, plants produce stiff, erect stems, and the plants are more disease-resistant. When insufficient or excess potassium is in the soil, plants contain too much water, are susceptible to cold injury, and growth is reduced.

4. *What do micronutrients do?*

Plants also need other chemicals in order to grow and remain healthy. Because smaller amounts of these nutrients are needed, they are called *micronutrients*. Calcium (Ca), magnesium (Mg), iron (Fe), sulfur (S), and many other chemicals are needed in small amounts. A lack of calcium in tomatoes causes the condition known as blossom end rot. A lack of iron can cause leaves to turn yellow. Most Georgia soils have enough micronutrients to keep plants healthy. If your soil is very sandy or is all clay, additional micronutrients may be needed. The best way to supply micronutrients is by mixing composted manure, homemade compost, or "enriched" fertilizer with your soil.

5. *What does garden lime do?*

Garden lime raises the pH of soil. Georgia soils tend to be acidic by nature, and regular applications of fertilizer tend to acidify the soil even further. Acid soil ties up many nutrients. They are less available to your plants even though they may be physically present in the soil. For this reason, lime is regularly applied to soil to counteract the soil's acidity and raise its pH.

6. *What is pH?*

pH is a numerical measurement of a soil's acidity. The pH number scale ranges from 0 to 14.

A number from 0 to 7 indicates acid conditions. A number from 7 to 14 indicates an alkaline soil. Most plants grow best when the soil pH is between 5.5 and 6.5. Some plants, like azaleas, blueberries, and centipede grass, tolerate more acidic soil than other plants and usually do not need lime.

## PREPARING A BED

Just as newlyweds select a cozy bed to share each night, plants must be given a comfortable bed (of a completely different nature) in which to grow. Preparing the bed is a simple but vital job. If you plant bulbs in hard clay, they will never look like the picture on the garden magazine cover. If you install a hosta in full sunshine and sandy soil in south Georgia, you'll have nothing but bleached leaves by July.

Preparing a bed requires a bit of work, but it is a chore that will reward you and your plants for years to come. Plant roots need three things: oxygen, moisture, and nutrients. The magic ingredient that provides these three things is organic matter. Whether you use composted pine bark, animal manure, or compost that you make yourself, it is almost always a good idea to mix organic matter into your existing soil before you plant.

Adding the right amount is important, too. A dusting of rotten leaves added to a bed does no good. Your goal should be to have a bed that is one-third organic matter and two-thirds existing soil.

## PREPARING A COZY BED

1. Use a shovel or rototiller to dig up the soil in the location you've chosen. The soil should be loosened to a depth of ten inches.

2. Thoroughly break up the big clods of earth. All clumps should be less than one inch in diameter.

3. Add a layer of organic matter two inches thick to the area you tilled. Mix it deeply and completely with the existing soil.

# BASIC HORTICULTURAL PRACTICES

There is an alternative to adding only organic matter to the soil. Expanded shale can be added to the soil to keep it loose on a long-term basis. Expanded shale does not hold moisture or nutrients very well, but unlike organic matter, it permanently loosens and does not disappear from your soil. Mix a two-inch layer of expanded shale plus a one-inch layer of organic matter into your bed if you use this product.

## REPLACING ORGANIC MATTER

Summer heat and Georgia rainfall will slowly cook away the organic matter in your garden soil. A few years after you worked so hard to make good planting beds, they will need another infusion of rich organic matter. This presents a problem if you have a bed of perennials or shrubs that you don't intend to move. The best way to replenish organic matter is to add a one-inch layer of composted manure on top of the soil each January. First rake away any mulch around your plants, add the manure, then cover with fresh mulch. When the soil warms, earthworms will go to work tilling the soil—without any more work on your part!

## COMPOSTING

The best source of organic matter for your garden is homemade compost. Why is it better than the store-bought stuff? Because it's alive!

Compost is full of tiny fungi, bacteria, and other creatures. These organisms can digest leaves, grass clippings, lettuce leaves, and wood chips. Euphemistically, we say they "break down" these items. In fact, they eat and then excrete organic materials. As anyone who has changed a baby diaper knows, poop is sticky. The sticky excreta of fungi and bacteria is made that way by a substance called glomalin. This glomalin glues together the tiny particles of clay in your soil. When tiny grains of soil become big soil granules, the soil becomes soft and loose. Sterilized cow manure can't do that. Composted wood fiber can't do that. Both are valuable soil amendments . . . but compost is best.

Composting is not rocket science! If you have a corner where two fences meet, pile your fall leaves there. In six months, you'll have compost. In fact, there are just two steps to making compost:

1. PILE IT UP. Compost bins can be purchased, or you can simply make one out of stiff welded-wire fencing. Join the ends of a piece of fencing that is four feet high and ten feet long. The hollow barrel you create is a perfect compost bin. Pile leaves and grass clippings in it during the year. Next spring, lift the bin off the pile and scoop out the rich compost underneath the top layer.

2. LET IT ROT. There is no need for "compost helper" products; Mother Nature will make compost without your help. Experienced composters turn their piles a few times a year to make the process go faster. However, organic matter will decompose whether the pile is turned or not. A good spraying with the garden hose while the leaves are being piled will help keep the pile moist. A shovelful of soil sprinkled over each successive bag of leaves will introduce all the fungi needed to make perfect compost by next summer.

You can also add grass clippings, raw kitchen vegetables, raked leaves, coffee grounds, and many other things. Eventually compost will happen!

## SUNSHINE VS. SHADE

Jekyll Island is a great place to sit on a sunny beach during the hot summer. Even the hardiest beach bums, though, know to apply lots of sunscreen before they sit down for a noontime picnic. Brasstown Bald is a magnificent mountain, but even locals don't climb it in January without dressing in their warmest clothing. The point is, people can adapt to their surroundings. In general, plants can't. The location you choose for your plants must match their tolerance for sunshine and other weather conditions.

This is not as hard as it seems. Nurseries do a good job labeling the conditions their plants prefer. Study the plant label before you purchase a plant to make sure it will be happy where you site it.

That said, sometimes nursery labels are less informative than you'd like. What does a sunshine icon on a label mean when it is half darkened? Does it mean the plant prefers constant partial shade or a half-day of full sunshine? Is the label truly accurate for Georgia's intense sunshine conditions? Would the plant be happy in full Ohio sunshine but scorched after a day's worth of Georgia's July heat?

## JUDGING LIGHT CONDITIONS

We realize that sunshine intensity differs across Georgia. Compare the noon sunshine in Savannah to noon sunshine in Blairsville: they're radically different! This is how we define sunshine conditions in Georgia:

**Full sunshine** in south Georgia is unfiltered sunshine for more than eight hours per day; in north Georgia, it is unfiltered sunshine from morning to night.

**Partial shade** (moderate shade) in south Georgia is all-day sunshine filtered through high pine or hardwood (oak, maple, poplar, etc.) foliage *or* three hours of direct sunshine between sunrise and noon followed by shade; in north Georgia, it is sunshine filtered through high pine foliage *or* four hours of direct sunshine between sunrise and noon.

**Shade** in south Georgia is all-day sunshine filtered through dense hardwood foliage OR direct sunshine that hits the plant less than two hours per day; in north Georgia, it is all-day sunshine filtered through scattered hardwoods OR direct sunshine that hits the plant less than three hours per day.

**Dense shade** means no direct sunshine hits the plant all day; this might be the shade under a southern magnolia, or the shade between two houses whose shadows prevent sunshine from hitting the earth at all.

## AND WHAT ABOUT THOSE TONGUE-TWISTING LATIN PLANT NAMES?

Latin plant names help gardeners know exactly which plant they have or want, regardless of the plant's physical appearance. A plant's common name is usually unique, but not always. The plant your neighbor calls wild honeysuckle is likely not the pestiferous vine—it is probably a native azalea. Neither rose of Sharon nor moss rose are true roses. Someone just thought they looked like a rose, and the names have been commonly used through the years.

When we want you to know about a specific plant in this book, we use the scientific name so you'll know exactly which one we are describing. You don't have to know or use Latin plant names, but it does help to know that there is a big difference between a magnificent dogwood *Cornus florida* 'Cherokee Princess' and a sparsely flowering *Cornus florida* 'Transplanted It Out of the Woods Years Ago'!

## SUMMARY

Gardening success can be summarized in just three rules:

1. Know your plants.
2. Know your site.
3. Even if you ignore the first two rules, plant anyway!

You might have success in spite of yourself or you might suffer failure. Either way, you'll learn and have fun and you will have started down the road to being A SUCCESSFUL GARDENER IN GEORGIA!

# INTRODUCTION

Gardening in Georgia is a year-round affair. Gardeners in the northern United States have a long rest each year during their severe winters. Not us! Even in winter there is a day or two each week when something productive can be accomplished in your landscape. Our growing season is such that many different plants can be grown in Georgia, from tropical fruit in Hahira to alpine evergreens in Hiawassee.

A beautiful landscape enhances your home in many ways. Not only does your property value increase when you landscape your home, your house has more curb appeal. Your landscape garden can serve as a retreat from the hectic pace of everyday life or an extension of the indoors, providing a place to entertain friends or dine outdoors. Like any other art form, gardening gives you an opportunity to be creative, whether you simply plant a few pots of brightly colored annuals or develop an elaborate landscape with shrubs, trees, annuals, and perennials, offering something of interest for every season. Gardening is also a stress reliever. Plants don't talk back, and many reward us with fragrant flowers, colorful foliage, and striking bark colors.

With all the gardening opportunities we enjoy, it is natural to feel a bit overwhelmed. There are weeks in April when it seems that everything must be done now! That's why we decided to write this book: to help guide you through your garden tasks all year long.

We have divided the book into nine chapters, each devoted to a group of plants we think is important. Each chapter follows the calendar year (January through December) with suggested tasks for each month, such as planning, planting, watering, fertilizing, pest control, and pruning. When possible, we have included lists of plant combinations or plants for special areas, such as ground covers for shade or annual vines with colorful flowers.

In addition to featuring each month in each chapter, we provide lists of plants recommended for our region. Our soil, heat, and humidity dictate what can be grown and require that you prepare the soil before you plant. Knowing which plants will thrive, and what they need, is half the battle. We also provide information about using (or not using) pesticides. The section on garden chemicals attempts to give you the information you need when you are deciding whether or not to use a pesticide.

Gardening in Georgia is, above all, a humbling experience. No one can know everything about every plant. Rosarians might not know rutabagas; fruit growers might not know a ficus from a fothergilla. Each of us will be an amateur at one thing and an expert at something else. Gardeners who have just begun to learn can be discouraged by failure. Every leafless plant or fruitless tomato seems to signify that the gardener did something wrong. Gardeners who have traveled farther down the path, though, think of failure as just one more way to make good compost.

We hope this book helps you find an area in your garden in which you can excel. There is no shame in trying small bits at a time, and there is great enjoyment when your efforts succeed. Read closely, work hard, look for miracles . . . and have a great time gardening in Georgia!

## GEORGIA'S GARDENING REGIONS

The United States Department of Agriculture has divided the country into hardiness zones based on the lowest temperatures expected in the region. Georgia spreads across two hardiness zones. The area below a line drawn between Columbus and Augusta is zone 8. The area above that line is zone 7. Colder parts of the country have zones with lower numbers. When purchasing a perennial plant or shrub, you will find its care tag often specifies the hardiness zone for which it is best suited.

Always consult plant tags to determine if plants are suited for your weather. If a plant is listed as "Hardy to zone 6," it is assumed that it can withstand any cold temperatures that zone 7 might present. On the other hand, a plant listed for zones 8 to 9 cannot be expected to survive a winter in the northern part of the state without extremely good care!

## GARDEN TOOLS

Gardening is not a mental exercise. It requires tools to help you accomplish a task quickly or properly. While we occasionally recommend motorized tools such as lawn mowers, aerators, and rototillers, the following list of basic tools should be adequate for you to start gardening with.

Basic tools for the garden or landscape:

1. **Long-handled, round-blade shovel.** The rounded point allows you to push it deeper into the soil than a flat-blade shovel. The long handle gives the leverage needed to lift and turn over the soil.

2. **Handpruners.** The kind with bypass blades usually lasts longer than the type with a blade and anvil.

3. **Spading fork.** It looks like a pitchfork, but the tines are shorter and wider. Great for digging bulbs or potatoes, a spading fork also penetrates clay soil better than a shovel.

4. **Bow rake (also called an iron rake).** It has short tines on one side attached to a steel frame (the bow). Useful for raking soil smooth.

5. **Hand trowel.** Solid, one-piece models like Corona™ and others last much longer than those with flimsy handles, which are only slightly less expensive.

6. **Leaf rake.** Plastic or metal, they are more useful and quieter than a leaf blower.

7. **Wheelbarrow.** Every time you have to carry a heavy bag of lime from your car or transport a pile of leaves to your compost pile, you'll be glad you have this handy tool.

As your interest in gardening increases, you will probably want to purchase additional tools, depending on the type of gardening you do. To save money, keep an eye out for tools at flea markets or yard sales.

# ANNUALS

Annual flowers are the workhorses of a summer garden. Many perennials bloom for only a few weeks, but annuals can provide colorful flowers for months at a time. As their name implies, annual plants live for only one growing season, although some seem to be perennial because they self-seed each year. Summer annuals, like impatiens, are planted in spring and die with the first frost. Winter annuals, like pansies, are planted in fall and bloom through spring until summer heat sets in.

Most landscapes include both annual and perennial plants, drawing on the strengths of each. While perennials set up housekeeping in one spot for the long haul and may not achieve blooming maturity before a year has passed, annuals have a "live fast, die young" attitude.

There is another class of flowering garden plants that take two years to reach maturity. These plants are known as biennials because they require a season of growth, followed by a period of rest, in order to produce their blooms. Foxglove is an example of a biennial. Seedlings should be planted in early fall in order to accomplish good growth before winter. After a rest during the cold months, the foxglove plant will grow even more before producing its spire of tubular blooms the following spring.

Though they may live in your garden for less than a year, annuals require the same attention to soil preparation as do other plants. See Horticultural Practices, p. 9, to find out how to make the soil ready for planting.

## CHAPTER ONE

## DESIGNING WITH ANNUALS

Because annuals are usually inexpensive to purchase or to grow from seed, they are excellent candidates for installation as a broad sweep or drift of color. They can also be used to define the edge of a specific area. If your landscape color seems to be mostly shades of green, annuals break up the color monotony of shrubs, evergreens, trees, and lawns.

Annuals are also excellent for use in patio containers and as temporary cover for an area where you'll later plant perennials or shrubs. Because they bloom for a long period, annuals give you the opportunity to cultivate a long-lasting personal garden spot just for your sentimental favorites or for cut flowers you can bring indoors or share with neighbors.

## PURCHASING

Flats of annuals can be purchased at garden centers every spring. If you have a large area to plant, it is very easy to grow annuals from seed yourself. You'll find instructions in February, as well as plans for a simple light stand to get the seedlings off to a good start.

## FERTILIZING

The main purpose of growing annual flowers is to have a long season of bloom. They will need regular feeding. April details a simple fertilizing schedule to follow. Though they are a bit more expensive, slow-release long-lasting fertilizers really do free you from remembering when to fertilize your beds. Note the October tips on fertilizing winter annuals. Cold soil slows root growth, and using the kinds of fertilizer recommended in October will make a lot of difference in your winter beds.

## WATERING

Watering during the year is obviously important, but it can be tricky when watering restrictions are mandated. The Xeriscaping tips in May will help you plan your landscape to accommodate dry weather. Keep in mind that annuals do not need watering every day. If your soil contains plenty of organic matter, a deep irrigation once or twice a week will keep your plants happy.

## REMOVING FLOWERS: DEADHEADING

Never forget that flowering plants are not blooming solely for your pleasure. Their purpose is to attract pollinators so the flowers can make seed and reproduce. Once pollinated, a flower sends hormonal signals to the rest of the plant, telling it to quit flowering. You might think that feeding and watering a plant are most important in determining flower quality, but regularly removing faded blooms is almost as important if you want flower-filled beds.

## PLANNING

The lists of annuals at the end of this introduction can be helpful when trying to decide what to plant. We have also collected lists of our favorite annuals for certain situations.

Once you have chosen your annuals, how close to each other should you plant them? In general, annuals should be spaced at the distance of their mature width, which can be determined from the chart at the end of this introduction. In other words, if a begonia's mature size is 12 inches, the begonias in a bed should be spaced 12 inches apart, center to center. To achieve a fuller look more quickly, the distance can be reduced a few inches. Ground cover petunias such as 'Purple Wave' may spread 2 to 3 feet in a season, but they are usually planted 12 to 18 inches apart so the bed will be covered in a short time.

You'll find that planting annuals, and most other plants, in staggered rows will look better to the eye than planting them in rigid ranks. One of the rules of landscaping is that an odd number of plants in a grouping looks better than an even number.

## ANNUALS THAT PLANT THEMSELVES

Certain annuals and biennials are known for their ability to self-seed without your help. Often these "volunteers" will appear in your garden year after year for generations. Because they are annuals, most are easy to control and can be easily pulled out if they threaten to take over an area. To take full advantage of these self-seeders, don't be too quick to remove seedlings you don't recognize. Good self-seeders include the following plants:

• Borage (*Borago officinalis*) has starry blue flowers and soft gray-green foliage.

• Bronze fennel (*Foeniculum vulgare*) 'Purpureum' has feathery anise-scented foliage.

• Common sunflower (*Helianthus annuus*) is quite versatile in a landscape, coming in 3-foot and 10-foot selections.

• Cosmos (*Cosmos bipinnatus*) comes in many colors and forms. It is used extensively in highway wildflower medians.

• Impatiens (*Impatiens walleriana*) are excellent for shady spots that receive little maintenance except a bit of water in summer.

• Johnny-jump-up (*Viola tricolor*) has purple-and-yellow spring flowers that look like pansy blooms.

• Larkspur (*Consolida ambigua*) is a good substitute for delphinium, and is much easier to grow in Georgia.

• Love-in-a-mist (*Nigella damascena*) blooms quickly in spring, but plants dry up in summer.

• Melampodium (*Melampodium paludosum*) is an attractive annual covered by yellow flowers throughout the summer.

• Mexican heather (*Cuphea hyssopifolia*) has tiny purple or white flowers scattered along slightly arching stems.

• Perilla (*Perilla frutescens*) has purple foliage that stands out against green backgrounds; it can be invasive.

• Shirley poppy (*Papaver rhoeas*) has red, pink, or white flowers on 2- to 5-foot stems. Excess seedlings can be removed once recognized.

• Spider flower (*Cleome hasslerana*) has spiky pink/purple flowers that sit atop wiry 3- to 5-foot-tall stems.

• Sweet Alyssum (*Lobularia maritima*) is a ground-hugger with tiny honey-scented white flowers.

• Wheat celosia (*Celosia spicata*) is grasslike in appearance—'Flamingo Feather' and 'Flamingo Purple' are excellent passalong plants.

## ANNUALS FOR CUT FLOWERS

One of the pleasures of growing flowers is having some to bring indoors or to share with neighbors. Some gardeners maintain showy beds of landscape annuals and a private, separate bed of flowers for cutting, so that landscape color will not be reduced when blooms are removed from the cutting garden. The following annuals produce wonderful flowers that you can enjoy in arrangements indoors:

| | |
|---|---|
| • Ageratum | • Phlox |
| • Bachelor's button | • Salvia |
| • Calendula | • Scabiosa |
| • Celosia | • Snapdragon |
| • Cleome | • Stock |
| • Cosmos | • Strawflower |
| • Dianthus | • Sweetpea |
| • Gomphrena | • Zinnia |
| • Marigold | |

## PLANTING FOR POLLINATORS

An environmental tragedy has quietly occurred in Georgia in the last decades: the wild honeybee population has been decimated due to mite pests. Many flowers and vegetables depend on bees and other insects to move pollen from flower to flower. The insects don't realize they are pollinating the plants they visit—they're just looking for food in the flowers. You can help the fruit, vegetable, and flowering plants in your neighborhood by planting a pollinator-friendly flower garden. Bumblebees, solitary bees, pollinating wasps, and other insects will try to fill in for honeybees. It is important to have something blooming almost year-round in order to attract these beneficial insects. The following list of plants that attract pollinators includes both woody and herbaceous plants and their monthly bloom times:

• February: Redbud
• March: Carolina jessamine
• April: Ajuga, crimson clover
• May: 'Schip' laurel, 'Otto Luyken' laurel
• June: Nandina
• July: Beebalm, chaste tree, sunflower
• August: Tall verbena (*Verbena bonariensis*), butterfly bush, glossy abelia
• September: Butterfly weed
• October: Mexican sage, pineapple sage
• November: Aster

## ANNUALS GOOD FOR DRYING

Some annuals are known for their good looks as dried flowers in winter as well as for their blooms in summer. Drying is easy—just cut the blooms after they dry in the morning, and hang them upside-down in a warm, dark place for a few weeks. The following annuals have attractive dried flowers:

• Celosia
• Chinese lantern
• Globe amaranth
• Gomphrena
• Money plant
• Statice
• Strawflower

## ANNUALS FOR THE COAST

Coastal gardens require annuals that tolerate sun, wind, and sometimes salt spray. The following plants are good for seaside conditions:

• Cape plumbago *Plumbago auriculata*
• Common lantana *Lantana camara*
• Creeping zinnia *Santivalia procumbens*
• Dusty miller *Senecio cineraria*
• Hibiscus *Hibiscus rosa-sinensis*
• Lily-of-the-Nile *Agapanthus africanus*
• Moss rose *Portulaca grandiflora*

# CHAPTER ONE

## Quick Reference to Common Annuals

| Name | Height[1] (in.) | Spacing[2] (in.) | Color[3] | Exposure[4] SU | S-S | SH |
|------|-----------------|------------------|----------|-----|-----|-----|
| Ageratum | 6–24 | 12 | WB | * | * | |
| Alyssum | 4–8 | 12 | WPL | * | * | |
| Amaranth | 12–60 | 12–24 | F | * | * | |
| Aster | 6–36 | 12–18 | All | * | | |
| Baby's Breath | 12–24 | 12–24 | WPL | * | * | |
| Balloon Vine | Vine | —— | F | * | * | |
| Balsam | 12–36 | 12 | —B | | * | * |
| Balsam Apple | Vine | —— | F | * | * | |
| Basil | 12–24 | 12–24 | F | * | | |
| Begonia | 6–12 | 12 | WPR | * | * | * |
| Bells of Ireland | 24–36 | 12–18 | F | * | * | * |
| Browallia | 6–18 | 12 | WB | | * | * |
| Calendula | 12–24 | 12 | YGO | * | | |
| Calliopsis | 18 | 12 | Y | * | | |
| Canary Bird Vine | Vine | —— | Y | * | | |
| Candytuft | 8–12 | 12 | WPRL | * | * | * |
| Castor Bean | 60–120 | 24–36 | F | * | | |
| Celosia | 6–30 | 12 | —B | * | | |
| Chinese Lantern | 18–24 | 12 | F | * | | |
| Chrysanthemum | 12–24 | 12–24 | —B | * | | |
| Cleome | 36–60 | 12–24 | WPL | * | | |
| Coleus | 12–36 | 12 | F | | * | * |
| Cornflower | 12–36 | 12 | WPRBL | * | | |
| Cosmos | 12–48 | 12 | YGP | * | | |
| Cup-and-saucer Vine | Vine | —— | LW | * | * | |
| Cypress Vine | Vine | —— | R | * | | |
| Dahlia | 18–72 | 12–36 | All | * | | |
| Dianthus | 6–12 | 12 | —B | * | | |
| Dusty Miller | 6–12 | 12 | F | * | | |
| Forget-me-not | 6–12 | 12 | BWP | * | * | |
| Four-o'-clock | 18–36 | 12–24 | WRYP | * | | |
| Foxglove | 24–60 | 12–24 | —B | * | * | |
| Gaillardia | 12–30 | 12 | YGR | * | | |
| Gazania | 6–12 | 12 | YGPRO | * | | |
| Geranium | 12–24 | 12 | —B —Y | * | * | |
| Gomphrena | 8–24 | 12 | WPL | * | | |
| Hibiscus | 36–96 | 24–36 | —B —Y | * | | |
| Hollyhock | 12–72 | 12–24 | All | * | | |
| Impatiens | 6–36 | 12 | —B | * | * | * |
| Kochia | 24–36 | 12–24 | F | * | | |
| Larkspur | 24–36 | 6–12 | BPWL | * | | |
| Lobelia | 3–6 | 6–12 | BLR | * | * | * |
| Marigold | 6–36 | 12–24 | YGRO | * | | |
| Melampodium | 12–24 | 12–18 | Y | * | | |

# CHAPTER ONE

## Quick Reference to Common Annuals

| Name | Height[1] (in.) | Spacing[2] (in.) | Color[3] | Exposure[4] SU | S-S | SH |
|------|-----------------|------------------|----------|------|-----|-----|
| Money Plant | 12–36 | 12 | F | * | * | |
| Monkey Flower | 6 | 6–12 | YR | | * | * |
| Moonvine | Vine | —— | W | * | * | |
| Morning Glory | Vine | —— | —Y —G | * | | |
| Narrow-leaf Zinnia | 12–18 | 12–18 | O | * | | |
| Nasturtium | 12–72 | 12–24 | YORW | * | * | |
| Nicotiana | 12–36 | 12–24 | —B | * | * | |
| Ornamental Kale | 6–12 | 18–24 | F | * | | |
| Ornamental Pepper | 6–12 | 6–18 | F | * | | |
| Pansy | 6 | 6–10 | All | * | * | |
| Petunia | 6–12 | 12–18 | All | * | | |
| Phlox | 6–12 | 12 | All | * | * | |
| Polka-dot Plant | 12–18 | 12 | F | * | * | |
| Poppy | 12–24 | 6–12 | All | * | * | |
| Portulaca | 1–3 | 12 | —B | * | | |
| Purple Fountain Grass | 30–48 | 12–24 | F | * | | |
| Salvia | 10–30 | 12–18 | RWBPL | * | * | |
| Scaevola | 4–8 | 10–20 | B | * | | |
| Scarlet Runner Bean | Vine | —— | R | * | | |
| Snapdragon | 6–36 | 12 | —B | * | * | |
| Snow On The Mountain | 24–48 | 12–24 | F | * | | |
| Statice | 18–24 | 12–24 | —R | * | | |
| Stock | 12–30 | 12–24 | All | * | | |
| Strawflower | 12–36 | 12–24 | YG | * | | |
| Sunflower | 24–120 | 24–36 | YG | * | | |
| Sweetpea | 12–96 | 6–12 | All | * | | |
| Thunbergia | Vine | —— | WYGO | * | * | |
| Tithonia | 48–72 | 24–36 | R | * | | |
| Torenia | 6–12 | 6–12 | WB | | * | * |
| Verbena | 6–12 | 12 | All | * | * | |
| Vinca | 6–18 | 12 | WPL | * | * | |
| Wallflower | 6–12 | 12 | WPRY | * | | |
| Zinnia | 6–36 | 12–24 | —B | * | | |

[1] Height may vary considerably among varieties.
[2] Spacing depends on ultimate size of plant and effect desired.
[3] G = gold, W = white, P = pink, Y = yellow, R = red, B = blue, L = lavender, O = orange, A = all colors,
— = one or two colors are absent, all others represented, F = grown for foliage or fruit.
[4] SU = full sun, S-S = semi-shade (filtered light or protection from midday and afternoon sun), SH = shade.

# JANUARY

## ANNUALS

 PLANNING

Although the weather is a mixture of chilly and cold now, this is an excellent time to plan how you will use annuals in your landscape this year.

1. Sketch a rough map of your property. Include your home plus existing large trees, shrubs, and flower beds. Make several copies of the sketch at a copy center.

2. Use colored pencils to shade the areas where you want annual flowers to provide landscape color. Remember that a mass of color in one spot is much more effective than a mixed "polka-dot" planting of several flower colors.

Rough Sketch of a Home Landscape

3. Indicate sunny and shady areas—this knowledge will dictate which annuals you can plant in those spots.

A word about color combinations: Professional garden designers spend hours looking for just the right flower color or hue to match a home's paint, or its shutters, or an adjoining bed of perennial blooms. While a carefully planned color combination can be a visual knockout, don't spend too much time aiming for perfection. Nature has designed flowers to look pleasant in combination with almost any other color. Until you have mastered the skills of raising healthy plants almost without fail, concentrate on the simple design ideas mentioned above, and leave the agonizing to those who are paid for their expertise.

 PLANTING

In south Georgia, colorful annuals can be planted even when the weather is cold. Flowering cool-season plants make an immediate impact in a bare landscape.

In north Georgia, winter annuals can be planted as long as daytime temperatures for the next few days are predicted to be above 40 degrees Fahrenheit accompanied by bright sunshine.

• Plant **dianthus, viola, snapdragon, pansy, ornamental kale, English daisy,** and **parsley.** All prefer a sunny spot. (See Annuals, October, for special planting directions.)

• Plant on sunny days, when the soil is more likely to be warm, and water the plants immediately.

• Purchase plants in 3-inch or larger pots so blooms will continue to appear (plants in smaller containers will stop blooming as they try to establish roots).

• Do not install "six-pack" plants now. They are too small to survive the cold temperatures and wind that surely will occur between now and spring.

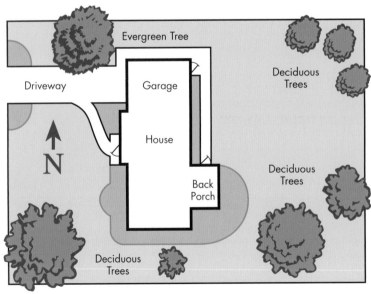

Evergreen Tree

Driveway

Garage

Deciduous Trees

House

N

Back Porch

Deciduous Trees

Deciduous Trees

## CARE

Don't worry if **pansy** leaves look pitiful in the morning; they will recuperate by noon as moisture fills the leaves. **Pansies** protect themselves during cold weather by wilting their leaves. Other plants use a variety of coping mechanisms.

Scatter pine straw loosely over flower beds if frigid, windy weather is predicted. When daytime temperatures are above 40 degrees Fahrenheit, lift the straw off the plants and use it for mulch around nearby shrubs.

## WATERING

If the soil is frozen or dry, the roots of winter annuals cannot absorb the moisture they need. Test soil moisture weekly by digging 4 inches into the ground and squeezing a lump of soil in your palm. If it is dry and crumbly, water is needed.

Water your flower beds as needed so moisture is available when plant roots require it after cold nights.

## FERTILIZING

Fertilize **pansies** and other cool-season annuals with a product containing nitrate nitrogen (see Annuals, October).

## PROBLEMS

Visit your flower beds each week to look for weeds such as chickweed, bittercress, and henbit. Pull weeds by hand, put them into a container, and remove them from the garden. This will eliminate the possibility of weed seeds being dropped onto the soil. Suppress further weed development by mulching with pine straw or pine bark mini-nuggets.

See Annuals, September, for information about preventing weeds with a pre-emergent herbicide.

## GROOMING

Remove faded blooms from plants as you notice them. This procedure (deadheading) is particularly important for **pansies**— these plants produce many more flowers if deadheaded regularly. Hold the plant stems with one hand while tugging on individual flowers with thumb and fingers. Garden scissors can also be used to remove flowers. Snip the blooms with one hand while gathering them with the other.

## HELPFUL HINTS

• Most garden centers keep a rack of helpful tip sheets and flower bed plans. Often the plan will specify exactly how many plants must be purchased to achieve a desired effect.

• Keep a disposable camera in the glove compartment of your car. When you see a design you like, snap a series of quick photos, both from a distance and up close. Take the pictures to your garden center, and ask an employee to identify the flowers and to estimate what will be needed to duplicate the look you admired.

• Subscribe to garden magazines. Almost every issue will have an article on design. Make sure the plants in the design are appropriate for your Georgia climate. If you are unsure, take the plan to a garden center, and ask a professional for advice.

# FEBRUARY

## ANNUALS

### PLANNING

Many annual flowers can be easily grown from seed. This month is a good time to purchase seed and to assemble materials needed for seed-starting.

Most homes do not have enough natural light in an appropriate spot to make seedlings prosper. Purchase or build a light stand, which uses fluorescent bulbs above the seed flats. PVC pipe is easily available at home-improvement centers and is quite easy to work with. The pipe fittings allow sturdy connections at the corners of the structure. Special "plant light" fluorescent tubes are not necessary; two

cool-white 40-watt tubes will be sufficient.

Here is a simple light stand described by Bob Polomski in *Month-by-Month Gardening in the Carolinas.* He attributes the design to Master Gardener Joe Maple. The dimensions shown are only suggested—you can lengthen or shorten the pipes to fit your own situation. One-half inch PVC pipe can be used, but 3/4-inch pipe will make a sturdier stand. Not all joints need to be glued. With a little planning, the light stand can be made so it can be disassembled after use and stored in an attic or closet.

### PLANTING

Since individual plants at a garden center cost between $.20 and $2, raising annuals from seed can save a lot of money!

1. Fill a plastic nursery flat (or an aluminum pan in which drainholes have been poked) with sterile seed-starting mixture.

2. Make several "furrows," 2 inches apart and 1/2 inch deep, across the surface of the growing medium with the point of a pencil.

Read seed packets carefully. Some seed, like **impatiens** and **poppy,** need light in order to germinate. They should simply be scattered onto the soil sur-

Portable Light Stand of PVC Pipes

face. Pat the soil with your hand to press them into good soil contact.

3. For tiny seed, mix 1/4 teaspoonful of seed with a tablespoon of dry sand. Fold an index card in half, and pour the seed/sand mixture in the center. Gently tap the card to direct the seeds and sand to drop in the furrows in the growing medium. Large seed can be placed by hand in the furrows. Cover the seed with a thin layer of vermiculite unless directed on the seed pack to expose the seed to light.

4. Spray-mist the medium with water to moisten the soil. It should be just slightly moist, not soggy.

5. Cover the tray or pan with clear kitchen plastic wrap. Affix masking tape to the ends of the container, and note the name of the seed, the date planted, and the date the seed should germinate.

6. Place the seed-starting trays in bright but indirect sunlight (a south- or west-facing window is ideal), or under the light stand described earlier (the fluorescent tubes should hang just a few inches above the plastic covering).

7. Remove the plastic when most of the seeds in a tray have sprouted. Raise the fluorescent tubes as the plants grow. If the plants become crowded, use a spoon to scoop individuals out of the tray, which can be planted in separate plastic pots.

In south Georgia, you can lightly scratch the soil and scatter **poppy** seed in your flower beds. Since they need light in order to germinate, do not cover with soil. **California, Iceland,** and **corn poppies** will sprout when the ground warms up.

## CARE

The fragrant flowers of **sweetpea** are a sure harbinger of spring. Most **sweetpea** varieties are climbing vines. Now is the best time to plant the seed. You can make an informal trellis with three slender pruned branches from your **crapemyrtle, apple,** or **flowering cherry** tree. Lean or tie the branches together at the top to make a 4- to 6-foot-high teepee form for the vines to ascend. Make a rich planting soil by mixing bagged manure, sand, and soil in a 1:1:1 ratio. When the seeds sprout, train them up your trellis. Flowers will appear March through May.

## WATERING

Windowboxes and other outside containers need watering more often than in-ground flower beds.

Dig 2 inches into the soil with your fingers. If the soil at that depth is dry, add enough water to the container until water runs out the bottom. Inspect and water flower beds as needed (see Annuals, January).

## FERTILIZING

Fertilize **pansies** (see Annuals, October).

## PROBLEMS

It is quite disappointing to observe seedlings suddenly fall over, as if broken at the soil level. A disease called damping off causes this problem—it is due to overwatering, crowding, or poor ventilation of the young plants. To prevent damping off, use fresh, sterile seed-starting medium each time you raise seedlings. Keep the medium moist but never soggy. Increase light and ventilation as soon as symptoms are noticed.

## GROOMING

Remove faded blooms from plants as they occur (see January).

# MARCH

## ANNUALS

 PLANNING

It is easy to get caught up in planting fever when you visit a garden center full of spring flowers. Before you visit, make an index card for each bed you'll be planting: Sketch the bed's shape on the card, particularly if it is irregular instead of rectangular. Write down the approximate square footage of the bed. Write down how much sunshine it receives and if parts of the bed are more shady than others. Jot down the flowers you intend to plant and the number you need to buy.

Design ideas for annuals:

• Choose a spot you want to highlight. Plant enough annuals of one color to draw the eye to that spot. White flowers can lighten a shady spot, but in bright sunshine brilliant red, orange, or yellow flowers are needed to compete with the existing light.

• Don't repeat the same mass of a single color throughout your landscape. One bed of **begonias** is fine—but six identical beds is as boring as hearing the same piano note repeated endlessly.

• Use beds in the backyard to intrigue viewers from the street. You can enjoy your private view from your kitchen window, but allow part of the bed to be seen through a side gate or around a corner of the house.

• A long bed edged in a single color tires the eyes. Try to make oval or irregular, rounded beds of distinct, single-color annuals that adjoin each other.

• Combine annuals and perennials to have a progression of blooms from spring to fall.

A spot planned to attract butterflies can be the most interesting area of your garden. The butterfly lifecycle requires different plants for the different life stages of the insect—the garden should have plants that feed caterpillars as well as plants whose flowers attract butterflies. Caterpillar-feeding plants include **parsley, dill, fennel, milkweed, clover, aster, snapdragon,** and **sunflower.** Butterfly-attracting plants include **lantana, butterfly weed, pentas, impatiens, cosmos, salvia, petunia, coreopsis, snapdragon, marigold, tithonia, aster,** and **black-eyed Susan.** Another ingredient for attracting butterflies is a source of water. Butterflies will not drink from large, open water areas. Wet sand or mud provides excellent watering holes. A saucer that is designed to fit under a clay

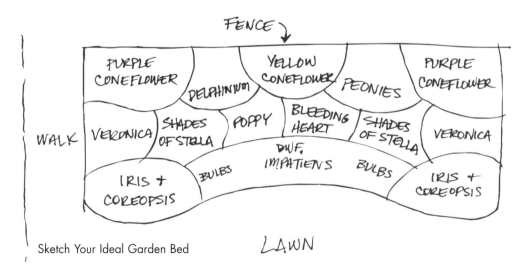

Sketch Your Ideal Garden Bed

or plastic pot makes a good watering hole for butterflies:

- Fill it completely with sand, and add water up to the rim. Make a few shallow depressions with your fingers where water can accumulate.
- A rock in the center of the saucer provides a resting spot for the butterfly.

## PLANTING

There's still time to start seeds of annual flowers indoors (see February).

If you like fragrant flowers, several "old-fashioned" varieties add spicy scents to your garden. Try planting **stock, sweet alyssum, sweetpea, nicotiana,** and **annual phlox.**

In south Georgia, plant cool-season annuals from six-packs as they become available at garden centers: **Viola, snapdragon, pansy, sweet William,** and **English daisy** will bloom in your landscape for the next six weeks or longer.

In north Georgia, you can't expect every plant you installed last fall to make it through the winter. Fill holes in your flower beds with new plants. Purchase 3-inch or larger pots; smaller plants will bloom for only a few days.

## CARE

Check for the seedlings of annuals you planted last fall. You should be able to see **poppy** and **larkspur** seedlings easily. Plants should be 6 to 12 inches apart. Gently transplant to an empty spot any seedlings that are too close. If you have more seedlings than space, remove some of the crowded seedlings by pinching them off at ground level.

## WATERING

Check the plastic covering on flats of seeds you are starting indoors. If a slight haze of condensed moisture isn't present, remove the plastic, and mist the soil until damp.

## FERTILIZING

Fertilize flowering annual plants (see October).

Fertilize the seedlings you have grown indoors with water-soluble houseplant food once the true leaves have appeared (true leaves are the leaves that emerge after the rounded first leaves unfold from the soil). Once plants are a few inches tall, fertilize them every two weeks until they are ready to be planted outdoors.

## PROBLEMS

Seedlings grown indoors may become infested with whiteflies if your houseplants have them. Spray with insecticidal soap, and use a yellow sticky trap.

## GROOMING

Remove faded flowers from **pansies.**

---

## HELPFUL HINT

If you can't find the seed of annuals you prefer at a local garden center, consider buying from a seed catalog.

Park Seed, 1 Parkton Avenue, Greenwood, SC 29647-0001, Phone: (800) 845-3369, **www.parkseed.com**

Seeds of Change®, P.O. Box 15700, Santa Fe, NM 87506 Phone: (888) 762-7333, **www.seedsofchange.com**

Johnny's Selected Seeds, RR 1 Box 2580, Albion, ME 04910-9731 Phone: (207) 437-4301, **www.johnnyseeds.com**

## ANNUALS

### PLANNING

One of the hottest landscaping trends in the last few years has been the "Tropical Look." While a year-round tropical landscape might be possible in Brunswick or Savannah, gardeners in other parts of the state usually settle for a tropical corner in the yard.

Two of the most popular plants for the Tropical Look are **elephant ear** and **banana.** **Common elephant ear** produces green leaves that gently sway in the breeze; 'Jet Black Wonder' has dusky black leaves; 'Frydek' sports velvety green leaves with white veins. **Fiber banana** (*Musa basjoo*) is reputed to withstand winter temperatures down to 10 degrees Fahrenheit; 'Rojo' displays green leaves with a red stripe. See October for tips on storing **elephant ear** corms and **banana** trees for the winter. Other annuals with that Tropical Look include **amaranth, chenille plant, coleus, dusty miller, perilla mint, polka-dot plant,** and **purple basil.**

### PLANTING

Soil temperatures determine when you can plant seeds outdoors. When the weather for several days in a row is warm enough to work outside wearing shorts and a T-shirt, it's time to plant! Annuals that are easy to grow from seed outdoors in spring include **marigold, cosmos, zinnia, celosia, cleome, sunflower,** and **nasturtium.**

### CARE

Though it may be warm during the day, nights are still chilly. The annual plants you have raised from seed for the past weeks can't tolerate cool temperatures. To accustom them to growing outdoors, they should be hardened off.

• If daytime temperatures are above 60 degrees Fahrenheit, take the plants outdoors and place them in a shady spot, for seven days in a row, bringing them indoors at night.

• When nighttime temperatures are 50 degrees or above, you can leave the plants outside both day and night. Bring indoors if temperatures fall below 50 degrees.

• Examine your plants daily to make sure they do not wilt.

• After two weeks outdoors, they are ready to be transplanted into your garden.

Less care will be needed if you select the healthiest plants when purchasing annuals. Be wary of buying a plant fully in flower—nursery techniques that force a plant to flower all at once can leave it weakened and bare in just a few weeks. Choose plants that have just one or two flowers and plenty of unopened flower buds. Gently pull one or two plants from the pot to examine their

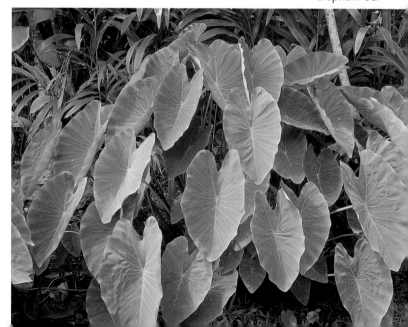

Elephant ear

roots. Soggy soil and brown, jelly-like roots can indicate root rot problems. Evaluate the nursery as a whole. Are most plants in good health, or do they seem to be underwatered or overgrown and floppy? Consider buying plants in 4-inch pots rather than in six-packs. Though they are more expensive, larger plants have more complete root systems and are likely to bloom earlier.

 WATERING

April is likely to have several days with temperatures in the eighties. Newly planted annuals can quickly dry out, especially on windy days. Water each plant immediately after planting.

1. Water again twenty-four to forty-eight hours later.

2. Water again four days after the initial planting.

3. Begin weekly watering for all your annuals once they seem adapted to their new homes.

FERTILIZING

Annuals need nutrients to get off to a good start. Water-soluble fertilizers (Miracle-Gro®, etc.) provide the quickest way to feed plants immediately. Slow-release fertilizers (Osmo-

## HELPFUL HINT

"Flowering Annuals for Georgia Gardens" is a free booklet available at your local Extension office (see Resources, p. 289), or download it from the Web at **www.gaurbanag.org** You can also refer to the *Georgia Gardener's Guide: Revised Edition* for more information about great annuals for Georgia.

cote®, Dynamite®, etc.) provide nutrients for the entire growing season.

• Use water-soluble fertilizer for the first watering, following label directions.

• Consider placing slow-release fertilizer granules in the bottom of each hole in which you plant an annual, following label directions.

• If you choose not to use slow-release fertilizer, you will need to feed your plants every six weeks with one pound of 10-10-10 for every 100 square feet of flower bed. Alternatively, use one of the water-soluble products according to label directions.

 PROBLEMS

Aphids love the lush tips of fast-growing plants. They can suck plant sap easily from stems or leaves and can disfigure the growing tip. Suspect aphids if you see many ants on a particular plant. Examine the undersides of leaves at the branch tips.

Aphids may be green, yellow, or black, and they are visible with the naked eye.

If you find aphids, blast them off the plant with a strong stream of water.

 GROOMING

Although it may seem harsh, the best way to help a plant establish a good root system is to remove blooms at planting— blooms take the energy needed for root growth and focus it on seed formation. Bloom removal is particularly important for plants purchased in "six-packs;" their root systems are small compared to their foliage. Plants purchased in 4-inch or larger pots do not require this clipping.

## ANNUALS

### PLANNING

Plant labels are quite useful in a garden. They help you remember the names of particular flowers, and they can remind you of a plant's source and special care. If you include a plant's scientific name, you can teach yourself the rudiments of botanical Latin! Labels can be made from plastic picnic knives, medical tongue depressors, aluminum window blind slats, strips of plastic cut from recycled non-dairy topping containers, or strips of aluminum cut from recycled aluminum pie pans. Most garden centers sell more attractive and permanent labels: fired clay markers for herbs, rectangular metal tags attached to steel hairpin legs, and copper tags that attach loosely to woody plant stems with wire.

### PLANTING

Good gardeners use planting tricks to avoid later chores. Here is the technique Dr. Gary Wade, Extension Horticulturist, uses to combat weeds, conserve water, and get rid of old newspapers:

• Thoroughly till the soil for your bed of annuals. You should have soft soil 6 inches deep.

• Unfold the Sunday newspaper, making a stack of all the sheets. Place near your planting spot.

• Fill a 5-gallon bucket with water; station it near your bed.

• Soak a group of three sheets of newspaper momentarily in the water. Spread them in a single stack over your tilled soil.

• Repeat this process, laying each group adjacent to the previous one, until the entire bed is covered with newspaper.

• Pour pine bark mini-nuggets in a layer 1 inch thick over the newspapers.

• Use a sharp trowel to stab through the mulch and wet paper, making a planting hole for each of your plants.

• Continue planting until the bed is completed.

Caution: Do not use the comics for this process. If you do, your plants will grow funny!

### CARE

Annual vines give lots of vertical interest and beautiful blooms to a flower garden, but they must be supported on a trellis, fence, or wall. Good annual vines include **moonvine, morning glory, purple hyacinth bean, scarlet runner bean, cypress vine, sweetpea,** and **thunbergia.** A few trellis possibilities include bamboo canes; long, limber branches pruned from your **crapemyrtle, flowering cherry, pear,** or **apple** tree; tuteurs (ornamental towers made from metal or wood, purchased at a garden center); and wire or strings attached to a wooden fence.

### WATERING

Nearly every year brings a drought to part or all of Georgia. You can prepare for water shortages by adhering to the principles of Xeriscaping (dry-weather landscaping).

1. **Planning and Design:** Establish low-, moderate-, and high-water-use zones. Group plants with similar water needs in the same zone.

2. **Soil Analysis:** Have your soil tested by your local Extension office (see Horticultural Practices, p. 8) to determine what is needed for your plants to develop drought-tolerant root systems.

3. **Appropriate Plant Selection:** Choose the plants that thrive naturally in your local environment.

4. **Practical Turf Areas:** Plan to have turf only in small areas near your home's entrance, in recreation areas, or on slopes where other plants would be impractical.

5. **Efficient Irrigation:** Zone your irrigation system to water plants with different needs separately.

6. **Use of Mulches:** Use mulch to prevent evaporation and to maintain even soil moisture.

7. **Appropriate Maintenance:** Water after midnight and before noon. Less water will be lost to evaporation, and it will have more time to soak into cool soil.

## FERTILIZING

One of the advantages of feeding annuals with slow-release fertilizer at planting (see Annuals, April) is that you don't have to rack your brain to remember if you fertilized recently. If you didn't use a slow-release fertilizer, you have two choices for applying nutrients: balanced, granular fertilizers (10-10-10, 8-8-8, Nursery Special™, etc.) and water-soluble products (Miracle-Gro®, etc.).

If you use a granular product:

• Note how often the product must be applied—usually every four to six weeks.

• Note, and follow, the application rate recommended on the bag.

• Determine how you will spread the granules evenly. Garden centers sell small "whirly bird" spreaders for this purpose.

---

## HELPFUL HINT

When shopping for annuals, choose plants having one or two blooms and lots of unopened flower buds. A six-pack that is covered with flowers may look pretty now but will lose the blooms quickly and won't put out new ones for weeks.

If you use a water-soluble fertilizer:

• Note how often the product must be applied—usually every two weeks.

• Mix at the recommended rate for the plants (annuals, perennials, shrubs, etc.) you are tending.

• Since these nutrients can be absorbed by plant leaves as well as roots, use a sprinkling can to get the best coverage. Otherwise, use a bucket and a comfortable dipper to pour the recommended amount beside each plant.

If you have a large area to fertilize, a special device called a siphoning mixer is very useful. This brass gadget attaches to your hose and injects concentrated liquid fertilizer into the water flowing through the hose. A water wand screwed onto the end of the hose allows you to sprinkle the enriched water quickly onto dozens of plants.

---

## PROBLEMS

Spider mites attack many plants and are common pests of **foxglove, verbena,** and **butterfly bush.** Symptoms include yellow-speckled leaves and wilted foliage (see Roses, July, for more information). The key to their control is regular inspection of your plants and sprays with horticultural oil if warranted. Prune nearby **butterfly bushes** down to 12 inches tall in March. Be vigilant about pulling weeds whenever you see them. If you can remove them before they drop seed, you'll save many headaches during the summer.

## GROOMING

As temperatures warm up, **pansies** will look like nothing more than green flowering spaghetti. Pull them out, and replace with **petunias, marigolds, coleus, geraniums,** or other colorful summer annuals.

# JUNE
## ANNUALS

### PLANNING

Gardeners know they can get just as much exercise from their activities as their neighbors who jog or visit a gym. Physical activity researchers have compiled the METs (metabolic equivalents) for hundreds of activities. A MET of 1 is the amount of energy you expend at rest. For an activity to help your body's circulation or strength, it should have a MET between 3 and 6.

| | |
|---|---|
| Weeding or planting | 4.5 MET |
| Digging or pushing a lawn mower | 5.0 MET |
| Riding a mower | 2.5 MET |
| Watering the lawn | 1.5 MET |

Doctors recommend that adults accumulate 30 minutes of physical activity above 3 MET each day. A gardener who weeds for 15 minutes in the morning and pushes a mower for 20 minutes in the evening has met his or her needs for daily physical activity.

### PLANTING

There's still lots of time to set out annual flowers for summer color. Try 'Wave' **petunias, narrow-leaf zinnia** (*Zinnia linearis*), **Mexican heather,** and **portulaca** in sunny spots.

### CARE

When planting transplants, don't just dig a small hole and shove the root system into it. Try to gently untangle some of the roots so they will quickly explore the soil around them. Firm the soil around each plant with your fingers to eliminate air pockets in the soil. Once a bed is finished, water each plant thoroughly (see below). Do not allow transplants to dry out.

### WATERING

Now that your plants are well along, it's time to think about how to water them, with the least effort, for the rest of the summer.

1. Black soaker hoses can be laid in a bed or down a row of flowers, and later covered with pine straw.

2. Drip irrigation systems are available at large garden centers. Though they are a bit more complicated to set up, you can be assured that plants will get the exact amount of water they need.

3. Some lawn and landscape irrigation systems can be adapted to water flower beds. The beds should always be on a different zone from the lawn—the water demands of flowers are completely different from those of lawn grass.

4. A water wand is indispensable for watering garden plants. The stream from a hose blasts plant leaves and scatters soil, but the gentle waterfall from the nozzle of a wand soaks the ground around a plant without disturbing it. Both metal and plastic wands work well.

An easy-to-operate valve is essential. Spend the money to buy a wand that has a valve with a long handle. Your fingers will thank you every time you turn the water on and off.

### FERTILIZING

If you use a ground pine bark soil amendment to prepare your beds (see Horticultural Practices, p. 9), the soil may be deficient in nitrogen for a month afterwards, and plant growth may be slow. Apply an extra dose of water-soluble fertilizer early this month to counteract this phenomenon. As the summer passes, nutrients from the breakdown of the woody materials will slowly be released for your plants to enjoy. Continue to fertilize at two- to six-week intervals as discussed in Annuals, May. When using granular products, be sure to water afterwards to carry the nutrients down to plant roots.

**Nasturtium** is one flower that actually prefers a sunny location with poor soil. Plant seeds now. Fertilize very lightly when sprouts are 6 inches tall. Do not fertilize again. Flowers will appear in fifty days.

 ## PROBLEMS

A great advantage of soaker hose and drip systems is that water is applied only to the roots of plants. By keeping the foliage dry, leaf diseases are reduced.

## GROOMING

Annuals produce flowers not for our enjoyment but to make seed to ensure their reproduction. On many plants, the flowering process stops if the flowers are allowed to fade as the seeds are maturing. It is therefore important to regularly remove withered flowers from your annuals. Deadhead **ageratum, calendula, cosmos, marigold, pansy, rudbeckia, scabiosa, verbena,** and **zinnia** each week. Remove the yellow flowers from **dusty miller** as they are produced in late June.

## HELPFUL HINT

If you do not recognize an insect pest or disease symptom, you won't know how to deal with it. No one is an expert on all plant problems, but you do have local resources which can help:

• Local University of Georgia Extension Service offices (see Resources, p. 289)—if you can't take a pest sample to them, photograph the damage or pest, and mail it to their office. All offices have email addresses to which digital photos can be sent.

• Experienced garden center personnel—call your local nursery, and ask who is their best pest identifier. Make an appointment to meet that person when it is mutually convenient.

• Longtime gardeners—if the pest is bothering you, it is probably bothering other folks as well. Ask neighbors and friends for their advice and expertise.

• Mass media—read the garden section of your local paper and listen to the local gardening radio show. Search the Internet for "garden problems."

Deadheading improves the appearance of your garden and promotes continued flowering.

# JULY

## ANNUALS

### PLANNING

Beds of annual flowers should be planned not only for beauty but also for ease of maintenance. A garden designed for a young or vigorous gardener should be different from a garden designed for a less vigorous gardener. Easy access gardens should have:

• narrow beds that are more easily reached from the lawn or a solid path.

• raised beds that demand less bending.

• flat, wide paths in the garden that allow wheelchairs or walkers to maneuver easily.

• tools designed for easy grasping (see Helpful Hint).

All gardeners should pay attention to these body-saving ideas:

• Alternate between movements. If you swap between digging, raking, weeding, and pruning, you can avoid repetitive motion injuries.

• Bend from the knees, not from the back. Lift large pots and sacks of fertilizer by first bending your knees, then grasping the object and straightening your knees. Avoid bending over to lift even light items—the lower back is prone to injury and should be spared whenever possible.

### PLANTING

Choose plants carefully. Avoid floppy or stretched-out plants. Ask your garden center manager when the next fresh shipment will arrive. Inspect plants for insects, like whiteflies or spider mites, before purchasing.

Plant **zinnia** seed. They will sprout in six days and bloom in just a few weeks. Plant dwarf **sunflower** seed now. Varieties like 'Teddy Bear', 'Sunspot', 'Pacino', and 'Prado Red' take up little space but delight the eyes of humans and birds alike. Plant more **caladiums** and **coleus.** They'll look better in fall than the early plants you put out in May.

Coleus are colorful additions to annual beds. New sun-tolerant varieties are great performers.

### CARE

When planting a large pot with summer annuals, there is no need to fill the entire pot with potting soil. After all, the roots of annual flowers rarely penetrate more than 10 inches into the soil. Fill the pot partially with empty plastic soft drink bottles. Add potting soil, and shake the pot vigorously to settle it around the bottles. When the soil no longer recedes below the bottles, fill the pot completely, and plant your annual flowers.

### WATERING

Watering restrictions and, sometimes, outright bans have become a way of life in the metropolitan areas of Georgia. When municipal water is in short supply, there are other sources of water for your plants.

• Water from a dehumidifier or from an air conditioner condensate drain is perfectly safe to use on plants. This water has been condensed from the ambient air—just like rainwater!

• Bathwater can be used to water most plants. The soap, shampoo, and conditioner are so diluted that they will not harm leaves or roots. Avoid using only bath water on **azaleas** and **rhododendrons;** these shrubs like acid soil, and soapy water is slightly alkaline.

• If you are lucky enough to live on a lake, it is theoretically possible to pump water from it for your landscape. Before you attempt this, consider: 1) An electrician will be needed to install a 220-volt power line for an electric pump (gasoline pumps are rarely adequate). 2) Irrigation sprinklers demand moderately clean water. How will the lake water be filtered and how often must the filter be cleaned? 3) The initial cost of an irrigation system is not insubstantial. Wouldn't it be cheaper to design a landscape that did not demand so much water? (See Annuals, May).

Avoid pumping water from a nearby creek without considering the effect the lower water level downstream will have. Small fish, frogs, and invertebrates depend on water for their lives. Birds and other predators depend on smaller animals for their food.

Some gardeners prefer to use "organic" fertilizers like manure, blood meal, and fish emulsion. These products are slightly more expensive but have the advantage of adding plenty of micronutrients to the soil. Research by Dr. Tim Smalley, horticulture professor at the University of Georgia, has shown that composted hen litter continues to release plant food for four years after a 2-inch layer is rototilled into flower beds.

Apply an organic fertilizer at the rate recommended on the container.

## PROBLEMS

It may seem contradictory, but the highest incidence of garden root rot problems seems to occur when summer watering restrictions are imposed. Perhaps gardeners fear that since water is limited, they should water all the more! Root rot is caused by soggy soil, which leads to weak root growth and an increase in soil fungi. Symptoms include yellow leaves, wilting, and plant stems that break at ground level.

Prevent root rot by watering annuals deeply once per week and mixing plenty of organic amendments into the soil before planting.

Continue checking for insect damage to your plants. The key to insect control is to identify the insect or other pest responsible. Many can be identified by their characteristic damage, like the lace doily effect of Japanese beetle feeding and the round leaf notches of black vine weevil.

## GROOMING

Continue deadheading annual flowers, as described in June.

## FERTILIZING

Continue to fertilize at two- to six-week intervals as discussed in Annuals, May. When using granular products, be sure to water afterwards to carry the nutrients down to plant roots.

## HELPFUL HINT

Here are some sources of tools for physically challenged gardeners:

Walt Nicke Co., P.O. Box 433, Topsfield, MA 01983
**www.gardentalk.com**

Lee Valley Tools Ltd., P.O. Box 1780, Ogensburg, NY 13669-6780, (800) 871-8158, **www.leevalley.com**

A. M. Leonard, Inc., 241 Fox Drive, Piqua, OH 45356-0816, (800) 543-8955, **www.amleo.com**

# AUGUST

## ANNUALS

### PLANNING

Concentrate on maintaining one or two blooming "oases" in your landscape—even if you have to allow the rest of the yard to dry out. Scavenge water from your bathtub or sink to keep your oases beautiful (see Annuals, May and July).

### PLANTING

Few Georgia gardeners manage to keep every plant alive over a hot summer. Remove annuals that have died or become unattractive. Replace plants whose removal leaves holes in a bed of flowers. Purchase mature plants of the same size as those in your bed.

### CARE

Mulches such as pine straw or shredded wood chips help conserve moisture by preventing evaporation. Placing about 3 inches of mulch 6 inches back from the base of a tree or shrub is an ideal way to maintain moisture under even the driest conditions. Fine-textured mulches hold moisture better than coarse-textured mulches. Good mulches are pine straw, pine bark mini-nuggets, and shredded hardwood mulch or chips. Avoid large-nugget pine bark, rock, gravel, and marble.

### WATERING

Water restrictions or bans make the task of scheduling irrigation in your garden a bit more difficult. Don't make the mistake of watering heavily every time watering is allowed. Many annuals can go for several days between waterings if they are irrigated heavily (by rain or your hose) once per week.

A heavy irrigation is 1 inch or more of rainfall or irrigation or 1 gallon of water per foot of plant height.

Examine plants for signs of water stress (wilting, blue/gray leaves) before you water.

When watering by hand, apply 5 gallons of water per 10 square feet. This is approximately the amount of water delivered by a garden hose operating at medium pressure for 1 minute.

A soaker hose can effectively water a swath 1 foot wide on either side of the hose. A 50-foot-long hose can water 100 square feet of landscape bed.

Apply 50 gallons of water per 100 square feet when plants show water stress.

Newly purchased soaker hoses are unwieldy at first as you stretch them among plants.

Use soil anchor pins made from surplus clothes hangers (see Annuals, December) to hold the hose in place.

Several granular products designed to conserve water have appeared in the last few years. The small granules look like grains of salt when dry; when mixed with water, they absorb the moisture and swell to many times their previous size. Manufacturers claim that by mixing the granules with the soil in a hot, dry flower bed, water can be stored and then released when plants need it. Research has shown these products hold some promise but are not "miracle" substances.

The best way to mix them with your soil is to sprinkle a few tablespoons of crystals in an empty wheelbarrow and add water. Follow the manufacturer's recommended rate. Once the crystals have become like jelly, slowly add garden soil to the wheelbarrow and mix thoroughly. Use the soil to fill your flower bed.

Some water-conserving products are diminished by fertilizer; others are consumed by soil organisms. In a few years you'll have to add more of the granules to your soil in order to continue reaping the benefits.

## FERTILIZING

Continue to fertilize at two- to six-week intervals as discussed in Annuals, May. When using granular products, be sure to water afterwards to carry the nutrients down to plant roots.

## PROBLEMS

The slug and snail population builds and wanes during the year, depending on the weather. The numbers can grow to such heights that most of an annual or perennial plant can be consumed overnight. Symptoms include large, irregular holes chewed in leaves, and silvery slime trails that can be seen on nearby leaves and mulch. There are several environmental controls you may wish to try:

• Press a saucer into the ground near affected plants, and fill with stale beer. Slugs and snails will fall into the beer and drown.

## HELPFUL HINT

Intense sunshine may be beneficial to some plants, but it is no friend to a gardener's skin.

• Keep containers of sunscreen in places convenient to the garden so you won't forget to apply it before working in the sun. If you dislike the greasy feel on your fingers, purchase the spray-bottle kind. Products with an SPF greater than 15 are best.

• It might be a good idea to anoint the skin under your shirt as well. A T-shirt has an SPF of only 5.

• Wear a hat to protect your face and neck.

• Long-sleeved, specially made sun-protective clothing is available at camping/hunting/outdoor equipment stores.

Regularly examine your skin for changes in moles and skin pigmentation. A yearly appointment with a dermatologist is a good idea if you work in the sun constantly.

• Support a 10x10-inch board slightly above the ground on small stones. Check it in the afternoon, and swipe the creatures into a pail of soapy water.

• Scatter inverted plastic plant "six-packs" or hollowed-out cantaloupe halves around affected plants. Check these slug and snail refuges every day, and discard those filled with the pests.

• Copper repels mollusks. Place a 1-inch-wide strip of copper screen around the top edge of the clay pot in which affected plants grow.

Some prefer chemical controls:

• Apply a band of iron phosphate paste or bait around plants.

• Place metaldehyde pellets in an empty small plastic soft drink bottle. Lay the bottle on its side. Use a rock, soil, or a twig to make a bridge from the soil level up to the neck of the bottle. Slugs and snails will feed on the pellets, but the poison will be inaccessible to pets and children.

## GROOMING

Cut back faded but healthy annual flowers by half, then water, and fertilize lightly with a water-soluble fertilizer. A second season of blooms will begin to appear in two weeks.

# September

## ANNUALS

 PLANNING

Most large flower beds contain several kinds of flowers—some may be perennial, some annual, some brightly colored, and so on. When you plan the layout of the flowers in the bed, a paper sketch might not be as helpful as physically marking where the groups of different flowers will be placed. Use a sharpened stake to draw onto the soil the outline of the different flower groups. When you are satisfied, sprinkle kitchen flour into the lines the stake has made. The white flour contrasts nicely with the soil. If you need to make a change, "erase" the flour with new soil, and draw a new line with flour.

 PLANTING

Though garden centers often have **pansies** and spring bulbs on hand in September, it is too early to plant them. If a bed of summer annuals is on its last legs, pull out the plants, and begin preparing the soil for the cool-season planting that will begin in October. See Horticultural Practices, p. 9, for the steps in preparing a bed.

 CARE

Though the weather is still hot, it's time to plan for saving the seed of some plants and rooting others to hold indoors during the winter.

### Saving Seed

1. As the seedpods on **impatiens, cleome, hollyhock, foxglove,** and **moonvine** dry out, collect them, and place each in a separate envelope. In a week or so, the pods will split and release the seeds.

2. Seedheads from perennials like **purple coneflower, Shasta daisy, black-eyed Susan,** and others can be collected when dry and gently crumbled above a sheet of paper. Separate the

Try rooting coleus, pentas, begonia, and geranium in fall. They can be wintered indoors until spring planting.

seeds from the pods, petals, and chaff as best you can. One way is to purse your lips and blow gently on a mound of seed. Place the cleaned seed in a small envelope, and label it clearly.

3. Insert several envelopes of seed into a pint jar. Enclose 2 tablespoons of dry milk powder in tissue paper, then wrap with a rubber band. Slip this into the jar with the seed.

4. Tighten the jar lid securely, and place it on a back shelf of your refrigerator. A storage temperature between 35 and 45 degrees Fahrenheit plus the drying action of the milk powder makes an excellent environment to keep the seed viable until next spring.

### Taking Cuttings

1. Several plants, including **coleus, pentas, begonia,** and **geranium,** can be propagated in fall and grown indoors until spring. Use a sharp knife to take 3- to 4-inch cuttings from the ends of vigorous, unflowering branches. Remove all lower leaves; allow just two or three leaves to remain on the cutting tip.

2. Dip the cut end into a rooting hormone such as Rootone™.

3. Fill several small pots with a 50:50 mixture of perlite and peat moss. Make a 2-inch-deep hole in the center of the rooting medium. Insert a single cutting 2 inches into a hole. Firm the

medium around the cutting. Repeat until all holes are filled. Water the pots, and let drain.

4. Put the pots into clear plastic bags, and seal. Set the pots in a bright east- or north-facing window (not in direct sunlight).

5. Open the bags in three weeks. Remove the plants, and care for each as a houseplant until the weather is warm enough to set them out in April.

## WATERING

Watch "indicator plants" like **impatiens** and **pentas** for signs of drought stress. When these plants are drooping, it's time to water your flower beds.

## FERTILIZING

Continue to fertilize at two- to six-week intervals as discussed in Annuals, May. When using granular products, be sure to water afterwards to carry the nutrients down to plant roots.

## PROBLEMS

The seeds of winter annual weeds such as chickweed, henbit, and annual bluegrass begin sprouting later this month. You can prevent them in your beds of winter flowers by applying a weed-preventer by mid-month. Read the label on any product you are considering to make sure it can be used on flowers. Be sure to irrigate thoroughly after applying the weed-preventer, to dissolve the chemical into the soil.

---

## HELPFUL HINT

Take care when weeding your landscape by hand this month. There are several stinging caterpillars that feed on plant leaves; they can make a nasty welt on your skin accompanied by an intense burning sensation.

• The bright-green saddleback caterpillar, 3/4 to 1 inch long, has a large brown "saddle" in its back and white poisonous bristles at each end of its body.

• The puss caterpillar, 1 to 1 1/2 inches long, has a flattened shape and is covered with brown hair that conceals stinging spines.

Control stinging caterpillars, if you choose to, with a contact insecticide or with a product containing *Bacillus thuringiensis*.

Other caterpillars are dangerous-looking but harmless. Let them go about their business, and you might be rewarded later with a glimpse of a moth or butterfly.

• A hickory horned devil, 4 to 5 inches long and blue-green with orange horns on its head, becomes a regal moth after it pupates.

• A hornworm (which comes in several varieties) has a characteristic horn on one end of its green body; it will become a sphinx moth if allowed to mature.

• Fall webworms form large colonies protected by a large web at the end of tree branches; these caterpillars are covered with white hair but are harmless.

• The spicebush caterpillar has fearsome black eyes at one end of its body; it will become a beautiful spicebush swallowtail butterfly after pupation.

---

## GROOMING

Reserve a day this month to tidy up plants that have tattered leaves, dead stems, and faded flowers. Even tired plants look better when they are neat.

# OCTOBER
## ANNUALS

### PLANNING

This is **pansy**-planting month throughout the state. Follow these tips in order to have color from their blooms in your landscape in winter.

**Timing:** In north Georgia, begin planting in early October as daytime temperatures fall into the seventies. In south Georgia, begin planting mid-October or later. Ideal conditions are when the weather is predicted to be cool for the next several days.

**Bed preparation: Pansies** have fine roots and need very soft soil in order to grow well. They cannot tolerate soggy soil. Rototill a 2-inch layer of organic material into prospective **pansy** beds.

**Spacing: Pansies** can be planted at a 6- to 10-inch spacing between plants. The smaller spacing results in a fuller bed but may make **pansies** more susceptible to disease due to crowding next spring. Use a 10-inch spacing when planting 3- or 4-inch-size potted plants.

### PLANTING

In north Georgia, plant **poppy, larkspur,** and **sweet alyssum** seeds now. Lightly scratch the ground around fading peren-nial flowers using an iron rake. Scatter seeds lightly. Press into place in the soil with the palm of your hand. Do not cover with earth, since these seeds need light to germinate. Do not water; allow nature to nurture the seeds. Little seedlings will germinate by November and they can be thinned. The seedlings will survive the winter without harm and will grow into larger plants next spring.

**Pansies** are not the only sources of flowers for fall through spring—**dianthus, snapdragon, stock,** and **viola** easily withstand winter weather conditions. **Ornamental kale** and **cabbage** as well as **lettuce** and **parsley** can lend their colorful foliage to your winter landscape.

### CARE

The magnificent leaves of **banana** trees and **elephant ear** tubers will not survive a freeze. Though it is a bit of work, they can be stored for winter and planted outside once again in late spring.

To store **banana:** Cut off all leaves close to the main trunk. Use shovels to excavate a rootball approximately 24 inches in diameter. Wrap the rootball tightly with burlap or sheet plastic. Invite friends to help you move the leafless trunk and its rootball to your basement or to a place where temperatures will not go much below freezing.

To store **elephant ear:** allow frost to kill the leaves. (use caution when chopping green stems: the sap can damage your eyes.) In the northern third of the state, dig the tubers, and allow them to dry in a covered spot. Store in a place where temperatures are between 50 and 70 degrees Fahrenheit. A cool basement is actually not as good as a closet upstairs. In the lower two-thirds of Georgia, **elephant ear** tubers will usually survive the winter when left in the ground.

It's pansy time in Georgia!

## WATERING

Plants dry out rapidly on sunny days, even when temperatures begin to cool off. Don't wait for plants to wilt; check soil moisture regularly with your fingers.

## FERTILIZING

**Pansies** and other cool-season plants bloom wonderfully during the winter as long as they receive proper nutrients. Fertilizing cool-season plants is different from fertilizing summertime annuals because the soil is cold while they are growing and blooming. Soil organisms that help release fertilizer nutrients in warm soil are not very active in chilly soil.

• Immediately after planting, fertilize with a water-soluble, quickly available fertilizer such as Miracle-Gro®.

• Repeat two weeks later if daytime temperatures are still in the seventies.

• Every four weeks, while the soil is cold, fertilize with a product such as Pansy Booster™, which contains a high percentage of nitrate nitrogen. Nitrate nitrogen does not rely on soil organisms to convert it to a form the plant can use. (Fertilizer products that do not contain nitrate nitrogen do very little for **pansies** that are

## OVERWINTERING GERANIUMS

**Geraniums** with an attractive flower color can be removed from the ground and kept indoors for the winter. Although keeping the plants in a sunny window will allow you to observe them daily, a **geranium's** fleshy stem and roots allow it to survive a few months in darkness.

• Water plants thoroughly a week before frost is predicted.

• Dig individual plants and place in separate paper bags. Medium-sized grocery bags are ideal.

• Place several bags in a cardboard box. Put the box in a cool place, such as a basement or garage.

• Check on the plants at Christmas; moisten the soil with a spray bottle; remove yellow leaves. Repeat in mid-February.

• In late March, bring the plants into a moderately shady, protected spot, and water thoroughly.

• In a week or so, sprouts will emerge from the stems, and the plant can be planted in its spring/summer home (remember to protect from freezing with a covering of pine straw if a late frost threatens).

growing in cold soil.) Continue to fertilize according to label directions until March 15.

• Resume fertilizing, with a water-soluble fertilizer, in late March. Fertilize every two weeks until you replace cool-season plants with summer annuals.

## PROBLEMS

Before the first frost, newly planted **pansies** are sometimes devoured by caterpillars of the fritillary butterfly. Symptoms are leaves that have been consumed back to the mid-vein. Look for small black droppings on the soil under the plant. Spray affected plants immediately with B.t..

If you plant in early October, or if you've had caterpillar problems before, consider applying a preventative spray of B.t. or a contact insecticide just after planting.

## GROOMING

Remove summer annuals as they deteriorate. It is usually easier to remove everything all at once from a bed, even though some annuals are still blooming. Rototill the soil, and add organic amendments (see Horticultural Practices, p. 10) before planting any winter annuals.

## ANNUALS

### PLANNING

Many gardeners dream of having a greenhouse in which they can putter with their plants throughout the weekend. Greenhouse kits can be purchased from home improvement centers or through special garden catalogs. Before you invest a great deal of money, consider the following questions:

**Do I have a proper site and enough room?**

The greenhouse should be in full sun to avoid high winter heating bills. Siting it near trees invites frequent damage to the glazing. Municipal building codes often limit how close you can build next to a property line. Check with your local zoning office.

**How will I provide heat to the greenhouse?**

Solar heating will not keep it warm on cold winter days. A natural gas or electric heater will be required.

**How will I provide electricity?**

The cost of running an electric line from your home to the greenhouse can be substantial. Installation should only be performed by a licensed electrician.

**How will I provide water?**

Extending a water line can be accomplished by a handy gardener, but a trench must be dug

---

### HELPFUL HINT

Local offices of the University of Georgia Cooperative Extension Service (see Resources, p. 289) have a free publication, *Managing the Hobby Greenhouse.* Other sources of greenhouse information and supplies are:

Charley's Greenhouse Supply, 17979 State Route 536, Mt. Vernon, WA 98273, (800) 322-4707, **www.charleysgreenhouse.com**

ACF Greenhouses, 380 Greenhouse Drive, Buffalo Junction, VA 24529, (888) 888-9050, **www. littlegreenhouse.com**

---

at least 12 inches deep in which to place the pipe.

**Would a cold frame serve some of my needs just as well?**

See Care in this month.

### PLANTING

Winter annuals, especially **pansies,** that are not growing vigorously by this time will not survive a severe winter. Replace weak plants with large ones. Examine the root systems of the replacements to make sure they are healthy. Roots should be white and numerous, and spread uniformly in the potting soil.

In north Georgia, look for already-sprouted seedlings of **foxglove, hollyhock, money plant,** and **flowering tobacco;** they should be no closer than 6 inches apart. Unless they are already in a favorable place, move the small plants to a "nurse bed" where they can grow for

the winter. Next spring you can move them from the nursery to their appointed spots.

Plant **poppy, larkspur,** and **sweet alyssum** seed now (see Annuals, October).

### CARE

On a warm weekend, make a final cleanup of your landscape:

1. Clip the dried stalks of annuals and perennials close to the ground.

2. Tuck pine straw around newly planted annuals.

3. Gently brush fallen tree leaves off flower beds. Use them for mulch under trees and shrubs.

A cold frame is a smaller, unheated version of a greenhouse. In it you can protect half-hardy annuals from brief freezes and can toughen annual seedlings before planting in beds next spring. Many cold frame designs have been tried.

Here is one you can make yourself from a double-hung storm window and some 2×6 lumber.

1. Purchase the storm window first. A large one (approx. 36 by 75 inches) is best. Make sure both sashes slide easily.

2. Using the storm window dimensions and the 2x6 lumber, construct a bottomless and topless box onto which the storm window can be mounted. Attach the storm window to the box frame with screws.

3. Using the same dimensions as the first one, construct two or three more bottomless/topless boxes.

4. Place a bottomless/topless box on the ground in a sunny, sheltered spot. Stack one or two boxes on top—use two if you need the additional height. (Whether you use two or three boxes in the stack, the one to which the storm window is mounted should be the very top one.)

5. Seal the joints between the boxes with duct tape on the inside and outside.

## HELPFUL HINT

Collect the bags of leaves (especially pine straw) that your neighbors stack so helpfully at the curb. Use the leaves to build several compost piles (see Horticultural Practices, p. 10). Use the pine straw immediately for mulch, or pile it under a plastic tarp to use later in the winter.

6. Open one of the storm window sashes, and place your plants inside. Leave it open on sunny days (so it does not overheat), and close it at night. Your plants will enjoy the mini-greenhouse in fall and spring even though you can't be in there with them!

## WATERING

Water **pansies** and other flowers that you have recently planted if no rainfall occurs. All these plants need to be growing vigorously as colder weather nears; make sure the soil is moist to 6 inches deep.

## FERTILIZING

Fertilize cool-season flowers (see Annuals, October).

## PROBLEMS

Pull weeds like chickweed and henbit now, before they have time to mature and drop seed. Dig out the roots of wild violet, wild onion, and dandelion; simply pulling off the leaves will not control these perennial weeds.

## GROOMING

Spend a warm afternoon clipping and removing the brown stems of annuals killed by frost. Accumulate your clippings in one spot and transport them to the compost pile when finished. Vacant beds can be covered with pine straw and left for the winter, or you can plant winter annuals (see Annuals, October). Remove faded flowers from the **pansies** you planted in October.

# DECEMBER

## ANNUALS

 **PLANNING**

December is a time for slow walks through your landscape, coffee in hand, to reflect on what has pleased you in the last year and what can be improved. If you have taken photographs regularly, you can spread them on the kitchen table to follow the progress of your flowers during the growing season.

**Were there times when nothing was blooming?**

Research the peak bloom time for different annuals. Make notes in your garden journal on what to plant in the bare spots next year. Don't forget that some selections of the same annual plant bloom before or after the variety you commonly use. If you are always successful with a particular annual, look for other selections that bloom at the time you need flowers.

**Did some plants grow larger than expected?**

Make notes of where to plant or move them next spring so they won't overshadow their neighbors.

**Was the backdrop for your flowers always effective?**

Extend the gardening season by covering your plants to protect them from the cold.

Refer to the lists of good trees, shrubs, and grasses in other chapters of this book for ideas. Consult the *Georgia Gardener's Guide: Revised Edition* for our recommendations of the best plants for Georgia's conditions.

 **PLANTING**

Cool-season annuals make great companions in a pot. Find a decorative container (or several!), and plant arrangements of **pansies, parsley,** and **snapdragons.** Keep the pots outdoors (by your front door, on your deck, etc.) for most of the winter, but bring them indoors for a few days at a time to decorate your home during the holiday season.

 **CARE**

Overenthusiastic gardeners may find there is not enough room in their home to carry over the plants that would normally reside outdoors. Rooted cuttings on windowsills, patio plants stacked by the sliding glass door, and houseplants may all vie for space.

Refer to the plans for a PVC light stand (Annuals, February) or an A-frame stand (Houseplants, February) for supplemental lighting options. Consider "lending" your plants to a school lobby or an assisted-living home. Both plants and people will benefit from the change of scenery.

Hoes, rakes, and shovels are expensive. It is easy to prolong their life by following a few good garden habits:

1. Rinse tools with fresh water as soon as you are finished using them to remove dirt. Soil left on wooden handles causes them to deteriorate quickly.

2. Paint boiled (not raw) linseed oil on wooden handles three times a year. Let it soak in overnight, then wipe off with a rag.

3. Use sandpaper on wooden handles that have become rough. They will feel much better to your touch. After sanding, give the handle a linseed oil treatment.

4. Spray a lubricant like WD-40 on the blades to protect them.

5. See Edibles, December, to learn how to sharpen tools.

A product called "floating row cover" is underappreciated for its usefulness in the garden. Made of very lightweight, translucent, woven plastic, a sheet of row cover can be spread over newly planted annuals to protect them from frost. Since the row cover is not opaque, it can be left on the plants for a few days until they are hardened off. Row cover is also useful for protecting annuals from unexpected frost in the spring. You can make soil anchors for the row cover from surplus clothes hangers.

## HELPFUL HINT

Good stocking stuffers are a water timer, solid aluminum trowel, indoor-outdoor thermometer, handpruners, indoor plant food, rain gauge, a garden book (see Resources, p. 288), and garden magazine subscriptions.

Use tin snips to make three cuts: in the center of the long, straight part and on both sides of the hook, under the twisted wire. Pliers may be needed to straighten the wire slightly so it slides into the soil easily.

## WATERING

Water winter annuals if rain has not fallen in the last seven days. Do not allow their roots to become dry.

An overlooked benefit of winter mulch is that it retains soil heat. Pine straw, in particular, traps an insulating layer of air close to the earth.

Keep an extra couple of bales of pine straw in a sheltered spot so straw will be handy if needed.

## FERTILIZING

Fertilize cool-season flowers again (see Annuals, October).

## PROBLEMS

Rabbits are often unfairly accused of eating the leaves of annuals in winter. It is more likely that the leaves wither due to insufficient roots during windy, cold days or to root rot. Visit your beds after a rain and note if water stands there for more than a few minutes. If so, the bed is not well drained.

Consider redirecting the source of the water (moving gutter drains, trenching around the bed, etc.).

Examine the roots of plants whose leaves have disappeared. If they are almost nonexistent, re-dig the bed, and add more soil amendments to raise it farther above the surrounding soil.

Plant large-sized replacements in the bed.

## GROOMING

Remove faded flowers from **pansies, dianthus,** and **snapdragons.**

# BULBS, CORMS, RHIZOMES, & TUBERS

Bulbs are amazing. A bulb in its dormant stage, whether a true bulb, corm, tuber, or rhizome, gives no hint of the beauty that lies within. Bulbs are all different, yet they possess similar characteristics in the way they store energy, actively grow, then go through a dormant period. During dormancy, growth is slowed to a minimum, roots die away, and new ones replace them. Portions of the underground plant contain stored food, leaves, flowers, and seeds. The dormant stage can be extended if bulbs are dug up when they are leafless and rootless. This means that unlike most other plants, bulbs can be shipped in their dormant state all over the country and world with relative ease, provided they are kept cool and dry.

There are types that bloom in spring, summer, and fall, and there are even a few that bloom in late winter, like snowdrops *Galanthus nivalis*. We in Georgia are fortunate. In most parts of the state, there is enough cold in winter to meet the chilling requirements that many bulbs have before they will bloom in spring, yet it is also mild enough that we can grow some of the tropical-type bulbs such as tuberose and alstroemeria. In coastal areas where temperatures are warmer than

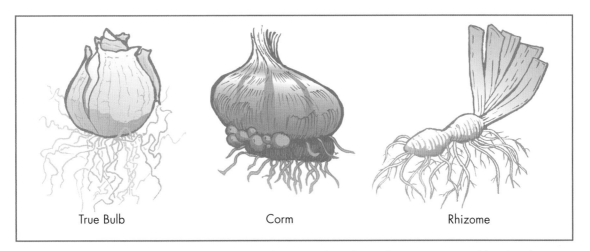

| True Bulb | Corm | Rhizome |

in other parts of the state, bulbs may need to be prechilled before they are planted to ensure good blooms (see October for details).

Some bulbs are swollen and fat and others are small and shriveled, but such characteristics do not determine the beauty of the flowers that individual bulbs produce. For example, the windflower *Anemone blanda* has a tuberous root that looks like a dried-up raisin, but the flowers, 1 to 1 1/2 inches across, are delicate and beautiful, sky-blue daisies that appear on stems 3 to 4 inches above soft ferny foliage.

Colchicums bloom even before you plant them, while other bulbs bloom five to six months after planting. Narcissus bulbs have been known to persist, blooming each spring in the same site for over one hundred years, surviving long after the generation of gardeners that planted them.

By selecting the right bulbs (see March for sun and shade preferences) for the right location, you can have large areas of bulbs that naturalize in a short period of time. With a well-thought-out plan, your garden can feature bulbs for every season.

## TYPES OF BULBS

A **true bulb** may be considered a bud. An onion (a true bulb) sliced lengthwise shows the budlike structure. Pale-green leaves in the center are protected by concentric layers of fleshy tissue called scales. The scales contain stored food and energy for the plant when it is actively growing, and the future flower is protected by the scales and the leaves. At the base of the bulb is a stem to which the scales and small leaves are joined; at the bottom of this is the basal plate, where roots emerge when the bulb is planted. If the basal plate is damaged, there may be fewer and smaller roots. It is for this reason that a healthy basal plate is important. The outer layer on a bulb is dry and papery and keeps the bulb from drying out. This layer is called a tunic. Daffodils, tulips, and hyacinths all have tunics; a lily bulb has scales that are short and fleshy, and there is no tunic or outer layer to protect them. A bulb is usually underground, but small bulbs called bulbils may appear in leaf axils of a plant like the blackberry lily, or in flowers and on stems of certain bulbous plants.

A **corm** is a short, enlarged, fleshy underground stem. Like a bulb, it is usually surrounded by a tunic, but the inside is solid. One or more buds give rise to leaves, stems, and flowers above ground; it roots from the base. Examples of corms are colchicum, crocus, and gladiolus.

A **rhizome** is a thickened stem that grows completely or partially underground, like rhizomatous iris, which should be planted so the rhizome is barely covered. Growing points initiate at the tip or along the length of the rhizome, and roots

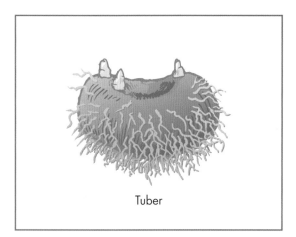

Tuber

develop from the underside. Rhizomes include calla lilies and bearded iris. (Dutch iris grow from bulbs.)

A **tuber** is a swollen underground branch or rootstock that contains a supply of stored food. It has "eyes" or buds from which stems are produced. Cyclamens, some of the anemones, and caladiums are examples of tubers. When you divide tubers, make sure each section has a growth bud. While cyclamen tubers continue to get larger over time, they never produce offsets as do caladiums. (Caladiums' offsets can be removed and planted.)

**Tuberous roots** store nutrients. Daylilies and dahlias are examples of tuberous roots. Their growth is such that the roots grow in clusters, radiating out from a center point, and buds are produced at the bases of old stems. When you divide tuberous-rooted plants, make sure each section has roots and shoots.

## PLANTING AND CARE FOR YOUR BULBS

When you purchase bulbs, select those that are firm and have the smallest number of nicks or bruises. If they are soft and mushy, they will probably die. If you buy your bulbs from a mail-order source, order from a company that grades its bulbs or specifies a size so you will have a better idea of their quality. You will save money in the

long run if you start with bulbs that are healthy. Open boxes or bags of bulbs as soon as you receive them, and keep them in a cool (60 degrees Fahrenheit or cooler), dry, airy place until you can plant them.

Most bulbs will grow in an average garden soil, provided it is well drained. Adding 2 to 3 inches of organic material, like compost or shredded pine bark, will help improve drainage if there is a problem. Mix in the organic material to a depth of 10 to 12 inches.

Take a soil test (see Horticultural Practices, p. 7) before you plant your bulbs, and the results will tell you what you need to add in the way of nutrients and lime. The pH for most bulbs should be between 6 and 7. As with all plants, the better the soil and the more vigorous the bulbs, the bigger the blooms will be. Prepare your planting area ahead of time. The sooner you get bulbs in the ground, the better.

Wait to plant spring-flowering bulbs when the soil temperatures are at 60 degrees Fahrenheit or cooler in the fall. Depending on where you live in the state, this varies from October to early January (see Lawns, Introduction to learn how to measure soil temperature).

There are several methods of planting bulbs. You can dig holes and plant individual bulbs, or you can dig out a large area (a circle, a square, or an irregular shape) and space bulbs out in the area, in a random pattern. The second technique is especially effective for naturalistic plantings that use large drifts of one type of bulb like daffodils or crocus.

As a rule of thumb, most bulbs should be planted at a depth that is three to four times the width of the bulb you are planting. There are exceptions, like the bearded iris, which should be planted shallowly (see January for details about planting depths).

Water deeply after planting, and apply a good layer of mulch. If you get 1 to 2 inches of rainfall

CHAPTER TWO

# TOOLS FOR PLANTING BULBS

### Bulb Trowels
Designed especially for planting blubs, these trowels have long handles and a narrow sharp pointed stainless steel blade, so they won't rust. They come in different sizes, and unlike traditional trowels which are designed to scoop out the soil, you simply stab the soil and pull the trowel toward yourself to create a planting hole. The 9- or 12-inch trowel is perfect for planting smaller bulbs like crocus or anemones. The 22-inch trowel has a blade that is 2 inches wide, making it suitable for planting larger bulbs whether in the lawn or the flower bed.

### Bulb Planter
There are different versions of this tool, but the basic construction is a planter that is 40 inches high from the tip of the stainless steel blade to the handle which is on a steel frame. These heavy–duty tools weigh 6 pounds or more. The blade is a cylinder. Using your feet, push the blade into the soil and then pull out a large plug of soil. Place the bulb in the hole and replace the cylinder of soil on top of the bulbs.

### Bulb Planter for Naturalizing or Soil That Is Unprepared
A heavy–duty steel tool 38 inches tall, it can weigh 8 pounds. Like the bulb planter, you operate this planter by standing on the foot bar. The notched 2 1/2-inch-wide blade is heavy enough that it is easy to push into the ground, whether it's the lawn, a border, or a meadow.

per week, that should be adequate. Use small cans like tuna fish or cat food cans to measure rainfall. Once there is 3/4 to 1 inch of water in the can, the bulbs have received enough moisture.

If watering by hand, apply 5 gallons of water per square foot. This is approximately the amount of water delivered by a garden hose operating one minute at medium pressure, and it should be enough water to penetrate at least 6 inches into a soil with a good percentage of clay. Repeat this step if bulbs are planted deeper than 6 inches.

## FERTILIZING BULBS
Spring-blooming bulbs should be fertilized in the fall and then again in spring when you see shoots emerging. Do not put fertilizer directly in the hole when planting bulbs, for it could burn tender new roots as it dissolves. Instead, topdress with a complete fertilizer. Use 1 to 2 pounds of 10-10-10 per 100 square feet. For topdressing in the spring, use a water-soluble formula (like 10-10-10) that will get to the roots quickly while the bulb is actively growing and before it blooms.

Do not fertilize spring-blooming bulbs while they are blooming or just after they finish blooming. See November for more information on fertilizing bulbs.

## PEST CONTROL
Bulbs are not bothered by many pest or disease problems, and good cultural practices can greatly reduce or eliminate most of the problems they do have. Most bulbs need plenty of moisture while they are actively growing, but during the dormant season, too much water can cause root rot. Make sure that you plant bulbs in a well-drained soil.

Aphids, thrips, and mites can attack the foliage and flowers of bulbs. Leaves and buds may be distorted, and leaves may be speckled. Inspect on a regular basis, and, whenever possible, use an insecticidal soap for pest problems before resorting to stronger pesticides.

# CHAPTER TWO

## Bulbs, Corms, Rhizomes, & Tubers for Georgia

| Common Name<br>Botanical Name | Size | Season<br>of Bloom | Culture and Remarks |
|---|---|---|---|
| *Allium christophii*<br>**Ornamental Onion** | 12 to 20 inches tall. | Blooms in early summer. Clusters of silvery amethyst flowers form a large head. | Sunny locations and well-drained soils. Combine with other perennials like **hostas** and **daylilies**. |
| *Allium giganteum*<br>**Giant Ornamental Onion** | Softball-sized heads of lilac-colored flowers on stems 40 to 48 inches tall. | Blooms in late spring. | Plant in full sun in well-drained soil. Combine with other bulbs and perennials like hardy **geraniums**, **Siberian iris**, and **peonies**. |
| *Allium spaerocephalon*<br>**Drumstick Allium** | Quarter-sized flowers on stems 18 to 30 inches high. | Maroon-colored flowers in midsummer. | Plant in full sun in well-drained soil. A great bulb to perennialize. Combine with **crinums**, **daylilies**, and **Asiatic lilies**. |
| *Alocasia* cvs.<br>**Elephant Ear** | 5 to 10 feet or taller and equal in width. | Grown for its handsome foliage, summer until frost. | Grows in full sun or shade. Prefers a moist soil. Great for containers, in ponds, or in the ground. A dramatic plant that gives a tropical flair. |
| *Alstroemeria psittacina*<br>**Parrot Lily** | Flowers occur on stems 24 to 30 inches tall. | Midsummer blooms in shades of marigold-orange with violet splotches. There are also pastel selections. | Plant in light shade in a well-drained soil. Keep roots cool. This plant makes a great cut flower. Look for hardy types 'Freedom' and 'Redcoat'. |
| *Anemone blanda*<br>**Windflower** | 3 to 4 inches tall. | Small daisylike flowers with fernlike foliage in early spring. | Plant in full sun or part shade in a moist soil. Soak tubers overnight before planting. Great for naturalizing. |
| *Caladium* cvs.<br>**Caladium** | Range in size from 8 to 40 inches tall. | Colorful foliage all summer until frost. Variegated green-and-white, red-and-green, pink, and spotted leaf types. | Wait until the soil is 60 degrees F. or warmer. Plant tubers 6 inches deep. **Caladiums** are great for the shade garden. They are happy in containers or in the ground. |
| *Canna* cvs.<br>**Canna** | Ranging in size from 2 to 8 feet tall, these lush perennials start as tuberous rootstock. | Lance-shaped leaves come in green, burgundy, variegated, and striped. Colorful flowers in summer to fall are a bonus. | Plant in containers, along the edge of a pond, or in the perennial garden. Great in the garden for a dramatic tropical flair. |

# Bulbs, Corms, Rhizomes, & Tubers for Georgia

| Common Name Botanical Name | Size | Season of Bloom | Culture and Remarks |
|---|---|---|---|
| *Colocasia esculenta* **Elephant Ear** | Leaves may be up to 2 feet wide and plants 4 feet or taller. | Grown for its colorful foliage, 'Black Magic' has dark purple-black leaves. | Part sun or shade is ideal. Prefers a soil that is rich in organic matter. A great plant to use for adding colorful foliage to the shade garden. |
| *Crinum* spp. and cvs. **Crinum** | Large sword-shaped leaves form large clumps, up to 3 or more feet across. | Lily-shaped fragrant flowers 4 to 6 inches long appear on tall stalks in mid- to late summer. | Full sun or partial shade. The bulbs resent being disturbed. Provide plenty of moisture. Rodents will not disturb this bulb. A good companion for perennials. |
| *Crocosmia* x *crocosmiiflora* **Crocosmia** | Swordlike foliage. Graceful 24- to 36-inch-tall stems, covered with flowers. | Flowers in shades of orange to orange-red appear in late summer. | Plant in full sun in a soil that is moist but well drained. Long-lasting as a cut flower. 'Lucifer' is a robust selection. |
| *Crocus* sp. and cvs. **Crocus** | **Crocus** range in size from 3 to 6 inches tall. | There are both fall- and spring-blooming types. | Plant corms 2 to 3 inches deep in a well-drained soil. **Crocus** prefer full sun to partial shade. Be warned, **crocus** is a favorite of chipmunks, who dig up and eat the flowers and the bulbs. |
| *Dahlia* cvs. **Dahlia** | The size of individual plants and flowers of this tuber ranges greatly from 12 to 80 inches high. | Flowers vary from the tiny pom-pom to the large dinner-plate type. Blooms summer through fall. | These showy flowers grow happily in full sun but will tolerate partial shade. A well-drained soil is best. Pest-resistant, **dahlias** come in a wide range of colors. |
| *Galanthus nivalis* **Snowdrop** | One-inch-wide, white, three-lobed, nodding, bell-shaped flowers on 6- to 9-inch stems. | Flowers appear as early as January and may continue on and of through March. | Plant these bulbs in full sun or partial shade in a moist, well-drained soil. Because the bulbs are so tiny and dry out easily, the best time to divide them is right after they finish flowering. |
| *Gladiolus* spp. and cvs. **Gladiolus** | Depending on the particular type, **gladiolus** range 1 to 5 feet tall with blooms 1 to 8 inches across. | If you plant a diversity of types, you can have **gladiolus** blooms from spring to fall. | Plant in a rich sandy soil. A corm should be planted at a depth that is four times the height of the corm. For a succession of blooms, plant in spring, after the soil has warmed, at one- to two-week intervals. |

# CHAPTER TWO

# Bulbs, Corms, Rhizomes, & Tubers for Georgia

| Common Name<br>Botanical Name | Size | Season<br>of Bloom | Culture and Remarks |
|---|---|---|---|
| *Hemerocallis* spp. and hybrids<br>**Daylily** | Lilylike flowers range from 2 to 8 inches across and appear in clusters on plants that are 1 to 6 feet tall. | Depending on the type, blooms occur from spring through fall. | Plant in full sun or light shade. **Daylilie**s tolerate most types of soil. **Daylilies** can be grown in containers, as a ground cover, or in a mass on a bank to control erosion. |
| *Hyacinthus orientalis*<br>**Hyacinth** | Grows to 1 foot tall with fragrant, bell-shaped flowers in shades of white, pink, blue, and purple. Narrow, bright-green leaves. | Blooms in early to mid-spring. | Plant in full sun or partial shade in a soil that is moist but well drained. This is an easy bulb to force to bloom out of season in winter. Extremely fragrant flowers. |
| *Iris* spp. and cvs.<br>**Iris** | There are many different types and sizes of iris, ranging from those that grow only 4 to 8 inches tall to those that grow 20 inches tall. | **Dwarf species iris** bloom in late winter to early spring. **Dutch iris** bloom in May or later. | Plant in full sun in a well-drained soil. Provide plenty of moisture fall through spring. Keep bulbs dry during summer when they are dormant. Dwarf iris make good rock garden plants. Both **dwarf** and **Dutch iris** make good container plants. |
| *Leucojum aestivum*<br>**Summer Snowflake** | Pendulous white bells with tips that look as if they've been dipped in green paint appear on stems 12 to 18 inches tall. | Blooms occur in mid- to late spring. | Plant in moist soils in full sun or partial shade. Great for naturalizing near streams or under trees and shrubs. Blooms in south Georgia occur November through winter. In other parts of the state they bloom in late winter and early spring. |
| *Lilium* spp. and hybrids<br>**Lily** | Many different sizes, types and bloom times. Flowers can be trumpet- or funnel-shaped or have recurved petals. | Depending on the type, blooms occur spring through summer. | Plant in a loose, deep, well-drained soil that is rich in organic material. Keep roots cool and tops in full sun or light shade. Viral or mosaic infection can cause problems. Purchase healthy bulbs from companies that specialize in bulbs. |

# CHAPTER TWO

## Bulbs, Corms, Rhizomes, & Tubers for Georgia

| Common Name Botanical Name | Size | Season of Bloom | Culture and Remarks |
|---|---|---|---|
| *Lycoris* spp. **Spider Lily** and **Naked Lady** | Flower stems range from 12 to 24 inches tall. **Spider lily** foliage is straplike and dark green with a silver-white vein. **Naked lady** leaves are wide, gray-green, straplike. | Naked ladies bloom in mid- to late summer, and spider lilies bloom in early fall. | Plant both types in a moist but well-drained soil. They grow in full sun or partial shade. Plant these fall-blooming bulbs July to August for best results. |
| *Narcissus* spp. and cvs. **Daffodil** | **Daffodils** range in height from 3 to 20 inches tall. They are divided into thirteen different divisions according to flower shape. | There are early, mid-season, and late-blooming varieties of these spring bulbs. | **Daffodils** prefer a soil that is moist but well drained. They need a minimum of six hours of direct sunlight to thrive. **Daffodils** are poisonous, and rodents will not disturb them. They are long-lived in the garden and require a minimum of maintenance. |
| *Polianthes tuberosa* **Tuberose** | Flowers shoot up 18 to 36 inches above foliage that is 1 foot high. | Twenty or more fragrant flowers on a stem; both single and double types bloom early to late summer. | Plant in a sunny site in a soil that is moist but well drained. Start bulbs indoors for early blooms. |
| *Tulipa* spp. and cvs. **Tulip** | Vary greatly in size depending on type, from species only 3 inches tall to Darwin hybrids that reach 28 inches tall. | Flowers occur from early to late spring in a range of colors and shapes. | In coastal areas, **tulips** need prechilling at 40 degrees F. for 2 to 3 months and should be planted December to mid-January. Plant in full sun in well-drained soil. Many of the species tulips bloom early. They are well adapted to the summer heat and will usually perennialize. |
| *Zephyranthes* spp. and hybrids **Rain Lily** | Grassy foliage 1 to 2 feet long. | Depending on the variety, flowers occur in spring, summer, and fall in shades of pink, white, and yellow. | Plant bulbs 1 to 2 inches deep in full sun. They tolerate periods of wet and dry. Flowers appear after a rain. Plant among ground covers for a good show. |

# JANUARY
## BULBS, CORMS, RHIZOMES, & TUBERS

 PLANNING

If you live in a coastal area, there is still time to plant spring-flowering bulbs, provided they have been prechilled (see October for more information). Plan for a sequence of bloom in the spring by planting bulbs that will bloom early, mid-season, and later, beginning with **snowdrops** and **crocus,** then **species tulips** and early **daffodils.**

Sometimes spring bulbs will begin to emerge (2 inches or so), and **snowdrops** may be blooming now in the northern parts of the state. Gardeners worry that these flowers might be damaged by the cold. Just cover them with some pine straw, and they should be fine.

 PLANTING

Once your **snowdrops** finish blooming, you can divide them. Because these bulbs are so tiny and dry out easily, the best time to divide is while they are still blooming or as soon as the blooms fade. Dig up a clump you want to divide, and gently tease apart the bulbs, making sure each division has bulbs with roots, shoots, and foliage. Replant them as soon as possible in their new location, leaving the

| Name | Planting Depth | Number of Bulbs or Spacing |
|---|---|---|
| *Allium giganteum* | 3 to 4 times the depth of the bulb measured from the base | large, 5 sq. ft.; small, 10 sq. ft. |
| *Alstroemeria* | 9 to 12 in. | 1 sq. ft. |
| *Anemone blanda* | 2 to 3 in. | 10 to 15 sq. ft. (soak overnight before planting) |
| *Caladium* | 6 in. | 1 sq. ft. (soil should be 60 degrees F. or warmer) |
| *Canna* | 5 in. | 10 to 18 in. apart (tuberous rootstock with 3 to 5 eyes) |
| *Colocasia* | 3 x the width of bulb | 18 in. on center |
| *Crinum* | plant so neck protrudes | 1 sq. ft. |
| *Dahlia* | 12 in. | 1 sq. ft. |
| *Galanthus* | 1½ to 2 in. | 10 sq. ft. |
| *Hyacinthus* | 4 to 6 in. | 5 sq. ft. |
| *Iris reticulata* | 4 in. | 10 to 12 sq. ft. |
| *Leucojum* | 3 in. | 5 to 6 sq. ft. |
| *Lilium* | small, 2 to 3 in.; medium, 3 to 4 in.; large, 4 to 6 in. exception **madonna lilies** - 1 in. deep | smaller bulbs 2 to 3 sq.ft; larger bulbs, 1 to 2 sq. ft. |
| *Narcissus* | larger bulbs (2 to 3 in. in diameter) 6 to 8 in. deep; medium-sized bulbs (1 to 2 in. in diameter) 3 to 6 in. deep; small or miniature bulbs (1½ to 1 inch in diameter) 2 to 3 in. deep | |
| *Polianthes tuberosa* | 2 in. | 3 sq. ft. |
| *Tulipa* | regular-sized **tulips,** 8 to 10 in. deep; small **tulips,** 4 to 6 in. deep | |
| *Zephyranthes* | 1 to 2 in. | 8 to 10 sq. ft. |

foliage intact. Water them in, and next year you should have blooms again.

Different types of bulbs should be planted at different depths, depending on the size of the bulb. (See the list on previous page.) Plant shallower in heavy clay soils and slightly deeper in light or sandy soils.

## WATERING

Water bulbs as soon as you plant them. Soak the planted area several times, once a week. Apply 2 inches of mulch (pine straw or pine bark) over the planted area.

## FERTILIZING

Wait until shoots emerge in spring, then apply a water-soluble fertilizer (10-10-10 is good) if you did not fertilize bulbs when you planted them in fall.

## PROBLEMS

In South Georgia, check for aphids feeding on new foliage and buds of bulbs. Use a strong blast from the hose to try to eradicate these hungry pests.

One of the frustrating things for gardeners who want to grow bulbs is that they have to deal

## HELPFUL HINTS

Gardeners with sandy soils, beware: Voles love such an environment, and if you grow **crocus** or **tulips,** these animals can be a challenge. To discourage voles, don't apply a layer of mulch that is too thick (2 to 3 inches is plenty), or the soil will become warmer and more inviting to the pests.

To avoid problems with voles, grow different types of *Narcissus* and other members of the Amaryllidaceae family (including *Leucojum* and × *Amarcrinum*), which are resistant to rodents and deer. *Narcissus* bulbs contain a poisonous alkaloid that acts as a natural pest-repellent.

Professional bulb growers Brent and Becky Heath of Gloucester, Virginia, have had success in controlling voles using two products, Mole-Med® and Ro-pel®. To discourage deer they recommend Deer-Off®. Look for all of these products at your local garden center.

with animals digging them up and eating them. One technique to discourage this is to plant the bulbs and then cover them with wire mesh. The holes in the mesh should be large enough (1 inch or so) so that the foliage and blooms can fit through. Cover the mesh with a layer of mulch. Squirrels and chipmunks like to dig up **crocus** and **tulip** bulbs for a tasty treat. They often dig them up before or while they are in bloom. Replant them quickly if you notice they have been pulled out of the ground.

## GROOMING

No pruning is needed at this time of year.

One bulb that is "safe" from voles and deer is summer snowflake, *Leucojum* species.

# FEBRUARY
## BULBS, CORMS, RHIZOMES, & TUBERS

 PLANNING

Record in your garden journal what's blooming or what bulbs are coming up in the garden. Depending on where you live in the state, early spring bulbs like **snowdrops** or **glory of the snow** (*Chionodoxa luciliae*) are beginning to bloom or are still blooming. Other early bloomers include *Narcissus* 'Rijnveld's Early Sensation', a classic **daffodil** with a yellow trumpet and petals; and the reliable heirloom **daffodil** *N.* 'February Gold', which is excellent for forcing and perennializing.

At the end of the month in the coastal part of the state, expect the old-fashioned *Narcissus jonquilla* to be in bloom. This species of **daffodil** (called "Sweeties" for its sweet perfume), which has rushlike foliage and extremely fragrant flowers, has naturalized throughout the Southeast.

While most gardeners are familiar with **daffodils** and **tulips,** there are a host of other bulbs that bloom in early spring. Following is a list of small flowering bulbs known to be among the earliest of the spring bloomers. Many of these same bulbs are also good candidates for naturalizing in lawns. Because they bloom early, the foliage has time to ripen before the first mowing of the lawn.

- *Chionodoxa luciliae* 'Alba'

**Glory of the snow** produces five to ten white starry flowers per stem in a spray.

- *Crocus* spp. and cvs.

**Crocus** is an easy-to-grow bulb with cup-shaped flowers and foliage only 3 to 6 inches tall. It can be tucked in pockets between tree roots, naturalized in the lawn, or featured in the rock garden.

- *Galanthus nivalis*

**Snowdrops** have white, nodding, bell-shaped flowers that appear as early as January. This woodland wonder grows anywhere from 4 to 10 inches tall, depending on the selection.

- *Ipheion uniflorum*

**Star flower** is a small bulb that has star-shaped flowers with six petals. The fragrant blooms range in color from almost white to soft violet. Be warned, though, the grasslike foliage smells like **garlic** when crushed.

- *Iris reticulata*

**Dwarf iris** offers little flowers (4 to 8 inches tall with leaves) that glisten like jewels when they bloom in shades of purple, blue, and lavender.

- *Puschkinia scilloides* var. *libanotica*

**Puschkinia** is an undemanding bulb that grows in sun or shade and produces many starry pale-blue to white flowers with dark-blue stripes. Growing only 4 to 6 inches tall, it is ideal for combining with other bulbs or planting in masses in the lawn.

- *Scilla siberica*

**Scilla** 'Spring Beauty' has clusters of dark-blue, loosely formed bells on 6- to 8-inch stems.

 PLANTING

If you have **daffodils** or other bulbs that you didn't plant in the fall and the bulbs are still firm, go ahead and plant them. You may not get any blooms this spring, or if you do, they may be shorter than normal, but don't worry! These bulbs should catch up with the rest of your bulbs in a few years. If you don't get your bulbs planted now, they will dry out completely by next fall and there will be nothing to plant.

 WATERING

Water bulbs immediately after you plant them, soaking the area thoroughly. Don't water bulbs that you planted last fall until they begin actively growing (the leaves and stems should be several inches high). Once they start growing, they will need to be watered only if you don't get any rain (at least 1 inch per week). If you have a small area of bulbs (several square feet), you can use a watering can to water. Apply water to the spot, let it soak in, and repeat. You will want to make sure that water gets to the bulb roots. If you apply 1 inch of water, it should reach roots at a depth of 6 inches in a soil with a moderate amount of clay (30 to 40 percent). Applying double this amount should be enough for bulbs that are planted as deep as 9 to 10 inches.

## FERTILIZING

In the southern parts of the state, if your bulbs are actively growing and 2 or more inches of foliage has emerged, you can topdress with a water-soluble formula like 10-10-10. It will get to the roots quickly while the bulb is growing and before it blooms. For **daffodils,** look for a formula such as "Peters Hydro-Sol®" (5-11-26).

## PROBLEMS

If you have problems with voles or chipmunks digging up your bulbs and you neglected to put

### HELPFUL HINTS

A slow-release fertilizer releases nutrients gradually over time at a rate at which bulbs can use them. A special "Daffodil Fertilizer" is recommended by Brent Heath, a third-generation nurseryman in the **daffodil** industry. A six-month slow-release, the 5-10-20 formula also contains trace amounts of manganese, iron, copper, sulphur, boron, and zinc. It is available from Brent and Becky's Bulbs (see Bulbs, August, p. 66). Apply this fertilizer in the fall, 1/2 pound (1/2 cup) per 10 square feet.

Other products known as bulb fertilizers can be used in sequential doses (refer to product label for detailed directions) with the addition of extra potash, which will fulfill the potassium requirements of daffodils.

Holland Bulb Booster™ is a choice slow-release fertilizer for **tulips** and members of the **lily** family including **alliums** and **hyacinths.** If you use this fertilizer for daffodils, be sure to add extra potash. A good source of potash is wood ash, which also contains trace elements bulbs need. Apply wood ash once per season (1 pound per l00 square feet). Wood ash also helps neutralize acidic soils because of its alkaline pH (be sure to keep it away from woody evergreens that prefer an acid soil; too much potash can cause evergreens to turn yellow and sickly).

down wire mesh when you planted, try this remedy: Mix some liquid dish detergent (a few teaspoons) and water in a quart spray bottle. Add some red pepper powder or hot sauce (a few teaspoons). Spray this around the area where the bulbs are coming up—this should discourage critters from digging up your treasures.

Another approach is to sprinkle red pepper directly on the soil where the bulbs are planted. Keep in mind that rain or dew will make these treatments lose their effectiveness.

## GROOMING

Remove faded blooms as they occur. Leave the foliage until it turns yellow and collapses.

# MARCH
## BULBS, CORMS, RHIZOMES, & TUBERS

 PLANNING

Now that spring bulbs are beginning to bloom, plan ahead for the bulbs you would like to have blooming in summer and fall. Keep in mind that even if summer bulbs like **caladiums** are available for sale in stores now, you should not plant them until the soil temperature is at least 60 degrees Fahrenheit or warmer and the fear of frost is past. **Caladiums** require warm soil and air temperatures of 70 degrees or above during the day and, ideally, not below 60 degrees at night. Depending on where you live in the state, these temperatures could occur in April or May. Purchase a soil thermometer or refer to Lawns, Introduction for information on how to measure soil temperature. Certain perennial summer-blooming bulbs like *Alstroemeria* should be planted in the fall.

Following is a list of bulbs that bloom in summer (including rhizomes, tubers, and tuberous roots) with brief descriptions, including whether they prefer sun or shade. While some begin blooming in late spring and continue through summer, others start in summer and continue until frost. There are a number of plants that have striking foliage and insignificant flowers, such as

elephant ear and **caladium.** There are also some types of **canna** that have fantastic foliage, colorful flowers, or both.

• *Alocasia* species and hybrids, including **upright elephant ear,** prefer partial shade to shade. There are many different selections, with large colorful leaves ranging in size from less than 1 foot to 2 feet across or longer and wider.

• *Bletilla striata* **(Chinese ground orchid)** prefers filtered shade. Plant in early spring. Lavender to magenta miniature orchidlike flowers occur May to June.

• *Caladium* hybrids (**Caladium**) prefer filtered shade to shade. Although some varieties that take sun have been bred, this tropical is indispensable when color is needed in the shade garden. Large (to 1 1/2-foot-long) heart- and arrow-shaped leaves on plants growing 2 to 4 feet tall (depending on the selection) come in a range of colors from almost pure white to dark green. They may be striped, banded, or blotched with rose, pink, silver, green, or bronze.

• *Canna* species and hybrids (**Canna**) prefer full sun to filtered shade. Their dramatic foliage, from dark red to variegated and all the variations, gives your garden a tropical flair. They range in size from 2 to 6 feet tall and

can be left in the ground year-round in coastal areas. Plant 5 inches deep and 10 inches apart.

• *Colocasia esculenta* (**Taro** or **elephant ear**) prefers filtered shade to shade. This tuberous herb is edible as well as ornamental; in lowland tropical areas, the starchy roots are a staple food. Selections of this plant can grow to 6 feet tall in the garden. Some have huge leaves, 2 feet long and even broader, in one growing season.

• *Dahlia* hybrids (**Dahlia**) prefer full sun. These summer bloomers, usually started from tubers, range from 15 inches to over 6 feet tall. The flowers come in almost every color and form imaginable.

• *Gladiolus* (**Gladiolus**) prefer full sun and bloom from spring until fall, depending on when you plant. The dwarf species *Gladiolus byzantinus* has maroon flowers, 1 to 3 inches, in clusters of six to twelve on 2- to 3-foot stems. Smaller and more refined than some of the larger types of **gladiolus,** this heirloom is also winter hardy.

• *Gloriosa superba* 'Rothschildiana' (**Climbing lily**) prefers sun to filtered shade. Flowers are made up of six bright red segments banded with yellow. Grow in pots. Start tubers indoors in February.

# PLANTING

You can start **caladium** tubers in pots indoors. Start **tuberose** indoors and plant outside when soil temperatures warm up. Plant the rhizomes 2 inches deep and 4 to 6 inches apart. In coastal areas, they can be left in the ground year-round.

# WATERING

Keep actively growing and blooming spring bulbs well watered. If you don't get at least an inch of rain per week in your garden, water. Apply 5 gallons of water to a 10-square-foot area.

# FERTILIZING

Fertilize spring bulbs after they emerge, before flowering. Top-dress with a water-soluble formula like 10-10-10 that will get to the roots quickly while the bulb is growing and before it blooms. For **daffodils,** look for a formula such as "Peters Hydro-Sol®" (5-11-26).

# PROBLEMS

You may notice that your early-blooming varieties of **daffodils**

# STARTING CALADIUMS

If you want to get a jump on the summer season, you can start **caladium** tubers indoors in March. If you use bottom heat when you start them, their growth will be accelerated (look for a heat mat designed for seedlings). Move them outside in late April or early May once soil temperatures are 60 degrees Fahrenheit or warmer. Use a mix that is equal parts coarse sand, compost, and ground pine bark or peat moss. For tubers that are 2½ inches long or smaller, use a pot that is 5 inches wide and deep. For larger tubers, use a pot that is at least 7 inches wide. You will encourage lots of side shoots if you scoop out the center growing tip. You can plant the tubers directly in a pot with the recommended mix, or scoop out the center growing tips first and then plant them.

1. Fill the pot with 1 inch of potting mix. Place the tuber in the pot. Position the tuber so the roots are at the bottom of the tuber toward the soil.

2. Add 2 inches of potting mix to cover the tuber. Water well until water rushes out of the holes in the bottom of the pot.

3. Keep the pot in bright light (a sunny window). Water when the soil feels dry to the touch.

have not yet come up and there is no indication that they will, even when you dig down several inches into the soil. They may have root rot. Dig up and discard bulbs. Don't replant without improving drainage.

# GROOMING

Remove faded blooms from flowering bulbs, but leave the foliage to ripen.

# APRIL
## BULBS, CORMS, RHIZOMES, & TUBERS

### PLANNING

Photograph your garden as more spring bulbs come into bloom. Make notes in your garden journal about which varieties are fragrant and which make good cut flowers.

After your **Easter lily** finishes blooming, you can plant it in the garden. Choose a site where the soil is well drained but rich in organic matter. Plant the bulb at the same depth it was in the pot. Let the stems ripen and die down before you remove them. Water the **lily** after you plant it. Next spring, fertilize with a complete fertilizer like 10-10-10. It may take several years before your **lily** blooms during its normal mid-summer season.

**Tulips** are a favorite of many gardeners, but not all **tulips** are created equal, especially when it comes to surviving in our hot, humid climate. While **tulips** are often treated as annuals in Georgia, there are a few that are good repeat bloomers. (This does not apply to coastal gardeners, whose **tulips** need to be prechilled before they are planted.) While their flowers are not as large and showy as those of the hybrids, most of the **species tulips** tolerate the heat better and bloom year after year

in the garden. Many of these have graceful, delicate flowers. Low growing and early blooming, **species tulips** are perfect for the rock garden or for growing in pots. If you're not already growing these **tulips,** think of adding some to your garden next year. Here is a list of some **species tulips** with brief descriptions.

- *Tulipa bakeri* 'Lilac Wonder', with a sunny yellow heart and lilac-pink petals, grows to 6 to 8 inches at maturity.
- *T. clusiana* var. *chrysantha* has 9-inch stems that produce flowers that are crimson when they're closed. When they open, the inside is bright yellow.
- *T. gregii* has scarlet flowers that measure 6 inches across, on 10-inch stems. The foliage is striped or mottled with brown.
- *T. kaufmanniana* is called the **waterlily tulip** for the flowers that occur on 6-inch stems. They are creamy yellow marked with red on the outside, and yellow in the center.
- *T. tarda* offers bunches of star-shaped **tulip** flowers of white and yellow, appearing on 6- to 8-inch stems in early spring.
- *T. turkestanica*, 6 to 8 inches tall, has white flowers with orange centers that perfume the air in early spring.

### PLANTING

Plant **Dutch iris** now for late-summer blooms. Check with your local Extension Service about the last frost date in your area. By mid-April in all but the most northern part of the state, it should be safe to plant many summer-blooming bulbs like **canna, elephant ear, dahlia,** or **gladiolus** outside—especially if you are planting them in containers. Before you plant, be sure soil temperatures are 60 degrees Fahrenheit or warmer.

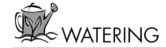

### WATERING

Now that spring bulbs are actively growing and blooming, make sure they get plenty of water. Water your bulbs once a week unless you get a good rain, 1 inch or more per week.

### FERTILIZING

Remember, the ideal time to fertilize bulbs is in the fall when they produce roots that absorb nutrients, but you might choose to fertilize now, too, when spring bulbs are growing and about to bloom. Use a water-soluble fertilizer (10-10-10) that will get to the roots quickly while the bulb is actively growing and before it blooms.

## PROBLEMS

Pull weeds that appear in your plantings of bulbs. Apply a weed-preventer in your established bulb beds. Read the label carefully before applying any pesticide.

One of the more perplexing problems observed by **canna** growers is leaves that refuse to unfurl in spring. On closer examination, they find that the edges of the **canna** leaves have been "stitched" together by silver webbing. Upon manually unrolling the leaf, a white grublike creature is found inhabiting the interior: the canna leaf roller. This grub is the larva of a moth that laid its eggs on the leaves as they emerged from the soil. Examine your **cannas** each week, and unroll any leaves that seem to be developing abnormally.

Make a note in your garden calendar to remove and destroy all **canna** stalks and foliage next November. The moth overwinters in the dead leaves, but not if you disrupt the life cycle.

## HELPFUL HINTS

If you love bulbs but are concerned about the awkward stage they go through when the foliage ripens, try companion planting. Plant your bulbs with companion plants and you can extend the blooming season and provide cover foliage to hide ripening bulb foliage. You can also layer your bulbs so that when one type finishes blooming, another begins. For example, you can plant **tulips** 10 inches deep, **daffodils** at 6 inches, and then **crocus** and **dwarf iris** on top at 3 inches deep. With this method you will have a long season of spring bloom from your bulbs. Here are some planting combinations:

- **Crocus** with **pansies** or lawn grasses
- **Daffodils** with **hellebores** and **hosta**
- **Daffodils** or **surprise lilies** with **English ivy** (use larger-type daffodils, not dwarf varieties, so they are robust enough to compete with the **ivy**)
- **Daffodils** with **ferns** like **Japanese painted fern**
- **Dwarf iris** with **ajuga** or **periwinkle**
- **Daffodils** with **daylilies** in a sunny border (this way you will have blooms in spring and summer in the same spot)

In a shady woodland composed of deciduous trees, bulbs get enough light in the fall, winter, and early spring to ensure good blooms; and when summer arrives, they are protected from the hot afternoon sun.

## GROOMING

Remove faded blooms of **daffodils** before they set seed. Remove the flowers, and leave the stems; the stems help with photosynthesis.

Once the **daffodils** finish blooming, some gardeners like to tie up their foliage with rubber bands or bunch them up. Not only is this practice unattractive, it prevents sunlight from getting to all the leaves, cuts off air circulation, and increases the chances of fungal problems.

It is important to let bulb foliage ripen. As leaves go through the process of photosynthesis, they store food for next year's blooms. The time to cut off the foliage is when it turns yellow and falls over. **Daffodil** expert Brent Heath recommends that you wait at least eight to ten weeks after bloom before cutting off bulb foliage.

# MAY

## BULBS, CORMS, RHIZOMES, & TUBERS

### PLANNING

Spring bulbs are finished, and summer will soon be here. Plan on adding at least a few summer bloomers to brighten the garden scene. You can easily grow summer bulbs in pots or in the ground. Think about combinations of different bulbs or bulbs and perennials. Stake **lilies** before they get too tall and the task becomes more difficult (see Perennials, April, for more information on staking).

One **canna** with dark or variegated foliage can make a dramatic statement in the perennial border. A combination that promises to light up the shade garden is made of **caladiums, cannas, elephant ears,** and **impatiens.** For sun, try combining **dahlias** with **ornamental grasses, butterfly ginger,** and one large **elephant ear.**

### PLANTING

Plant **cannas, caladiums, dahlias, elephant ear,** and **gladiolus.** Transplant **tuberose** that you started indoors to the garden. **Dahlias** are usually planted as tubers but can also be grown from seed; they range in size from only 15 inches to over 6 feet tall. For dwarf types, sow the

Dahlias can be stunning in a bed or border.

seed directly in the spot where the **dahlias** will grow. Start seed for taller varieties indoors in February or March.

Before you plant **dahlia** tubers, make sure the soil has been amended with organic materials like compost or ground bark. Here are a few tips for planting the tubers:

• Space the largest types 4 to 5 feet apart, and make sure the hole is 1 foot deep.

• Space medium-sized tubers 3 feet apart and 1 foot deep.

• Space small tubers 1 to 2 feet apart and 1 foot deep.

• If you use fertilizer, use a complete fertilizer like 10-10-10. Mix in 1/4 cup thoroughly with the soil in the planting hole, then

add another 4 inches of soil over this before you plant.

• With large tubers, it is a good idea to put the stake in the hole when you are planting. This way you won't risk damaging the tuber later with the stake. After you place the tuber horizontally, position the stake a few inches from the eye (growing point). Fill in and cover the tuber with 3 inches of soil. Water thoroughly. Gradually fill the hole with soil as the shoots grow.

Plant summer-flowering **garden gladiolus** at one- to two-week intervals, and this will give you a long season of bloom, up to six weeks. Before planting, treat them with bulb dust, an insecticide-fungicide. Some of the hybrids grow 5 feet high and don't require staking. They offer spikes of flowers with twelve to fourteen blooms at one time. For the most productive corms, select those that are 1½ to 2 inches wide.

# WATERING

Keep bulbs watered while they are growing and blooming. One inch per week should keep them happy.

# FERTILIZING

Keep fertilizer out of direct contact with **gladiolus** corms. Instead, mix a complete fertilizer into the soil thoroughly before planting, or use superphosphate 0-46-0 (4 pounds per 100 square feet).

# PROBLEMS

Look for aphids on **lilies, dahlias, and gladiolus.** Spray them with insecticidal soap or a synthetic pesticide. Aphids spread mosaic virus, which attacks **lily** foliage and for which there is no cure. If any of your **lilies** exhibit mottled leaves or stunted growth, they may have mosaic. Dig and destroy the bulbs. The best way

# HELPFUL HINTS

**Dahlias** are great for growing in the border, for cut flowers, or in containers. With pinching and thinning you can increase the number or size of the flowers. For tall varieties, remove all but one or two of the strongest shoots. When the shoots develop three sets of leaves, pinch off tips just above the top set. This should lead to the development of two side shoots from each pair of leaves, and more flowers. If you want to have large flowers, remove all but the terminal flower buds on the side shoots. This will encourage the plant to put its energy into making fewer but larger flowers.

When cutting **dahlias** from the garden, cut them in early morning or evening. Remove any leaves below the top 2 inches of the stem. Place the base of the cut stems in 2 to 3 inches of hot water. Let the water cool for several hours or overnight. Once the water has cooled, fill the remainder of the container with water up to where the leaves begin on the stem.

**Keeping Cut Flowers Fresh:** Cut flowers will last longer if you use a container that is clean and free of dirt and bacteria. Changing the water daily will also help keep flowers fresh.

to avoid this infection is to buy only healthy bulbs and remove injured portions before planting.

You may notice that your **bearded iris** have notches in the leaf margins, about ⅛ inch wide, and there is also a dark trail in the leaves. This means leaf borers. While you can use an insecticide like Cygon to control these pests, you can also kill the borers by squeezing the infested leaves between your thumb and forefinger in the areas where you notice them feeding (the dark, water-soaked areas).

# GROOMING

Keep plants groomed. You can prevent diseases from spreading by removing diseased pr dead leaves as soon as you notice them.

# JUNE
## BULBS, CORMS, RHIZOMES, & TUBERS

 PLANNING

Gardeners agree that there is really no such thing as "low-maintenance gardening," but there are some bulbs that are proven winners in the low-maintenance quest. **Daylilies** are at the top of the list for choice summer-blooming bulbs (although not true bulbs, these members of the **lily** family have tuberous fleshy roots). Lily-like flowers appear above clumps of arching, sword-shaped leaves. One or two divisions (a division is also called a fan, as the foliage looks similar to a fan) can quickly multiply and fill an area of your garden. **Daylilies** come in a wide range of colors and shades of red, orange, yellow, pink, purple, and more.

With just a minimum of care, **daylilies** reward you every year with a long season of bloom and lush healthy plants. Plant them in full sun or light shade in a soil that is well drained. There are numerous selections, including types that bloom only once a season and those that bloom for weeks, rest, and then produce more blooms. Combine **daylilies** in the same planting bed with spring-blooming bulbs and you will have a succession of blooms. Plant them in masses, mix them in with other perennials, or use them as ground covers or in containers. Most types offered for sale are hybrids with improved flowers and foliage. The modern hybrids include deciduous, evergreen, and semi-evergreen types. Evergreen types are well suited for coastal gardens; the hardier deciduous types are better for gardens in the middle and northern parts of the state.

For maximum impact, plant early, midseason, and late-blooming varieties. Modern **daylily** hybrids range in size from dwarf, 1 foot tall, to the giant at 6 feet tall with flowers 3 to 8 inches across. The flower types are diverse, too, from spidery to ruffled. Some of the species and older varieties have flowers that are not only colorful but fragrant as well. Following is a list of a few **daylilies** to consider for your Georgia garden. For more information about **daylilies,** contact The American Hemerocallis Society. The website **www.daylilies.org**) lists **daylily** groups and display gardens in Georgia under a link for regional activities (Georgia is Region 5).

• *Hemerocallis fulva* **Orange daylily** is a deciduous species that is also called **ditch lily** because it is commonly seen in roadside ditches or old gardens. A tough plant, it grows to 6 feet high and has leaves that are 2 feet or longer. The orange-red flowers, 3 to 5 inches wide, appear in summer and look great in combination with the old-fashioned blue "mophead" **hydrangeas.** Although it is not as refined as many of the hybrids offered for sale, this tough "doer" is still a good choice for a care-free perennial bulb.

• *H.* 'Happy Returns', a long-blooming **daylily** hybrid, offers yellow flowers, at about 2 to 3 feet high, for months, beginning in May and continuing until frost. Its compact size, about 18 inches high by 18 inches wide, makes it ideal for small gardens, containers, or masses.

• *H. lilio-asphodelus* (*H. flava*) **Lemon daylily** is a deciduous type, growing to 3 feet tall or taller. This old-fashioned favorite is grown for its fragrant yellow flowers that appear in late May or June.

 PLANTING

Plant **caladiums, dahlias, daylilies,** and **gladiolus.**

## HELPFUL HINT

**Daylily** blooms open for one day and then fade away. As a general practice, it is best to pinch off dead blooms as soon as you notice them. This way the plant will not only look better but will put its energy into making more flowerbuds instead of seeds.

Divide **daylilies** (refer to illustration in Perennials, March).

## WATERING

Keep summer-blooming bulbs watered. Check containers daily; feel the top 1 to 2 inches of soil and if it is dry to the touch, water until the water runs out the bottom of the pot. Check bulbs planted in the ground weekly. If you haven't received at least 1 inch of rain per week, water well.

Mulching your bulb plantings not only helps conserve moisture but cuts down on weed infestations. Apply 1 to 2 inches of mulch on top of the soil in areas where you plant bulbs.

## FERTILIZING

Once they're planted, **dahlias** don't need supplemental fertilizer unless they are growing in poor soil. If this is the case, you can sidedress when first flowerbuds appear. Apply the fertilizer in rows between the plants with a fertilizer that is high in phosphates and potash, like 5-10-15.

Fertilize **caladiums** with a complete water-soluble fertilizer like 20-20-20 once a month during the growing season.

Fertilize **gladiolus** with a complete fertilizer like 8-8-8 or 10-10-10 once they have developed five or more leaves. Keep the fertilizer 6 inches from the main stem of the **gladiolus.** Water well after you fertilize.

## PROBLEMS

Check **dahlias** for thrips (see Roses, May)—new growth and buds will look distorted and flowers will fail to open normally. Leaf surfaces may look silvery or bronze. Black specks on the leaves are another indication that thrips are present. Use a strong blast from the hose, and wash them off. If you have a severe infestation, you may have to use a systemic insecticide.

Pinch off dead blooms as soon as you notice them.

Your **dahlia** leaves may have tiny dark specks and a silvery cast, and the undersides of the leaves may have a fine webbing. This means spider mites. Spray with horticultural oil, insecticidal soap, or a synthetic miticide.

## GROOMING

Cut off the yellowing foliage of **daffodils** that bloomed in early spring. (If it is mostly yellow and lying on the ground, it is safe to cut it off.)

# JULY
## BULBS, CORMS, RHIZOMES, & TUBERS

### PLANNING

If you have large clumps of **daffodils** that are healthy but have produced very few blooms in the spring, it is time to divide them. While **daffodils** welcome the sun in winter and early spring, they benefit from some shade in the summer. If you need to divide them, the best time is after the foliage has turned yellow and fallen over. Late-blooming varieties may still have foliage that is visible in July.

If there is still a bit of foliage to mark where the **daffodils** are growing, it makes it easier to divide them. When you dig up a clump, dig around and under it with a digging fork or spade. Use caution so as not to cut off roots or slice into the bulbs. Shake soil off the bulbs, and gently untangle the roots. Do not break apart bulbs that are firmly attached to one another or you may injure them, which makes them more susceptible to disease. They will split apart in their own time once they are replanted. If you are moving your bulbs, have the new planting site prepared ahead of time.

If you don't replant immediately and want to store your bulbs, make sure you dry them completely. Use mesh bags like those used to store fruit or onions to store your bulbs. Nylon stockings make a good substitute if you don't have a mesh bag. Use a fan to provide good air circulation while you dry the bulbs. Keep them in a cool, dark, dry place until you replant them in fall.

There are a number of late-summer/fall bloomers that can be planted in the summer as soon as you receive them, including **spider lily** *Lycoris radiata,* **surprise lily** *L. squamigera,* and **autumn daffodil** *Sternbergia lutea.* These bulbs are normally dug and shipped anytime between June and August. Order them now for planting. They may not bloom the first season, but once they are established, they will reward you every year with flowers at a time when few other bulbs are blooming.

### PLANTING

Plant another crop of **gladiolus** so that you will have blooms all summer and into fall.

If your **daffodils** are in a spot that is hot and sunny all summer, plant a summer crop of annuals over the bulbs. This will provide them with some shade and the annuals will use up excess moisture, helping the bulbs stay dry.

*Crocosmia's striking blooms and graceful stems help it to be an exceptional cut flower.*

### WATERING

Stop watering **daffodils** and other spring-blooming bulbs once they are no longer blooming. **Daffodils,** especially, require well-drained soils when they are dormant or they will develop basal rot.

### FERTILIZING

Fertilize **caladiums** with a complete water-soluble fertilizer like 20-20-20.

## PROBLEMS

Pull weeds in your bulb beds when they are young and before they flower and set seed. This will prevent them from spreading freely by seed.

Your **dahlias** may look wilted even after you water them; some plants may have stunted growth, others have died, and when you cut open a stem you see brown streaking on the inside. This means your **dahlias** have a fungus called Verticillium wilt. This fungus destroys tissues responsible for transporting water throughout the plant. There is no chemical control. Destroy infected plants, and dispose of them in the garbage, not the compost pile.

Do not plant **dahlias** in the same area again or you may have the same problem.

Some of your **daylilies** may have yellow and brown streaks, others may have dark brown spots that are irregular in shape, and some of these leaves eventually die. All this means your **daylilies** are probably suffering from a leaf spot caused by a fungus. Remove and destroy any infected leaves. During hot, humid weather, plants are more susceptible to attack by certain fungi. Use drip irrigation or other alternatives to overhead watering. The faster leaves dry, the less chance fungi will have to attack.

Select varieties of **daylilies** that are recommended for your region. Check with The American Hemerocallis Society (**www.daylilies.org**).

## HELPFUL HINTS

While many summer-blooming bulbs are great in the garden, there are a number of types that also make great cut flowers.

• *Alstroemeria* hybrids, or **Peruvian lilies,** produce clusters of orchid-like flowers on tall stems (24 to 36 inches high) that last for weeks.

• *Crocosmia* cultivars have graceful arching stems, 24 to 36 inches high, with tubular flowers in brilliant red, orange, or yellow.

• *Dahlia* hybrids offer many different sizes, shapes, and colors from 1 foot high to 6 feet or higher.

• *Gladiolus* offers colorful blooms that alternate up the 4- to 5-foot-tall stem.

• *Iris xiphium* (**Dutch iris**) blooms in late spring to early summer, with tall slender stems and foliage. Flowers tend to be two-toned in shades like violet and blue, yellow and white, or silvery white and yellow.

• *Ixia* cultivars (the **corn flower**) produce 8- to 16-inch spikes with upfacing, six-petaled flowers on wiry stems. Flowers range from white to fuchsia pink and purple.

• *Liatris* species and cultivars have 2- to 3-foot spikes of bottlebrush-type flowers opening from top to bottom. Flowers are rosy-lavender or white.

• *Lilium* **Asiatic, Oriental,** and **species lilies** have flowers that open from late spring until frost in a wide range of colors.

• *Polianthes tuberosa* has fragrant white flowers with a waxy coating. One stem will perfume an entire room.

• *Tritonia* cultivars, called **blazing star,** offer charming flowers that look like stars in the garden in shades of white, red, orange, and pink.

• *Zantedeschia* hybrids and cultivars, or **calla lilies,** have white, yellow, and red flowers.

For more information about bulbs, check out **www.bulb.com**.

## GROOMING

Remove dead flowers from **daylilies** and **dahlias.**

# AUGUST
## BULBS, CORMS, RHIZOMES, & TUBERS

### PLANNING

It's time to begin planning for this fall and next spring. Make a list of bulbs you would like to add to your garden. This is a good time to place your order for spring bulbs. They are usually shipped for fall planting beginning in August and continuing through November.

While there are many spring-blooming bulbs, there are also late summer- and fall-blooming bulbs. Some fall bloomers have foliage that appears in spring and then disappears. When the flowers appear in autumn, it's almost like magic. Plant fall-blooming bulbs with ground covers like **English ivy** or **pachysandra**. The dark-green background will help mask the bulb foliage as it ripens and will show off the flowers when they appear in fall. Double your pleasure, and plant **daffodils** in the same spot. This way you will have blooms in spring and fall. Fall-blooming bulbs also complement fall perennials like **sedums, asters,** and **ornamental grasses**. Here are some fall bloomers:

• *Colchicum* species and cultivars—often called **autumn crocus** because they look like a giant **crocus**, these tough bulbs are pest-proof. Flowers are up to 4 inches across in white, lavender, and rose. Plant these bulbs where they will get partial shade in a well-drained soil.

• *Crocus* species—there are a number of **crocus** that bloom in autumn. They vary in color and size, from 3 to 6 inches, in shades of white, lilac, and blue. Plant in a sunny location in a well-drained soil.

• *Lycoris radiata*, also called **spider lily**, has bright-red spidery flowers on naked stems that stand out in the early fall garden. This bulb thrives in a shady garden with a well-drained soil.

• *Sternbergia lutea* is called the **autumn daffodil,** but the flowers of this small bulb look more like a yellow **crocus** on 4- to 5-inch stems. This fall bloomer produces foliage and flowers at the same time. Plant these bulbs and be patient. Some may take two to three years before they bloom well. Once they are established, wait at least six to eight years before dividing them.

### Mail-Order Sources of Bulbs:

Brent and Becky's Bulbs
7900 Daffodil Lane
Gloucester, VA 23061
(804) 693-3966
**www.brentandbeckybulbs.com**

McClure & Zimmerman
P.O. Box 368
Friesland, WI 53935-0368
(800) 883-6998
**www.mzbulb.com**

When dividing iris, separate healthy rhizomes by breaking them off with your hands or using a sharp knife.

Old House Gardens
Heirloom Bulbs
536 Third Street
Ann Arbor, MI 48103
(734) 995-1486
**www.oldhousegardens.com**

# PLANTING

Plant late-summer/fall-blooming bulbs like **spider lilies, surprise lilies,** and **autumn daffodil.**

Plant spring-blooming **bearded iris,** and divide those that are overgrown. By doing this now the rhizomes will have plenty of time to acclimate before cold weather sets in. When planting the rhizomes, space them 1 to 2 feet apart, and cover them lightly with soil so the rhizomes are just below the soil surface. Growth is initiated from the end of the rhizome with leaves; point this end in the direction you want the **iris** to grow.

If you are dividing a clump of **iris** that is crowded and producing very few flowers, lift the entire clump, and break off the healthy rhizomes. Discard any that are shriveled or leafless. You can break apart rhizomes with your hands, or separate them with a sharp knife. Let the cut ends heal for at least a few hours or up to a day before you replant them. Trim the leaves back to a height of 2 to 3 inches, and replant. The best soil to plant

in is one that has been amended with lots of organic material. After planting, water well. Continue watering (check the soil on a weekly basis until frost arrives) as the plant puts down roots.

# WATERING

Water summer bulbs that are actively growing or blooming. **Cannas, elephant ear, caladiums,** and **ginger lilies** should be putting on a show now. There's no need to water spring bulbs that are dormant. Water fall-blooming bulbs when you plant them.

Mulch any new bulb plantings with 1 to 2 inches of mulch. Use buckwheat hulls, cocoa hulls, pine straw, pea gravel, or other products.

# FERTILIZING

When you add bulbs to the garden, topdress with fertilizer such as Bulb Booster™. Fertilize **cala-**

## HELPFUL HINTS

**Rain lilies** belong to the genus *Zephyranthes*. There are both native and exotic types of this charming bulb. The autumnal flowers of *Z. candida* are triggered by rain at the end of the summer and continue through fall. The starry white blooms stand out against the dark-green rushlike foliage and pop into bloom as soon as it rains. Because the bulbs are so tiny and dry out easily, it is best to purchase them when they are actively growing.

**diums** with a complete water- soluble fertilizer like 20-20-20.

# PROBLEMS

Chipmunks and other rodents love to dig up your favorite **crocus** while it's blooming. When you plant bulbs that critters like, cover the planted area with a wire mesh. The squares should be 1 inch wide, allowing the bulbs room to emerge while discouraging animals from digging them up.

Handpull any weeds as soon as you notice them.

# GROOMING

Cut fall-blooming bulbs and bring them into the house to enjoy.

# SEPTEMBER
## BULBS, CORMS, RHIZOMES, & TUBERS

### PLANNING

There is still time to order your spring bulbs.

Take a soil test. Most bulbs will be happy with a pH that is slightly acid to neutral (a pH of 7 is neutral, and less than 7 is acid). If you're not sure about the specific requirements of a particular bulb you're growing, check with your local Extension Service (see Resources, p. 289).

Prepare the soil in areas where you will be planting bulbs. All bulbs benefit from a soil that is rich in organic matter and well drained. To prepare the soil, spread 3 to 4 inches of organic material evenly over the area you plan to amend. Use composted horse or cow manure, leaf compost, or similar materials. You can also broadcast a complete fertilizer like 10-10-10 (follow the directions to determine the amount per square foot) evenly over the area, or you can fertilize at the time of planting. Rototill the soil to a depth of 1 foot or deeper. Bulbs need a good 6 to 8 inches of good soil underneath them for their roots. Soils that have a high percentage of organic matter make it easier for nutrients to get to your plants.

Make notes in your garden journal about what bulbs are blooming in your garden now and how your summer bulbs fared.

### PLANTING

Continue planting fall-blooming bulbs like **spider lilies, crocus,** and **colchicums.**

Plant **lily** bulbs as soon as you receive them, or keep them in a cool, dry place until you plant them. There are many different

Plant spring-blooming crocus bulbs now so you'll have lots of color early next year.

types of **lilies,** differing in size, habit of growth, and time of bloom. Before you plant, treat **lilies** with a fungicide. This usually comes in the form of a dust. **Lily** bulbs should be spaced 1 foot apart, but for a mass effect, you can plant them as close as

6 inches apart. Dig a hole to the required depth (see below), and place the bulb in the hole, spreading out the roots. Make sure it is firmly in place.

- Plant small bulbs (1 to 2 inches wide) 2 to 3 inches deep.
- Plant medium-sized bulbs (2 to 3 inches wide) 3 to 4 inches deep.
- Plant larger bulbs (3 inches or wider) 4 to 6 inches deep.
- One exception is **madonna lilies.** Never plant them deeper than 1 inch.

Don't worry if you plant your **lily** bulbs too shallowly—they have special roots that will pull them down to the proper planting depth as long as the soil below is soft.

## WATERING

Continue to water **lily** bulbs until the foliage turns yellow and begins to collapse. Adjust the watering to reflect the change in season. Don't let **lily** bulbs dry out, but don't overwater either. Push your finger into the soil. When the top 2 inches is dry to the touch, water thoroughly. For one plant that is well established, use 1 gallon of water. Let it soak in, then apply another gallon.

## FERTILIZING

Fertilize bulbs when you plant them, using a complete fertilizer like Bulb Booster™. You may choose to use a special formula for **daffodils** (see February, Helpful Hints).

To help improve drainage and make nutrients readily available, add lots of organic material and mix it in with the existing soil.

If you use a complete fertilizer, like 8-8-8 or 10-10-10, it is safer to topdress after you plant the bulbs. If you add it directly to the hole when you plant a bulb, there is the possibility of burning young, tender roots.

---

**HELPFUL HINTS**

The best time to fertilize your spring-blooming bulbs is in the fall. Often we forget where we planted bulbs until they come up in spring. Use golf tees to mark the location of your bulbs; place them in a circle around a clump of **daffodils** or other bulbs. When fall arrives, you will know where to fertilize. You can also use plants to mark where you have bulbs planted. If you plant **daffodils** in a bed of ground cover, fertilize the ground cover in autumn and the bulbs will be fertilized, too. Because **grape hyacinth** foliage comes up in the fall, you can plant it to mark where clumps of **daffodils** are.

---

## PROBLEMS

Your **bearded iris** leaves may have turned yellow and have dark streaks. If the leaves pull off easily and the plant dies, you probably have borers. Borers can hollow out the rhizomes, which then become infected with a bacterial rot. To prevent this problem, pull off and destroy old brown leaves in the fall and winter. Provide excellent drainage and, if necessary, spray new foliage in spring when it is 5 inches high. Use Cygon, and read the product label completely before spraying.

To prevent unwanted crops of chickweeds and other winter weeds in established beds, apply a granular weed preventer. **Note:** Read the label carefully before applying any pesticide. A pre-emergent weed control should be used only if bulbs are established (they have been growing and thriving in the same area for two or three years). Some bulbs may be sensitive to this type of chemical.

## GROOMING

If you still have **daylilies** blooming, pinch off dead blossoms before they form seed unless you want to save the seed. Cut off and save any ripe seedpods from bulbs that you want to grow from seed next year. Once the pods turn from green to brown and they begin to dry out, the seeds inside should be ripe. Store the seed in a dry, cool place (see Annuals, September). If the foliage on your **lilies** has turned yellow or brown, it is now safe to cut them back to a height of 2 to 3 inches.

# OCTOBER
## BULBS, CORMS, RHIZOMES, & TUBERS

 PLANNING

Gardeners who live in the warmest parts of the state (coastal gardeners and those who live in zone 8 or 9) need to prechill some of the spring-flowering bulbs before they plant them. Although it is possible to purchase bulbs that have already had a prechilling treatment, it is easy to do yourself. When purchasing bulbs, be sure to read the fine print. If bulbs are prechilled, that should be stated on the package; otherwise, it is safe to assume they are not prechilled.

Many of the large **tulips** require ten weeks of prechilling. Place them in a breathable bag in the refrigerator. Keep them away from any ripe fruit that releases ethylene gas, as ethylene gas can interfere with the production of flowers. After this prechilling they will be ready to plant in the garden once the soil temperatures are 60 degrees Fahrenheit or cooler.

Some **daffodil** cultivars require a minimum of fourteen to sixteen weeks of constant cold before they will initiate flowerbuds. (Check with your local Extension Service about the best bulbs for your region. Bulb suppliers should provide specific information about cold requirements for specific bulbs.) Store them in a breathable bag in the refrigerator for six to eight weeks. They will be ready to plant in the garden when the soil temperatures are 60 degrees Fahrenheit or cooler at a depth of 3 to 4 inches.

You can force bulbs to bloom early for blooms indoors, or you can bring them out to the garden and place the pots around for additional color in the spring.

If you want to force bulbs to bloom earlier than they normally would, you can pot them up and store them in the refrigerator or in a room where the temperature can be held below 60 degrees Fahrenheit while the bulbs are rooting for six to eight weeks. After this period, store them at a temperature of 35 to 45 degrees for another six to eight weeks. If it is cold enough outdoors (35 to 45 degrees), you can place the pots under a mulch pile. **Daffodil** expert Brent Heath recommends using a potting mix that is coarse so that roots will be able to penetrate easily and there will be good drainage. Mixes that contain peat moss, ground pine bark, perlite, and granite sand work well. Water the bulbs when you pot them up, and then only when the soil surface feels dry to the touch. When potting up the bulbs, they should just be touching one another, depending on the size of the pot—for example, five bulbs are good for a 6-inch pot.

Once roots begin to emerge from the bottom of the pot, bring it into the house or greenhouse. A temperature of 70 degrees is ideal—the top of the refrigerator is usually this warm or warmer. Give your bulbs the maximum amount of daylight so that they develop strong stems; grow lights can be used to provide supplemental light in the evening.

Check pots regularly now to see if they need water. Water when the soil is dry to the touch, but don't overwater. There is no need to fertilize your bulbs unless you want to plant them in the garden after they finish blooming (be sure the threat of frost has passed). In this case, use a water-soluble fertilizer that is high in phosphorus, potash, and trace elements.

 PLANTING

In the middle and northern parts of the state, you can plant spring bulbs provided the soil temperatures have cooled off to 60 degrees Fahrenheit. Use a soil thermometer to measure the temperature at 3 to 4 inches deep.

Start **paper-whites** in pots so you will have blooms for Thanksgiving. By staggering the times you plant **paper-whites,** you can have fragrant blooms indoors from Thanksgiving well into the New Year. **Paper-whites** do not require a chilling period before they grow and bloom, and some will be in bloom three to four weeks after you pot them up. Keep them in a cool, dark place until they put on a good bit of growth (the foliage should be 3 or more inches tall). At this point, move them gradually into the light.

If you are potting up lots of bulbs for forcing (**paper-whites** and other types, too), use a potting mix that is one part coarse builder's sand, one part perlite, two parts peat moss, and two parts ground pine bark. All pots must have drainage holes. You may place a pot with drainage holes in a decorative pot that doesn't have holes if you like.

Fill the pot 3/4 full with the soil mix. Place the bulbs in the pots, with the sides barely touching, then fill in with small gravel or pebbles to hold the bulbs in place. As the bulbs begin to grow and the stems stretch, stake them so they won't fall over once they begin to bloom. Try placing three attractive bamboo stakes in the pot, at equal distances from one another, and use a natural jute twine or raffia to form a ring around the stakes. Water the bulbs after you pot them up, and then only when the soil is dry to the touch.

## HELPFUL HINTS

Forcing **daffodils** is fun and rewarding. Below is a list of the best varieties to force as recommended by Brent Heath.

- All **paper-whites**
- *Narcissus* 'Abba'
- N. 'Bridal Crown'
- N. 'Cragford'
- N. 'Garden Princess'
- N. 'Ice Follies'
- N. 'Johann Strauss'
- N. 'Jumblie'

- N. 'Kassels Gold'
- N. 'Little Beauty'
- N. 'Little Gem'
- *Narcissus obvallaris*
- N. 'Pipit'
- N. 'Rijnveld's Early Sensation'
- N. 'W.P. Milner'

See the Helpful Hints for the best varieties of **daffodils** to force. These can be enjoyed indoors or brought out to the garden when they are ready to bloom.

## WATERING

Water your bulbs as soon as you plant them. Give them a good soaking. If you apply 1 inch of water, it should reach roots at a depth of 6 inches in a soil with a moderate amount of clay (30 to 40 percent). Applying double this amount should be enough for bulbs that are planted as deep as 9 to 10 inches.

## FERTILIZING

If you plant spring bulbs now, you can topdress with a complete fertilizer like 10-10-10 or Bulb Booster™. If you mixed fertilizer into the soil when you tilled it, there is no need to fertilize again.

## PROBLEMS

Clean up any dead or diseased leaves on your summer bulbs. Dispose of these in the garbage. This will reduce the spread of potential insect or disease problems that might otherwise overwinter.

## GROOMING

There is no pruning required at this time.

# NOVEMBER
## BULBS, CORMS, RHIZOMES, & TUBERS

### PLANNING

If you don't have any **daffodils** in your garden, consider adding some this fall. **Daffodils** are among the most satisfying of bulbs to grow because they thrive with just a minimum of care once they are established. Knowing the best varieties for our Georgia climate will help ensure your success (see December). Prepare the soil where bulbs will be planted (see September, Planning).

### PLANTING

Plant spring-flowering bulbs. Don't forget to replant any spring-flowering bulbs that you dug during the summer. Early-flowering types can be planted under deciduous trees since they will be going dormant by the time trees leaf out fully and create heavy shade.

Most spring-flowering bulbs thrive if they are planted in full sun or part shade, but the flowers will last longer if they are protected from the hot midday sun.

In the middle and northern parts of the state (zone 7 or colder), summer bulbs like **dahlias, cannas, elephant ear,** and **caladiums** should be dug up

and stored for the winter. Here are some tips for digging up **Dahlia** tubers and other summer-blooming bulbs like **caladiums.**

• Wait until a frost kills back the foliage. Cut back the stem to a height of 12 inches.

• Use a digging fork, and carefully dig around and under the clumps. Lift them out of the ground.

• Follow this technique if you divide the clumps long after you dig them. Use a sharp knife, making sure each tuber has a stalk about 1 inch and an eye (this is where new growth will initiate).

• Dust **dahlia** tubers with sulfur, and then cover them with sawdust, sand, or vermiculite. Store them over the winter in a dry, cool (40- to 50-degree-Fahrenheit) place.

If you decide to store the clumps whole and divide them in the spring, cover them with sawdust, sand, perlite, peat moss, or vermiculite, and keep them in a cool, dry place. Separate the tubers two to four weeks before you plant them, using the method described above.

If you have **elephant ear** that you want to save, you can dig up the tuberous roots and keep them cool and dry over the winter. The roots can be as big as a softball. If you grow them in containers, cut back the foliage after

there is a hard frost (to about 12 inches high). Use caution when you cut back the foliage, as the sap contains microscopic crystals of oxalic acid, which can be very dangerous to your eyes. Cover the stems with an old cloth as you prune off the leaves. Keep the container in a cool, dark space, and provide a minimum of moisture to keep the plant alive until spring when you can bring it back outside.

### WATERING

Water bulbs after you plant them. Apply 2 to 3 inches of mulch on top of newly planted bulb areas.

### FERTILIZING

Fertilize bulbs when you plant them, with a complete fertilizer like 8-8-8 or 10-10-10 (see February, Helpful Hints, for tips on fertilizing **daffodils**).

Topdress bulbs that you planted last fall (see Helpful Hints in September for tips on how to remember where you planted your bulbs).

Bonemeal is not considered a complete fertilizer, because it does not provide all the nutrients that bulbs need. If you want to use an organic-type fertilizer,

## TIPS FOR DRYING AND STORING YOUR BULBS

These tips apply to both spring- and summer-blooming types of bulbs.

**DRYING:** Find a dry, shady spot in which to spread your tender bulbs as they dry completely. This step is important because the bulbs harden their skin and heal wounds as they slowly dry. This process helps prevent rot later while they are stored inside. Some gardeners wipe their bulbs with a 1:10 solution of bleach and water in order to kill fungi. Others dust the bulbs with sulfur or garden fungicide to protect them. Neither practice is absolutely essential, but each does add a measure of protection. Let the bulbs dry outdoors until the foliage is withered and the stems begin to shrink. Do not let them freeze or get wet.

**STORING:** Separate the bulbs by variety and color. Small cardboard boxes make good containers. Spread a 1-inch-thick layer of dry peat moss in a box, then place bulbs so they do not touch each other. When one layer is finished, cover it thickly with peat moss, and make another layer.

Label each box clearly. Unlike spring bulbs, which are best stored in cool temperatures, tender bulbs like it warm during the winter. A good storage place is in a closet where temperatures do not fall below 50 degrees Fahrenheit.

When you store your tender bulbs for the winter, you can plant winter annuals like **pansies, parsley,** and **ornamental cabbage** in their beds. Next spring, in May when the soil is quite warm, you can plant your treasures and enjoy their foliage and flowers once again.

look for "Bulb Mate," which has a 5-10-12 formula. It contains cricket manure, rock phosphate, bonemeal, granite meal, dolomitic limestone, and organic compost.

## PROBLEMS

Clean up any remaining leaf litter. It should be safe to put most leaves on the compost pile even if they were affected by insects or disease, unless the disease is a virus, such as mosaic virus. Any bulbs or plant parts infected with a virus should be disposed of in the garbage.

## GROOMING

If there are any seeds you want to save, cut off the pods while they are still brown and before they turn mushy.

Label each container of bulbs you're storing; you don't want to mix them up next spring!

# DECEMBER
## BULBS, CORMS, RHIZOMES, & TUBERS

 PLANNING

In coastal areas, there is still time to plant spring-flowering bulbs this month and next month. If you have a large area and you want to grow spring-flowering bulbs, naturalizing or mass planting might be a good technique to try. Prepare the soil ahead of time.

Dig out large areas to the depth required by whatever type bulb you are planting. If you are planting **crocus** in the lawn, you won't need to dig as deeply as you will if you plant large **daffodils.** After you dig out an area, set aside the soil. Place the bulbs in the planting space, which can be an irregular shape. This will result in a more natural-looking planting when the bulbs bloom in the spring. If you want a more formal look, plant in rows or a definite geometric shape, and space the bulbs at a regular distance from one another. A cluster of 100 in one spot will make for a more dramatic effect. If you use the same variety, it will also have more of an impact than having a scattering of types blooming at all different times. You can do this easily with **crocus, daffodils, snowdrops,** and **snowflakes.**

You can also use this technique to create a meadow garden. After you plant the bulbs, add other perennial plants that will bloom at times other than when the spring bulbs are blooming. If you have weeds and want to use a nonselective weedkiller, use a glove (or two gloves, one on top of the other for safety), and wipe the weedkiller on the plants. This way you can control what the chemical touches.

While all **daffodils** belong to the genus *Narcissus,* not all *Narcissus* are **daffodils.** The genus *Narcissus* is represented by thirteen different divisions. The divisions are determined by the type of flower such as the Classic Trumpet, Large-cupped, Small-cupped, Double, Jonquilla, and so on. Jonquilla and Tazetta represent two of the divisions of **daffodils** that do well in Georgia gardens. Below are selections that perennialize well:

• 'Carlton', in the Large-cupped Division, offers upfacing two-toned yellow flowers with a vanilla scent; it grows 14 to 16 inches tall.

• 'Erlicheer', a vigorous double-flowering **daffodil,** produces clusters of fifteen to twenty creamy-white-and-gold fragrant flowers per 12- to 14-inch stem.

• 'February Gold', a Cyclamineus hybrid, has gold petals that are recurved (curved back away from the trumpet part of the flower).

• 'Ice Follies', in the Large-cupped Division, has flowers with creamy white petals and a yellow cup that turns almost white as it matures.

• 'St. Keverne', in the Large-cupped Division, is an heirloom that is all yellow and grows 16 to 18 inches tall. It performs well in coastal gardens, too.

• 'Tête-a-Tête', a Cyclamineus hybrid, grows only 6 inches tall and has buttercup-yellow flowers.

• 'Thalia' is a Triandrus hybrid with two or three white flowers per stem.

In coastal areas, gardeners can grow **paper-whites** and other **daffodils** in the Tazetta and Jonquilla division with great success because they don't require a chilling period.

• 'Avalanche' grows 16 inches tall and produces clusters of flowers (up to twenty) with white petals and a yellow cup.

• 'Chinese Sacred Lily' is similar to a **paper-white**; this **daffodil** has white petals with yellow cups, grows 10 to 14 inches tall, and needs staking.

• 'Galilee' flowers are pure white with a musky fragrance. They grow 12 to 14 inches tall.

## PLANTING

If you haven't planted yet and the ground is not frozen, get those spring-flowering bulbs in the ground. In coastal areas, this is a great month to plant spring bulbs.

If you want to force **paper-whites** for the New Year, plant some today. You can plant them in soil and top off the pot with pebbles. Another method that works well is to use a decorative container: Use pebbles to hold the bulbs in place. Fill up the pot with water, but don't cover the top 1/4 of the bulb. Keep the bulbs in a cool spot with dim light until they put up 3 to 4 inches of stems and leaves. At this point, move them into a bright room; as they grow, move them to the sunniest window you have.

## HELPFUL HINTS

If you want to force other spring-flowering bulbs to bloom, there is still time. Below is a list of bulbs that are relatively easy to force. While some bulbs like **paper-whites** and **hyacinths** can be forced in water with pebbles, most spring bulbs need oxygen and should be potted up in a pot with soil and drainage holes. You can force these bulbs to enjoy indoors or to bring out into the garden after the danger of frost has passed in early spring.

- **Crocus**
- **Daffodil**
- **Dwarf iris**
- **Glory of the snow**
- **Hyacinth**
- **Siberian squill**
- **Tulip** 'Apricot Beauty'

Check with your local Cooperative Extension Service for more information on forcing bulbs.

## WATERING

Water bulbs you planted this fall for the next two months while they are putting energy into forming roots and before they go into a semi-dormant state for winter. If you are forcing bulbs to get them to bloom earlier, check the pots and make sure they don't dry out completely.

## FERTILIZING

Topdress any bulb plantings that you plant this fall (see February, Helpful Hints).

## PROBLEMS

If you haven't cleaned up the garden yet, now is the time to remove leaf litter from summer bulbs and other perennials. A clean garden means fewer places for pest and disease problems to overwinter.

## GROOMING

No pruning is needed at this time.

# EDIBLES

Before there were landscapes to beautify, before there were lawns to tend, "gardening" was all about food. It was a major step for hunter-gatherers to settle down and build permanent communities; they could make their homes in one spot because they learned to cultivate food rather than catch it.

Nowadays, growing food in a garden is not as common as it once was. It is usually cheaper to purchase fresh food at the grocery, and it is a lot less work! Nothing, however, can compare to the taste of a vine-ripened tomato plucked from the vine on a summer morning and consumed in the middle of your garden. Nothing is as juicy as

fresh sweet corn that fifteen minutes before being boiled was standing tall in your patch. Few things are as pleasant as sharing the surplus of your garden with neighbors or the local food bank.

Food gardening is not about cost or labor. It is about taste, productivity, and connection to the earth. Georgia is blessed with a long growing period—so long that it is divided into three parts: spring season, summer season, and fall season. This chapter will help you organize your efforts to have food available from your garden in all three seasons. If you want to preserve your food, you can have food from your garden all year long! Maximizing your yield starts with planning.

## CHAPTER THREE

### PLANNING

Late winter weather plays a big role in determining which vegetables can be planted in the different parts of the state. In general, the south Georgia cool-season vegetable planting period begins in the last week of January. The north Georgia season begins around the first week of March. The Small Garden Plan on p. 281 will give you information on the proper dates to plant your crops.

### WHERE TO PLANT

Vegetables need full sunshine in order to produce to the fullest. A few hours of light shade is acceptable, but few things will grow where they receive less than four hours of direct sunshine per day. If you have a semi-shaded spot, concentrate on leafy vegetables and bean family members, not tomatoes, watermelons, and corn, which require lots of sun. Remember that vegetables can be grown in containers if the sunniest place available is your patio.

A late frost can freeze the blooms on fruit trees, leaving a healthy tree but no fruit for the season. Pick a planting site that gets plenty of sunshine—but not at the bottom or top of a hill, where temperatures are usually colder. Refer to the fruit variety charts on p. 282 for fruit varieties that bloom later and avoid damage.

### ORGANIC GARDENING

If you are growing food for yourself or your family, you certainly do not want the food to harm you. While researchers and government agencies have stated that synthetic pesticides can be safely used on edibles, some gardeners prefer to use only naturally derived pesticides on their plants. They use beneficial insects, botanical insecticides, and improved varieties so they can avoid using synthetic pesticides. Many organic pesticides are included in the Chemicals section (p. 277). Though organically grown produce may have a few cosmetic flaws, organic growers take pleasure in producing their food in the most natural way possible.

Our recommendations for proper soil preparation (see Horticultural Practices, p. 9) will help you produce strong plants that can tolerate insects and diseases but still grow acceptably. For more information, contact Georgia Organics (770-621-GOGA). You will also find much information in *Organic Gardening* magazine (800-666-2206).

If you prefer organic fertilizers for your garden, the publication "Converting Soil Test Results to Organic Fertilizer Recommendations" is available from your local Extension Service office (p. 289).

### PREPARING THE SOIL

A thorough tilling of your vegetable garden is necessary each year to break up soil clumps and old rootballs. See Horticultural Practices, p. 9, for complete instructions on preparing a bed.

### POLLINATION

In order for a plant to produce vegetables, fruit, or nuts, the flowers must be pollinated. Nature will usually take care of this for you. For tips on vegetable pollination, see the June, August, and September months. If you do not see many pollinating insects in your garden, see the introduction to the Annuals chapter, and learn how to attract more of them.

Some fruit trees are self-fruitful (pollen from a single plant is sufficient to pollinate its own flowers). Others are partially self-fruitful or even self-incompatible. Follow these general guidelines when deciding whether you need one or more of each:

- Apple: Plant at least two different varieties.
- Blueberry: Plant at least two different varieties.
- Bunch grapes: Self-fruitful.
- Fig: Self-fruitful.
- Muscadine grape: Plant at least two different varieties; one must be self-fruitful.
- Peach: Self-fruitful.
- Pear: Most are self-fruitful.
- Pecan: Plant at least two different varieties.
- Plum: Plant at least two different varieties.
- Raspberry, blackberry: Self-fruitful.

## CHAPTER THREE

### FINDING SPECIAL SEED

Seed packets of the common vegetables can be found at your local garden center. If you want to grow vegetable varieties that are a little less common, catalogs may have what you are looking for. Check the Internet for listings.

Memories of the taste of a particular tomato variety send some gardeners on a fruitless search for that plant at their local nursery. If it is not available there, seed may be available from specialty suppliers. Sources of heirloom tomato seed include:

Totally Tomatoes, P.O. Box 1626,
  Augusta, GA, 30903-1626, (803) 663-0016
Tomato Growers Supply, P.O. Box 2237,
  Fort Myers, FL 33902, (888) 478-7333

Rachel's Tomatoes, SBE Seed Co.,
  3421 Bream St., Gautier, MS 39553,
  (800) 336-2064

If you are looking for a certain variety of fruit or vegetable that just can't be found through normal channels, the *Georgia Farmers and Consumers Market Bulletin* is a good source to try. This free weekly newspaper is full of items for sale to farmers and gardeners statewide. The pictures of oddly shaped and overlarge vegetables submitted by their owners are consistently entertaining.

19 M.L.K. Jr. Drive, Atlanta, GA 30334-4250,
  Phone: (800) 282-5852

## WHEN TO HARVEST YOUR VEGETABLES

When will you know it is time to harvest your vegetables? The following are signs that different vegetables are ready to be harvested:
- Asparagus: stem 6 to 8 inches long, has no fiber or strings. (Begin harvesting asparagus when the plants are well established in their bed.)
- Broccoli: bright-green color; head still closed.
- Cabbage: head is firm, leaves tight.
- Cantaloupe: stem breaks easily from vine when gently pulled; netting on skin is raised and distinct.
- Collards: bright-green color; small midvein on each leaf.
- Corn, sweet: most kernels plump and filled with milky liquid.
- Cucumber: skin dark green, seeds soft.
- Eggplant: skin glossy; skin springs back when pressed.
- Lima bean: bright-green pod; seeds visibly swollen in the pod, not flat.
- Okra: pods 2 to 3 inches long and tender.
- Onion: tops are yellow and three-fourths fallen over.
- Pea, southern: seeds fully developed but soft.
- Pole green bean: bean seems full; seed half-grown, not overmature or dry.
- Potato, Irish: tops begin to die back.
- Potato, sweet: most tubers 2 to 3 inches in diameter.
- Snap bush bean: pods firm when pinched; seeds just visible.
- Squash, summer and winter: skin can be penetrated by thumbnail.
- Tomato, mature green stage: color changes from green to light green, no pink color on blossom end (these tomatoes can be stored one to two weeks in your refrigerator).
- Tomato, pink stage: pink color about the size of a dime on blossom end (these tomatoes will ripen in three days at room temperature).
- Tomato, ripe: flesh full red but still firm (may be refrigerated to slow ripening, but these tomatoes should be used immediately).
- Watermelon: skin that was lying on the soil turns from light straw color to rich yellow. When slapped, sounds hollow (unripe ones sound as if you're hitting solid wood).

(Courtesy of Dr. McLaurin, "When to Harvest Vegetables," UGA

# VEGETABLE GARDEN FERTILIZATION

Run a soil test (see p. 7) to determine lime and fertilizer needs (see Horticultural Practices, p. 8). If the pH is low, apply the recommended amount of lime before rototilling the soil so the lime can be mixed with the soil as you till. A pH of 6.0 to 6.5 is recommended for all vegetables except Irish potatoes, which require a pH of 5.5 to 5.8. Vegetables are classified as Light, Medium, and Heavy feeders, based on their fertilizer needs.

<u>Heavy Feeders</u>

| | | |
|---|---|---|
| Cabbage | Irish potatoes | Onions |
| Celery | Lettuce | Tomatoes |

<u>Medium Feeders</u>

| | | | |
|---|---|---|---|
| Artichoke | Corn, sweet | Okra | Rhubarb |
| Asparagus | Cucumbers | Peas, English | Squash |
| Beans, all | Eggplant | Pepper | Sweet potatoes |
| Beets | Greens, all | Pumpkin | Swiss chard |
| Cantaloupes | Herbs | Radish | Watermelon |
| Carrots | | | |

<u>Light Feeders</u>
Southern peas

The results of your soil test will detail the exact fertilizer needs of your vegetables. In the absence of a soil test, use the following recommendations:

## BEFORE PLANTING (ALL VEGETABLES)
Broadcast 30 pounds of 5-10-10 (or 6-12-12) fertilizer per 1,000 square feet. This can be done just after planting but it is preferable to mix the fertilizer with the soil before the final rows are laid out. Lime and fertilizer can be broadcast and rototilled into the soil at the same time.

## DURING THE GROWING SEASON
<u>Heavy Feeders</u>
Side-dress (see June, Fertilizing) with 1 pound of 10-10-10 per 100 feet of row, beginning when plants are 6 inches tall. Repeat twice more, at four week intervals.

<u>Medium Feeders</u>
Side-dress with 1 pound of 10-10-10 per 100 feet of row, beginning when plants are 6 inches tall. Repeat once more six weeks later.

<u>Light Feeders</u>
Side-dress with 1 pound of 10-10-10 per 100 feet of row when plants are 6 inches tall.

## ORGANIC FERTILIZERS
Organic fertilizers can be used in your garden instead of synthetic nutrients. Composted hen manure, bloodmeal, steamed bonemeal and Sulfate of Potash magnesia (Sul-Po-Mag) are excellent organic sources of nutrients. As the soil test report you receive will recommend synthetic fertilizers (10-10-10, 33-0-0, 0-46-0, etc.), ask your local Extension Service office (See Resources) for a free copy of "How to Convert an Inorganic Fertilizer Recommendation to an Organic One."

# JANUARY
## EDIBLES

 PLANNING

Bare-root fruit trees will soon be available at nurseries. Ask the manager when he or she expects the shipments to arrive. If you want to plant a particular variety, ask if it can be special-ordered for you. If you plan to have dwarf trees, do some research to learn the ultimate size of a mature plant—some semi-dwarf varieties grow larger than you might expect.

Having fruit plants is not a simple matter of planting now, then enjoying fruit for years to come. Most fruit trees, especially **peaches,** require careful management to control insects and diseases. Smaller fruit plants like **blueberry, raspberry, blackberry,** and **fig** need much less care. They also take up less room!

 PLANTING

Rototill garden beds where you will plant cool-season vegetables. If the soil is ready, you will not have to tend to this task when the early gardening season begins next month.

 CARE

**Raspberry** and **blackberry** stems (canes) are not permanent. On most plants, the canes that bore fruit last season will die during the winter to make room for fresh growth. Now is a good time to remove the brown, dead canes from your plants and tie the green canes to your wire trellis.

Leather gloves are a must when working with brambles. Use jute twine to loosely tie up the canes. The twine will rot by the end of the year.

 WATERING

In south Georgia, sandy soil loses water rapidly. Plan to add 1 cubic foot of organic material for each foot of hole diameter before planting a fruit or nut tree. The organic particles will act like a sponge during the summer, storing water when it is available and releasing it when dry weather occurs.

Make a habit of mulching plants with shredded leaves each fall. As the leaves break down, earthworms will mix them with the soil beneath.

 FERTILIZING

Fruiting plants are deciduous, losing their leaves in winter in most parts of Georgia. Mature plants don't need fertilizer now, since there are no leaves present. New plants, on the other hand, need phosphorus immediately.

Mix 1 tablespoon of 0-46-0 (triple superphosphate) per foot of height into the soil when you plant a fruiting plant. This will give the roots the phosphorus they require when they begin to grow.

 PROBLEMS

Many insects overwinter under the bark of fruit trees.

Spray dormant horticultural oil on fruit tree branches and trunks to suffocate dormant insects. Thoroughly cover the entire trunk and all branches with the spray.

 PRUNING

Prune your **muscadine grapes** now, removing the long whips that grew last year. Actually, you'll prune back to the first two buds on each long stem, leaving only these to make new growth this year. It is on this new growth that the **grapes** are produced!

After several years of pruning back to two buds, a series of spur clusters (staghorns) will protrude from the main vine arms. If the clusters crowd each other too much, remove a few to give the rest more room to grow.

**Pear** and **apple** trees often suffer broken limbs due to an excess of fruit in August.

Shorten long and slender limbs by 1/3 to 1/2.

Limbs that cross through the branches in the center of a fruit tree rarely bear fruit. They also shade the leaves of more productive limbs.

This is a good time to examine the structure of your trees. Remove crossing limbs, dead limbs, and limbs that deviate from the appropriate form (see February).

**Fig** bushes that have become too large for their space can be severely pruned now.

If the space is small to begin with, consider moving the bush to a spot where it can grow at least 8 feet tall and 8 feet wide.

## HELPFUL HINTS

Most dwarf trees are made to grow that way by grafting a twig from a regular-sized tree onto a "dwarfing rootstock." You can tell you have a grafted tree by noticing the swollen lump near ground level where the two plant parts were joined together.

Sometimes a strongly dwarfing rootstock does not have a brawny root system like a normal tree—this makes it prone to falling over during a forceful windstorm or a severe ice storm. To prevent this, install a deeply-driven post 12 inches from the tree when it is planted. Tie the post loosely to the tree trunk so it is anchored against abnormal wind or weather.

Check your pear or apple trees; remove any branches that cross over or that deviate from their proper form.

# FEBRUARY

## EDIBLES

 PLANNING

**Asparagus** is easy to grow in a permanent bed. The key to success is to prepare the soil properly at the beginning, since you won't be able to improve it for several years. Raised beds, deeply dug and amended with copious amounts of organic matter, will give your **asparagus** a happy home for years.

- Try to find a hybrid **asparagus** variety like 'Jersey Giant' or 'Jersey Male'. These newer hybrids produce twice as many spears as the old-timers' favorite 'Mary Washington'.
- Purchase crowns that are more than one year old—two- or three-year-old crowns are best.
- Avoid harvesting spears the first year. The plant needs at least a year to grow vigorous roots.

 PLANTING

**Blueberries** are among the easiest-to-grow backyard fruit plants. They make a good hedge, and the leaves are colorful in fall. **Blueberry** plants should arrive at your nursery any day now.

- Buy the largest **blueberry** plant you can find, preferably in a 3-gallon pot. A plant this size has a good chance of bearing lightly in its first growing season.
- Dig a 3-foot-wide hole for each **blueberry** plant, mixing in ¹/₂ cubic foot of peat moss for every foot of hole diameter. The peat moss yields the acidic soil that **blueberries** love.
- Do not fertilize with synthetic fertilizer (10-10-10, etc.) for one year after planting. Use manure or blood meal instead.

 CARE

It is common to have several days of warm weather in February, followed by a frigid Siberian Express. **Fig** bushes come out of dormancy readily during warm weather, and they can be frozen to the ground if not protected:

1. Make plans to have ready a sheet of black plastic large enough to cover your plant entirely if icy weather threatens.

2. Anchor the plastic on all sides with stones or limbs. It is a waste of time to perform this task if you can't cover the entire plant.

3. Remove the plastic when the sun comes out the next day. This is especially important if you use clear plastic. Under clear plastic, temperatures rise rapidly!

 WATERING

One of the best water-saving investments for a garden is a rubber soaker hose.

- Make a tentative layout of your garden rows and measure the length to determine how much hose to buy.
- A continuous stretch of soaker hose should be no longer than 100 feet.
- You might have to invest in a faucet "splitter valve" so you can send water to each length of soaker hose in its turn.

 FERTILIZING

Late February is a good time to plant **strawberries,** if this was not accomplished in the fall (see October).

Once your bed is planted, water it with a high-phosphorus (12-55-6) water-soluble fertilizer at ¹/₄ strength (usually 1 tablespoon per 4 gallons of water). This will give the **strawberry** roots the available phosphorus they need without stimulating tender leaf growth.

Fertilize **pecan** trees in south Georgia with 1 pound of 10-10-10 per inch of trunk diameter (and again in June).

 PROBLEMS

Nematodes are microscopic soil-dwelling worms. Most of them are harmless to plants, but some are parasites of vegetable plant roots. If your **tomato** or **okra**

roots were swollen and gnarled last year, you may have nematodes in your soil. No nematicides are available for purchase by the homeowner, so you may deter nematodes these ways:

• The best nematode control is to till your garden soil when it is cold and windy. Many nematodes will die due to exposure to wind and cold.

• Soils kept high in organic matter deter nematodes by nurturing competing soil organisms. Add lots of organic material whenever you rototill a garden bed.

• It is best not to plant nematode-susceptible plants in the same spot for three years after discovering this pest. Plant **corn, beans,** or **peas** there instead.

## PRUNING

**Blueberries** have a tendency to grow tall sprouts in the center of the bush. Now is a good time to remove them.

Don't prune any branches that are within picking distance. The horizontal branches within 6 feet of the ground will bear most of your fruit.

**Apple** and **pear** trees are rarely hurt by winter cold. The story is not the same for **peach** and **plum** trees. A week of unseasonably warm weather can force the buds of a **peach** or

## HELPFUL HINTS

Good pruning shapes a tree to maximize the leaf surface facing the sun. Prune **apple, pear,** and **pecan** trees to a single leader. Prune **peach, plum,** and **cherry** trees to an open leader.

**plum** to swell and come out of dormancy.

For this reason it is better to wait until mid-March to prune these trees, after the threat of a frigid blast is all but gone.

Apple tree pruned to a central leader.

Peach tree pruned to an open leader.

# MARCH

## EDIBLES

 PLANNING

Start seeds of **tomatoes** indoors. You'll need six weeks to grow strong plants. They will be ready just in time to plant outdoors when the soil is warm.

• Use peat pots filled with sterile potting soil. Plant two or three seeds per pot.

• When the seeds have sprouted and grown 2 inches, pinch out the weakest one(s), leaving the strongest plant to thrive.

 PLANTING

Pinching (or cutting with scissors) some of your new seedlings allows the strongest ones to survive.

Plant **beet, cauliflower, mustard, radish,** and **turnip** seeds outdoors. Plant **strawberries** as soon as they become available at your local nursery.

 CARE

If you planted a cover crop on your vegetable garden last fall, mow it first, then till the leaves and stems into the soil.

 WATERING

Water fruit trees you planted in the last six months.

• Apply 1 gallon of water per foot of height per week.

• Keep a 2- to 3-inch-thick layer of mulch over the root system.

• Pull the mulch back 3 inches from the trunk in all directions.

 FERTILIZING

Plants can't use much fertilizer if they don't have leaves. Fertilize established fruit and nut trees when their leaves are expanding. A typical amount is 1 pound of 10-10-10 per inch of tree-trunk thickness. Repeat the feeding in May or June.

The feeder roots of a woody plant may extend twice as far as the tips of its branches. Few feeder roots exist close to a plant's trunk. Be sure to scatter the fertilizer evenly in a "doughnut" around the plant, applying at least half the fertilizer past the branch tips.

PROBLEMS

**Peach** and **plum** fruit are particularly susceptible to a disease called brown rot. It infects the bloom, waiting until the fruit is nearly ripe to exhibit itself. To treat this problem:

1. Spray a fungicide labeled for fruit trees on the tree when almost all the blooms are open.

2. Repeat when 50 percent of the blooms have fallen.

3. Be sure to remove all mummified fruit left on the tree from last season before blooms appear—this will reduce the chances of infection of this year's fruit.

Spray **apple** and **pear** tree blooms with bactericide if you have had problems with fire blight in past years.

 PRUNING

**Peach** and **plum** trees can be pruned when you are reasonably sure severe cold will not come again.

• Remove dead limbs or branch stubs.

• Remove limbs that cross through the center or droop too low.

• Remove pencil-sized water sprouts in the center of the tree.

• Try to keep the center of the tree open so sunshine can easily penetrate.

**Bunch grapes** are not pruned like **muscadine grapes,** because their old canes harbor disease more readily than do those of **muscadines.** Instead of having permanent fruiting arms, **bunch grapes** should be pruned to leave only four healthy canes from last year's growth. The new growth from these canes will produce the fruit.

---

**HELPFUL HINTS**

Digging in your garden will be much easier if your shovel is sharp. To minimize injuries, most shovels are sold with a dull blade. You'll be amazed at the difference a sharp shovel will make:

• Clamp the shovel in a vise, placing the blade upwards.

• Draw a mill file slowly across the edge of the blade, trying to keep the file at a 30-degree angle to the blade.

The blade does not need to be as sharp as a razor, but it should not have a thick or rounded edge.

---

• Select four healthy canes arising from the **grape** trunk. Two should be growing in one direction, and two should grow in the other along your two-wire trellis.

• Examine the four canes and note the somewhat swollen buds that occur along each one.

• Count the buds on a cane, starting at the trunk, and proceeding toward the tip. When you reach twelve, clip the cane.

• The result should be four canes, each having twelve buds.

• On young vines, or on those that did not fruit strongly last year, leave only eight buds per cane.

Finish pruning all grapevines by mid-month (see January). If you wait until later, much bleeding of sap from the cut ends will occur. (Although ominous-looking, bleeding does not harm the vine.)

Finish pruning out dead canes of **blackberry** and **raspberry.** Tie green healthy canes to a wire trellis.

Do not delay pruning **figs** past mid-month. The longer you wait, the more trouble you'll have with rampant, unproductive growth in summer.

It is not necessary in all instances to cut away fruit tree limbs that are growing too close together. Instead, make a spacer from a 12-inch-long (or longer, if needed) piece of 1×2 wood.

1. Cut a deep notch in each end of the wood.

2. Force the limbs apart and insert the spacer.

3. Leave it in place for at least two years.

# APRIL

## EDIBLES

### PLANNING

If you have never grown vegetables, you might wonder how many you'll have to plant to have fresh produce all summer. The following chart shows the length the planting rows should be for a family of four to have vegetables all summer long. Remember that some of the vegetables should be planted more than once in order to spread the harvest over the summer. Double the amounts if you plan to freeze or can your vegetables.

| Vegetable | Row Length (in feet) |
|---|---|
| Cabbage | 25 |
| Collards | 25 |
| Corn | 40 |
| Cucumber | 5 |
| Eggplant | 4 |
| English pea | 20 |
| Irish potato | 20 |
| Lima bean | 20 |
| Okra | 10 |
| Onion | 10 |
| Pepper | 3 |
| Snap bean | 40 |
| Southern pea | 30 |
| Summer squash | 5 |
| Sweet potato | 12 |
| Tomato | 12 |
| Turnips/mustard | 12 |
| Winter squash | 5 |

When **apples** are in full bloom you can count 150 days forward to determine when to start checking for ripeness.

### PLANTING

Plant warm-season garden crops such as **tomato, eggplant, pepper,** and **squash** when the soil is quite warm. In south Georgia, this planting time is in late March or early April. Gardeners in the northern half of the state should wait until April 15 to be safe. Of course, some gamblers will plant earlier—but they run the risk of losing everything to a late frost, and even if that doesn't happen, their plants will just sit there, not growing, waiting until the soil is warm.

Fruit trees can be purchased bare-root, balled-and-burlapped, or container-grown. Because the first two types have limited root systems, they are best planted in winter or very early spring. Fruit trees that have been grown in containers have a much more robust root system and can be planted in April and May.

### CARE

Nematodes (see February) can greatly limit your harvest. These tips will help minimize their damage to susceptible plants if you have nematodes in your small garden:

- Determine where you will place each plant.
- Shovel the soil out of a 1-foot-diameter hole at each spot.
- Fill the hole with good-quality bagged planting soil.
- Plant seedling plants in the center of the hole.
- By the time nematodes have moved from the contaminated soil into the clean planting soil, you'll have harvested plenty of produce. Remove the entire plant and root system from your property.

### WATERING

Water newly planted vegetables, herbs, and fruiting plants weekly, providing 1 to 5 cups for small plants, 1 to 2 gallons for shrubs and trees.

Mulching vegetable seedlings immediately after planting is a good practice for three reasons: moisture retention, weed control, and disease control. A thin layer of pine straw or grass clippings works well, or try using newspaper mulch:

1. Unfold a section of the paper, and select a stack of three sheets.

2. Tear the stack halfway down the center, and slip it around the stem of an individual plant.

3. Wet it down to hold in place, then cover with straw or leaves.

## FERTILIZING

You can make a simple starter fertilizer solution at home to use on new vegetable transplants:

1. Add 2 tablespoons of 5-10-15 fertilizer to 5 gallons of water.

2. Mix thoroughly and allow to settle.

3. Pour the solution around new transplants to settle them into the soil.

The jury is still out on the value of commercial root-stimulator solutions for new plants. It is not likely that the products cause harm, so go ahead and use them if you wish.

Fertilize **pecans** in north Georgia with 1 pound of 10-10-10 per inch of trunk diameter (and again in June).

Do not fertilize **blueberries** with granular fertilizer during the first year after planting. In later years, fertilize lightly in April, June, and September.

## PROBLEMS

Keep a vigilant eye out for chickweed in your garden. Pull it from among your cool-season vegeta-

## HELPFUL HINT

If you are short on space, **beans, cucumbers,** and **melons** can be grown on a trellis. A wire tomato cage (see June) is a bit small, but serviceable and easy to use. A more permanent trellis can be constructed using two sturdy posts erected at each end of a row:

1. Post tops should be 5 feet from the ground. Stretch heavy wire from post top to post top, anchoring it securely.

2. Stretch another heavy wire between the posts 1 foot from the ground.

3. Weave jute twine (up-down-up-down, etc.) between the wires to form a web on which the vines can crawl.

A permanent trellis can be constructed from stakes and wires.

bles, hoe it from the middles of the rows—just don't let it go to seed!

Mulch **tomato** plants right after you plant them, a practice that will help prevent leaf diseases. Early blight is a fungus that splashes onto leaves from the soil during rainstorms or overhead watering. Once the fungus is on the leaves, it will continue to splash up the plant as it grows.

Control with fungicides is difficult; immediate mulching is much more effective.

## PRUNING

Remove the thin "sucker sprouts" as they arise from the lower trunks of **apple, pear,** and **peach** trees.

# MAY

## EDIBLES

### PLANNING

**Kiwifruit** is delicious, but the vines are not very cold hardy. The fruit can be grown in south Georgia, but is not always cold hardy north of Macon. The vine is grown on a double-wire trellis identical to a grape trellis.

• Yearly pruning in March is required because the vine grows so fast. The technique is the same as for **muscadine grape-vines** (see January).

• A male vine is needed to provide pollen for one to five female vines.

• Don't expect fruit for two years. The vine needs at least this long to establish itself.

• Make plans to protect the vine with a plastic sheet whenever temperatures fall below 30 degrees Fahrenheit.

### PLANTING

Select **bush-type** or **cherry tomatoes** for patio planting. A huge pot is a must! Five gallons of soil for one plant is a bare minimum.

Use light-colored pots. Dark ones absorb sunshine and cause the soil to become too hot.

Plant **rosemary, dill, oregano, mint,** and **basil** for savory summer meals.

The soil has to be very warm (above 65 degrees Fahrenheit) to encourage **corn, squash, bean,** and **field pea** seed to germinate. Plant by mid-April in south Georgia and mid-May in the northern part of the state. Make another planting in two weeks to spread out your harvest.

### CARE

A weekly inspection of your fruit plants can reveal problems that need attention.

1. Prune out any dead limbs or twigs.

2. Add mulch if needed. Make sure to keep it pulled back 6 inches from the trunk in all directions.

3. Look for insect or disease damage. Determine if the problem merits control before automatically reaching for a pesticide.

### WATERING

Georgia summers are famous for prolonged dry periods. The best time to prepare for a drought is before it occurs.

• Lay a soaker hose alongside your **blueberry, grape,** or **raspberry** plants.

• Place a soaker hose on the ground under the branch tips of fruit and nut trees.

• Consider using drip irrigation to water individual plants.

### FERTILIZING

Fertilize vegetables when they have grown enough to demonstrate that the root system has firmly established itself. This is generally two weeks after planting, or when the plant has grown 3 to 6 inches. (See p. 8.)

Fertilize small fruit trees with 1 cup of 10-10-10 per foot of height; large trees: 1 pound of 10-10-10 per inch of trunk thickness.

### PROBLEMS

Watch for blackened leaves at the ends of **apple** or **pear** limbs. This could be fireblight disease.

• Spray with a bactericide before every rain to protect new leaves.

• Prune out diseased branches. Sterilize your pruner between every cut with a 1:10 mixture of alcohol or bleach in water.

• Mark your calendar to spray again next year when the tree is blooming. Fireblight is spread by honeybees as they travel from flower to flower.

Apply *Bacillus thuringiensis* to **cabbage, broccoli,** and **cauliflower** to ward off cabbage looper caterpillars.

To prevent leaf diseases, place a newspaper mulch three sheets thick under **tomato** plants immediately upon planting. Cover the paper with pine straw.

Rabbits are cute, but they can be a real nuisance when they visit your garden. A short (18 inches tall) fence will keep them at bay while allowing you to easily step over it.

1. Purchase a roll of 1-inch mesh chicken wire 2 feet wide and long enough to encircle your garden. Purchase 2-feet-long sharpened surveyor's stakes onto which you can staple the wire.

2. Dig a shallow trench 4 to 6 inches deep around the garden. Drive the stakes into the trench at 4-foot intervals around your garden.

3. Use heavy-duty staples to fasten the wire to the wooden stakes.

4. If you like, slip the bottom 6 inches of the wire into the trench and cover with soil. This will prevent the bunnies from digging under your fence.

## HELPFUL HINT

Be sure to throw away the fruit you remove when thinning your fruit trees—don't drop it on the ground.
1. Tie the handle of a small bucket to your belt buckle.
2. Thin fruit with both hands, dropping them into the bucket.
3. When your pants begin to fall down, empty the bucket into a larger container and destroy the fruits.

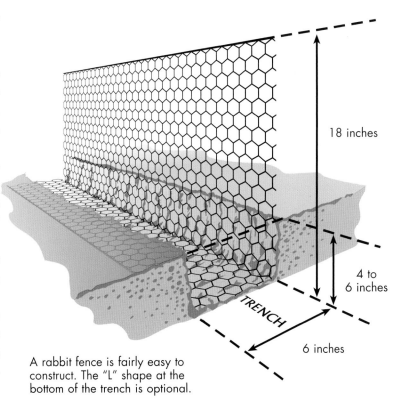

18 inches

4 to 6 inches

TRENCH

6 inches

A rabbit fence is fairly easy to construct. The "L" shape at the bottom of the trench is optional.

## PRUNING

Healthy fruit trees usually produce many more young fruit than the tree can comfortably bear by late summer. Surplus fruit should be thinned out and discarded by mid-May. It may seem wasteful to throw away the green fruit, but the tree will put its energy into ripening properly sized fruit if you thin corectly. Correct fruit spacing after thinning is:

• **Peach:** adjacent fruit on a limb should be no closer than 8 inches.

• **Apple:** adjacent fruit on a limb should be no closer than 6 inches.

• **Plum:** adjacent fruit on a limb should be no closer than 6 inches.

• **Pear:** adjacent fruit on a limb should be no closer than 8 inches.

# JUNE
## EDIBLES

### PLANNING

The different varieties of **sweet corn** each require a fixed number of days between planting and harvest. Unless you want a great deal of **corn** all at once, plant **sweet corn** seed every two weeks. As the different plantings mature, your **corn** season will be much longer.

- Plant **corn** through mid-July.
- Try a different variety of **corn** each year. You might like the new "super-sweet" types ('Kandy Korn', 'Seneca Sweet', etc.) better than the old standards ('Silver Queen' and 'Truckers Favorite').

Though it is not as critical as with **corn**, it is also beneficial to make successive plantings of other vegetables: **Summer squash, lima beans, pole beans,** and **field peas** can be planted every three weeks.

### PLANTING

**Corn** is pollinated by wind currents, not by insects. Plant your seeds in several parallel rows side by side instead of in one long row.

Vegetable transplants are still available at garden centers, but they might not always be the best quality:

- Examine each plant to make sure it does not have leaf disease.
- Short, stocky plants are better than the stretched-out ones that have flopped over each other.
- Try to purchase freshly delivered transplants rather than those that have been on display for several days.

Many vegetable plants can be grown on a trellis to minimize the space they need. Use strips of cloth or jute twine to tie vines to the trellis.

**Tomatoes** can be caged or staked to hold the vine off the ground:

- Purchased tomato cages are good for **bush** and **patio tomatoes,** but they are usually too small for other varieties.
- A homemade tomato cage may be made from a 6-foot-high section of heavy-duty fence wire 7 feet long. Join the ends of the fence wire to form a tube 6 feet high and 2 feet in diameter. Slip the tube over a plant. Attach the cage to a sturdy stake driven into the ground to keep it from blowing over.
- To stake **tomatoes,** drive a long wooden stake next to each plant; tie the vine loosely to the stake as it grows longer. Pinch the tips of limbs that sprout from the main stem when they have grown 12 inches. Fruit will then be produced close to the stake.

Tomatoes can be caged to keep the developing tomatoes off the ground.

**Watermelon, winter squash,** and **pumpkin** can also be trellised. Follow these steps to build a structure that will serve one plant:

1. Drive two sturdy posts into the ground 6 feet apart.

2. Stretch a 6-foot-long and 6-foot-wide piece of wire fencing between the posts; nail it to the post securely at both ends.

3. When fruits form, use a large square of cloth to cradle each one; tie the diagonal corners of the cloth to the trellis.

Do not attempt this trellising technique with large-fruited varieties.

## CARE

Remove stakes from fruit trees that have been planted for several months. They are now strong enough to stand on their own.

## WATERING

A drip irrigation system uses emitters that slowly drip water wherever you want it to be applied. The emitters are inserted into a plastic pipe that carries water from your faucet throughout your garden.

The best way to learn about drip irrigation is to purchase a starter kit that contains the components needed to water a small area. It can be expanded as necessary.

Soaker hoses laid down the row beside your vegetable plants will water them well without waste.

Water **cucumbers** regularly to prevent a bitter taste.

## FERTILIZING

Side-dressing is the practice of applying fertilizer to the ground beside plants as they grow. If your garden vegetables are growing in a row, it is simple to sprinkle fertilizer on the ground as you walk between rows.

You may also choose to fertilize in a circle around individual plants or broadcast it over the whole plot.

It's a common complaint of **tomato** growers that they have huge vines but few fruit. This condition might be caused by overfeeding with liquid fertilizer.

Once your **tomatoes** have grown to 2 feet tall, stop fertilizing until blooms appear.

(See Vegetable Garden Fertilization, p. 79.)

## PROBLEMS

Blossom end rot is a common disorder of **tomato** fruit. It is caused by a lack of calcium in the fruit when it is small.

• Add 2 tablespoons of lime to the soil when planting individual **tomatoes.**

• Keep soil moisture levels constant; avoid wide fluctuations of water around the roots. Use mulch under the **tomatoes.**

• If you notice the fruit has a rotten bottom (the blossom end), spray immediately with a product containing calcium chloride.

## PRUNING

Use garden herbs often in your kitchen, snipping and nipping leaves as you need them. Herbs grow best when the branches and leaves are harvested regularly.

---

## ORGANIC GARDENING REFERENCES

*Organic Gardening Magazine*, Rodale, Emmaus, PA 18098

*The Encyclopedia of Organic Gardening*, by J.I. Rodale, Rodale Press

*Common-Sense Pest Control*, by William Olkowski, The Taunton Press

# JULY
## EDIBLES

### PLANNING

Early this month is the time to plant **pumpkins** for Halloween. Most varieties need at least 100 days of growth to make a suitable jack-o-lantern. Varieties that produce "baby" pumpkins are often more successful. Varieties with shorter vines take up less space. If you are still short on space, build a heavy-duty trellis (see June) on which to train the vine.

### PLANTING

You can root new **tomato** plants now to keep your garden productive into October:

If you want to harvest pumpkins in time for Halloween, plant seeds this month.

1. Put the lower 6 inches of a 12-inch-long **tomato** branch in a jar of water. Keep it in a shady area outdoors.

2. When roots are 1 inch long, the **tomato** can be transplanted into a pot.

3. In two weeks the plant will be ready to move to your garden.

If you are conscientious about keeping the soil moist, you can root **tomatoes** right in the soil. This is how Walter's neighbor Harry does it:

1. Cut a 12-inch branch from your **tomato** plant. Strip off all the leaves except the two or three around the tip of the branch.

2. Poke a hole in the garden soil deep enough to insert all but the top 3 inches of the branch.

3. Water the soil thoroughly every two days.

4. Make a temporary umbrella for the tender plant using an unneeded branch from a **holly** or **aucuba** shrub. Remove the umbrella ten days later. Your new plant is rooted in place and ready to grow!

### CARE

Don't let fruit tree limbs break: prop them up with poles, or remove some fruit to lighten the load.

Pick **squash, cucumbers,** and **okra** regularly. A single fruit left to overmature on the vine will stop bloom production completely.

### WATERING

It is sometimes said that watering vegetable plants on a hot, sunny afternoon will cause spots to be burned in the leaves because the water droplets focus sunlight on the leaves. This is hogwash.

Quick afternoon showers are common throughout the summer. Neither vegetables, nor trees, nor flowers, nor any other plant are harmed by water on their leaves on a sunny afternoon.

Water weekly your fruit trees and vines that were planted in the last six months. They need approximately 2 gallons of water per foot of plant height.

## FERTILIZING

Continue to fertilize summer vegetables. (See Vegetable Garden Fertilization, p. 79.)

Don't forget to water the fertilizer into the soil afterwards.

**Patio tomatoes** need to be fed regularly because the constant watering rinses fertilizer out of the soil.

You can also mix up a large storage container of water-soluble houseplant fertilizer at $1/4$ strength and simply use it to water the plants each time.

## PROBLEMS

**Tomato** leaves disappearing overnight? Suspect the tomato hornworm, a big green caterpillar camouflaged among the plant stems. Hornworms are easiest to find in late evening, using a flashlight. Look for black excrement pellets on the ground underneath their feeding site.

---

### HELPFUL HINT

All members of the **squash** family (**watermelon, pumpkin, gourd, cucumber,** and **squash**) form separate male and female flowers on the same vine. Male flowers are first to arrive. They regularly appear for weeks before a female flower materializes on the vine. A healthy vine will eventually produce lots of fruit . . . don't worry if at first you have lots of flowers but nothing to eat!

Bees must be present to pollinate the flowers. If you are getting only a few well-shaped fruit, transfer pollen between male and female flowers. Use a cotton swab or camel hair brush, shaking it gently inside the flowers three times each day.

---

Some gardeners prefer not to kill the hornworm caterpillar. After all, it will eventually turn into a sphinx moth.

**Tomatoes** are susceptible to several diseases, so researchers have bred varieties that are resistant to disease. Look for the letters VFN or VFNT after the variety name. The letters mean the **tomato** is resistant to:

- Verticillium wilt
- Fusarium wilt
- Nematodes
- Tobacco mosaic virus

There is no defense against **tomato** bacterial wilt. The plant wilts markedly during the day but may partially recover overnight. After a week of successive wilts, the plant dies. Bacterial wilt remains in the soil for five years. Do not plant **tomato, pepper,** or **eggplant** in a bacterial wilt spot; plant **beans, peas,** or **corn** instead.

If you have no other place to plant **tomatoes,** follow the recommendation for thwarting nematodes described in April, Care.

## PRUNING

Prune **figs** lightly now. Remove the tall shoots in the middle of the bush.

Remove the vertical "water sprouts" that emerge from **apple, peach,** and **pear** limbs.

# AUGUST

## EDIBLES

### PLANNING

By now you have likely become tired of harvesting **beans, corn, peppers, tomatoes,** and **squash.** You can choose to let the whole garden wither for a few weeks . . . but don't forget to plan a fall garden: you can start buying seeds and finding out when transplants will be available at your nursery.

• **Collards, kale, mustard, beets,** and **turnip** are best planted from seed.

• **Broccoli, cabbage, cauliflower,** and **green onion** are best grown from transplants.

### PLANTING

If you are not tired of summer vegetables, several can be planted now and still yield a good harvest:

• **Bush beans** can be grown from seed.

• **Tomato, bell pepper, cucumber,** and **squash** can be grown from transplants.

### CARE

Look on the ground around your **blackberry** and **raspberry** plants. The canes snaking across the ground should be trained back to their wire arbor.

Winter Garden

Trellised English peas

Broccoli · Butterhead lettuce · Beets · Mustard · Bulbing onions · Kale · Onion sets · Cauliflower · Leaf lettuce · Cabbage · Celery · Collards · Crisp lettuce · Turnips · Carrots · Radishes · Parsley

### WATERING

Water **figs** and **apples** regularly now as they begin to ripen. Harvest every morning, before the birds can do their damage.

Water vegetables deeply once each week. (Avoid giving them light sprinkles several days in a row.)

### FERTILIZING

Fertilize newly planted vegetables with starter solution only. Do not fertilize heavily, since this increases the water needs of your plants.

Do not fertilize established vegetables and fruit now. (See Vegetable Garden Fertilization, p. 79.)

### PROBLEMS

Whiteflies are a common pest of **tomatoes** and **peppers,** (and **gardenias**). You can make a trap and catch hundreds of them:

1. Cut out two pieces of cardboard 3 inches by 4 inches in size.

2. Spray-paint the cards bright yellow.

3. Cover the cards with sticky motor oil treatment (STP®, etc.).

4. Nail the cards to stakes driven on both sides of a plant.

5. When trapped whiteflies cover the card, clean it and reapply the sticky stuff. Or, just start with another fresh card.

Deer can devastate a garden overnight. Many repellents have been tried, but few are effective more than a day or two. Repellents that deter deer with their bitter taste are not good choices for something you intend to eat! Wire mesh fencing is effective but expensive. You might want to try a different kind of fence: an electric fence that does not harm deer but gives them a mild electric shock when they touch it. Follow these steps to build a "Peanut Butter Electric Fence":

1. An electric fence consists of a small wire supported above the ground on insulated stakes. A special electric charger is attached to the wire and to a ground rod which has been driven into the ground. You can buy the materials from a hardware store or home improvement center for less than a hundred dollars. After you string the wire around your garden, it's time to train the deer.

2. Turn off the charger and grab a jar of peanut butter and some aluminum foil.

3. Take a tablespoon-sized wad of peanut butter in your fingers and mold it around the wire at some point.

4. Tear off a strip of aluminum foil 3 inches wide and 12 inches long, and center it over the gob of goober-butter. Drape the foil

strip on both sides of the wire. Crumple the foil where the foil touches the peanut butter. You should now have a wad of aluminum foil protecting the peanut butter from rain and a narrow flag of shiny foil hanging beneath it.

5. Repeat this procedure at 5-foot intervals along the entire circumference of the garden.

At night, when hungry deer approach your garden, they will smell the peanut butter and investigate with their nose. *Kazaaap!!!* Those **beans** don't look quite as inviting when they are accompanied by a side dish of electricity! When the deer wander by the next night, they will be reluctant to come close to any shiny, dangling objects—no matter how good they smell and no matter how inviting the plants

inside the wire seem.

6. When you install the electric fence, clear a strip of ground 3 feet wide on either side so you can walk along it every week to keep the wire clear of weeds.

**Caution:** Do not use an electric fence where children or unknowing visitors might come in contact with it. Post signs identifying your fence at intervals around it.

## PRUNING

Harvest **squash, okra,** and **cucumbers** regularly. If one fruit gets too big, the plant will stop blooming.

> ## HELPFUL HINT
>
> Even though you added organic amendments to the soil when you planted in spring, some of the material has already disappeared, cooked away by the heat and rainfall of the summer. Cover the soil with a 1-inch layer of organic amendment (compost, manure, ground pine bark, etc.), and rototill it into the earth before planting fall vegetables.

# SEPTEMBER

## EDIBLES

### PLANNING

Just because you can find a particular fruit in the grocery store does not mean it will grow in Georgia. Varieties of fruit that do not grow well in our Georgia climate are:

• 'Bing' or any other **sweet cherry**—winter temperature fluctuations and late frosts kill **sweet cherry** blooms. (**Pie cherries** such as 'Montmorency' or 'North Star' produce moderately well in the northern half of Georgia.)

• 'Bartlett' **pear**—fireblight disease is severe on this variety.

• 'Santa Rosa' **plum**—late frosts kill blooms, and Pierce's disease causes severe leaf drop. It seems to have a limited life span in south Georgia, although it might grow better in north Georgia.

• **Currants, gooseberry**—high summer temperatures doom these plants.

• The **pomegranate** is a fruiting shrub familiar to south Georgia gardeners, but it is not as common in the north Georgia; cold winter temperatures can freeze the plant back to its roots or kill it outright. If you would like the juicy fruit and the colorful foliage of a **pomegranate,** plant it in a spot protected from cold winter winds.

### PLANTING

In north Georgia, it's time to plant cool-season vegetable seeds and seedlings. **Cabbage, lettuce, collards,** and **broccoli** transplants are available at garden centers. **Lettuce, beets, turnip, spinach,** and **radish** seeds can be planted. **Onion sets** (small bulbs) and **garlic** can be planted now as well. Be sure to soak the soil after planting. Rainfall may not occur as often as you'd like.

Plant **parsley, rosemary, sage,** and **thyme** from transplants. Examine the small pots before you buy. Sometimes several plants will be growing in one pot; you can gently separate them just before planting and get several plants for the price of one!

### CARE

Show your kids how to eat a **muscadine:** pop it in your mouth, suck the pulp out of the skin, enjoy the juice, then spit out the skin and seeds. What a delicious mess!

Wrap cheesecloth around **sunflower** heads to keep the birds away. The head is ready to harvest when the back has turned from green to brown.

If your late **tomatoes** aren't setting fruit, the reason could be poor pollination due to heat and humidity.

Use an electric toothbrush to vibrate each flower cluster two to three times a day for three days.
*or*
Lightly tap each flower cluster with a pencil four to five times a day for three days.

### WATERING

This month is typically dry and hot in all parts of Georgia. Late-maturing vegetables need plenty of water for their fruit to ripen. Water deeply at least once per week.

Check the soil with a trowel after you water. Make sure the moisture has penetrated 6 inches.

Water **pecan** trees if rainfall is scant. This is a critical month for the nuts—they will not fill out if water is lacking.

## FERTILIZING

Fertilize newly planted cool-season vegetables. Since the soil is quite warm, water-soluble liquid fertilizers will push the plants off to a fast start.

Apply lime to your garden according to the results of your soil test.

## PROBLEMS

Big green caterpillars on **parsley** and **fennel** are the precursors of beautiful swallowtail butterflies. Try not to kill them all.

Better yet, plant plenty of **parsley** and **fennel** so there is enough for you and the caterpillars.

Fall webworms construct ugly nests at the end of **pecan** and other tree branches. The webbing protects the caterpillars from weather and predators.

The best control is the simplest: poke a long, limber branch into the web and pull it from the tree to expose caterpillars to the elements.

## PRUNING

Remove dead limbs from fruit trees and vines. Remove short stubs that have weak sprouts growing from them.

## HELPFUL HINTS

Herbs can be harvested and preserved throughout the summer and early fall. Here are two methods of keeping them for wintertime use:

**Freezing**

1. Rinse the herbs quickly in cold water, shake off the excess, then chop coarsely.

2. Place large pinches of herbs in an ice cube tray, cover with water, and freeze.

3. Transfer the cubes to plastic bags or airtight plastic containers. Freeze until needed.

Do not refreeze herbs after thawing.

**Drying**

1. If the herbs are clean, do not wet them. Otherwise, rinse the foliage, shake off excess water, and spread the herbs out to dry on paper towels until all surface moisture has evaporated. Remove any dead or damaged foliage.

2. Tie the stems into small bundles with string, and hang them upside down in a warm, dry place out of the sun. Make small, loose bundles, and allow for good air circulation around each bunch.

3. To air-dry herbs with seeds, tie the herbs in small bundles and suspend inside a paper bag with holes punched in the sides. Suspend the bag in a dark area with good air circulation. Collect the seeds when they are dry, and store in dark containers.

**Sage, thyme, dill,** and **parsley** are easy to dry. **Basil, tarragon,** and **mint** may mold if not dried quickly.

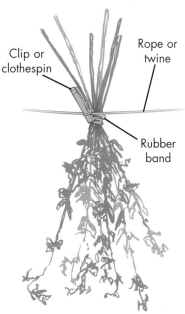

Clip or clothespin

Rope or twine

Rubber band

Herbs can be dried for later use.

97

# OCTOBER

## EDIBLES

### PLANNING

One of the joys of gardening in Georgia is our long growing season. Gardeners in Minnesota report that their two seasons are "winter and the Fourth of July!" North Georgia gardeners are fortunate to experience 200 to 250 frost-free days per year; south Georgia gardeners may enjoy close to 300 days without freezing temperatures.

- The average date of first frost in Atlanta is November 13. Frost has been recorded as early as October 25 and as late as December 6.
- The average date of first frost in Tifton is November 21. The earliest recorded frost date

occurred October 26, while the latest was December 20.

- The most likely date for a last frost in Atlanta is March 27. The earliest date for a last spring frost was February 16, and the latest frost in spring occurred on April 23.
- The average date for the last frost in Tifton is March 6. The earliest date a final frost occurred was January 27, while the (surprise!) date for a late spring frost was April 1.

### PLANTING

Dream of strawberry shortcake for next June! Plant **strawberries** in a well-tilled bed. Good **strawberry** varieties are 'Florida 90', 'Earliglow', 'Cardinal', and 'Delite'.

- Plant them 12 inches apart, preferably in a raised bed.
- Cover plants lightly with pine straw to protect them for the winter.

In south Georgia, all fall vegetables can still be planted. **Cabbage, lettuce, collards,** and **broccoli** transplants are available at garden centers. **Lettuce, spinach,** and **radish** seeds can be planted. **Onion sets** (small bulbs) can be planted now as well. Be sure to soak the soil after

planting. October is typically a dry month, and rainfall may not occur as often as you'd like.

Clip out the woody flower stems of mature **parsley** at ground level, taking care not to damage new leaves that have emerged there. Dig the plants and plant in 6-inch pots to bring indoors to a sunny window.

Although **parsley** is usually winter hardy outdoors, you'll have fresh **parsley** handy to use through November if you bring it indoors.

### CARE

Prepare your composting area for fall leaves. You can make an inexpensive bin from a piece of wire fence 4 feet wide and 10 feet long:

1. Join the two ends to form a hollow wire barrel.

2. Place a pile of small limbs 6 inches high on the bottom for best air circulation.

3. Pile leaves and other compostables on top of the limbs.

Bring some **rosemary** inside to dry for winter use.

Dig **sweet potatoes,** but let them "cure" in a warm place for five days before you store them in a cool basement or unheated garage.

Harvest **winter squash and pumpkins** before they are

Pot up some parsley to overwinter indoors.

damaged by frost. They can be stored in a cool, dry spot for months.

## WATERING

Though you may need one hose to keep fall vegetables watered, you won't need all the components you used during the heat of summer. Drain and store water hoses, sprinklers, and soaker hoses to avoid winter damage.

## FERTILIZING

If parts of your garden will not be used until next spring, you can improve the soil and prevent erosion by planting a cover crop now. Plants can be tilled into the soil just before you plant next spring. Good cover crops are:

| Cover Crop | Seeding Rate per 1000 Square Feet |
|---|---|
| **Crimson clover** | 3.3 ounces |
| **Winter wheat** | 40 ounces |
| **Annual ryegrass** | .5 to 1.0 pounds |
| **Alfalfa** | 80 ounces |

If you decide not to plant a cover crop over your garden for the winter, at least mulch the garden with wheat straw to prevent erosion. The straw will be

---

## HELPFUL HINTS

Cool weather brings a reminder that **tomato** vines can't bear freezing temperatures. Follow these tips to store green **tomatoes**:
- Leave fruit on the vines up to the last week before a frost is imminent.
- After picking, remove stems and dry-wipe to remove dirt.
- Sort out fruit that have a bit of pink showing around the stem. These will ripen quickly in a sunny window.
- Select remaining green fruit that have reached mature size and turned whitish-green.
- Wrap individual **tomatoes** in sheets of newspaper. Place gently in a cardboard box in your basement or a very cool room.
- Green **tomatoes** will ripen very gradually in storage. Check weekly for rot.

For best flavor, remove from the box and place in a warm window a few days before you need them. If you still have leftover "love apples," look for a good fried green tomato recipe

---

almost completely decomposed by spring.

## PROBLEMS

Use a hoe or rake to remove sprouts of chickweed in your garden. The plants may be small now, but they will cause a big problem if left unattended until spring. Rake out and replace all the mulch and dead leaves under **peach, pear, apple,** and **crabapple** trees. You'll prevent diseases on next year's leaves. Clean all the old vines from tomato cages before putting them in storage. Many pests

---

overwinter in plant debris such as vines, stems, and leaves.

Pull out withered plants and put them on your compost pile or rototill them into the soil.

## PRUNING

Do not prune (except for dead limbs) during this time of year. Pruning causes plants to delay going dormant and can increase their susceptibility to cold damage.

# NOVEMBER

## EDIBLES

PLANNING

One of the most important practices of a smart gardener is to keep notes on what happened in the garden during the year. The notes can be kept formally in a journal, or informally in a shirt pocket–sized spiral notepad. Now that the growing season is all but over, take time to jot down anything you would change for next year.

• Did your **tomatoes** perform as you expected?

• Was brown rot a problem on your fruit? How (and when) can it be prevented next year?

• Were the rows spaced properly, or should you make adjustments next year?

• Were you able to harvest something almost every month? Were some months heavier than others? Did this overload your ability to use the produce? Should more or less of some items be planted?

• How well did your weed- and insect-control measures work? Should your prevention methods be put into action earlier?

PLANTING

You can have a winter garden even if you don't own a plot of land. Plant winter container gardens on your sunny patio or porch. Utilize the same large pots that contained your summer annuals.

• Use greens such as **arugula, parsley, mustard, lettuce,** and **spinach.** Even **green onion** bulbs will grow very well if you have plenty of sunshine.

• Don't be afraid to mix **pansies** and **snapdragons** with your edible plants.

• Fertilize with houseplant fertilizer according to label directions.

• Move the container(s) to a sheltered spot if frigid or windy weather threatens.

This is a great time to plant bare-root fruit and nut trees—but be sure to plant varieties that grow well in your area! (See the Fruit Varieties charts, p. 282.)

Brambles are highly productive and have few pests. Plant **blackberries** and **raspberries** now, in the sunniest spot possible. See Care for a trellis plan. (See Fruit Varieties charts, p. 282.)

In south Georgia, plant **carrots** now. They can also be planted in north Georgia, but some winter injury may occur. 'Nantes', 'Danvers', and 'Chantenay' are good varieties. Do not fertilize **carrots;** splitting will result. Let them absorb nutrients left over from your summer garden.

CARE

**Blackberry** and **raspberry** plants should be grown on a wire trellis. You can build a sturdy trellis easily in an afternoon:

1. Set 4x4 pressure-treated posts 10 feet apart. The posts should be 5 feet tall after installing in the ground.

2. Stretch three heavy-gauge wires between the posts, at 24, 42, and 60 inches from the ground.

3. Plant brambles 24 inches apart.

4. Tie the canes to the wires as they grow longer.

A cold frame offers the opportunity to enjoy fresh cool-season vegetables for much longer than might be possible with a normal garden. Construct several, using the plans in Annuals, November. To simplify management, you can devote each frame to a different crop: **lettuce, spinach, beets, turnip greens.**

WATERING

Fall is an excellent time to plant fruiting trees, vines, or shrubs, but even though air temperatures are cool, the soil may be dry. Give newly installed plants at least five gallons of water each week unless rain occurs.

At full pressure, most hoses deliver five gallons of water in one minute.

 FERTILIZING

It is not necessary to fertilize fruits, vegetables, or herbs during the cold season.

Make sure your fertilizers are stored where they will not get wet during the winter.

 PROBLEMS

When leaves have fallen, thoroughly spray fruit trees with a dormant oil. Dormant oils are heavier than other horticultural oils; the oil suffocates insects that hide on and under the bark.

## HELPFUL HINTS

This is a good month to clean tools and pots. Items that might be contaminated with disease spores or pesticides should be thoroughly cleaned. Clean your pesticide sprayers thoroughly with a 1:10 mixture of bleach and water:

1. Disassemble the wand; clean the nozzle.
2. Pressurize the tank and shoot some of the cleaning mixture through the nozzle.
3. Partially fill the tank with clean water and circulate it through the wand and nozzle.
4. Turn the tank upside down to drain. Afterwards, reassemble loosely and store in a covered spot.

Empty any caked potting soil from pots. Dump it on an empty garden bed for rototilling next spring. Rinse out any remaining soil with a hose.

Soak clay and plastic pots, seed trays, and seed-starting items in a bucket filled with a 1:10 mixture of bleach and water.

Allow to dry afterwards, and stack neatly where you can find them when you need them.

 PRUNING

Remove the foliage of **asparagus** plants now, before the red berries fall off. Otherwise, seeds will sprout, and the **asparagus** bed will become too crowded.

Once the leaves fall from fruit and nut trees, examine the trees' form. Make plans to prune them during the winter. (See February for illustrations of correct form.)

A cold frame allows you to enjoy some veggies, such as lettuce and spinach, far longer than normal.

# December

## EDIBLES

### PLANNING

If space is limited, you'll find that several raised beds produce more vegetables than an equivalent amount of flat ground. Choose a warm weekend to construct your beds. Treated or untreated wood, stones, or concrete blocks can be used to line the bed.

• The sides of a bed should be at least 8 inches tall.

• Beds can be any convenient length, but it is easier to weed and maintain beds that are 30 to 40 inches wide.

• Dig and loosen the soil inside the bed, rototilling in a 2-inch-thick layer of soil amendment (see Horticultural Practices, p. 9).

• Fill the remainder of the bed completely with good-quality planting soil. Mix it deeply with the undersoil. Buy extra—after a few weeks the bed will settle and will need refilling.

### PLANTING

After leaves have been nipped off by frost you can transplant any of your small fruit trees to new sites.

• Don't try to transplant trees larger than 8 feet tall. You'll be more successful buying a new tree rather than waiting for a transplanted tree to start growing again. If the tree is 8 to 12 feet tall, you can reduce its height to 6 to 8 feet by pruning.

• Dig a 6-foot-wide hole into which the tree will be planted.

• No need to fertilize now. Wait until next summer, when the tree has fully leafed out.

### CARE

If you still have **beets, collards, mustard,** or **turnip greens** in your garden, don't be afraid to eat them. Old-timers say they have the best taste when the leaves have endured a frost or two. A thin layer of pine straw will protect them from temperatures below freezing.

### WATERING

Be sure to turn off the water supply valve and drain your watering system before hard freezes arrive. Wrap outdoor faucets that cannot be drained with insulating foam. Coil up soaker hoses and water hoses, and store them in an out-of-the-way spot so you can work in your garden easily next spring.

### FERTILIZING

Have a bag of lumpy fertilizer? It doesn't go bad . . . and your plants will appreciate it next year:

1. Spread a sheet of plastic on your garage floor and place the fertilizer in the middle.

2. Use a hammer to break up the lumps into pieces no larger than $1/2$ inch in diameter.

3. Scoop the fertilizer into a lidded 5-gallon plastic bucket. Seal the lid tightly.

4. Use a permanent marker to label the bucket's contents.

### PROBLEMS

Much can be done now to prevent pests and diseases next year in your fruit and vegetable garden. Fruit that didn't get picked during the summer may still be hanging on your trees—these "mummies" should not be left on the tree. Pick them off and remove them completely from your garden to prevent potential disease problems. Rake dead leaves under fruit trees, vines, and shrubs; replace them with fresh mulch. Spray trees with dormant horticultural oil to kill overwintering insects.

The value of good pruners cannot be overemphasized.

 PRUNING

A good pair of handpruners and long-handled loppers are essential for maintaining fruit trees and vines. When purchasing pruning tools, the motto "You get what you pay for" is quite true. While inexpensive pruners may cost less than ten dollars, they become dull quickly and are difficult to maintain. Here are some buying, sharpening, and care tips:

## HELPFUL HINT

Store all your garden tools (shovel, spading fork, trowels, etc.) neatly for the winter—don't pile them in a heap. Spray metal surfaces with a lubricating spray to thwart rust.
• Firmly attach an 8-foot-long 2×4 to the wall of your storage building.
• Hammer twelve-penny (12d) finishing nails into the 2×4 at 12-inch intervals.
• Drill $1/4$-inch-diameter holes in the handles of wooden tools and hang them from the nails.

• Plan to spend $25 to $40 for good pruners. The best models can be disassembled easily and have a replaceable blade (Felco® #2 is a favorite of many gardeners).

• In general, anvil-type pruners are less versatile than bypass (scissor-type) pruners.

• Brightly colored handles are a plus if you tend to misplace your tools.

Handpruners and loppers can be sharpened after hard use.

1. Disassemble the pruner and place the handle in a vise. The blade should be upwards and easily accessible from all sides.

2. Use a whetstone (available at hardware stores) lubricated with oil. Some whetstones have a "fine" side and a "coarse" side for more versatility. Shine a light on the blade so you can see the manufacturer's original bevel.

3. Holding it at the original bevel angle, slide the whetstone up the blade from the base to the tip of the blade. Use many light strokes. Strive for a uniformly bright and sharpened edge.

4. Slide the stone against the flat backside of the blade once or twice to break off the tiny metal curls that were formed when the beveled side was sharpened.

5. Use oil or a lubricating spray to lubricate your pruners after each use.

6. Examine the blade regularly for nicks and chips. Replace if badly damaged.

Never use a pruner to cut wire unless it has a special notch designed for that purpose.

# LAWNS

Warren Schultz, author of *A Man's Turf—The Perfect Lawn*, begins his informative book with these words: "The lawn works in mysterious ways." For too many people that is true. Many find lawn maintenance a mysterious process. From selection to planting to fertilizing to pest control, lawn work seems to require more knowledge than do other landscape chores.

Yet grass grows easily beside the highways with no fertilizer, mown only once a year, and almost no pests beyond lit cigars and errant SUVs. Does having a nice lawn require a college degree, or can just about anyone achieve an attractive turf?

With the information in this chapter, you'll find that nice lawns are the result of common sense, occasional maintenance, and attention to a few details. In each month you'll see the tasks that need to be done for the various lawn grasses we cultivate in Georgia. If you follow our recommendations, your lawn will look as good as, or better than, your neighbors'—and you will soon find that the "mysteries" of lawn cultivation are quite easy to solve. Following are some lawn basics to get you started.

## WHICH GRASS SHOULD YOU CHOOSE?

Choosing the right grass for a lawn is initially based on how much sunshine the site receives and how much water you are able to apply in the summer. Consider also the amount of labor you are willing to invest in your lawn.

Tall fescue is classified as a "cool-season" grass, and it stays green all year long. Bermudagrass, zoysiagrass, centipedegrass, and St. Augustinegrass are all classified as "warm-season" grasses. They are green most of the year, but turn brown

# CHAPTER FIVE

(or light green, in the case of St. Augustinegrass) and go dormant in winter. The descriptions below will help you decide which grass will grow in your area and which ones match your requirements for appearance and maintenance.

TALL FESCUE grows best when daytime temperatures do not exceed 80 degrees Fahrenheit—at higher summer temperatures, tall fescue has all it can manage just to survive. Best for semi-shade sites or lawns that have a mixture of sunny and shady areas, it can be successful in full sunshine if the soil is tilled properly before planting and you can irrigate in the summer. It is green year 'round under proper management and adequate irrigation; it's usually best for the northern half of Georgia. Dozens of new varieties of tall fescue are introduced each year. Proponents of each variety claim theirs is the most shade- and drought-tolerant and the most resistant to disease. Most support these claims by quoting the results of grass-growing trials at research facilities scattered across the country.

• The "turf-type" tall fescues are indeed superior to the "pasture-type" tall fescue that is commonly called 'Kentucky 31'.

• While there are differences between the "turf-type" tall fescue varieties, no one variety surpasses the rest at all research facility trials.

• The work you do to prepare the soil before planting is *much* more likely to produce a great-looking lawn than the tall fescue variety you plant.

BERMUDAGRASS can be planted by seeding or by sodding. Common Bermudagrass produces fertile seed, which is sold at most garden centers. Hybrid Bermudagrass does not produce fertile seed; the only way to propagate this, and other sodded grasses, is to grow it from sprigs taken from a "mother" plant. On the flat soil of south Georgia, millions of sprigs are planted each spring to become the sod you purchase during the year.

• Common Bermudagrass is always grown from seed. It is lighter green in color than hybrid Bermudagrass, and its leaves are coarser in texture. Seedheads pop up quickly after mowing, and it invades flower beds rapidly.

• Tifgreen (Tifton 328) Bermudagrass sod is low-growing and spreads rapidly. It has fine texture and soft leaves.

• TifSport Bermudagrass is more cold-hardy than other Bermudagrasses. It is dark emerald green, resists drought, and does well in low-maintenance situations.

• Tifway (Tifton 419) Bermudagrass sod is darker green than Tifgreen. It is more frost-tolerant, stays green longer in fall, and turns green earlier in spring.

ZOYSIAGRASS is typically installed as sod.

• 'Emerald' zoysiagrass has a very fine leaf texture and good shade tolerance. It is less cold-tolerant than other zoysia varieties.

• 'Meyer' zoysiagrass has a wider leaf than 'Emerald'. It has good cold tolerance but less shade tolerance than 'Emerald'.

• 'El Toro' zoysiagrass sod grows rapidly and has a leaf width similar to that of 'Meyer'.

• 'Zenith' zoysiagrass can be planted from seed, grows rapidly, has a dense growth habit, and tolerates light shade.

CENTIPEDEGRASS may be established from seed or sod. Its appearance is like that of St. Augustinegrass, but the leaves are smaller and lighter green in color. It requires less mowing than Bermudagrass or St. Augustinegrass. It requires no lime and minimal amounts of nitrogen.

ST. AUGUSTINEGRASS is always sodded or sprigged for establishment. It is the most shade-tolerant of the warm-season grasses, but the least winter hardy. Injury is likely if the temperature dips below 10 degrees Fahrenheit. St. Augustine never becomes completely dormant in winter and must begin spring growth from above-ground buds. Newer varieties include 'Floratam' and 'Seville' for south Georgia. 'Raleigh' is suitable for north Georgia up to northern Atlanta.

## CHAPTER FOUR

## SEEDING VERSUS SODDING

As we will point out in April, there are two ways to establish a lawn: by planting seed and waiting for it to sprout, or by laying sod and gaining an instant lawn. Some grasses are better planted from seed, while others can only be planted with sod. See April for a complete comparison of seeding versus sodding.

## PLANTING GRASS FROM SOD

Warm-season grass sod is best planted in early summer; cool-season grass sod grows best if planted in early winter.

1. Kill all weeds by spraying the area with a non-selective weedkiller two weeks before planting.

2. Till the soil to a depth of 6 inches, mixing in the recommended amount of lime and fertilizer (see Horticultural Practices, Soil Test, p. 7).

3. Rake the area smooth, removing rocks, clumps, and grassy debris.

4. Roll the area with a water-filled roller to reveal low spots. Fill low spots with soil.

5. Starting along the longest straight edge of the area, lay sod pieces end-to-end. Make sure each piece is tightly placed next to its neighbor. Stagger sod pieces in adjacent rows so seams do not line up. Use a small hatchet or sharp shovel to trim pieces to fit around obstructions.

6. Roll the entire area once more, to ensure good sod-to-soil contact.

7. Water the sod thoroughly (see Watering New Sod, p. 107).

## PLANTING GRASS FROM SEED

1. Kill all weeds by spraying the area with a non-selective weedkiller two weeks before planting.

2. Till the soil thoroughly to a depth of 6 inches, mixing in the recommended amount of lime and fertilizer (see Horticultural Practices, Soil Test, p. 7).

3. Rake the area smooth, removing rocks, clumps, and grassy debris.

4. Roll the area with a water-filled roller to reveal low spots. Fill low spots with soil.

5. Scatter seed according to rates below. Cover very thinly with wheat straw (3/4 bale per 1000 square feet).

6. Follow the watering guidelines on page 107.

Do not use weed-control products on your lawn for at least six weeks after planting tall fescue.

## SEEDING RATES FOR NEW LAWNS

- BERMUDAGRASS: 1 to 2 pounds per 1000 square feet
- CENTIPEDEGRASS: .25 to .5 pound per 1000 square feet
- TALL FESCUE: 5 to 10 pounds per 1000 square feet
- ZOYSIAGRASS: 1 to 3 pounds per 1000 square feet

## GROWING GRASS IN SHADE

All lawn grasses have a difficult time growing in shade. If the shade is too dense for the grass, it will become thin and weed-infested. Tall fescue is the most shade-tolerant cool-season grass. 'Emerald' zoysiagrass and St. Augustinegrass can sustain themselves in light shade. Bermudagrass, centipedegrass, and 'Meyer' zoysiagrass can grow in the shade cast by high pine trees, but no more shade than that.

Even though tall fescue is the most shade-tolerant grass, it must have at least four hours of direct sunshine per day to remain attractive. There is no great difference in the shade tolerance of the various "named" turf-type tall fescues. A thoroughly rototilled seeded lawn (see the process described above) is the best way to help fescue tolerate shade. To maximize tall fescue's shade tolerance:

- Apply only 1/2 the recommended fertilizer rate to shaded lawn areas.

• Raise the mowing height of your mower to 4 inches if possible.

• Irrigate weekly, as weather conditions dictate, but never water after 3:00 p.m.

## WATERING

The best time to water a lawn is in the morning, preferably before noon. This allows the grass to dry before nightfall, reducing the risk of disease. If the only time you can water is after 5:00 p.m., be sure to water thoroughly only once each week, not every day. Here's how to measure the amount of water applied by irrigation:

1. Place six identical containers randomly in the area wetted by your sprinkler. Plastic cups can be used, but weight them down with a heavy washer in the bottom of each.

2. Let your sprinkler run for an hour.

3. Measure the amount of water that has accumulated in each cup. Calculate the average of the depths. This gives you the amount (in inches) that has been applied in an hour. Make a mental calculation of how long it will take to apply an inch of water.

Don't be surprised if your sprinkler must run for more than an hour to apply the water your lawn needs.

## WATERING NEW SOD

Water newly planted sod deeply and regularly so the roots will explore the soil beneath the original sod. Use a trowel to check how far water soaks into the soil after an irrigation. Heavy clay soil absorbs water slowly. If water runs off before it is absorbed, split the irrigation into two sessions an hour apart. Sandy soil absorbs water rapidly but dries out quickly. Consider splitting the recommended inch of water per week into two irrigations of $1/2$ inch of water three days apart. Here's one example of followup watering after sod has been laid:

• Apply $1/8$ inch of water daily for seven days

• followed by $1/4$ inch of water every third day for nine days

• followed by $1/2$ inch of water every five days for ten days

• followed by 1 inch of water per week for the rest of the growing season.

## WATERING NEWLY SEEDED LAWNS

• Apply $1/8$ inch of water daily until seedlings are 1.5 inches tall

• followed by $1/4$ inch of water every third day for nine days

• followed by $1/2$ inch of water every five days for ten days

• followed by 1 inch of water per week for the rest of the growing season.

## MOWING

Every lawn grass has a height at which it should be mowed. The rule is that only $1/3$ of a grass plant should be removed in one mowing. As an example, if you intend to mow your tall fescue lawn at a 3-inch height, you can allow it to grow to 4.5 inches between mowings. If you fertilize moderately, mowing should be needed only once per week.

## MOWING HEIGHT

• CENTIPEDEGRASS: 1 to 1.5 inches

• FESCUE: 2 to 3 inches

• RYEGRASS: 1 to 2 inches

• SEEDED BERMUDAGRASS: 1 to 2 inches

• SODDED BERMUDAGRASS: .5 to 1.5 inches

• ST. AUGUSTINEGRASS: 2 to 3 inches

• ZOYSIAGRASS: .5 to 1.5 inches

## CHAPTER FOUR

## LEVELING YOUR LAWN

Despite your best efforts, your lawn may have spots that are lower than their surroundings. The best time to level lawns is while they are growing rapidly (tall fescue in the fall, warm-season grasses in early summer). There are two ways to correct low spots:

1. Topdressing: Mix a bag of dry topsoil with a bag of sand in a wheelbarrow. If the mixture tends to clump, spread it over a tarp in a covered spot to finish drying. Shovel the mixture, no more than $1/2$ inch deep, into low spots. Sweep the soil off the grass blades and sift it down as far as possible. Maintain the lawn normally until the grass has grown over the first layer of topsoil. Repeat the steps above until the low spot is filled.

2. Fill and patch: Use a flat shovel to remove grass from the low spot in large clumps. Set the clumps to the side, and fill the low spot with topsoil. Plant the grass clumps back in place. Water thoroughly, and maintain normally for the rest of the growing season.

## AERATING

Aeration is the process of mechanically poking thousands of holes in the soil. This allows water, oxygen, and nutrients to better penetrate to the roots of your grass. Motorized aerator machines can be rented from hardware or tool rental stores. The best aerator is one that has hollow tines (spoons) that pull up plugs of earth as the machine travels along. Solid-tine spike aerators pulled by lawn tractors are of little benefit.

• Use a crisscross pattern. First guide the mower over the entire lawn, going back and forth in one direction. Second, direct the machine back and forth at right angles to the first series of trips.

• Examine a square-foot area of the lawn. It, and every other square foot, should have at least twelve holes in it. If not, crank up the machine again!

• If the plugs of soil on the surface are objectionable, let them dry a few days, then drag a 5×5-foot piece of carpet across the lawn to pulverize them.

May and June are good months to aerate Bermudagrass, centipedegrass, zoysiagrass, and St. Augustinegrass lawns. March and September are the best months to aerate tall fescue.

Even though aeration damages the grass a bit, it is able to recover rapidly. As the soil plugs disappear from the soil surface, they inoculate the thatch layer with organisms which help it decompose more rapidly. Even if you are not planting seed, plan to aerate lawns growing on clay soil every two years.

## FERTILIZING

Lawn fertilizer is manufactured by many companies. Each manufacturer uses a slightly different blend of plant nutrient chemicals to arrive at a final product. Chemicals such as urea, ammonium nitrate, urea formaldehyde, and ammonium phosphate provide a high percentage of the nutrient nitrogen (which rapidly growing lawns need more than they need phosphorus and potassium). Most lawn fertilizer products are granular, but some are designed to be applied after they are dissolved in water. Granular fertilizers tend to last longer (up to three months) in the soil. Slow-release fertilizers are generally better for a lawn than fertilizers that release their nutrients quickly during the first rain.

## LIMING

Turfgrasses need soil that is only slightly acid in order to thrive. In most parts of the state, the soil is more acid than grass prefers. Garden lime neutralizes acidity and should be applied when needed. It is never the wrong time to lime your lawn . . . but how much lime should you apply? Forty pounds per 1000 square feet of lawn area is probably enough, but a soil test (see Horticultural Practices, p. 7) will tell you exactly how much you need. Adding too much or too little lime can harm your lawn in the long run. Don't guess—soil test!

Garden lime can be purchased in bags in one of two forms: powdered or pelletized. Neither form is inherently better. Pelletized lime flows through a lawn spreader more easily, and powdered lime is slightly less expensive.

## SELECTING A FERTILIZER SPREADER

Broadcast spreaders are best for large areas. They can apply a lot of material in a short time. For small lawns or lawns that have many corners and tight spaces, a drop spreader is the best choice.

## CALIBRATING A FERTILIZER SPREADER

It is important to know how much material your spreader is applying when you use it for seeding or fertilizing. Many lawn products list the appropriate spreader setting for several models—but what should you do if your spreader is not listed?

1. Measure an area of 1000 square feet (10 feet by 100 feet, 20 feet by 50 feet, etc.) in your lawn.

2. Set your spreader to one-fourth open.

3. Load the spreader with a weighed amount of cat litter. (Ten pounds is usually enough.)

4. Operate the spreader over the 1000-square-foot-area.

5. Weigh the amount left in the spreader. Subtract from the amount originally in the spreader. The result is the application rate of the spreader for that particular material per 1000 square feet.

Example: After loading the spreader with 10 pounds of cat litter and operating it over 1000 square feet, 5 pounds are left. At that setting,

and for that material, your spreader dispenses 5 pounds per 1000 square feet.

• Use a permanent marker to write on the spreader the results of your calibration.

• Each different type of seed or fertilizer will require its own spreader calibration.

## PEST CONTROL

It is a common tendency to blame an unsatisfactory lawn on diseases or insects, but lawn problems can usually be traced to improper grass selection for the site and/or improper soil preparation. We have included several tips for identifying and controlling pests in the months that follow. Though they do not attack grass directly, fire ants can make lawn maintenance miserable. Their control is discussed in May. One bit of knowledge to always keep in mind is that soil temperature governs many stages of lawn growth and pest appearance.

## MEASURING SOIL TEMPERATURE

Weeds and insect pests emerge based on the warmth of the soil surrounding them. Crabgrass requires several days above 55 degrees Fahrenheit in order to sprout. Tall fescue seed sprouts best when the soil temperature is above 50 degrees. Bermudagrass and centipedegrass seed should not be planted if soil temperatures are below 65 degrees. For these reasons, checking the temperature of your soil occasionally will help you time your lawn activities.

Soil temperature can be measured directly by slicing the ground open with a shovel or trowel and inserting a household thermometer. If this is too much trouble, you can visit the Georgia Environmental Monitoring Network (www.georgia weather.net). Find the site closest to your home and follow the directions to see local soil and air temperatures for the previous thirty days.

# JANUARY
## LAWNS

### PLANNING

Are you spending more time than you would like taking care of your lawn? Do you really need as much lawn as you now have? Consider these lawn-shrinking tips:

- Eliminate the sparsely growing grass in a shady area. Cover the area with mulch, or plant it with a ground cover such as **mondo grass, periwinkle,** or **pachysandra.**

- Grass growing in sharp corners is difficult to mow. Round the corners of your lawn with flower beds, shrubs, or mulch.

- A grassy walkway between the front lawn and backyard is likely to have so much traffic in the center that it will never look nice no matter how hard you try. Install walking stones to keep footsteps off the grass.

### PLANTING

**Tall fescue** sod can theoretically be planted any time the soil is not frozen, but professional growers have the same trouble that you do growing **tall fescue** in summer—it's a lot of trouble to get seed to survive in the heat. Because they find it impossible to grow **tall fescue** year-round, the growers wait until fall to plant

their sod fields. This means that **tall fescue** sod has limited availability during the prime planting time in fall; it becomes widely available only in December or early January each year.

See Lawns, April, for sodding tips.

Since **tall fescue** does not naturally form a mat of roots, sod is often grown on plastic mesh:

- Clip loose ends of plastic with scissors as you work.

- Do not attempt to aerate your newly sodded **tall fescue** until next fall—the aerator tines will quickly become entangled in the mesh.

- Once the sod is rooted deeply, the mesh will not be a problem.

### CARE

Avoid heavy traffic on dormant lawns in winter; dry grass is easily broken. The living crown of your grass plants may be damaged even though the grass is brown. Since the grass is not growing and able to recover, even a short game of football can cause scars you'll regret in spring.

### WATERING

**Bermudagrass** sod can be successfully laid at any time of year, even if it is brown and dormant. The key to its survival is watering the sod after installation, even when it looks brown and lifeless. Roots are growing into the soil below—they need moisture. In the absence of rainfall, apply $1/4$ inch of water per week (see Lawns, Introduction, for more information).

**Tall fescue** sod installed in the last six months should also be watered regularly ($1/2$ inch per week). The green leaves transpire a great deal of moisture on sunny, windy days.

### FERTILIZING

You have probably heard of people who "burn off" their **Bermudagrass** lawns in winter: they literally set their lawn afire in the mistaken belief that the ashes contain fertilizer that will feed the grass.

- There is a tiny bit of potassium in ashes, but not nearly enough to risk causing a tragedy in your neighborhood. The flames can easily ignite pine straw islands and cedar siding.

- In most municipalities, outdoor burning is illegal.

There is no need to fertilize any warm-season grass at this time.

## PROBLEMS

If you have a **Bermudagrass** lawn in the northern half of the state, it is easy to spot the green leaves of unwanted **tall fescue,** chickweed, or wild onion in your brown turf. If you are very careful, you can spray the weeds lightly with a nonselective herbicide now. The weeds will be killed, but if the **Bermudagrass** is dormant, you won't hurt your lawn. It is important to examine your **Bermudagrass** closely to make sure it is fully dormant before attempting this task:

• Get down on your hands and knees. Pull back the dead grass foliage and inspect the stems where they come out of the ground. Do you see any green stems? If so, the grass plant is not dormant.

• Repeat the examination at several spots across the lawn before spraying.

# HELPFUL HINT

On a warm day, chop or mow unwanted kudzu, **English ivy**, and **bamboo** to the ground. Spray with glyphosate or triclopyr on the new leaves in April.

Watch out for poison ivy (see Lawns, June) when working outdoors. Even leafless vines and branches can cause a powerful skin reaction if they are touched accidentally:

• If you see the vine climbing a tree, don disposable gloves and clip the vine at ground level.

• Carefully pull the vine from the tree bark. If it adheres too tightly to pull by hand, use a long-bladed screwdriver to pry it away from the bark. Wash the tool thoroughly afterwards.

• Do not attempt this winter weedkilling trick on **zoysiagrass, centipedegrass,** or **St. Augustinegrass** lawns. These turfgrasses can be severely harmed by nonselective weedkillers, as can **Bermudagrass** if it is not fully dormant. Hand-weeding is your best option for these turfgrasses.

## MOWING

As winter wears on, the tree leaves you failed to rake last fall can blow across your lawn and build up in piles at the edges:

• Don't let leaves pile up and suffocate your grass. Without sunlight, disease will attack grass crowns and roots.

• Rake up the leaves and add them to your compost pile, or run over the leafy spots with a lawn mower to shred the leaves into tiny pieces.

Don't store mowers or other motorized lawn equipment near a gas water heater or furnace:

• If the gas tank leaks accidentally, the fumes can ignite and burn down your garage or home.

• Most manufacturers recommend draining the gas tank each winter.

• Never store gasoline, even in "spillproof" cans, indoors.

# FEBRUARY

## LAWNS

### PLANNING

When caring for a lawn, there is one basic fact you need to know: how big is it? Application rates for fertilizer and weed-killers are based on applying a certain amount for each 1000 square feet of lawn. Here's how to measure the area—you will need several soft drink cans, a pencil, and a piece of paper:

• Roughly sketch the lawn and divide it into rectangles.

• Put a can on each corner of each rectangle.

• Walk from can to can; count your paces between each can, and mark the figure on the sketch. Assuming your pace is 2.5 feet long, multiply the number of steps by 2.5 to find the length, in feet, of the sides of each rectangle. If you have a longer or shorter stride, adjust your calculation accordingly.

• For each rectangle, multiply the length of the short side by the length of the long side. This tells you the number of square feet in that rectangle.

• Add the area of all rectangles together to find the total square footage of the lawn.

• Note your measurements in your garden journal.

Remember, we're not trying for "exactly"—just "close"!

### PLANTING

If your **tall fescue** lawn is thin now, late February is a good time to plant seed. The soil is cold, so seed will not germinate quickly. However, you need to get started so the seed can take advantage of any warm days that come along:

1. Aerate before seeding (see the Introduction).

2. Scatter 3 to 4 pounds of seed per 1000 square feet if you already have 50-percent grass coverage. Coverage with wheat straw is not needed.

Scatter 6 to 8 pounds per 1000 square feet if planting on newly tilled soil. Cover very thinly with wheat straw (1 bale per 1000 square feet).

3. Plan to water each week between now and August. See the Introduction.

Do not use weed-preventer products on your lawn for at least six weeks before or after planting **tall fescue**.

### CARE

It is tempting to consider using a "weed 'n' feed" product to fertil-

You can easily make a weed guard to spot treat weeds, if you need to protect nearby plantings.

ize your grass and kill weeds simultaneously. Consider these points before making your decision, remembering that there are two kinds of "weed 'n' feed" products:

1. A weed 'n' feed that promises to *prevent* weeds contains chemicals that will inhibit all seeds from germinating. If you are planning to plant **tall fescue** seed now, this type of product cannot be used beforehand. Weed-preventers vary in the length of time the chemical is active in the soil, affecting how long you must wait before planting any seed. If you used one in a previous season, make sure you read the label—if any of the chemical is still present in the soil, you will not be successful when you plant seed.

2. A weed 'n' feed product that promises to kill existing weeds can be used on well-established grass. Do not use on newly planted **tall fescue** or on other turfgrass that is not yet 50 percent green. Read the label of your weed 'n' feed carefully, and follow directions to the letter.

Notice lawn areas where the shade from a tree has caused grass to grow thinly. Now is a good time to prune out low limbs to allow more sunshine on the grass. (See Trees, February, to learn how to prune properly.) **Southern magnolia** and other densely leaved trees are notori-

If you have a dog, it is likely there is a well-worn path along the fence or in a line stretching from your back door to the doghouse. No grass can sustain daily trampling, even from a small dog. Large pine bark mulch chunks, not grass, are best for these trails. Sooner or later the chunks will be scattered, but they can easily be raked back into place.

ous for severely limiting grass growth. Consider covering the ground under them with mulch.

 WATERING

On a rainy day, notice how water flows or stands on your lawn. Frequent flows of water over one spot will cause erosion. Water that stands for more than a half-day in one spot will drown the grass roots.

• Correct the erosion problem by redirecting the water source, slowing it down, or eliminating it.

• Correct the wet spot problem by eliminating the source of water or making the soil level higher so water does not stand. Plant new grass on the spot.

FERTILIZING

How much fertilizer does your lawn really need? The only way to know for sure is to have a soil test done (see Horticultural Practices, p. 7).

Fertilize **tall fescue** lawns now (repeat in April, September, and November).

 PROBLEMS

If your weed problem is minor or your lawn is small, hand-digging weeds is effective and permanent. If you choose to use chemical herbicides, here are some options:

• Spot-spray chickweed with a broadleaf weedkiller. Don't soak the ground—a light spray is best.

• On a warm, windless day, spray wild onions with a herbicide containing 2,4-D, and MCPP. Because many concealed bulblets will remain after spraying, hand-digging wild onions is almost as effective as using a herbicide.

# MARCH

## LAWNS

### PLANNING

The calendar is not a very accurate way to determine when to plant grass or apply a weed-preventer. The timing of many lawn tasks is best determined by the temperature of the soil. For example:

• **Tall fescue** or **rye** seed germinates when the soil temperature is above 55 degrees Fahrenheit.

• **Bermudagrass** or **centipedegrass** seed germinates best when the soil temperature is above 70 degrees.

• Crabgrass seed germinates when the soil temperatures are above 55 degrees for seven days in a row.

• Chickweed seed germinates when the soil temperature is 70 degrees and declining. (See Measuring Soil Temperature, p. 109.)

### PLANTING

Aerate **tall fescue** lawns and overseed them (see Lawns, Introduction) if grass is thin. Wait until soil temperatures are warm, as specified above.

• Listen to the weather forecast to see when a few days of warm weather are predicted. After a couple of days above 50 degrees

Fahrenheit, **tall fescue** seed can be planted in bare spots.

• The seed will germinate as conditions allow. Even if low temperatures occur for a few days, the seedlings will not be harmed.

• Remember that if you are planting **tall fescue** seed, you can't use a weed-preventer herbicide for six weeks after planting.

Lay **tall fescue** sod (see Lawns, January).

### CARE

Just as the leaves of your **Bermudagrass, zoysiagrass,** and **centipedegrass** grow and wane over the course of a year, the roots of these grass plants do too. Each plant stores a great deal of energy in its central crown in late fall. As grass blades turn brown, roots also die back. When the weather warms in spring, the crown sends out new, green shoots—and roots begin to grow once again. If anything interferes with root growth or a grass's aboveground green-up this month, your lawn will suffer.

• Avoid using weed-killing chemicals on warm-season grasses in March (occasional spot-sprays are fine). Most weed-preventing chemicals (pre-emer-

gents) can be used without harm to turfgrass.

• Do not fertilize warm-season grasses (see below) except in extreme south Georgia.

• Postpone aerating and dethatching until the grass has turned completely green and is growing vigorously.

A late freeze can wreak havoc on warm-season grasses by killing the lush green growth that has begun to appear. To help your lawn recover from an unexpected freeze:

• Do not fertilize. Wait until April or May to determine which areas have been killed.

• Irrigate the dead spots lightly with 1/4 inch of water per week, no more.

• If green grass does not emerge by May, plant sod or large plugs of grass in each dead area.

• Fertilize the lawn on your normal schedule beginning in May.

### WATERING

Windy days cause grass to dry.

• Water **Bermudagrass** or **tall fescue** sod that was planted within the last six months.

• Water **tall fescue** lawns that were recently seeded (see Lawns, Introduction, for a watering schedule).

FERTILIZING

Lime raises the pH (the acidity or alkalinity) of soil. This is important because soil pH determines how efficiently plants can absorb fertilizer (see Horticultural Practices, p. 7).

• Most grasses thrive in soil that has a pH of 6.0 to 6.5. If your soil pH is 5.5, only 50 percent of the phosphorus you apply will be used by your lawn.

• Have your soil tested now (see Horticultural Practices, p. 7) to determine the pH.

• If you are unable to have your soil tested, 40 pounds of lime per 1000 square feet of lawn is a good recommendation.

Lawn grass that is dormant cannot use fertilizer. Don't fertilize your **Bermudagrass, centipedegrass,** or **zoysiagrass** lawn now—wait until the whole lawn is at least 50 percent green. Fertilizer that is applied too early may be washed into nearby streams before it is used by your grass. Excess nutrients pollute waterways and the lakes into which they drain.

## HELPFUL HINT

Grass clippings provide nitrogen and moisture, both vital to a good compost pile. If your pile of leaves from last fall looks about the same as it did the last time you visited it, mix lawn clippings into your compost heap to jump-start the process of decomposition:

1. Use a garden fork to temporarily move the compost pile to the side.

2. Pile 3-inch-thick layers of leaves and grass clippings alternately as you rebuild the pile.

3. Spray dry leaves with a hose to moisten them thoroughly before adding to the pile.

See Horticultural Practices, p. 10, for composting details.

 PROBLEMS

It's time for the first application of a weed-preventer for all types of lawns. Next application will be in May.

• Remember to irrigate your lawn after applying a weed-preventer herbicide. The water dissolves the chemical, making the top $1/2$ inch of soil inhospitable to weed germination.

On a warm, windless day, kill weeds in your driveway and walks with a nonselective herbicide.

Spot-spray dandelions, curly dock, mugwort, and other perennial weeds with a broadleaf herbicide; you can also dig them out with a dandelion fork.

 MOWING

Have your mower blade sharpened now:

• A sharp blade ensures that grass blades are sliced rather than torn apart. Clean cut grass is healthier and uses less water.

Dormant lawn grasses can be cut low (scalped) now to speed green-up. Set your mower just low enough to remove only the top of the brown foliage.

If your **Bermudagrass** was overseeded with **ryegrass** last fall, mow it to a height of 1 inch so that the **Bermudagrass** can begin growing again.

# APRIL

## LAWNS

### PLANNING

Not all grasses can be grown from seed. Scientists have hybridized some grass species, particularly **Bermudagrass,** to develop superior varieties. Hybridization results in seed that will not germinate. Therefore, sod farmers grow hybrid **Bermudagrass** from sprigs. When the sprigs have grown to cover an area, the grass can be lifted as uniform sod pieces that are shipped to you for planting. Grasses typically installed as sod include the following types:

• **Hybrid Bermudagrass** (Tifgreen, Tifway, 'Tifton 419', 'Tifton 328', TifSport, etc.)

• **Zoysiagrass** ('Meyer', 'El Toro', 'Emerald', 'Zenith', etc.)

• **Centipedegrass**

• **St. Augustinegrass** ('Floratam', 'Raleigh', 'Palmetto', etc.)

• **Tall fescue** (available only in northern half of Georgia)

Sod can be ordered from brokers who arrange for it to be shipped to your site. In small amounts it can be bought from garden centers. Don't wait until the day before sod is delivered to prepare the area. Make sure you have plenty of help to lay the sod. Each sod piece may weigh twenty pounds; carrying hundreds of them in one day can lead to exhaustion.

Laying sod will give you an "instant" lawn.

Some lawn grasses grow readily from seed. The key to establishing a lawn from seed is to control weeds while the seeds are germinating. **Centipedegrass** and **zoysiagrass** seed do not germinate rapidly. Chemicals that might kill weeds also harm the emerging grass seedlings. Frequent hand-pulling is necessary to keep the weeds at bay. Lawns that can be grown from seed include the following:

• **Tall fescue**

• **Common Bermudagrass**

• **Centipedegrass** (somewhat difficult)

• **Zoysiagrass** (somewhat difficult)

### PLANTING

There are two ways to establish a lawn: by planting seed and waiting for it to sprout, or by laying sod and gaining an instant lawn. The following steps ensure a successful sod installation:

1. Kill all weeds by spraying the area with a nonselective weedkiller two weeks before planting.

2. Till the soil thoroughly to a depth of 6 inches, mixing in the recommended amount of lime and fertilizer (see Horticultural Practices, Soil Test, p. 9).

3. Rake the area smooth, removing rocks, clumps, and grassy debris.

4. Roll the area with a water-filled roller to reveal low spots. Fill low spots with soil.

5. Starting along the longest straight edge of the area, lay sod pieces end to end. Make sure each piece is tightly placed next to its neighbor. Stagger pieces in adjacent rows so seams do not line up. Use a small hatchet or sharp shovel to trim pieces to fit around obstructions.

6. Roll the entire area once more, to ensure good sod-to-soil contact.

7. Water the sod thoroughly (see Lawns, May).

## CARE

When you operate a spreader to apply fertilizer or pesticides, avoid casting the materials onto your street. Rainfall will wash these chemicals into municipal water-treatment systems or local waterways. The pollution may harm plants and animals that live near water.

## WATERING

After sod has been laid, the lawn must be watered regularly to keep the sod alive while it establishes new roots. Unlike newly-seeded lawns, the initial watering of sod should be sufficient to moisten the soil under it to a depth of 6 inches.

This will take more than an hour in most cases. Lift a piece of sod and use a trowel to measure the depth of water penetration. See Lawns, Introduction, for more sod-watering information.

## FERTILIZING

In late April, most warm-season grasses can receive their first fertilization, while **tall fescue** is ready for its last. Any turf fertilizer will suffice unless otherwise noted.

• **Tall fescue:** Fertilize now, but wait until September to fertilize again.

• **Bermudagrass:** Fertilize only when the lawn is fifty percent greened-up.

• **Zoysiagrass:** Fertilize only when the lawn is fifty percent greened-up.

• **Centipedegrass:** In south Georgia, fertilize with 6 pounds of 15-0-15 per 1000 square feet of lawn.

• **St. Augustinegrass:** In south Georgia, fertilize if the lawn is fifty percent greened-up.

## PROBLEMS

The presence of big green patches of thin-bladed grass in your **Bermudagrass** or **zoysiagrass** lawn is usually a sign of annual bluegrass (*Poa annua*). One way to kill it is to soak a foam paint brush with a nonselective herbicide and carefully wipe it on the weed but not on your grass. (Be sure to wear plastic gloves on your hands.) Otherwise, make a mental note to use a weed-preventer that is

effective on grassy weeds next September; this will prevent the bluegrass seeds from sprouting.

Watch for the bright-green leaves of chickweed in your lawn. Spot-spray with broadleaf weedkiller.

## MOWING

Two types of mowers are generally available: rotary and reel. Here are the pros and cons of each:

**Rotary Mower Pros**
• Readily available
• Can be used on all types of grasses
• Easy to repair
• Easy to replace blade
• Mulching models recycle your grass clippings

**Rotary Mower Cons**
• Wheel may fall into low spots, yielding half-moon shaped scalped areas
• Blade must be kept sharp to achieve best cut

**Reel Mower Pros**
• Yields an even, manicured cut on **Bermudagrass** and **zoysiagrass** lawns
• Less likely to be affected by uneven surface conditions

**Reel Mower Cons**
• More expensive than rotary mower of comparable width
• Blade must be sharpened by an expert

# MAY

## LAWNS

### PLANNING

It is possible to purchase seed for warm-season grasses like **centipedegrass, Bermudagrass**, and **zoysiagrass,** but establishing these lawns is not as easy as establishing a **tall fescue** lawn from seed. Before deciding to plant warm-season grass from seed, carefully consider whether you are willing to spend weeks babying your lawn. These grasses have tiny seed which may take many days to germinate, even under the best conditions; weeds will sprout as the seedlings struggle to grow, and they may overpower the grass seed.

### PLANTING

Warm soil temperatures usher in the very best months for planting all warm-season grasses. Seeding is less expensive, but you must nurture the seed for several weeks before it makes a respectable lawn (see Lawns, Introduction, for seeding rates). Sodding is more expensive, but you will have the satisfaction of an instant lawn (see April for sod planting procedures).

The seeds of **Bermudagrass, zoysiagrass,** and **centipedegrass** are tiny. In order to spread them evenly, they can be mixed with sand:

1. Use very dry sand. A large bucket or a wheelbarrow makes a good container in which to mix.
2. Mix one part (by volume) of seed to ten or twenty parts of sand. In other words, mix 1 cup of seed with 10 to 20 cups of sand.
3. Apply half the recommended rate traveling back and forth in one direction, and the other half traveling at right angles to the first.

### CARE

**Tall fescue** lawns that were heavily seeded in the past six months may have large patches of straw-brown dead grass. This is caused by too many seedlings growing in a small space. When dead patches appear, rake out the dead grass and sprinkle seed very lightly over the spot. Irrigate evenly, and nurture it until the spot matches the rest of your lawn.

Remember when planting in the future to use the correct amount of seed per thousand square feet (see p. 106).

### WATERING

Lawns need approximately 1 inch of water per week. An inch of water is the amount of rainfall or irrigation it takes to fill a rain gauge or a soup can to a depth of 1 inch (see Lawns, Introduction, for more information).

### FERTILIZING

Don't apply fertilizer when the grass is wet. The granules will stick to the grass blades and burn them temporarily. Use a drop or a broadcast spreader (see Lawns, December) to apply fertilizer to dry grass. Hand-casting results in streaks of under- and overfertilization. Try to fertilize just before it rains, or be sure to irrigate the lawn afterwards.

• **Tall fescue:** If the lawn has not been fed in the past eight weeks, fertilize again, preferably before the middle of the month. Otherwise, wait until September.

• **Bermudagrass:** Fertilize now (and again in June, July, August, and September).

• **Zoysiagrass:** Fertilize now (and again in June and August).

- **Centipedegrass** in north Georgia is usually green enough to fertilize by now. Use 6 pounds of 15-0-15 per 1000 square feet of lawn. **Centipedegrass** grows best at a pH of 4.5 to 5.5. Lime is rarely needed.

- **St. Augustinegrass:** Fertilize now (and again in June, July, and August).

# PROBLEMS

If you missed the March application of a weed-preventer, crabgrass sprouts will have begun to appear. Use products containing MSMA, CAMA, or DSMA to control them. Read the herbicide product label carefully, and follow it exactly.

Fire ant mounds are quite visible now. Several months of control can be gained by using the "Georgia Two-Step" method:

1. Treat the area with a fire ant bait. The best time to treat is on a warm day, after 10:00 a.m.

2. Apply a powdered or liquid insecticide to individual mounds 48 hours later.

Repeat the procedure again in September.

# MUSHROOMS

After a few days of rain, mushrooms may sprout in your lawn overnight. Mushrooms can be thought of as the "flowers" of a fungus. These "toadstools" are nothing more than the reproductive portion of a fungus that has quietly been consuming organic debris underground. With warm soil and a bit of rain, the fungus decides the time is ripe to reproduce. It is impossible to eliminate fungi from the soil. The best treatment for mushrooms is to simply pick them and discard them. They are not edible. Use a five-iron on the largest ones to improve your golf game!

# MOWING

As the summer mowing season begins in earnest, check the height of your mower to make sure it is clipping your grass at the correct height (see Lawns, Introduction, for more information).

Apply fire ant treatment to individual mounds.

# JUNE
## LAWNS

### PLANNING

A sharp border on a lawn can make all the difference in its appearance. Whether it is a straight edge next to the sidewalk or a gentle curve next to a flower bed, the observer's eye finds comfort in a neatly defined edge. Make sure the edges of your lawn do not include sharp angles or dead-end corridors—both are difficult to mow. Before constructing a new edge, push your mower along the boundary of your lawn to gain a feel for how easy or difficult it will be to mow. See hints for edging in the Mowing section of this month.

### PLANTING

When the soil has warmed above 65 degrees Fahrenheit, you can plant sprigs (small plugs) of **Bermudagrass, centipedegrass, zoysiagrass,** and **St. Augustinegrass.** Sprigging saves money because you can divide a sod piece into hundreds of individual sprigs. On the other hand, sprigging is labor intensive, and you must water and weed your newly-sprigged lawn frequently. Sprigging is best done on a small lawn:

1. Till the soil 6 inches deep, adding organic matter, starter fertilizer, and lime as recommended by a soil test.

2. Level the area and roll it with a heavy roller to highlight any low spots. Fill low spots with soil before you begin sprigging.

3. Run a motorized core aerator over the lawn twice. This will make hundreds of small holes. The holes should be 3 to 6 inches apart.

4. Soak a piece of sod in a tub of water. Pull apart the sod into as many pieces as possible. Make sure each sprig has roots attached.

5. Keep the sprigs damp in a bucket, and insert them individually into the aerator holes.

6. Water thoroughly and regularly (see Lawns, Introduction, for a watering schedule) until sprigs take root. Remove weeds by hand.

This is the very best month to plant **centipedegrass** or **zoysiagrass** seed (see Lawns, Introduction, for seeding rate). Don't go on vacation—you will need to water the lawn daily and pull weeds conscientiously for four weeks to ensure success.

### CARE

It may take weeks for the seed of warm-season grasses to sprout and show green leaves. Keep the soil moist and pull any weeds by hand during this time.

### WATERING

Water hoses will leak if stepped on or driven over too often:

• Buy a hose reel to wind up your hose after use.

• Inspect the rubber washer and replace if necessary.

### FERTILIZING

Lawn fertilizers are usually labeled as such. Typically the first number (nitrogen) is the highest among the three fertilizer analysis numbers on the front of the bag. Though the fertilizer numbers differ among brands, any of them can be used successfully if you follow the directions on the bag.

• **Tall fescue:** Do not fertilize this month.

• **Bermudagrass:** Fertilize now (and again in July, August, and September).

• **Zoysiagrass:** Fertilize now (and again in August).

• **Centipedegrass:** Do not fertilize unless you skipped the feeding in May

• **St. Augustinegrass:** Fertilize now (and again in July and August).

## PROBLEMS

Check your lawn for circular dead spots. It could be "brown patch" (see Lawns, August), but correct your watering and fertilization practices before reaching for a fungicide.

Use a broadleaf weedkiller to spot-spray for violets, wild strawberry, and dandelion in your lawn.

## MOWING

Thatch is a layer of undecomposed grass stems and debris that accumulates under grass plants. As the layer of thatch becomes thicker, the grass grows on top of it. During severe cold or drought, grass growing on thatch will be harmed.

• Check the thickness of your thatch layer by scratching at the base of a grass plant with your fingers.

• A layer less than 1/2 inch in depth is not harmful.

Grass growing on a layer of thatch can be harmed during periods of severe cold or drought.

Thatch

Mat

Thatch Layer

Soil

• Improper mowing, not grass clippings, causes thatch.

If you have a thick layer of thatch, it can be corrected by using a vertical mower (dethatcher). The height of the blades should be adjusted so they lift up the thatch but don't harm the grass too much.

• The best time to dethatch warm-season lawns is when the grass is growing rapidly, typically in May or June.

• Apply a light fertilization (1/4 the normal rate), a weed-preventer, and 1/2 inch of water after dethatching.

Yearly aeration of your lawn (see Lawns, Introduction) with a motorized core aerator will also decrease thatch. The cores of soil deposited on the grass surface inoculate it with fungi which consume thatch.

There are a couple of ways to achieve a neatly defined edge for your lawn:

• Use a power edger or string trimmer to slice through grass that grows along the edge of your street, driveway, or flower beds.

Be sure to wear eye protection when using a powered edger. Warn children to stay away.

• If you have a small lawn, non-motorized edgers are available. They are a bit more work, but they are easy to store.

# JULY
## LANWS

LAWNS

### PLANNING

Another option for making a defined edge where your lawn borders a flower bed is to dig a trench between grass and bed. This procedure is called trench edging:

- Use a thin shovel to dig a trench 6 inches wide and 2 inches deep along the edge of your grass.
- You can choose whether to leave the trench empty or to mask the bare soil with a shallow layer of pine straw.
- If the trench slants downhill, interrupt the downward flow of water by placing stones or half-bricks in the trench at regular intervals.

### PLANTING

Too hot for the kids outdoors? Now is a good time to lay sod in the bare areas where the kids have been playing ball.

Remember to dig the soil to a depth of 3 to 6 inches, and rake it smooth before laying sod.

It will be hard to keep children off the lawn when you water the thirsty young sod.

Plant sod pieces on half the lawn this month and half next month so the children can at least get some enjoyment from the sprinkler when the first part of the lawn has been repaired.

Can't afford to sod the bare spots in your **St. Augustinegrass, zoysiagrass,** or **Bermudagrass** lawn? Buy sod pieces at the nursery, and cut them into dozens of plugs with a hatchet or sharp knife. Some garden centers sell special tools that cut sod plugs to the right size. They can be used to dig matching holes as well.

Plant 3-inch-diameter sod plugs 12 inches apart. They will cover the ground by fall. (**Zoysiagrass** will be the slowest to spread.)

### CARE

Whether you have sodded or seeded a new lawn, it is important to keep the family and pets off the area until the grass is well established. Compaction from just a few trips across the lawn in

The premier turf for drought tolerance is Bermudagrass.

one path can prevent good grass growth there for years.

• Sod that is well established cannot be pulled up from the ground. Well-established seeded lawns should appear to be 100 percent covered with grass seedlings.

• Even on a well-established lawn, mowing in the same pattern over and over will result in compaction where the wheels roll. It is best to use a different mowing pattern (vertical, horizontal, or diagonal) each time you mow.

 WATERING

Turfgrasses have varying degrees of drought tolerance. Ranked from highest drought tolerance to lowest:

First: **Bermudagrass**

Second: **St. Augustinegrass**

Third: **centipedegrass, tall fescue,** 'Emerald' **zoysiagrass,** and 'El Toro' **zoysiagrass**

Fourth: 'Meyer' **zoysiagrass**

It is a shame to discard a perfectly good hose because you accidentally crushed one end with a car tire. Hose repair kits are inexpensive, available at any hardware store, and easy to use. Take the hose with you when you purchase a kit, just to make sure you get the right size. If you can't bring along the hose,

look for "universal" kits that work on two or more hose sizes.

 FERTILIZING

**Bermudagrass:** Fertilize now (and again in August and September).

**Zoysiagrass:** Do not fertilize unless a previous feeding was missed.

**St. Augustinegrass:** Fertilize now.

**Tall fescue:** To avoid disease and drought problems, do not fertilize **tall fescue** during the summer. If your **tall fescue** is more yellow than you prefer, apply a product containing plant-available iron.

Ironite™ is one such product. Apply 1 to 2 pounds per 100 square feet.

 PROBLEMS

Insect damage to lawn grass is difficult to diagnose. Symptoms might include numerous dead patches or grass blades that seem to disappear in an area overnight. One way to check if you have harmful insects is to "float" them out:

1. Mix 2 ounces (4 tablespoons) of lemon-scented dish detergent in 2 gallons of water.

2. Pour the mixture over a 2-foot-square area.

Insects such as sod webworms and chinchbugs will come wriggling to the surface of the soapy froth.

3. Collect the insects and have them identified by your local Extension Service (see Resources, p. 289) or garden center.

 MOWING

Grasscycling is the practice of leaving grass clippings on the lawn rather than collecting them. Grasscycling saves time and energy, plus it reduces the amount of yard waste that might be taken to the landfill.

• Because clippings contain the nutrient nitrogen, grasscycling allows you to reduce the amount of fertilizer you apply by one-fourth.

• Specially-designed mulching lawn mowers do an excellent job of chopping the clippings so fine they cannot be seen.

• Older, side-discharge mowers can also be used if mowing is done often enough that only a third of the grass height is removed in one mowing.

• Scorching sunshine can make the soil so hot that grass roots can't grow.

Raise the height of your mower by one notch. It will help the grass withstand hot, dry weather by shading the soil and by raising the humidity at soil level.

# AUGUST

## LAWNS

 PLANNING

This is an excellent month in which to compare your lawn to others in your neighborhood. The stress of drought, heat, disease, and insects will be evident on lawns whose owners have neglected some facet of their care. If yours is the best on the block, congratulations! If yours is not quite on par with the rest, make notes on what practices you can improve in other parts of the year to make your lawn look its best.

 PLANTING

If your lawn is thinning in dense shade, why not replace the sparse grass with a ground cover like **mondo grass, ajuga, pachysandra,** or **liriope**? Even pine straw or wood chip mulch will look better than grass that's struggling along in semi-darkness.

 CARE

If there is a secret to having an outstanding lawn, it is regular, leisurely observation of the grass and making time to do a little "problem correction" each week. Weed, insect, and disease problems don't appear out of thin air—they develop over time. Even though it is hot and sultry outdoors, take time each week to walk across your lawn, ice-cold drink in hand, noting small problems and planning your response.

 WATERING

Water restrictions are common summer occurrences in metropolitan areas of Georgia. Don't fall into the trap of believing that you should water your lawn whenever allowed. A deep soaking, one per week, is all a lawn needs. (See Lawns, Introduction, for watering information.)

 FERTILIZING

• **Tall fescue:** Do not fertilize.

• **Bermudagrass:** Fertilize now (and again in September).

• **Zoysiagrass:** Fertilize now.

• **St. Augustinegrass:** Fertilize now.

• **Centipedegrass:** Do not fertilize. **Centipedegrass** is naturally a lighter green than other grasses. Fertilizing with an iron sulfate product will make **centipedegrass** greener. Apply 1 to 2 pounds of Ironite™ per 100 square feet.

 PROBLEMS

"Brown patch" and "dollar spot" are two common lawn diseases. Both are best controlled by attention to proper watering and fertilization.

Brown patch symptoms are large circular areas of dead grass, in which the edge and center of each area may be dark green. To control brown patch:

• Keep grass as dry as possible between weekly waterings. Water between midnight and noon.

• Follow recommended fertilizer rates. Do not overfertilize.

Dollar spot symptoms appear as dozens of small dead spots. To control dollar spot:

• Water deeply each week. Do not allow the lawn to become drought-stressed.

• Keep grass healthy with a regular fertilization program.

If caught in time, both diseases can be controlled with fungicides. Fungicides are expensive and will not cure an advanced case of either disease.

If you had tremendous numbers of Japanese beetles, you might get some control by poisoning the grubs now. There is no need to use an insecticide if you find only a few grubs when you dig. Eight to ten grubs per

White grub

square foot is the threshold at which a poison should be considered.

This is the most effective time to apply grub poisons, but remember to water heavily after application, which will wash the chemical down into the soil where the grub lives. Consider using milky spore disease powder for organic grub control.

If your predominant grass is **tall fescue,** now is the time to kill other grasses in preparation for planting **tall fescue** in September.

• Spray any **Bermudagrass, centipedegrass** or **zoysiagrass,** with a nonselective, systemic weedkiller.

• Seven days after spraying, irrigate thoroughly to encourage sprouts of the invading grass to emerge.

• Seven days after irrigating, spray the sprouts of weed grasses with nonselective weedkiller.

---

## HELPFUL HINT

The biggest reason lawn mower oil goes unchanged and the blade goes unsharpened is the difficulty of working on the machine while it is on the ground. Removing a blade is particularly difficult. If you have an aluminum extension ladder, a cinderblock, and an outdoor flight of steps, you can lift a mower to make it more accessible:

• Place one end of the ladder on the second or third step. Rest the other end on the ground.

• Position the mower at the lower end of the ladder, facing the steps.

• With a great grunt, push the mower up the slanted ladder. As the wheels leave the ground, the underside of the mower frame will scrape along the ladder frame. Shove the mower up the ladder as far as you can.

• Move the upended cinderblock close to the low end of the ladder. Lift the ladder with one hand and place the end rung on top of the cinderblock set on its end.

• The mower should now be supported 18 inches off the ground by the ladder frame. You can easily reach under it to loosen the blade attachment bolts or the oil drain plug.

**Caution:** Always disconnect the spark plug when working on a lawn mower.

---

Now is also a good time to control broadleaf weeds. Use a selective weedkiller labeled for use on such pests.

## MOWING

How long has it been since your lawn mower blade was sharpened? Cleanly cut grass is healthier and does not look yellow after mowing. Your lawn mower blade should be sharpened once each summer to avoid shredding the grass when you mow.

Often **zoysiagrass** does not appear to need mowing even though it may be growing higher than the recommended .5 to 1.5 inches.

• Mow your **zoysiagrass** lawn regularly to avoid thatch buildup.

# September

## LAWNS

### PLANNING

Whether you're planting seed or spreading fertilizer, an even application of material is important. The best way to accomplish this with a lawn spreader is to use the crisscross method:

1. Apply half your material in several passes going in one direction.

2. Apply the second half in several passes that are at right angles to the first application.

### PLANTING

**Tall fescue** is a common lawn grass in the northern half of the state. Fall is the best time to plant it if you are using seed. The planting can be done successfully until mid-October, but the longer you wait, the cooler the soil becomes and the longer it will take for the seed to germinate.

• Planting a new **tall fescue** lawn from scratch? Use 6 pounds of seed per 1000 square feet.

• Overseeding an old lawn? Use 3 to 6 pounds of seed per 1000 square feet, depending on how much **tall fescue** already exists.

• Before spreading seed, either aerate thoroughly or scratch the soil hard with a bow rake.

South Georgia lawn-lovers still have time to plant **common Bermudagrass** seed and get acceptable growth before winter.

**Bermudagrass** sod can still be planted successfully, but it would be better to not plant **zoysiagrass**, **centipedegrass**, and **St. Augustinegrass** sod until spring.

### CARE

After planting **tall fescue** seed, it must be mulched with wheat straw to protect it from birds and to hold soil moisture.

Use no more than one bale of straw per 1000 square feet.

### WATERING

After **tall fescue** seed has been planted, it must be watered regularly until the seeds have established a good root system. If you are under watering restrictions, getting good seed-to-soil contact is very important. (See Lawns, Introduction, for watering information).

Apply seed or fertilizer using a crisscross pattern.

## FERTILIZING

**Tall fescue:** Fertilize after the middle of the month (and again in November). Use a starter fertilizer (which usually has a high percentage of phosphorus) for the first application if you planted **tall fescue** seed. Use any brand of turf fertilizer for subsequent feedings.

**Bermudagrass:** These lawns benefit from a "winterizer" fertilizer application now when growth has slowed but before the grass turns brown. The best date is six weeks before you estimate the first frost will occur in your region. A winterizer fertilizer helps **Bermudagrass** get off to a strong start in spring— this fertilizer contains a moderate percentage of nitrogen and higher-than-usual percentages of phosphorus and potassium.

**Zoysiagrass:** Do not fertilize at this time.

**Centipedegrass:** Do not fertilize at this time.

**St. Augustinegrass:** Do not fertilize in north Georgia. Fertilize in south Georgia only if the August feeding was missed.

## PROBLEMS

The seaport of Brunswick has the honor of being the introduction point of a destructive lawn pest in south Georgia: the mole cricket. Adult insects tunnel just below the surface of the soil. They feed on grass roots, but the grass suffers great harm just from the drying out of loosened soil. The best first step to mole cricket management is correct watering, fertilizing, and mowing height. Insecticides are most effective when applied in June, although cricket damage is most noticeable in September.

After applying sprays or granular poisons, irrigate immediately to dissolve the poison in the soil.

The Georgia Two-Step fire ant control technique (see Lawns, May) is extremely effective when applied now. The combination of a bait and a mound treatment now can bring them to their knees.

Armadillos can be a pest on lawns in south Georgia. They root through the turf looking for grubs to eat. Your lawn will look like a group of small bulldozers visited during the night!

• Use 24-inch-tall fence wire and short wooden stakes to construct a simple funnel trap facing the area from which the animals come each night.

• The mouth of the funnel should be 30 to 50 feet wide.

• The trap sides should taper down to a width of 12 inches— just wide enough to place the opening of a large live trap in the armadillo's path.

• Transport the animals you capture several miles away, and release them.

"Winter" weeds germinate in fall but wait to make their appearance the following spring. Chickweed, annual bluegrass, and henbit are common winter weeds.

Mid-September is the best time to put out a pre-emergent winter weed-preventer.

Before planting **tall fescue** seed, wipe out weeds with a fast-acting but short-lived weedkiller.

Use a nonselective weedkiller now, and you can plant grass seed in seven days.

Many tough-to-control summer weeds are at their weakest now from summer stress.

Apply a broadleaf weedkiller to violets, wild strawberry, and wild onion in your lawn.

## MOWING

If you raised your mowing height to help your grass during the summer, lower it to the proper height now. See the mowing height chart in Lawns, Introduction.

# OCTOBER

## LAWNS

 PLANNING

Before you can move into a new home, it must pass a final inspection and receive a "certificate of occupancy." The county housing inspector won't grant a certificate of occupancy if the lawn has not been planted or sodded. The installation of grass is often the last thing done by the builder before the home sale.

• If you have any input into the decision, make sure the appropriate grass has been chosen for your lawn (see Lawns, Introduction).

• **Annual ryegrass** is sometimes allowed, but remember that it must be replaced with a permanent grass in spring.

• Ask the builder how the soil was prepared before seed or sod was planted.

• Test the softness of the soil by pressing a pencil into the earth—if it penetrates more than 2 inches easily, grass can grow readily. If the soil seems rock hard, you will have endless problems with your lawn in the future.

• If you are not satisfied that the new lawn will succeed, negotiate appropriate guarantees or concessions at closing.

 PLANTING

**Bermudagrass** turns brown and dormant in winter. To avoid this brown look, one can overseed the **Bermudagrass** with **annual ryegrass.** The **ryegrass** will be green in winter but will die out in early summer.

1. Mow the **Bermudagrass** as low as possible without your mower blade hitting the ground.

2. Spread **ryegrass** seed evenly at a rate of 5 to 10 pounds per 1000 square feet.

3. Fertilize with starter fertilizer.

4. Water thoroughly (see the watering information in Lawns, Introduction).

**Caution:** Overseeding with **ryegrass** may weaken the underlying **Bermudagrass** because it competes for available nutrients during the winter. Follow all **Bermudagrass** maintenance recommendations during the year to help it withstand the stress of being overseeded in the winter. Do not overseed thin or weak **Bermudagrass** lawns.

**Tall fescue** seed can still be planted, but don't delay. Cold soil causes the seed to germinate unevenly.

 CARE

Moss is a common inhabitant of lawns that are shady or constantly moist. Moss-control chemicals are available, but they are not permanent solutions to the problem. For permanent moss control:

• Loosen the soil deeply to make it drain faster.

• Reduce shade by removing low limbs of nearby trees.

• Correct the water-flow problems that cause the soil to be wet.

**Important:** Lime does not eliminate moss. Although moss prefers acid soil, liming will not control the moss unless the environmental conditions mentioned above are corrected.

 WATERING

Water newly planted **tall fescue** lawns regularly.

Water recently sodded lawns deeply so the water penetrates 4 inches into the soil below the sod layer.

Drain your lawn irrigation system before winter arrives:

1. Turn off the water valve that supplies your system.

2. Allow the system timer to run through all its cycles in its normal manner. Much of the water in your pipes will run out of the lowest irrigation heads. What water remains will not be under pressure and will not hurt components if it freezes. The system should be fine when you turn it on next year.

An alternative is to purchase a maintenance contract from an irrigation contractor. The workers will check the operation of all of your heads before draining the system in winter. They may also want to shoot compressed air through the pipes to remove all remaining water. They will also check the system again in spring.

Store water hoses where you won't be tempted to move them when they're frozen. A hard-frozen hose is brittle; leaks may result if it is flexed when cold. A hose reel is very handy for hose storage throughout the year.

## FERTILIZING

**Tall fescue:** There's still time to give **tall fescue** lawns that first fall feeding. Use any turf fertilizer. Use a starter fertilizer for the first application if you planted seed.

**Bermudagrass:** It may be fertilized with a winterizer product in south Georgia.

**Zoysiagrass:** Do not fertilize at this time.

**Centipedegrass:** Do not fertilize at this time.

**St. Augustinegrass:** Do not fertilize at this time.

Fireplace ashes can be scattered over your lawn rather than disposing of them. They provide a bit of phosphorus and potassium, plus they counteract acidity, just like garden lime. Spread no more than 10 pounds per 1000 square feet per month. **Caution:** Never store ashes in a flammable container; always place them in a covered metal pail.

## PROBLEMS

Don't forget to spread a weed-preventer as soon as possible on established lawns to suppress weeds such as chickweed, *Poa annua*, and hairy bittercress next spring.

Remember that weed-control chemicals can harm germinating seed as well as grass that is going dormant:

• Do not apply a weed-preventer to newly seeded **tall fescue** lawns.

• Do not use "weed 'n' feed" products or a broadcast application of broadleaf weedkiller on any turfgrass at this time.

• Spot-spray broadleaf weeds that pop up this fall.

The effectiveness of the Georgia Two-Step fire ant control (see Lawns, May) depends on ants that are actively foraging for food:

• In south Georgia, you can use the Two-Step technique until the weather becomes chilly.

• In north Georgia, treat individual mounds with contact insecticide.

## MOWING

Mow warm-season grasses as needed while the weather cools. You can stop mowing after the first frost.

Mow **tall fescue** as needed (see Lawns, Introduction, for mowing heights).

# NOVEMBER

## LAWNS

### PLANNING

On a warm day, walk across your lawn and note any problems that could be cured during the next growing season.

- Does the grass grow evenly in all areas?
- Are particular spots prone to weed and disease problems?
- Was it easy to mow all areas?
- Could the size of your lawn be reduced to save water and maintenance time?

It is a common practice of builders to install **Bermudagrass** sod in the front lawn and to plant **tall fescue** in the back. Remember that if you have two different grasses, they will have two different management schedules:

- **Tall fescue** is fertilized and mowed in the cool months but not in summer.

- **Bermudagrass** is fertilized and mowed in summer but not in winter.

If the backyard is sunny, consider converting to **Bermudagrass**.

### PLANTING

It is very late to be planting **tall fescue** seed in the northern half of Georgia except in the area south of Atlanta and north of Macon. In areas north of Atlanta, you can do it, but germination will take weeks. See the Helpful Hints for a possible solution.

**Tall fescue** sod should be available now. It can be installed anytime between now and next summer.

There's still time to plant **annual ryegrass** for erosion control, or just to use as a green spot in a brown landscape.

Do not plant **zoysiagrass, centipedegrass,** or **St. Augustinegrass** sod in the northern half of Georgia now. These grasses do not have enough time to grow good roots before cold weather sets in.

In the southern half of the state, all sods can be planted, but use caution. Avoid planting in sunny or windy weather.

Mondo grass can be an excellent grass substitute for those areas that are not "grass friendly."

Remember to water new sod regularly until it is well established. (See Lawns, Introduction, for watering schedule).

**Bermudagrass** sod can be planted now if you are certain you can water it regularly during the winter to keep the roots moist.

This is an excellent month to plant **liriope** or **mondo grass** in shady spots where grass refuses to grow:

- The easiest way to get plants is to divide a clump already growing in your yard or that of a friend. Ask your neighbors if they have an area where one of these ground covers is growing.
- Dig the clump, wash it off, and divide it into individual plants.
- Replant some of the sprouts where they grew originally. Take the rest to your landscape and install 6 inches apart.
- Water twice, at three-day intervals. No further care should be required.

### CARE

Are your neighbors raking up pine straw and putting it in bags for the garbage man? If they can't use it in their landscape, ask if you can have some for yours. If you have the space, stockpile bags under a tarp so you'll have plenty of mulch next year.

Keep the leaves raked (or blown) off your newly planted **tall fescue** lawn.

## WATERING

Drain your irrigation system (see Lawns, October) and outdoor faucets. If the faucets can't be drained, cover them with insulation for the winter. Hardware stores stock foam pipe wrap and faucet covers that are easy to install.

## FERTILIZING

Lawn fertilizer does not "go bad," even when it becomes lumpy and breaks through the bottom of the bag. If it can be pulverized enough to flow through your spreader, apply it to your lawn on the usual schedule. If the lumps are too hard to break, throw them, in moderate amounts ($^1/_2$ cup per plant), under your woodland trees and shrubs in spring. Fertilize **tall fescue,** preferably in the early part of the month. Do not fertilize **Bermudagrass, zoysiagrass, centipedegrass,** or **St. Augustinegrass.**

## HELPFUL HINTS

If you have a **tall fescue** lawn spot that simply must be planted in cold weather, here is a trick that can be used to extend the season.

### Greenhousing
- Rake the area with a hard-tined garden rake (a bow rake).
- Scatter seed lightly and evenly over the spot. Water and cover very thinly with wheat straw.
- Cover the whole area with clear plastic sheeting; anchor it loosely with stones or large limbs.
- Sunshine will warm the soil and encourage the seed to sprout quickly.
- Lift the plastic when the grass is green underneath.

**Caution:** Do not attempt this technique if the weather is unusually warm or sunny. Your seed may overheat and die under the plastic.

## PROBLEMS

Squirrels may dig holes in your lawn in order to hide acorns. The holes are unsightly, but little can be done to deter the rodents. If the holes bother you greatly, use a live trap, baited with peanut butter, to capture a few of the creatures and give them a nice trip out of town.

## MOWING

Fall leaves are much easier to handle when they have been shredded. If you have a bagging mower, simply rake up a pile of leaves and mow through them until you fill the bag. Shredded leaves can be used as mulch under trees and shrubs or can be added to your compost pile. High-performance mulching mowers can shred leaves so finely they won't be noticed on your lawn; the particles simply add organic material to your soil.

# DECEMBER

## LAWNS

 PLANNING

No law says you have to have a lawn (although neighborhood covenants may require one). It is possible to have a very attractive front yard without enduring the work and management details a lawn requires. On a warm December day, walk across your lawn and envision what it would look like if it were filled with beds of flowers or shrubs or tree islands.

 PLANTING

**Tall fescue** sod can be planted anytime it is available. **Bermudagrass** sod can be successfully installed in the northern half of the state throughout the winter as long as it is kept from drying. Do not plant **zoysiagrass** or **centipedegrass** sod. In the southern half of the state, all sods can be planted, but use caution. Avoid planting in sunny or windy weather. Remember to water new sod regularly until it is well established (see Lawns, Introduction, for watering schedule).

 CARE

Rake the last of the fall leaves from your lawn. A pile of wet, matted leaves now can lead to big dead spots next spring. Use them for mulch under shrubs and trees.

 FERTILIZING

**Fescue:** Fertilize only if the November feeding was missed.

**Bermudagrass:** Do not fertilize at this time.

**Zoysiagrass:** Do not fertilize at this time.

**Centipedegrass:** Do not fertilize at this time.

**St. Augustinegrass:** Do not fertilize at this time.

 PROBLEMS

Watch for the bright-green leaves of chickweed in your lawn. Spot-spray with a broadleaf weedkiller.

Spray for wild onions in your lawn. Do this a second time in February, and another time in April. If you'd rather not use a herbicide, a stiff dandelion fork can be used to dig out the underground bulbs.

**Tall fescue** lawns that were planted in fall may appear slightly yellow after a December cold snap. This minor frost damage will disappear in just a few days. It will not reoccur once the grass has become well-established.

 MOWING

Mow **tall fescue** and **ryegrass** regularly, removing only $1/3$ of the height each time. Mowers are tough machines, but a little maintenance now will make them much easier to operate:

• Don't leave your lawn mower out in the rain. Water can get in the gas tank and prevent starting next spring. It is best to drain the tank completely, or run the mower until it is out of gas.

• Flip your mower on its side and clean the underside of the mower with a sturdy stick. Remove caked grass. Check the mower shaft for string or wire wrapped around it.

• Use a spray lubricant, such as WD-40, to protect and lubricate wheel axles, control cables, and blade height adjusters. A 5-minute task today can save hours of frustration next spring.

• This is a fine time to have the blade sharpened if this was not done earlier in the year.

**Caution:** Always disconnect the spark plug before maintaining a lawn mower.

# PERENNIALS & ORNAMENTAL GRASSES

Perennials, also called *herbaceous plants*, produce fleshy stems that die down each winter, but their roots stay alive and send up new growth in spring. Many perennials will thrive and bloom in the same spot year after year with a minimum of care. Others need to be divided or replaced after two or three years. In the milder parts of Georgia, certain perennials stay evergreen all year long.

Perennials can be grown from seed, but you may have to wait several years before they will bloom. The availability of a wide range of container-grown perennials makes it easy to start a perennial garden and have blooms the same season you plant. Perennials that catalogs describe as "blooming for weeks" may actually be fleeting in our hot, humid climate—because of this, it is best to grow a variety of perennials, including those with striking foliage and distinctive forms as well as those with colorful flowers. This way your garden will not rely solely on flowers to create interest. Plants such as hostas and ferns offer colorful foliage that persists for months, often when little is blooming in the shade garden. In the sunny garden, plants like lamb's ear and artemisia provide a transition from one group of colors to another, and they, too, look good for months at a time.

While it's true that annuals must be replaced every year, growing perennials is not necessarily more cost-effective. Unless you grow your plants from seed, perennials initially cost more than annuals, and once you get bitten by the perennial bug, you may find you are making lots of trips to the local nursery. Still, when the perennial garden is established, you won't have to replace plants every year the way you do with annuals, and you will have plenty of divisions and cuttings to share with friends and neighbors.

## PLANNING THE PERENNIAL GARDEN

If you're not sure about which perennials will do well in your garden, start with a small area. Examine the environment that your existing trees and shrubs are growing in to help guide you in your choices. Is it a hot, sunny spot, or is it cool and shady? Determine how much sun you get in a particular area. Start by observing the sun at different times of day, beginning in early morning, then at noon, and again in the afternoon. Record how many hours of direct sunlight an area receives. If you want to grow sun-loving plants, four to six hours of direct sunlight is ideal. If you garden in the shade, plants will still need a minimum of light to thrive, perhaps a half-day of bright indirect light. High shade from mature deciduous trees will allow a good bit of light into an otherwise dark area. If there is not enough light and plants are weak and not thriving, you may have to do some selective pruning and open up the canopies of large trees nearby.

Draw a plan on graph paper, indicating which plants you would like to include. While you don't have to have a scale drawing, you can use your house as a reference point to help you locate plants in relationship to one another.

When selecting perennials, consider not only the season of bloom and the flower color, but the color of the foliage, the texture of the plant, and what the plant looks like when it is not in bloom. List the attributes of plants you want to grow: flowers, foliage type, and whether or not there are decorative seedheads. Note which plants attract

bees and butterflies, and which plants die back after they finish blooming (like the one that seems to disappear soon after its flowers fade). Remember that just one plant of many different varieties will not make an effective display. Think about grouping plants—two or three of the same type will make an impact.

Grouping plants that have flowers with similar colors will also make an effective display. Spring may feature pastel blooms of pink, white, and blue, while summer may be reserved for hot colors like red, orange, and yellow. Remember that green in all its shades is also a color.

Spacing is important, too. Do a little research on the cultural requirements and growth rate of the plants you would like to grow before you purchase them. While you don't want to wait three years for your plants to fill in, you don't want your garden to become overgrown in only one year either.

Ornamental grasses are herbaceous plants that add flair to the garden with their striking forms, foliage, flowers, and seedheads. When planted in masses, they add a sense of drama. When mixed in with your flowers or used as part of a mixed border with shrubs, trees, and perennials, they add a touch of elegance and grace as they sway in the breeze. Many are long-lived, offering colorful foliage and flowers year after year, beginning in summer and continuing well into winter when their decorative seedheads persist. These plants demand little in the way of care, although division of mature clumps may be required to keep the plants healthy (grasses should be divided in spring). While grasses are often associated with full-sun gardens, there are also types that thrive in shade. Although there are both annual and perennial selections of ornamental grasses, the varieties recommended in this chapter are perennial in most parts of Georgia.

Most important, no matter what types of perennials you grow, remember to let the garden tell you what to do. Is the soil well-drained, or does it stay wet and compacted? Knowing the answers to these questions will help you when you make your plant selections. Use your garden journal to record what you plant where, including information on sources, the condition of the plant when you plant it, and how many plants you purchased and planted. Photograph your garden before you plant, and then after you plant, at least once a month. This will provide useful information in the future.

On page 136 is a chart of a few ornamental grasses for Georgia, including varieties that thrive in sun and some for shade. Certain grasses will also thrive in containers, and can be moved around to add instant interest to the garden.

## SOIL PREPARATION

There's an expression that sums up the importance of good soil preparation when growing perennials: Prepare a ten-dollar hole for a one-dollar plant. This means that if you invest in the soil by preparing it before you plant, you can start with smaller plants that will become large and robust in no time.

Eliminate existing weeds before you add soil amendments. If you use a nonselective herbicide like Roundup™, you can spray weeds, wait ten days to two weeks, then begin adding soil amendments.

A slower method that involves no chemicals is to cover weeds with a layer of newspaper, at least one inch thick, and then put two to three inches of mulch over the newspaper. This technique is effective, but it takes six months or longer before the weeds are killed and the newspaper breaks down. You can also place a sheet of black plastic over the weeds, and then put a two-inch layer of mulch over the plastic. Check after six months to see if weeds are dead and gone. Both of these techniques are for patient gardeners.

Once the site is weed-free and the soil is mostly dry, rototill the area to a depth of twelve to eighteen inches, adding soil amendments as you go.

Avoid working soils that are waterlogged. If you have a heavy clay soil, incorporate organic material and coarse sand into the existing soil. A good amended soil recipe calls for one-third organic material, one-third coarse sand (river sand or builder's sand), and one-third existing soil. Mix these well and use as backfill. A few examples of organic material are leaf compost, horse or cow manure that has been composted for at least six months, and mushroom compost. These materials are available at local garden centers.

Plan to add more organic material to the soil every season. While mulch will help keep soil temperatures cooler in the summer and warmer in the winter, and will conserve moisture, it does not offer the same benefits that topdressing with an organic material does. Once the garden is established, you can topdress with organic material once in spring and once in fall. These materials will break down over time and provide welcome nutrients for the soil.

## FERTILIZING

If you take the time to prepare your soil before you plant perennials, you should not have to fertilize on a regular basis. Still, some gardeners may want to fertilize new plants with a dilute solution of a liquid fertilizer like Peters® or Miracle-Gro®, at half the recommended rate. Spreading a thin layer (one to two inches) of compost or organic material such as well-composted manure over your perennial beds in spring and then again in fall will help ensure that your soil stays healthy. If you want to fertilize, three times a year is adequate, in spring, summer, and fall. When perennials are dormant, there is no need to fertilize.

## PEST CONTROL

Like all plants, perennials are susceptible to their share of insect and disease problems. One of the best ways to keep infestations to a minimum is to maintain healthy plants. Start with vigorous plants, and provide the proper environment like healthy soil, good air circulation, and water on a regular basis.

Monitor your garden by checking plants weekly during the growing season for signs of damage (chewed or discolored leaves). If there is a slight infestation of an insect or disease (less than one-third of the plant), try washing off the affected area with water or using insecticidal soap. If you use chemicals to control a particular pest, take extra caution, and always wear protective clothing and gloves. Treat problems before they get out of control. Whenever possible, consider an organic alternative before resorting to chemicals.

## WATERING

Too much water can be as harmful as too little. When perennials are newly planted, they will benefit from regular watering if there is not adequate rainfall (one inch per week—measure this by using a tuna fish can).

Here is a method to determine watering time: Dig down 2 inches, and if the soil is dry to the touch, it's time to water. Sandy soils may need watering more frequently than those that have a high clay content. Container gardens may need more frequent watering than perennials that are planted in the ground.

## BEST PICKS PERENNIALS FOR SHADE

Rick Berry, Nurseryman and Co-Owner of Goodness Grows, Lexington, Georgia, has been growing perennials for Georgia gardens for over twenty years. The list below represents some of his top contenders for gardening in the shade.

- *Amsonia hubrectii* (Arkansas blue star)
- *Arum italicum* (arum)
- *Asarum* spp. (ginger)
- *Begonia grandis* (hardy begonia)
- *Dryopteris erythrosora* (autumn fern)
- *Epimedium* hybrids (barrenwort)
- *Heuchera* 'Amethyst Myst' (alumroot)
- *Polygonatum odoratum* 'Variegatum' (variegated Solomon's seal)
- *Rohdea japonica* (sacred lily)
- *Saxifraga stolonifera* (strawberry begonia)
- *Tricyrtis* spp. (toad-lily)

## Ornamental Grasses for Georgia

| Botanical Name / Common Name | Cultural Requirements | Average Height and Width | Comments |
|---|---|---|---|
| *Acorus gramineus* 'Ogon' **Golden Variegated Sweet Grass** | Full sun or shade; moist soil. | 6 to 12 inches by 6 inches | Great in containers or to brighten the edge of a woodland pond. |
| *Calamagrostis* spp. **Feather Reed Grass** | Full sun; moist well-drained soil. | 2 to 4 feet by 2 to 3 feet | In north Georgia the fall color is orange yellow. |
| *Carex hachioensis* 'Evergold' **Variegated Japanese Sedge** | Full sun in coastal areas, partial shade in other parts of the state; moist, well-drained soil. | 2 feet by 2 feet | Effective in rock gardens or when planted in masses. |
| *Chasmanthium latifolium* **Northern Sea Oats** | Tolerates a wide range of growing conditions; full sun and dry soil if kept watered; partial shade and moist soil is best. | 2 to 3 feet tall by 2 feet wide | Handsome flowers and foliage. Cut off seedheads in June if you want to prevent this grass from spreading by seed. |

CHAPTER FIVE

# Ornamental Grasses for Georgia

| Botanical Name<br>Common Name | Cultural<br>Requirements | Average Height<br>and Width | Comments |
|---|---|---|---|
| *Miscanthus sinensis*<br>**Maiden Grass**<br>**Japanese Silver Grass** | Full sun and moist soil; tolerates drought when established | 5 to 8 feet by 2 to 3 feet | Good for coastal gardens; along edge of a pond, or at the back of the border. |
| *Pennisetum alopecuroides*<br>**Fountain Grass** | Adapts to a range of soil types; prefers moist soil and full sun. | 2 to 3 feet by 2 to 3 feet | Great for the fall garden; attractive flowers and colorful foliage. |

# Perennials for Georgia

| Botanical Name<br>Common Name | Cultural<br>Requirements | Average Height<br>and Width | Comments |
|---|---|---|---|
| *Achillea* x 'Coronation Gold'<br>**Yarrow** | Full sun; well-drained soil | 2 to 4 feet by 3 feet | Yellow flowers in late spring. Divide in spring or fall. Good for drying. |
| *Alcea rosea* cultivars<br>**Hollyhock** | Full sun; well-drained soil | 4 to 8 feet by 2 feet | Many selections both single and double forms; blooms in late spring or early summer. Easy to grow from seed. |
| *Amsonia hubrectii*<br>**Arkansas Blue Star** | Full sun or partial shade; water during periods of dry weather. | 2 to 3 feet by 3 feet | Feathery foliage, pale blue starlike flowers in spring. Plant turns golden yellow in fall. |
| *Anemone* x *hybrida* 'Honorine Jobert'<br>**Japanese Anemone** | Partial shade; well-drained soil. | 2 to 4 feet by 2 feet | White flowers in fall. Not a good choice for coastal gardens. |
| *Aquilegia canadensis*<br>**Columbine** | Shade, a moist soil, although they will tolerate sun. | 2 to 3 feet by 1 foot | This native columbine has yellow and red flowers, which appear in early spring and last for weeks. A prolific seeder. |
| *Artemesia* hybrids and cultivars<br>**Wormwood** | Sun; well-drained soil. | 2 to 4 feet by 4 feet | Silver-gray foliage looks good most of the year. Prune in spring or summer only. Not a good choice for coastal areas. |
| *Arum italicum*<br>**Italian Arum** | Shade; a moist soil. | 12 to 20 inches by 18 inches | New foliage appears in fall and lasts through winter. |
| *Asarum shuttleworthii* 'Callaway'<br>**Mottled Wild Ginger** | Moist, well-drained woodlands. | 4 to 9 inches by 8 inches; a very slow grower | Mottled evergreen heart-shaped leaves, this native is an aristocrat. |
| *Asclepias tuberosa*<br>**Butterfly Weed** | Sun; average garden soil. | 2 to 3 feet by 2 feet | Flowers in spring for up to six weeks in shades of red, orange, and yellow. Happy in a meadow or the garden. |

# Perennials for Georgia

| Botanical Name<br>Common Name | Cultural<br>Requirements | Average Height<br>and Width | Comments |
|---|---|---|---|
| *Aster* species and cultivars<br>**Aster** | Sun; average garden soil. | Range in size from 6 inches to 8 feet tall by 9 inches to 4 feet wide. | No fall garden should be without asters. Cutting them back early in the season will keep plants compact and bushy. |
| *Baptisia australis*<br>**Wild Indigo** | Full sun or partial shade; tolerates poor soil but moist, rich soil is best. | 3 to 4 feet by 4 feet | Indigo blue flowers in spring followed by attractive seedpods in summer. |
| *Begonia grandis*<br>**Hardy Begonia** | Shade; moist well-drained soil. | 1 to 2 feet by 1 foot | Blooms with pink flowers late summer to early fall. Handsome leaves, reseeds easily. |
| *Belamcanda chinensis*<br>**Blackberry Lily** | Full sun or partial shade; average garden soil. | 3 to 4 feet by 2 feet | Easy to grow; this iris relative produces orange flowers with red spots in summer and lots of shiny black seed in autumn. |
| *Chrysanthemum* hybrids<br>**Fall-Flowering Mums** | Full sun; well-drained soil. | 1 to 3 feet by 3 feet | Cut back three times during the growing season (until August 15) for full, more compact plants. |
| *Coreopsis* species and cultivars<br>**Coreopsis, Tickseed** | Full sun; well-drained soil. | 12 inches to 3 feet by 3 feet | Yellow flowers in summer; 'Moonbeam' and 'Zagreb' are good selections for Georgia. |
| *Dianthus gratianopolitanus* 'Bath's Pink'<br>**Cheddar Pinks** | Full sun; well-drained soil. | 9 to 12 inches by 12 inches | Fragrant pink flowers in spring; gray-green foliage. |
| *Dryopteris erythrosora*<br>**Autumn Fern** | Shade; average garden soil. | 18 to 30 inches by 2 to 2½ feet. | Evergreen in most parts of Georgia; new growth has bronze and pink tinges. |
| *Echinacea purpurea*<br>**Purple Coneflower** | Full sun; well-drained soil. | 2 to 3 feet by 2 feet | Purple ray flowers surround a brown cone. Deadheading helps prolong flowering. |
| *Epimedium* hybrids<br>**Barrenwort** | Partial shade; moist, well-drained soil is best. | 6 to 15 inches by 15 inches | Good groundcover for shade. |
| *Eupatorium purpureum*<br>**Joe-Pye Weed** | Full sun to partial shade; moist soil. | 5 to 7 feet by 3 to 4 feet | Big heads of mauve flowers in fall attract butterflies. |
| *Gaillardia* x *grandiflora*<br>**Blanket Flower** | Full sun; well-drained soil. | 2 to 3 feet by 2 feet | A mix of red and yellow, the flowers bloom summer until fall. Great for coastal gardens. |
| *Geranium macrorrhizum*<br>**Bigroot Geranium** | Partial shade; moist, well-drained soil. | 15 to 18 inches by 15 inches | Magenta flowers in spring; fragrant foliage. |

CHAPTER FIVE

# Perennials for Georgia

| Botanical Name<br>Common Name | Cultural<br>Requirements | Average Height<br>and Width | Comments |
|---|---|---|---|
| *Helleborus orientalis*<br>**Lenten Rose** | Partial to full shade; moist, well-drained soil. | 15 to 18 inches by 15 inches | Evergreen foliage looks good year-round; flowers in late winter to early spring in white, purple, and maroon. |
| *Heuchera* hybrids<br>**Alumroot, Coralbells** | Partial shade; moist, well-drained soil is is best; will tolerate full sun with adequate moisture. | 12 to 36 inches by 18 inches | Many great selections with colorful foliage; wonderful woodland plant. |
| *Hosta* x 'Royal Standard'<br>**Fragrant Hosta** | Sun or partial shade; moist, well-drained soil. | 2 to 3 feet by 3 feet | Tolerates sun more than most hostas; fragrant flowers in later summer. |
| *Iris tectorum*<br>**Japanese Roof Iris** | Full sun or partial shade; moist, well-drained soil. | 12 to 18 inches by 18 inches | Blue or white flowers in spring; light green fanlike foliage looks good year-round. |
| *Lantana camara*<br>'Miss Huff'<br>**Hardy Lantana** | Full sun; well-drained soil. | 3 to 6 feet by 3 to 6 beet | Yellow, orange, and pink flowers attract butterflies in summer and fall. Good for coastal gardens. |
| *Liatris spicata*<br>**Blazing Star, Gayfeather** | Full sun or partial shade; moist, well-drained soil. | 3 to 4 feet by 2 feet | Spikes of mauve flowers in summer. |
| *Phlox subulata*<br>**Moss Phlox** | Full sun; well-drained soil. | 6 to 9 inches by 12 inches | A carpet of flowers in early spring; found in blue, white, pink, and purple. |
| *Polygonatum odoratum*<br>'Variegatum'<br>**Variegated Fragrant Solomon's Seal** | Shade; moist soil. | 18 to 24 inches by 2 feet | Great foliage plant for the shade garden. Green leaves edged with a broad strip of creamy white. |
| *Polystichum acrostichoides*<br>**Christmas Fern** | Partial shade to shade; moist soil. | 12 to 18 inches by 12 inches | Tough evergreen fern; easy to grow. |
| *Rosmarinus officinalis*<br>**Rosemary** | Full sun; moist, well-drained soil. | 3 to 6 feet by 3 to 4 feet | Fragrant culinary herb; great for cooking. |
| *Rudbeckia fulgida*<br>'Goldsturm'<br>**Black-eyed Susan** | Full sun; well-drained soil. | 2 to 3 feet by 2 feet | Blooms summer to fall wth bright orange-yellow flowers. |
| *Sedum* 'Autumn Joy'<br>**Autumn Joy Sedum** | Full sun or partial shade; well-drained soil. | 12 to 24 inches by 24 inches | Flowers start out green in summer and then turn pink and maroon in fall. |
| *Tricyrtis* species<br>**Toad-Lily** | Full or partial shade; moist, well-drained soil. | 1 to 3 feet by 2 feet | Orchidlike flowers in late summer to autumn. |
| *Verbena* 'Homestead Purple'<br>**Homestead Purple Verbena** | Full sun; well-drained soil. | 8 to 18 inches by 3 feet | Rich purple flowers in spring and then on and off until frost. |

# JANUARY
## PERENNIALS & ORNAMENTAL GRASSES

### PLANNING

This is the ideal time to plan your perennial garden.

- Begin by making a wish list of the plants you'd like to include, grouping those that have similar cultural requirements. Include varieties that shine for each season so you can have a progression of blooms and interesting foliage.
- Sketch potential designs on graph paper, remembering that once you begin to plant your plan may change.
- Leave space in your plan to add annual color.
- When you design your garden, remember that several plants of one variety will make more of an impact than single examples of many different varieties.

Siting your perennials against a backdrop of evergreens, a hedge, a fence, or a stone wall will help define your garden and provide structure all year long.

- Record weather conditions in your garden journal. Keep track of areas in your garden where the soil stays wet all the time. Plan to correct this problem before you plant, or select perennials that will tolerate this environment.

- Record what you plant, when you plant it, and the source of your plants.
- Take a photograph of the garden while everything is dormant.

### PLANTING

In south Georgia, perennials can be planted any time they are available.

In north Georgia, it is best to begin planting in late February or early March unless the weather is extremely mild and plants have been grown in containers outdoors for one full growing season ("extremely mild" means the ground isn't frozen and the temperatures have not dropped down to freezing every night). Hardy perennials normally stay outside all year long. This means they are acclimated to the fluctuations that occur with the weather. If they have been grown in a greenhouse, they will not be ready to plant outside until the threat of frost has passed.

If you are uncertain about the frost-free date in your region, check with the Cooperative Extension Service.

Certain unusual varieties of perennials may only be available as seeds. Order seeds now

to start indoors under lights. (See Annuals, February.)

### WATERING

If temperatures are mild, plants can dry out. Keep them watered and mulched.

Water newly planted perennials (those planted within the past twelve months) once a week if there is not adequate rainfall (1 inch). Use a tuna fish can to measure rainfall.

If you can't tell by a physical inspection whether plants need water, feel the soil. If it is dry to the touch when you dig down 2 or more inches, it's time to water. If you don't have many perennials and want to water by hand, 2 gallons of water for a 1-gallon-size plant should be adequate.

### FERTILIZING

In south Georgia, you can fertilize newly planted perennials with a half-strength mix of a liquid like Peters® or Miracle-Gro®.

In north Georgia, there is no need to fertilize your perennials when they are dormant. Now is a good time to amend soil in new beds so you will be ready to plant in the spring. Spread 2 to 4 inches of compost or manure across an area, and mix it in a good 12 inches deep with the rototiller.

## PROBLEMS

Look for infestations of chickweed, a mat-forming winter annual. The leaves are opposite and densely hairy; the white, notched flowers appear in clusters at the ends of the stems. If a crop appears, pull them out before they set seed.

The best time to weed is the day after a gentle rain when plants are easy to pull up, roots and all.

Remove any dead leaves that have accumulated around perennials. This will help eliminate insects that may be overwintering.

Scale can be white or brown and often look crusty. They appear in clusters on the bark, stems, and leaves of plants. Use horticultural oils to suffocate insects like scale or other pests.

## GROOMING

Remove any dead stalks, seedpods, or leaves you missed in the fall. Wait until early spring, just before perennials begin to put out new growth, before you prune plants back hard, to a height of several inches. Some perennials don't need to be pruned back hard, but you can tidy them up by removing dead flower stalks. Perennials that don't require much pruning include:

- *Anemone × hybrida*
- *Asarum shuttleworthii* 'Callaway'
- *Begonia grandis*
- *Heuchera americana* cvs.
- *Saxifraga stolonifera*
- *Sedum kamtschaticum*
- *Veronica prostrata*

In south Georgia, cut back clumps of **pampas grass** and other ornamental grasses to a height of 12 to 24 inches.

January is a good month to cut back ornamental grasses to prepare for spring growth.

# FEBRUARY
## PERENNIALS & ORNAMENTAL GRASSES

 PLANNING

Take a soil sample and have it tested by your local Cooperative Extension Service (see Horticultural Practices, p. 7). You will receive a report that describes the nutrients present in your soil, the amounts in which they are present, and specific recommendations for correct fertilizer use. A soil test will also determine the pH of your soil and the amount of lime it needs.

The pH affects the availability of nutrients and whether they are soluble in the soil. A pH of 7 indicates that the soil is neutral. A pH below 7 indicates acidity, and one above 7 indicates alkalinity. Acid-loving plants like **rhododendrons, camellias,** and **azaleas** are happiest in a soil with a pH of less than 5.5. Lime is applied in gardens primarily to raise the pH.

Lime also has a physical effect on soil: in clay soils, it causes particles to form larger units and therefore enables water and air to move more easily through the soil (for information on lime applications refer to Lawns, p. 108). In sandy soils, lime holds particles together so that water is held for a longer time.

As a rule, the rate of application for lime is 4 pounds per l00 square feet. When you apply lime, it is best to make sure that you rototill it in to a depth of 4 to 6 inches. This can be done when you prepare the soil for planting as you add other soil amendments.

 PLANTING

In milder parts of the state you can begin to prepare the soil for planting now, provided it is not too wet (wet soils with a high percentage of clay can turn into large impervious clods). Scoop up a handful of soil and squeeze it. If it crumbles easily, the soil should be dry enough to work.

Rototill to a depth of 12 inches, adding soil amendments as you go. The particular materials you add to the soil will be determined by the type of soil you have. Heavy clay soils will need lots of organic materials (this helps improve drainage, adds microbes, and improves the overall soil structure) and some coarse sand; sandy soils will benefit from incorporating some clay along with organic materials. Organic materials such as mushroom compost, cow manure, horse manure, cottonseed meal, or ground pine bark are all good choices for amendments.

Start perennials from seed indoors under lights (see Annuals, February). Some seeds require stratification before they will germinate. Referred to as

Gather the materials you'll need to start seeds, including flats, cell-packs, and individual peat pots as needed by specific plants.

"after-ripening" they may require either a cold or warm treatment. Leaving seeds in a polyethylene bag in the refrigerator for one to four months at 40 degrees Fahrenheit will accomplish this. Other seeds need to be soaked in hot water and then given the cold treatment described above. Some seeds need to have their seed coats broken mechanically before they will germinate. Some need light to germinate and should not be covered with soil.

Read the backs of seed packets to determine what conditions individual perennials require to germinate.

As a general rule, allow six to eight weeks from the time you sow perennial seed indoors until the seedlings will be ready to transplant to the garden.

Certain perennials like **hollyhocks** are difficult to transplant.

Seeds should be sown in individual peat pots so the roots won't be disturbed when you plant them in the garden.

You can also sow seeds in flats, plastic cell-packs, or individual pots. Whichever type of container you use, make sure to punch holes in the bottom for drainage.

If you use fluorescent lights to start seedlings, your setup should provide 15 to 20 watts per square foot of growing area.

## HELPFUL HINT

To learn more about growing plants from seed, check course offerings at your local botanical garden.

## WATERING

Water containers during mild spells. Water perennials in the ground if the weather is windy for several days. Check them weekly—if there is not adequate rainfall (1 inch or more per week) and the ground is not frozen, plan to water.

Keep the seedlings you're starting indoors moist; a spray bottle of water is an effective way to water seedlings.

## FERTILIZING

Once seedlings germinate and are a few weeks old, fertilize them with a complete liquid fertilizer at half-strength like Peters® 20-20-20 or another with a similar ratio.

## PROBLEMS

During mild spells (when temperatures are such that working outdoors in a long-sleeved shirt is comfortable—in other words, you don't need a hat and gloves), reapply a granular weed preventer (the best time to apply it is in September in established perennial beds to prevent future crops of chickweed and other winter weeds from taking over). Read the label carefully before applying.

In extreme South Georgia, inspect your perennials for signs of aphids or other insects.

Use a strong blast from the hose or an insecticidal soap to control them. Horticultural oils are also an option; they work by smothering insects.

# MARCH
## PERENNIALS & ORNAMENTAL GRASSES

### PLANNING

If a scoop of soil holds together but crumbles easily, it is dry enough so you can begin planting hardy perennials. Have a list of plants and a plan ready. Local garden centers and nurseries should have a fresh supply of plants for sale now.

### PLANTING

When you purchase perennials, remember that you are investing in a root system. If you start with a weak plant, it will take twice as long as a strong healthy plant before you can expect a big flowering show, as the plant will put all its energy into developing a strong root system. When you ease a rootball out of the pot,

Daylilies can be divided easily by separating a clump with two pitchforks, back to back.

you should see fleshy roots covering at least 50 percent of the soil. If they are dried out and brittle, or if there are only a few, this indicates a weak root system.

This is the time to plant bare-root perennials, while temperatures are mild and many plants are still dormant. **Peonies** are often sold bare-root, as are certain varieties of perennials that are available only by mail-order. Before you plant bare-root perennials, cut off any broken roots or those that are dried up; soak the roots in a bucket of water while you prepare the planting hole.

Tips for dividing perennials:

1. Perennials with lots of fibrous roots can be dug up with a spade or shovel. Get a big clump—more roots are better than fewer roots.

2. Gently pull apart the roots by hand. Cut off any damaged or dead roots.

3. Replant divisions at once.

4. Water, and apply a 2-inch layer of mulch.

Some perennials should be divided by hand, not with a sharp spade or digging fork, but by digging up a large clump and then teasing apart the roots, making sure shoots are attached to each section. You can use two pitchforks back to back, or a

pitchfork (or digging fork) and a spade to pull apart the rootballs. Try this method with the following plants:

- *Aquilegia* spp. **columbine**
- *Epimedium* hybrids **epimedium** (after they flower)
- *Gaillardia* spp. **blanket flower**
- *Geranium* spp. **hardy geranium**
- *Helleborus* spp. **hellebore** (after they flower)
- *Heuchera* spp. **coralbell**

Other perennials can be divided with the fork or spade technique, in early spring:

- *Achillea filipendulina* **yarrow**
- *Anemone x hybrida* **Japanese anemone**
- *Aster* spp. **aster**
- *Boltonia asteroides* **boltonia**
- *Chrysanthemum* spp. **chrysanthemum**
- *Coreopsis verticillata* **coreopsis**
- *Dianthus* spp. **pinks, carnation**
- *Echinacea purpurea* **coneflower**
- *Hemerocallis* spp. **daylily**
- *Hosta* spp. **hosta**
- *Monarda* spp. **beebalm**
- *Phlox paniculata* **garden phlox**
- *Rudbeckia* spp. **black-eyed Susan**

## WATERING

Water all new plantings and transplants once a week for the first month after they are planted.

Water established plantings once every two weeks if you don't get 1 or more inches of rain.

## FERTILIZING

If your perennials are in a healthy soil, it is not necessary to use a commercial fertilizer on a regular basis. Instead, consider topdressing with an organic material such as compost, cow manure, horse manure, or other bagged product. Spread the organic material about 1 inch thick, keeping it away from the stems and crown of the plant (the crown is the center of the plant where stems and buds originate). If you do use a chemical fertilizer, apply 1 pound of a complete fertilizer such as 10-10-10 per 10x10-foot square. Water in the fertilizer. Too little fertilizer is always better than too much.

## PROBLEMS

Look for yellow or discolored leaves, stippling (dark tiny spots) on leaves, sticky sap, and other signs of insects.

---

## DOUBLE DIGGING

This labor-intensive method for preparing a planting bed is a favorite of many longtime gardeners.

1. Using a spade, dig up the top 10 inches or more of the soil and set it aside.

2. Dig the subsoil layer, incorporating organic material to a depth of about 10 inches.

3. Amend with organic material the topsoil layer that you set aside, and then place it back on top of the amended subsoil.

The new planting bed will provide a healthy planting bed for years. If you use this method, you can work on one area of the garden each season instead of tackling your entire garden at one time. Amending and tilling the soil this thoroughly is sure to reward you with lush, healthy plants. Continue to feed your soil by topdressing it with organic materials once or twice a year.

---

Treat with horticultural oils or insecticidal soaps as needed. Handweed on a weekly basis to help keep weeds at a minimum.

It's not too late to use a granular weed-preventer in your perennial beds if you didn't use one in February.

Read the directions carefully before applying.

## GROOMING

Cut back your ornamental grasses to a height of about 6 to 12 inches just before or just as new growth is beginning in early spring.

If you have evergreen ornamental grasses such as *Carex*, pull out the dead, brown sec-tions. New growth will fill in within a few weeks.

Clean up any remaining leaf litter, dead stalks, or seedpods from the previous season. Now is the time to cut back perennials, before new growth begins.

Certain perennials like *Artemesia* 'Powis Castle' and other **artemesias** can get large and overgrown in one season; it is best to cut them back now, at the beginning of the growing season, rather than in the fall. If they are cut back in the fall, they may not have time to recover before the winter, and the plant is sometimes killed back.

Reduce the size of an individual **artemesia** by $1/2$ or more. Provided you keep it watered, it will fill out within a few weeks.

# APRIL
## PERENNIALS & ORNAMENTAL GRASSES

### PLANNING

If you don't have a plan for your perennial garden, now is the time to create one (see January).

### PLANTING

Divide and transplant perennials.

The best time to divide ornamental grasses is in the spring, just as new growth is beginning. Certain grasses like *Miscanthus* spp. and *Pennisetum* spp. can develop into large clumps and may require a handsaw to divide them. Make sure each division has roots and shoots before you replant it.

Certain perennials such as *Amsonia* spp. and *Astilbe* hybrids can also be divided with a handsaw in the spring; make sure each division has new shoots and roots.

Harden-off perennial seedlings:

1. Take seedlings outside, and place them in a shaded area, gradually exposing them to more sun each day.

2. Once they are acclimated to the outside environment, you can plant them in the garden. A week to ten days should be long enough for the acclimation.

If seedlings were sown in individual peat pots, you can plant the pot directly into the ground. A few cuts with your pruners into the bottom of the pot will stimulate roots to become established more quickly. Keep peat pots moist while seeds are germinating and when you transplant them to the garden.

If you want to purchase plants, local nurseries and garden centers should have a good selection of perennials from which to choose.

Space plants to allow enough room for growth. Keep in mind that you may have to move or divide plants next year if they get too large.

### WATERING

For the first few months you may need to water every few days if temperatures are high and plants are planted in full sun. After this initial period, check plants once a week for the first growing season. If you do not receive 1 inch of rainfall per week, applying 2 gallons of water per 1-gallon-size perennial should be adequate.

Containers should be checked daily and may need more frequent watering than plants that are planted in the ground. Water when the soil 1 to 2 inches deep is dry to the touch.

### FERTILIZING

If you haven't fertilized yet, you can apply a complete fertilizer like 10-10-10 at a rate of 1 pound per 100 square feet. If you have soil that has been amended with organic amendments, you won't have to fertilize your perennials every month. If you want to fertilize, three times a year (spring, summer, and fall) is plenty.

### PROBLEMS

Check perennials for aphids or other insects; if needed, treat with insecticidal soap.

If 50 percent or more of the plant is infested, it is an option to spray with a contact insecticide.

Look for signs of slugs or slug damage on plants like **hostas:** the leaves may be chewed, and often there is a silver trail on the leaves or on the ground near the plant.

Use a slug bait to control them.

Continue handweeding. Spot-spray weeds in perennial beds with a nonselective weedkiller.

Single Stake
Support

Metal Hoop Support

# HELPFUL HINTS

If you have any perennials that need staking, plan ahead. Right about the time the flower buds begin to show color is the best time to stake. You can use a single stake or a series of stakes for multistemmed plants; bamboo stakes work well. For tying, use green or natural-colored jute twine, which will blend in better than white string.

• Certain perennials like **peonies** or *Phlox paniculata* can be staked now with a circular gridded ring placed on top of three stakes. The stakes should be evenly spaced and adjustable. As the plant grows up through the openings, the ring will keep the plant from flopping over when it is in full flower. This type of stake is called a "grow thru" or a metal hoop support.

• For single-stem plants like **lilies,** place the stake about an inch from the main stem, and tie jute to the stake, leaving 2- to 4-inch loose ends. Bring the **lily** stem close to the stake, and tie the loose ends around it.

• Another method for staking is to use the twiggy prunings from your trees, cut into various 16- to 20-inch lengths. Stick them into the ground all around young plants when plants are about half their expected height, and in no time the plants will cover the stakes. This works well when there are lots of perennials in one area or for plants like **beebalm** that have many stems.

If you want to keep the amount of staking to a minimum, plant your garden so that one variety of perennial supports another. Early-blooming **Shasta daisies** make a good mass to plant in front of **salvias,** which will bloom later.

Cover perennials with a piece of newspaper to keep any spray from drifting onto desirable plants.

 GROOMING

Prune back **lantana** unless you live in south Georgia where it is evergreen. Even if these plants were overgrown last fall, it is best to prune them now in early spring when they are actively growing. You can cut back $1/3$ to $1/2$ of the total plant, and it will quickly recover.

# MAY
## PERENNIALS & ORNAMENTAL GRASSES

### PLANNING

Many perennials are now in bloom or beginning to bloom. Think about the rest of the season and what the garden will look like. Incorporating perennials that have interesting foliage and distinctive forms will help the garden have interest even when there are no flowers. When you plant your perennials, remember to leave space for colorful annuals. And remember that white flowers combine well with most other colors in the garden or help to separate one area of color from another.

Photograph the garden at least once in spring, and write the names of the the spring bloomers in your garden journal.

### PLANTING

Continue adding perennials to the garden, including varieties that will bloom in summer and fall like **salvias, asters, chrysanthemums,** and *Helenium autumnale*. Start with healthy plants that have clean foliage and a good root system.

Gently ease the plant out of the pot before you purchase it. If the rootball is covered with roots that are white and fleshy, then the roots are healthy. If there are more roots than soil, the root system may be stressed. If you have purchased a plant that has been grown in the same container for a long period of time it may be "potbound."

If it is potbound, cut the container down one side and ease out the plant. Make two or three clean cuts into the rootball at various points around the ball to loosen the roots. Gently pull them apart, and spread them out in the planting hole. The plant should adjust and begin to grow where you plant it.

The perennials listed below should be divided in spring after they finish blooming:

• *Dicentra* spp. **bleeding heart** (divide by hand)

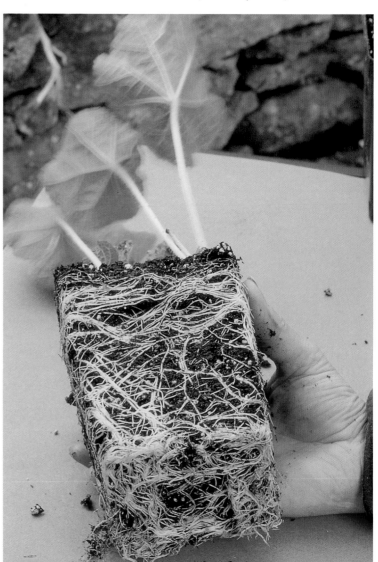

A good, healthy root system, like this example, is essential.

148

- *Iris sibirica* **Japanese iris** (use a spade or hand saw to divide)
- *Iris tectorum* **Japanese roof iris** (use a spade or handsaw to divide)

## WATERING

Continue watering new plantings on a weekly schedule. If you have an automatic irrigation system, you will need to adjust its schedule according to the amount of rainfall.

- It is better for your plants if the system comes on once a week or every few days rather than every day.
- Keep track of how much water plants receive. Note this in your garden journal.
- Long, slow, thorough watering is best. Allow the soil to dry out between waterings.

## FERTILIZING

Applying a dilute solution of a liquid fertilizer such as 15-30-15 directly to the foliage of new plantings will give them an added boost. Young leaves absorb the fertilizer quickly. It is best to apply foliar feeds early in the day before the intense heat sets in.

## PROBLEMS

Use insecticidal soap to control insects like aphids, spider mites, thrips, and whiteflies. Apply spray during the early morning before temperatures get too hot (check the label for recommendations).

Spray the plant to the point where the spray is dripping, being sure to cover the undersides of the leaves.

Continue to handweed. Pulling weeds before they flower or set seeds will help reduce future weed infestations.

Spot-spray with a nonselective weedkiller to control weeds, using extreme caution around perennials and other desirable plants.

If the leaves of your **columbine** are discolored and have a series of silver trails running through them, the problem is leaf miners. The best and easiest treatment is to shear off plants to the ground and destroy the infected foliage after the **columbine** finishes flowering. A new flush of growth will quickly replace the old leaves.

Although it is not immune to pests, the native **columbine**, *Aquilegia canadensis* is less susceptible to leaf miners.

## GROOMING

Depending on the type of plant, deadheading (removing spent blossoms from flowers) can encourage perennials to produce more flowers. Experiment with your favorite plants. Plants that send up more flowers if you deadhead include:

- *Gaillardia* × *grandiflora*
- *Gaura lindheimeri*
- *Scabiosa* 'Butterfly Blue'
- *Verbena bonariensis*
- *Veronica* 'Sunny Border Blue'

Cut or pinch back fall-blooming **chrysanthemums** and **asters** by 1/3 and you will have fuller plants in the fall.

Cutting back certain perennials will often delay their flowering by a few weeks and prevent them from flopping over when they finally do bloom. This type of pruning should be done about eight weeks before plants are expected to bloom. Plants that respond to this procedure include *Phlox paniculata* and **asters.**

Experiment with pruning. If you have a group of one type of plant such as **beebalm,** cut back some of the plants and let the others progress naturally. This method will give you staggered bloom times, which means you will have flowers over a longer period of time.

# JUNE
## PERENNIALS & ORNAMENTAL GRASSES

### PLANNING

Make notes in your garden journal about how plants are performing, color combinations that you like, and plants that, based on their performance, may be in the wrong spot. Be sure to list the sources of plants you like so you'll be able to get more of the same. Have you included a variety of perennials to ensure that there is always something of interest in your garden, be it flowers, leaf form, or texture?

Use perennials that complement the existing shrubs and trees in your garden. For example, *Robinia pseudoacacia* 'Frisia' has golden-yellow leaves, and so does *Spiraea* 'Ogon'; two perennials that complement a planting of these two are the **variegated Solomon's seal** (green leaves with white edges) and the white-flowered **fleabane** called *Erigeron karvinskianus* 'Profusion'.

### PLANTING

Continue adding container-grown perennials to your garden. Make sure the soil is prepared before you plant. Water and mulch as soon as you get new plants in the ground; this

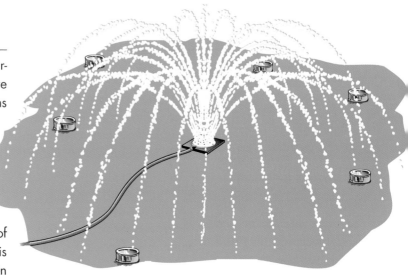

Time the flow of your sprinker (once is enough) to know how long it takes to provide ¾ inch of water.

will help keep soil temperatures cooler.

Late spring or early summer is a good time to propagate certain perennials by division, including *Lysimachia nummularia* and *Astilbe*—you may have fewer blooms for one season, but the plants will be robust next year.

Propagate the following perennials by cuttings:

- *Amsonia tabernaemontana*
- *Dianthus plumarius*
- *Monarda didyma*
- *Phlox divaricata*
- *Salvia × superba*
- *Sedum kamtschaticum*
- *Sedum spectabile*
- *Verbena tenuisecta*
- *Veronica spicata*

### WATERING

Water new plantings once a week if there is no rain. As a rule of thumb, apply 2 gallons of water for a 1-gallon-size plant; if plants are smaller, they will need a bit less water. If you use a sprinkler, set out a couple of shallow cans (tuna fish cans work great) to measure the water. You will have applied enough water as soon as the cans contain ¾ inch of water.

### FERTILIZING

Apply a foliar fertilizer to newly planted perennials for a quick boost. Use a dilute solution of a water-soluble fertilizer like Peters® or Miracle-Gro®, following the label direc- tions for half the recommended rate or less. Wait until fall to fertilize established plants.

## PROBLEMS

During hot, humid weather, problems like powdery mildew on **phlox, beebalm,** and other perennials may be a problem. To make an organic spray for powdery mildew, combine 1 tablespoon baking soda and 1 tablespoon Ultrafine Sun Spray oil in 1 gallon of water. Mix well, and spray the plants completely, being sure to wet both tops and undersides of the leaves.

Apply spray early in the day before temperatures get too hot. Avoid spraying when temperatures get above 90 degrees Fahrenheit, as this may burn the plants.

Check for insects, and treat as needed, using insecticidal soaps whenever possible to control problems like aphids, spider mites, and whiteflies.

If you have small infestations of Japanese beetles on **hollyhocks** or other plants, approach them slowly, handpick, and drop them into a jar of soapy water. (See Roses, June.)

## HELPFUL HINTS

Dry shade is a challenge that many Georgia gardeners face when they have a landscape where tree roots are competing with perennials for moisture. Here is a list of perennials (including a few perennial ornamental grasses) that will thrive in dry shade, even under a large mature tree:

• *Carex* 'Evergold' (variegated green-and-white foliage lights up the shade garden)
• *Carex* spp. (there are a number of selections of this adaptable ornamental grass)
• *Epimedium* spp. **Barrenwort** (many different selections)
• *Euphorbia robbiae* **Mrs. Robb's bonnet**
• *Helleborus orientalis* **Lenten rose** (evergreen foliage, and showy flowers in early spring)
• *Polygonatum odoratum* 'Variegatum' **Variegated Solomon's seal** (grows to 3$\frac{1}{2}$ feet tall)
• *Sedum ternatum* **Whorled stonecrop**
• *Senecio aureus* **Golden groundsel** (evergreen foliage, yellow daisylike flowers in early spring)

Spot-spray weeds in your perennial beds with a nonselective weedkiller.

Handpull weeds that are immediately next to desirable plants that might be harmed by chemical controls.

## GROOMING

Keep leaf litter at a minimum by pruning off any dead or diseased stems, leaves, or branches.

Continue deadheading perennials to encourage more blooms (refer to Perennials, May; and Horticultural Practices, p. 7).

Cut back fall-blooming **chrysanthemums** now, and you will have bushier plants which won't be as likely to fall over once they begin blooming.

Cut back fall-blooming plants like **Joe-Pye weed, swamp sunflower,** and **ironweed** now so that you won't have to stake them in autumn.

# JULY
## PERENNIALS & ORNAMENTAL GRASSES

 PLANNING

During these hot months, early morning or evening is the coolest time to work in the garden. This is a good time to edge your flower beds and think about planting projects for the fall. It's amazing how edging your flower beds with stone or brick can give your garden a more refined look, setting it off from lawn areas. Here are some ideas for edging flower beds:

• Use a straight-edge shovel to dig into the soil at a slight angle toward the flower bed; be sure to dig down at least 4 inches. Fill the trench you have created with the same mulch you use on your flower beds—this will delineate the bed line and separate it from the lawn.

• If you use brick or stone for edging, be sure to start with a level area if the bricks are upright, making sure $1/3$ is buried in the soil; sand is a good filler and will help the bricks settle.

• Other materials to use for edging include treated wood strips, metal, or plastic buried several inches in the soil.

Photograph your garden, and make a list of summer bloomers in your garden journal.

 PLANTING

If you add any plants to the garden now, keep in mind that they will probably not put out many roots until soil temperatures cool off. Here are a few tips for planting in the summer:

• Start with healthy plants that already have a robust root system.

• Restrict your planting and transplanting to the shade garden during the hot summer months. Minimize planting in sunny areas since root growth is at a minimum in high temperatures.

• Water and mulch immediately after planting.

Edging can provide an amazing transformation to the appearance of beds and borders.

 WATERING

Water established perennials during a prolonged dry spell (a month or longer without significant rainfall). About 1 inch per week should be enough.

• Attaching a water wand to your hose can make this chore much easier. Not only is the water more evenly dispersed through the many holes on the end of the breaker, an on/off valve will mean a lot less wasted water.

• Soaker hoses are also an option. Place them in your perennial flower beds, and cover them with a light coat of mulch. Be sure to inspect them periodically to see how well they are working.

• If you are growing perennials in decorative containers, you can add a granular product designed to absorb and release water in the soil (see Annuals, August). If you do this, be sure to adjust your watering frequency— you will have to experiment, but if you want to be certain you do not overwater, water only when the top 2-inch depth of the soil is dry.

• If you use sprinklers that are set according to timers, you will have to adjust them when there are changes in weather such as rainy days.

# ORGANIC METHODS OF CONTROLLING SLUGS

• Use orange or grapefruit rinds or black plastic cell-packs (six- or eight-packs in which annuals or vegetables are sold). Place the rinds or cell-packs under and near the leaves of susceptible plants. Mostly nocturnal, slugs seek dark, moist areas. In the morning, remove the rinds and cell-packs along with the slugs.

• Use a physical barrier like a 3-inch-wide strip of copper around susceptible plants.

• Slugs avoid areas that are dusty and scratchy. Sprinkle diatomaceous earth, sharp sand, or crushed eggshells around plants that slugs prefer (**hostas** are a favorite of slugs). Their soft bodies are sensitive to sharp edges, and they can die from dehydration.

• Another popular method for controlling slugs is to place the lid of a large mayonnaise jar next to the plants that may be attacked. Fill the lid with beer, and the slugs will drown.

## FERTILIZING

Don't fertilize now. The hot weather makes plants more susceptible to problems, especially if they are encouraged to put on lots of new growth.

## PROBLEMS

Check for aphids, spider mites, and thrips. Sometimes a strong blast of water will get rid of them; insecticidal soaps and horticultural oils can also be effective.

Southern blight is a soilborne fungus that causes stem rot at the soil level and can spread to surrounding plants. If plants are infected, remove and destroy them. Leave the area unplanted for six months (if you do plant in the infected area before six months are up, be sure to amend the soil with coarse sand, which will improve drainage). Plants often affected include **artemisia, aster, columbine, liatris, phlox, salvia,** and **Shasta daisy.** To reduce this problem:

1. Keep mulch away from plant stems.

2. Avoid overwatering.

3. Don't grow the same varieties of plants in the same spot year after year.

4. Good sanitation is also critical. Collect and destroy dead and diseased leaves.

Spot-spray weeds in perennial beds with a nonselective weed-killer. Use extreme caution around desirable plants. Continue to handpull weeds.

## GROOMING

Prune back by ⅓ to ½ fall-blooming perennials like **asters, chrysanthemums,** *Heliopsis,* and *Helianthus.* This will result in fuller plants that shouldn't require staking, although sometimes the flowers will be a bit smaller. Be sure to do this pruning at least eight weeks before the plants would normally bloom.

Fall-blooming perennials begin blooming in September, with other varieties continuing well into October and November.

Continue to deadhead repeat bloomers like *Echinacea purpurea, Rudbeckia* 'Goldsturm', *Scabiosa, Stokesia, Salvia,* and *Verbena.* This will encourage more blooms over a longer period. Plants like **yarrow** (*Achillea* spp.) may or may not bloom again but will be much tidier if you cut off the dead flower stalks.

Shear *Coreopsis verticillata* 'Moonbeam' for a second flush of bloom.

# AUGUST
## PERENNIALS & ORNAMENTAL GRASSES

### PLANNING

This is a good month to assess the successes and failures in your perennial garden. Make a list of plants you would like to add to the garden in fall once the weather begins to cool off a bit.

Plants for fall blooms or colorful foliage:

FL = colorful foliage

F = flowers

- *Amsonia hubrectii* FL
- *Anemone x hybrida* 'Honorine Jobert' F
- *Aster* spp. F
- *Chrysanthemum* 'Apricot Single' F
- *Eupatorium purpureum* F
- *Helenium autumnale* F
- *Sedum* 'Autumn Joy' F

Make a list in your garden journal of plants that will need to be divided in fall. If plants are healthy and thriving, you don't have to divide them unless they are getting too large for the space they are growing in.

### PLANTING

You may want to refurbish your decorative container plantings by adding perennials that offer fall blooms or colorful foliage. Another way to brighten up your perennial garden is to add some fall and winter annuals (refer to Annuals, August).

Plant container-grown ornamental grasses that bloom in fall or that have colorful autumn foliage. After they finish blooming, many of the seedheads provide interest well into winter. Grasses with attractive foliage or persistent seedheads include:

- *Miscanthus sinensis* 'Gracillimus' **maiden grass** (5 to 6 feet tall)
- *Miscanthus sinensis* var. *strictus* **porcupine grass** (yellow band on green foliage)
- *Panicum virgatum* 'Shenandoah' (a selection of **switch grass** with burgundy-red and green foliage)
- *Pennisetum* spp. **fountain grass** (flowers look like foxtails and persist into winter)

### WATERING

Keep perennials watered during the hot dry days, but don't overwater. Feel the soil, and if the top 2-inch depth is dry, it's time to water. A thorough soaking once a week should be adequate if there is no rain. Water plants using a hose at the base of the plant. If you do use a sprinkler, place small cans nearby (tuna fish cans work well), and water until there is $3/4$ to 1 inch of water in the can.

Avoid overhead-watering plants like *Phlox paniculata* or *Monarda* spp. that are susceptible to powdery mildew. Keeping the foliage dry will minimize this problem.

### FERTILIZING

Don't fertilize until fall. Fertilizing now will encourage new growth at a time when plants are under stress from heat and drought, making them more susceptible to pest and disease problems.

Scrape away old mulch and add a new 2- to 3-inch layer; this will dress up your garden and help conserve soil moisture.

### PROBLEMS

Continue to check perennials for insect and pest problems. Whenever possible, use insecticidal soaps to control infestations of aphids, mites, whiteflies, and other bugs.

Whether you use organic or chemical controls, apply them only as needed.

If your plants have white powder or black spots on their leaves, they could be suffering from a fungus.

If more than 50 percent of the plant is infected, you may want to throw the plant out and start

## PERENNIALS WITH ATTRACTIVE SEEDHEADS FOR FALL OR WINTER INTEREST

- *Baptisia australis* **Blue false indigo** (black pods 2 to 3 inches long)
- *Clematis macropetala* and *C. tangutica* (both these species have silky seedheads that persist into winter)
- *Iris foetidissima* **Gladwin iris** (large seed capsules open in fall to display orange-scarlet seeds)
- *Rudbeckia fulgida* var. *sullivantii* 'Goldsturm' (brown balls of seeds)
- *Sedum* 'Autumn Joy' (flowers start out looking like a head of broccoli, then turn pink, and finally maroon)

with a new plant. If only a portion of the plant is infected, there are fungicide sprays you can apply.

Keeping plants groomed will also help reduce problems. Apply any sprays during the coolest part of the day, in early morning or early evening.

This way you will avoid a chemical reaction which can occur when the insecticide reacts with high temperatures and bright sunshine, causing leaf scorch.

**Columbines** are often affected by leaf miners, which damage the foliage and leave it looking unsightly.

Simply cut off the foliage to within an inch of the base and you should get a flush of new growth that will be pest-free.

Groom plants like **lamb's ear** *Stachys* 'Helen Von Stein'. Remove leaves that are yellow, brown, or mushy.

This will increase air circulation and encourage the plant to put out new growth.

Continue handweeding.

Removing weeds while they are in flower and before they set seed will help reduce weed infestations next year.

## GROOMING

- Perennials like **salvia** will continue to bloom well into fall if you keep them deadheaded: pinch or snip off the faded blossoms so that the plant puts its energy into making more flowers and not setting seed.
- Remove yellow or diseased leaves of **iris,** but leave the seedpods for winter interest.

Collect seeds from your favorite perennials as the seedheads dry. Seeds that require no pretreatment, such as cold stratification or scarification, can be stored in the refrigerator until spring when they can be sown outdoors; store them dry in airtight containers or tightly sealed plastic bags. Plants with such seeds are:

- *Aquilegia canadensis* **columbine**
- *Asclepias tuberosa* **butterfly weed**
- *Aster* spp. **aster**
- *Belamcanda chinensis* **blackberry lily**
- *Liatris* spp. **blazing star**
- *Scabiosa caucasica* **pincushion flower**

(See Annuals, September.)

# September
## PERENNIALS & ORNAMENTAL GRASSES

## PLANNING

This is a good month to refurbish your perennial garden if it is getting overgrown and tired-looking. Decide which plants to add and which to divide or move to another location. Think about the form and texture of individual plants; include types with attractive foliage as well as those with beautiful flowers. Consider all the seasons. Here is a list of plants that offer three to four seasons of interest:

S = sun lover.

SH = shade lover.

• *Amsonia hubrectii* **amsonia** (green feathery foliage in spring, blue flowers, yellow fall color, tawny foliage in winter) S

• *Artemisia* 'Powis Castle' (feathery gray-green foliage all year) S

• *Asarum shuttleworthii* 'Callaway' **ginger** (glossy green mottled foliage all year) SH

• *Carex* 'Evergold' (green-and-white variegated ornamental evergreen grass) SH

• *Helleborus orientalis* (glossy evergreen foliage and flowers in late winter to early spring) SH

• *Heuchera americana* cultivars and hybrids (colorful evergreen foliage) SH

• *Selaginella uncinata* **peacock moss** (evergreen blue-green foliage) SH

• *Stachys* 'Helen Von Stein' **lamb's ear** (gray-green foliage all year) S

## PLANTING

If you don't have any perennials that bloom in fall, now is the time to add some—try **Joe-Pye weed, asters, sedums,** and **chrysanthemums.**

This is also a good season to work on improving the soil by adding organic amendments and rototilling. A soil test before you add amendments will help you determine the best amendments to add. Then you will be ready to plant this fall or next spring.

1. Prepare the soil ahead of time. If you are planting a large area, rototill 12 inches deep and add soil amendments to the entire area before you plant.

If you are planting only a few plants, you can prepare individual holes. Dig down 12 inches, and mix organic material with the existing soil. The planting hole should be twice as wide as the rootball, and the depth should be equal to the depth of the container the perennial is growing in.

2. After you plant, water well.

3. Mulch new plantings with a 2-inch-thick layer of mulch, keeping it away from the crowns of plants.

Pine straw, shredded pine bark, bark nuggets, leaf compost, or products such as ground pine bark are effective mulches that help keep roots cool and reduce weed infestations.

Once temperatures cool off a bit, it is a good time to divide and transplant perennials that have outgrown their spots in the garden or may not be performing as well as they could be. Perennials to divide in the fall include:

• *Amsonia* spp.
• *Asarum europaeum*
• *Astilbe* (can also be done in spring or summer)
• *Baptisia australis*
• *Boltonia asteroides*
• *Chelone lyonii*
• *Coreopsis verticillata* 'Moonbeam'
• *Epimedium grandiflorum*
• **Ferns** (many different types)
• *Hemerocallis* spp. and cultivars
• *Heuchera americana*
• *Lychnis chalcedonica*
• **Irises**
• *Phlox paniculata*
• **Rudbeckias**

Minimize transplant shock by cutting back the foliage by 1/3 to 1/2 at the time you transplant. This will help compensate for root loss.

## WATERING

Even as the weather begins to cool off, it is important to keep plants watered. If there is no rain, water perennials about once a week, especially transplants and new plantings. Apply 2 gallons of water for a 1-gallon-size perennial.

 ## FERTILIZING

While it is not necessary to fertilize, you can topdress your perennial plantings with mushroom compost, horse manure, cow manure, or a similar product. (To topdress means to spread a thin layer 1 to 2 inches deep on top of the soil). This will help keep the soil healthy, and plants will respond by developing strong root systems.

 ## PROBLEMS

Continue to pull weeds before they set seed in order to reduce weed populations next spring.

This is a good time to use a granular weed-preventer in established perennial beds. It will greatly reduce infestations of winter weeds like chickweed.

Check for slugs, and control as needed.

## HELPFUL HINTS

Add some fall bloomers to extend the season in your garden. Here are a few to consider:
- *Aster* (many different species and selections)
- *Boltonia asteroides*
- *Ceratostigma plumbaginoides*
- *Chrysanthemum* 'Apricot Single' or 'Hillside Sheffield'
- *Eupatorium purpureum*
- *Helenium autumnale*
- *Helianthus angustifolius*
- *Salvia leucantha* (a tender perennial, it often blooms until frost)
- *Salvia* 'Indigo Spires'
- *Tricyrtis hirta*

You can still use insecticidal soaps to control aphids and whiteflies.

Be sure to get good coverage of all the plant surfaces.

Certain poisonous caterpillars and other chewing insects blend in with plant foliage and are difficult to see. Wear gloves that cover you up to your elbows if you are handchecking leaves for pest problems.

The saddleback caterpillar is common now, and the sting is painful like a bee sting. Its name comes from the purplish-brown saddle on its green back.

There are also greenish-yellow caterpillars with black stripes that run horizontally instead of lengthwise. You don't want to kill these caterpillars even though they eat the plant, because eventually they will turn into beautiful monarch butterflies.

This late in the season the monarch larvae won't harm the plant permanently.

You may notice that your *Asclepias tuberosa* **butterfly weed** is covered with yellow aphids.

The safest way to get rid of the aphids in this case is to blast them off with the hose.

 ## GROOMING

Cut back flowers when they finish blooming, and remove any foliage that is diseased or dying. This will reduce the number of places for unwanted pests to overwinter.

Leave attractive seedheads, like those of *Sedum* 'Autumn Joy' or *Baptisia australis*, for winter decorations.

# OCTOBER
## PERENNIALS & ORNAMENTAL GRASSES

 PLANNING

This is an ideal month to add spring-blooming perennials to your garden. Make sure the soil is well prepared and that you have an idea of "what blooms when" before you start adding more plants. Make up a planting list, including information about flower color and the size of the plant and its texture.

Photograph your garden and make notes in your garden journal about plants that offer autumn interest.

 PLANTING

Amend planting beds with organic materials. Rototill to a depth of 12 inches if possible; add perennials to your garden.

Now is the time to plant and transplant herbaceous **peonies.** Follow these steps:

1. Dig up the area where they will be planted a few days ahead of time, and let the soil settle.

2. Add lots of compost and some superphosphate (refer to product label for amounts).

3. The **peony** roots should be planted so the buds (eyes) are 1 to 1¹/₂ inches deep. (Deeper planting will prevent **peonies** from flowering.)

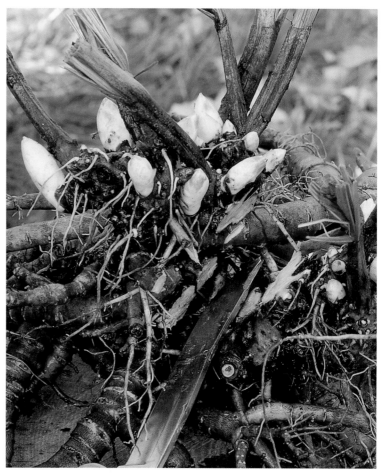

To divide an established clump of peonies, wash off the roots after digging and cut them into sections using a sharp knife.

Established clumps of **peonies** have stopped blooming. The clumps are large and healthy with lots of foliage, they have been fertilized regularly, and are growing in a spot where they receive four to six hours of sun per day. They may need to be divided.

1. Dig up the roots (rhizomes).
2. Wash soil off the roots.

3. Divide rhizomes into sections.

4. Dig a hole that is 1¹/₂ feet wide and about 1 foot deep. Mix in organic matter.

5. Replant the sections. Each section should have at least three buds (eyes), and healthy roots. It is important not to plant too deeply.

6. Space plants on about 1- to 2-foot centers.

Herbaceous **peonies** generally love cold weather, but there are a few varieties that perform well in southern gardens. Tips for growing herbaceous **peonies** in Georgia:

• Plant single or Japanese forms.

• Plant varieties that are early-flowering.

• Provide afternoon shade.

• Provide support for heavy flowers. Stake early with rings they can grow through.

• Some varieties for southern gardens are 'Festiva Maxima', an old-fashioned favorite with double white flowers flecked with red; 'Sarah Bernhardt', with double pink flowers; 'Imperial Red', with single red flowers; and 'Seashell', which has single pink flowers.

Divide plants of *Arum italicum,* **Italian arum,** after the leaves appear. This shade-lover provides handsome foliage in the fall and winter garden.

## WATERING

Be sure to keep plants well watered, especially new plantings and recent transplants. If you don't get 1 inch of rain, set out sprinklers, and water until there is $3/4$ inch of water in a nearby tuna fish can.

---

# HELPFUL HINTS

If you add new perennials to the garden this fall, draw a rough sketch indicating where they are in relation to existing plants. This will make it easier next spring when plants begin to sprout to separate the flowers from the weeds. Save the labels for any new plants that you add to the garden. This way you can refer to them if you forget the name of a certain variety once it begins to grow and bloom, and you will be able to match descriptions to names.

Some perennials grown for their foliage look good most of the year, even in winter on a frosty morning:

• *Dianthus gratianopolitanus* 'Bath's Pink'
• *Epimedium grandiflorum* **Epimedium**
• *Heuchera americana* (and many selections of this plant)
• *Phlomis fruticosa* **Phlomis**
• *Stachys* 'Countess Helen von Stein' (a selection of **lamb's ear** with larger leaves)
• *Yucca filamentosa* 'Bright Edge'

---

## FERTILIZING

Topdress perennials with 2 inches of organic materials like composted manures (cow or horse), mushroom compost, or composted leaves. Take care to keep compost away from the stems and crowns.

Fertilize established herbaceous **peonies** with 8-8-8 and bonemeal. Read the product label for recommended amounts.

## PROBLEMS

Keep beds free of diseased or dead leaves. This helps eliminate conditions that encourage insects to overwinter.

Use insecticidal soap for minor insect problems.

## GROOMING

Cut back spring-blooming perennials now, but wait until early spring to cut back fall-blooming types as well as certain other perennials like **artemesias,** which overwinter better when you leave them unpruned.

Cut back **lantana,** but just enough to keep it from blowing around in the winter wind—any hard pruning should be done in early spring.

# NOVEMBER
## PERENNIALS & ORNAMENTAL GRASSES

### PLANNING

In all but the most northern parts of the state, this is a good month to add container-grown perennials to your garden before the ground freezes.

Make notes in your garden journal about how your plants performed over the past season. Catalog the photos you took throughout the year.

### PLANTING

Hardy ferns add color and texture to the shade garden. Here is a selection of **hardy ferns** for Georgia gardens:

- *Athyrium felix-femina* **lady fern** (dies back in winter, upright habit, 2 to 3 feet)
- *Athyrium nipponicum* 'Pictum' **Japanese painted fern** (deciduous, wonderful variegated grayish-red/silver foliage, grows 1 to 2 feet)
- *Cyrtomium falcatum* **Japanese holly fern** (glossy evergreen, 2 to 3 feet tall)
- *Dryopteris erythrosora* **autumn fern** (evergreen, new foliage is a coppery color, grows to 3 feet)
- *Osmunda cinnamomea* **cinnamon fern** (deciduous, large upright fronds, grows 3 to 5 feet)

- *Osmunda regalis* **royal fern** (deciduous, 4 to 6 feet, native to swamps and wet areas)
- *Polystichum acrostichoides* **Christmas fern** (evergreen, 12 to 18 inches, has a prostrate habit)
- *Thelypteris kunthii* **southern shield fern** (deciduous, 2 to 3 feet, tolerates more sun than most ferns)

Plant **hellebores** now for late winter/early spring bloom. Perfect for the shade garden, these evergreen plants look good twelve months of the year.

- *Helleborus foetidus* **Bearsfoot hellebore** (light-green flowers, blooms from February to June)
- *Helleborus orientalis* **Lenten rose** (flowers range from white to purple, February to May—the plant tolerates drought and a half-day of full sun, although it will thrive in a moist woodland)

Sow seed of perennial **poppies,** including the scarlet *Papaver orientale,* which is best grown in the more northern parts of the state:

Japanese painted fern

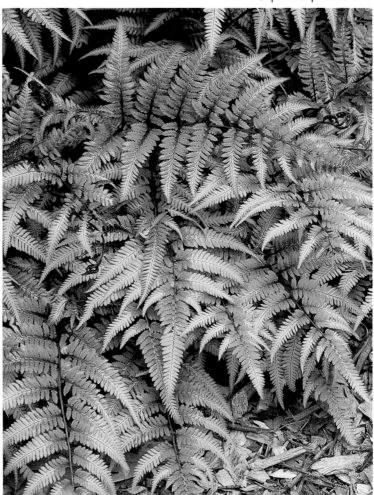

1. Prepare the soil by adding soil amendments and rototilling. Rake out the area where you will sow seeds.

2. sow seeds; barely cover them—**poppy** seeds need light to germinate.

3. Water until the soil is wet down 1 inch.

Sow seed of *Asclepias tuberosa* **butterfly weed.** These spring bloomers produce a range of flower colors from yellow to orange to scarlet. Germination rate is low, so plant thickly.

Propagate perennials once they are dormant: *Anemone* × *hybrida* by root cuttings; **geranium** species and hybrids by division; *Hemerocallis* **daylilies** by division into plantlets, each with a single fan; and *Heuchera* cultivars and hybrids by division.

## WATERING

Water new plantings and transplants weekly unless there is adequate rainfall (1 inch per week). If you use a sprinkler, use tuna fish cans to measure the amount of water plants receive. Once the can has $3/4$ to 1 inch of water, you have watered long enough.

## COMPANION PLANTS FOR POPPIES

When **poppies** finish blooming by mid- to late summer, they will disappear, leaving a bare spot in the garden. These perennials bloom at different times and can help fill the gaps:
- *Boltonia asteroides* **White boltonia**
- *Gypsophila paniculata* **Baby's breath**
- *Perovskia atriplicifolia* **Russian sage**

Once the ground freezes, apply a fresh layer of mulch (about 2 inches, keeping it away from stems and crowns) to perennial beds. This will help conserve moisture and reduce weed infestations.

## FERTILIZING

There's no need to apply fertilizer now.

## PROBLEMS

Pull weeds when they are young.

## GROOMING

Once there is a frost, prune back dead stalks and leaves of perennials such as **asters, chrysanthemums, salvias,** *Perovskia atriplicifolia*, and other late-blooming plants. Don't cut stems all the way back—leave 3 to 4 inches to help protect the crowns. This will also help you keep track of where perennials are planted so you won't accidentally dig them up when they are dormant.

Prune off the stems and leaves of herbaceous **peonies** to minimize the chances of fungus spores overwintering.

# DECEMBER
## PERENNIALS & ORNAMENTAL GRASSES

 PLANNING

It's time to begin thinking about next year's spring and what you will plant.

Sketch a plan that shows which perennials you want to include in your garden, paying attention to placement, color schemes, time of bloom, and ultimate size. If you're not sure where to begin when designing your perennial garden, try this technique:

• While the perennials are still in their pots, place the pots in the spot where individual plants will grow. Move them around until you are pleased with the design, keeping in mind what plants will look like when they're blooming and during the rest of the year, including the dormant season.

• Once you plant your perennials, if you think two colors clash or if one variety turns out to be too aggressive for the spot you've planted it in, you can move plants to another location—perennials are resilient and forgiving.

 PLANTING

In the most southern parts of the state you can add perennials to your garden throughout the year. In areas where the ground freezes, wait until spring to add new plants.

Sow seed that requires a cold treatment (*Aquilegia* spp. **columbine**, *Chelone* spp. **turtlehead**, *Echinacea purpurea* **purple coneflower**, and *Phlox paniculata* **garden phlox**). Start them in pots, and leave them outside through the winter, in areas where the temperature stays cool, next to the house in the shade.

Prepare your soil now for spring planting. Wait until a warm, sunny day when the soil is dry. Rent a small rototiller, and till the soil, adding amendments as you go—remember, the better the soil, the better the gardening results. Mix $1/3$ organic material, $1/3$ coarse sand, and $1/3$ existing soil. After you mix all the ingredients together, mulch the bed with a good 2 to 3 inches of mulch, and let it sit until spring when you can turn it under and begin to plant.

 WATERING

Water new plantings and transplants once a week unless there is adequate rainfall (1 inch per week).

Mulch is an insulator and helps reduce weed infestations. If you have not mulched your perennials this season, apply a fresh layer now, about 2 inches, being sure to keep it away from the stems and crowns of plants.

 FERTILIZING

You can still topdress with composted manure (cow or horse) or mushroom compost. Apply 2 inches of the organic material, then apply a fresh layer of mulch.

 PROBLEMS

Pull any weeds that are left in the garden.

 GROOMING

If you haven't cleaned up the perennial garden yet, do it now. Prune dead stalks and leaves—remember to leave 3 to 4 inches of stem as a marker (you will cut down the remaining dead stalks in early spring once new growth begins to emerge). Discard any diseased leaves or plants.

# ROSES

The rose is sometimes called "The Queen of the Garden." The variation in flower color, the heady scent of some (but not all) blooms, and the romantic associations in our culture make it one of the most versatile plants in a landscape. Roses vary in size from miniature to "monster," as anyone who has seen a 'New Dawn' grow over a garage would agree. Their flowers range in color from purest white to almost black.

Roses have had a reputation for being difficult to grow, but public opinion has begun to change in the last decade. Modern roses' prickly reputation developed when breeders began growing roses for competition. The flowers on the plants they bred were beautiful, but hybridization left behind the fortitude of the original roses. Native roses grow very well in the wilds of North America, China, and Europe.

Today's breeders have developed (and gardeners have rediscovered) roses that exhibit fortitude and beauty. The roses offered by catalogs (see January) and knowledgeable growers provide plenty of choices for your rose garden. Gertrude Stein was correct in literary terms that a "A rose is a rose is a rose," but her advice should be discarded when you select a rose for your garden.

# CHAPTER SIX

The pretty picture on the rose tag may not be possible to match if the plant cannot stand up to Georgia growing conditions. Look for roses described as "hardy in the South," "tolerates heat and humidity," and "little maintenance required" for your first plants. We have scattered lists of recommended roses throughout this chapter.

With roses, it is best to start small and build on your success. In addition to the variety you choose, rose experts agree that the key to success is providing the best environment for your plants from the beginning. Your rose should be planted in well-prepared soil and should receive plenty of sunshine. See January and October for descriptions of the best techniques for preparing a planting site. You'll get years of enjoyment from your roses if you put the right roses in the right spot.

## PURCHASING

Once you have discovered a rose variety you think will grow well in your garden, be sure to purchase the best plant you can find. If the rose has been grown in a container, do not buy it without checking its root system. Pull the plant from the pot to make sure roots spread throughout the potting medium. Don't be surprised if you find a plant that has vigorous growth above the soil line but few roots below—these roses have been moved too quickly through the production process. Do not buy a rose with weak roots.

You'll find some roses that are promoted as "growing on their own roots." Some producers feel that "own-root" roses are superior because they are less susceptible to stress. Own-root roses also avoid the problem that arises when the lower part of a grafted rose sends forth sprouts that are not like the upper part. If you garden in the north Georgia mountains, own-root roses will sprout back true from the roots even when the upper part of the plant is frozen to the ground.

Rooting rose cuttings, enough to market in sufficient numbers, is a slow process. Many more units of a beautiful rose can be produced if cuttings are grafted onto the roots of a less desirable variety.

Grafted roses are graded according to their size when they are harvested. A #1 grade rose has larger and more vigorous canes than a #1½ or a #2 grade rose. In general, you get what you pay for when buying a rose. Although it might be possible to buy a lower grade rose and wait for it to achieve its potential, this is usually not a good idea. In future years, you will get more pleasure from a single energetic plant than from two that began a bit runty in size.

Since Georgia has such a favorable climate for rose diseases, do not bring a diseased plant into your garden. Examine all the leaves for the yellow splotches that are symptoms of black spot (see March).

## FERTILIZING

Any of the commercial rose fertilizers or organic fertilizers will keep your plants happy. Our recommendations in March and the tips in following months will result in strong, vigorous roses. Once you have had several years of experience, you can experiment with the exotic mixtures rosarians sometimes employ.

## WATERING

Like most other garden plants, roses like to grow in soil that holds water a day or two after irrigation or rain but which dries before a week has passed. The only two times when attention to watering is needed is when a rose is first establishing itself in your garden and during times of extreme drought. Follow our recommendations on soil preparation plus our monthly watering tips and your roses will thrive, even in summer heat.

## CHAPTER SIX

### PRUNING

Trees and shrubs might grow for years before they need pruning. Most roses, however, grow and bloom best when pruned properly each year. Old-fashioned roses might need only an occasional touch-up pruning. Hybrid tea roses require heavier pruning to look their best—this is because they make their blooms on "new wood" (the stems that grew in the past few months). If you want copious blossoms (and what's the point of growing roses if this isn't your goal?), prune your roses properly. The important pruning dates to remember are February (for shrub roses) and June (for climbers). Our calendars for both those months will help you understand how to prune correctly.

Pruning is not limited to February and June, however. Remove dead stems and leaves regularly. Your roses will look neater and will be less susceptible to disease if you follow our monthly tips on what to look for as you wander through your rose garden each week.

### KINDS OF ROSES

Roses are grouped by growth and blooming habit. As you choose the roses you'd like to grow, you'll find the following classifications:

HYBRID TEA. These traditional one-flower-per-stem roses are used mainly as cut flowers. The roses usually have long pointed buds with high centers. Most hybrid teas have an upright growth habit.

FLORIBUNDA. They are similar to hybrid teas but shorter, bushier, and flower in clusters. They provide an abundance of color to any border, hedge, or container.

GRANDIFLORA. Basically, grandifloras are tall floribundas with clusters of hybrid tea–like flowers. This classification can be very confusing, though, because some floribundas grow taller than grandifloras.

SHRUB ROSES. These are colorful roses that are continuously in bloom from spring to late autumn. They provide beautiful flowers with very little care. Shrubs are excellent to use in borders and as hedges, and some do very well in containers.

CLIMBERS. Climbers are tall, upright, and spreading in growth habit, covering large areas. They are excellent for arbors, fences, and hiding an unattractive view.

### LEARNING

Growing roses in Georgia is not like growing them in Connecticut or Oregon or Michigan. Gardeners who move to Georgia, bringing their favorite no-care roses with them, quickly find that what works in one part of the country may not be so successful here . . . and the reverse would also be true if you moved out of the South. Rose culture in Georgia has been made more successful by the enthusiastic rose societies that meet throughout the state. If you want to be the "Queen (or King) of Roses" in your neighborhood, find a rose group or garden club (see October), and prepare to learn about and enjoy the exciting culture of roses in Georgia.

# JANUARY
## ROSES

## PLANNING

This is a good time to order roses from a rose catalog. Catalog ordering gives you many more choices of color and ultimate plant size than most neighborhood nurseries can offer. Local rose societies and botanical gardens maintain lists of roses that have performed well for their members. If one of their recommendations meets your needs, a catalog from a specialty rose nursery will help you find it.

## PLANTING

How to achieve the best planting bed is a topic of much discussion among rose fanciers. Some prefer amending their native soil and

Remove existing grass from the planned bed. If the grass is Bermudagrass, dig down 6 inches.

## ROSE CATALOGS

**ANTIQUE ROSE EMPORIUM**
9300 Lueckemeyer Rd.
Brenham, TX 77833
(800) 441-0002
**http://www.antiqueroseemporium.com**

**JACKSON & PERKINS**
1 Rose Lane
Medford, OR 97501
(877) 322-2300
**http://www.jacksonandperkins.com**

**ROSES UNLIMITED**
363 N. Deerwood Dr.
Laurens, SC 29360
(864) 682-7673
**http://www.roseunlimitedownroot.com**

**WAYSIDE GARDENS**
1 Garden Lane
Hodges, SC 29695
(800) 845-1124
**http://www.waysidegardens.com**

giving their roses a "natural" environment. Others construct raised beds, either mounded or lined. Either way has merit; make your choice and get to work before rose planting season arrives.

- Estimate how many roses you plan to grow in an area.
- The bed should be 4 to 8 feet wide. Plan at first on 6 feet between plants. You can make a closer calculation later, after the plants have been purchased.
- Remove all grass from the area. If **Bermudagrass** was growing there, remove and discard all soil to a depth of 6 inches.
- Shovel up the remaining soil to a depth of 10 inches.
- Pour a 2-inch-thick layer of soil amendment over the bed.
- Add 4 pounds of bonemeal and four pounds of garden lime per 100 square feet.
- Rototill the soil and amendments together.
- If the bed is not mounded 8 inches above the surrounding soil, add bagged planting soil to the mound. Rototill it completely into the existing bed.

If you choose to line the bed to hold the soil in place, several materials work well:

- Treated lumber (remember to wear gloves when handling)
- Untreated lumber (will last only four to five years)
- Brick (attractive, but mortar joints are beyond the skills of most folks)
- Cinderblock (not very aesthetically appealing; use a cap block to cover the holes)
- Stacked stone (very attractive, but requires a lot of work to build)

## CARE

Existing roses need care during the winter, even during deepest cold.

1. Winter winds can whip **climbing rose** canes against their trellis, damaging the bark. Use jute twine to tie the loose canes firmly in place.

2. Prune out blackened canes whenever you notice them.

3. Keep a 3-inch-thick layer of pine straw mulch under plants at all times.

## WATERING

Roses cannot tolerate soggy soil—even in winter. If your rose bed is constantly damp, make a mounded bed.

- Dig up the rose after pruning.
- For each rose, pour a bag of topsoil and a bag of gritty paver leveling sand over the area, and mix it with the existing soil.
- Plant your rose(s) in the resulting mound.
- Tamp down the soil around the rose roots with your shoe.

Water any plants you put in last fall. One to 2 gallons of water per plant is sufficient. Remember to drain the hose after every use so it does not freeze and crack.

## FERTILIZING

Roses are dormant in winter and do not need fertilizing.

## PROBLEMS

The pine vole is a rodent about the size of a mouse. Voles live under brushpiles and in hollow logs; they scurry about, hidden under mulch and groundcovers, looking for plant stems to gnaw

on. A vole-damaged rose may suddenly break off at ground level and show clear evidence of gnawing at the soil line.

- Pull back mulch 6 inches from the stem(s) of each plant. Be sure to keep the mulch away from the stems at all times.
- Do not pile brush near your rose garden. Put it at the far edge of your property.
- Keep the weeds at the edge of your property line cut short.
- Voles may be killed with a mousetrap baited with peanut butter. Be sure to cover the trap with an upturned plastic pot so no other animals are harmed. Some gardeners put a slice of apple under the pot to lure the vole to his last lunch.

## PRUNING

Bright winter days make it easy to see dead branches in the center of a rosebush. Though it is too early to perform your spring pruning, dead limbs can be removed any time you notice them.

## HELPFUL HINTS

Many **climbing roses** bloom only at the ends of the canes. This is due to the uneven distribution of plant hormones along the cane. You can encourage flowering all along the cane by arching the tip of the canes outward—almost horizontally at the end. Another technique is to loop back the ends of the canes so they point toward the base of the bush. Allow horizontal stems to develop along the canes. These will then produce the majority of your flowers.

# FEBRUARY

## ROSES

 ### PLANNING

Roses need at least 4 to 6 hours of full sunshine each day. A location that receives morning sunshine and afternoon shade is best because the leaves dry off faster, offering some protection against black spot and powdery mildew diseases.

 ### PLANTING

Plant **potted** and **bare-root roses** now, a few weeks before the last frost. Before planting, prune away any dead or broken branches.

**Bare-root Roses**

• Dig a hole 12 inches deep and 18 inches wide in your prepared bed.

• Form a cone of earth in the middle. Spread the rose roots on all sides of the cone.

• Fill the hole with the soil that has been removed, tamping it firmly as you go.

**Potted Roses**

• Dig a hole 12 inches deep and 24 inches wide in your prepared bed.

• Gently untangle and spread the roots in all directions in the planting hole.

• Fill the hole with soil that has been removed, tamping it firmly as you go.

Plant bare-root roses over a mound of soil in the planting hole; drape the roots over the mound.

 ### CARE

If you order roses from a catalog, they will be shipped bare-root in order to minimize costs. **Bare-root roses** are also available at local nurseries; the roots will usually be wrapped in damp wood shavings.

• When your roses arrive home, decide if you can plant immediately or if the plants must be held for awhile.

• If the holding interval will be only twenty-four to forty-eight hours, simply spray water on the roots and rewrap them.

• If holding for several days, plant them in potting soil in 2- or 3-gallon pots. Protect them from freezing while you prepare their new home (see January).

 ### WATERING

After planting roses, soak the soil around them thoroughly. This settles the soil and drives out air pockets.

 ### FERTILIZING

Roses bloom best when the soil has a pH of 6.0 to 6.5. For existing rose beds, have your soil tested (see Horticultural Practices, p. 7), and add garden lime and other nutrients to your beds if recommended.

• Phosphorus and lime do not move rapidly down to the plant root zone; it is best to mix them both with your soil when planting a rose.

• In the absence of a soil test, thoroughly mix 1/2 cup lime and 2 tablespoons 0-46-0 (triple superphosphate) with the soil you pack around the roots of each rose.

## PROBLEMS

Few sights are more heartbreaking than roses chewed to the ground by deer. If deer constantly enter your garden, spray valuable roses with a deer-repellent. Many products are available, but their success rate varies. Deer will eat just about anything if they are hungry enough. Plan to spray every week, or more often if damage is evident. Year-round spraying is often necessary, switching products at monthly intervals. Some gardeners fall back on deerproof fencing as their best defense (see Edibles, August).

## HELPFUL HINTS

Roses are the most popular flower given on Valentine's Day. Follow these hints to keep yours looking their best:

• When purchasing cut roses, look for flowers with petals that are just starting to unfurl and buds that are springy to the touch.

• Buy a package of floral preservative. Bleach, aspirin, and soft drinks do not help a rose, but commercial products are specially blended to prolong rose beauty.

• When you arrive home, cut at least 1 inch from the bottom of the stems. Hold the stems completely under water as you do this.

• Place in a vase with lukewarm water to which preservative has been added.

• Every two days, clean the vase, recut the stems, and add warm water and more preservative.

• You can remove one or two outer petals from a bloom if they begin to fade.

• If roses begin to droop, submerge the whole stem in water and let it soak for a few hours.

## PRUNING

Prune **bush roses** severely between now and March 15; the new growth that is produced will bear most of this year's rose blooms. Wait until June to prune **climbing roses.**

• Remove dead, weak, or damaged canes. Make a flat cut 1/2 inch below the dead or damaged portion.

• Cut away limbs that rub against another or cross through the center of the plant.

• To shorten a living branch, make a 45-degree-angle cut 1/4 inch above a bud that points outward from the plant.

• If your rose has been pruned every year, prune back the size of the plant by 1/3.

• If the rosebush is completely overgrown, 1/2 to 2/3 of the plant might need to be removed.

# MARCH

## ROSES

### PLANNING

**Climbing** and **trailing roses** can surprise you with their appetite for space. Study the label that comes with a new rose and space it accordingly.

• Plant roses at least 30 inches from a building. Otherwise, they will lean outward, and the lower branches will become bare.

• Plant roses at least 4 feet from other large plants. Roses are heavy feeders and will compete with their neighbors for nourishment.

### PLANTING

If a nearby tree has begun to shade your rose bed, you can either remove the tree or move your roses. Most gardeners prefer the latter.

1. Prune the rose first so you can work without suffering too many wounds.

2. Use a spading fork to lift and explore the soil 2 feet in all directions from the trunk, looking for shallow main roots.

3. When you have identified the main roots, lift them completely from the ground, working from 3 feet away from the plant towards its center. Use hand-pruners to cut roots that plunge vertically.

4. Thrust a sharp shovel into the soil around the plant, 1 foot from the trunk. Continue in the same manner around the plant, avoiding the previously excavated roots, until you have gone all the way around the plant.

5. With a mighty heave, lever the plant rootball out of the ground. Mist the roots with water and cover with plastic to keep them moist.

6. Plant in a new, sunny bed as soon as possible. See January, Planting, for tips on making a new bed.

### CARE

It is important to coat both the tops and the undersides of leaves when applying pesticides. This is difficult to accomplish with dusts but easier with sprays. Spray the underside of leaves first, follow with a light spray over the top.

**Important:** Read and follow all label directions when using a pesticide.

### WATERING

Newly planted roses, especially bare-root plants, need regular watering. Give each plant at least 3 gallons of water per week in the absence of rain.

Allow the soil to dry somewhat between waterings.

### FERTILIZING

Roses need regular fertilization in order to grow the leaves and branches that will support new blooms. Follow these steps to fertilize newly planted roses:

1. In March, topdress the soil under each plant with 1 cup bonemeal and 1 cup cottonseed meal. Scratch them into the soil, and water with 1 gallon of water in which $1/4$ cup Epsom salts (magnesium sulfate) has been dissolved.

2. Add 1 cup bloodmeal under each plant in April.

3. When the plant has grown many new leaves and seems healthy, begin using 2 tablespoons of 10-10-10 per foot of plant height each month until September. Use half the rate in July and August . . . *or* . . . use water-soluble fertilizer (Miracle-Gro®) at the rate and frequency recommended on the label.

To fertilize established **shrub** and **climbing roses,** follow these steps:

1. In March, topdress the soil under each plant with 1 cup bonemeal, 1 cup cottonseed meal, $1/2$ cup bloodmeal, and $1/4$ cup Epsom salts (dissolved in water). Scratch into the soil and water lightly.

2. Beginning in April, use 3 tablespoons 10-10-10 per foot of height per plant. Repeat monthly until September. Use half the rate in July and August . . . *or* . . . use water-soluble fertilizer (Miracle-Gro®) at the rate and frequency recommended on the label.

## PROBLEMS

Our heat and humidity make Georgia a prime site for rose black spot, a fungus disease of rose leaves. **Old-fashioned roses** tolerate the disease by shedding some, but not all leaves. Many of the newer **hybrid tea roses** will shed most of their leaves by July

A rose leaf with blackspot.

### HELPFUL HINTS

Sealing cuts is usually not necessary if rose pruning is done during chilly weather. On canes larger than $1/2$ inch, or if you have previously had problems with rose cane borers, smear white glue onto the cut end of the cane. Cane borers are the immature form of one of several insects. Borers damage a rose by tunneling into the stem or boring around the stem under the bark. Swollen or cracked stems signal their presence.

if black spot is not controlled. Here are some organic strategies for black spot control:

• Plant only roses that are known to have tolerance or resistance to the disease.

• Pick off and discard diseased leaves as soon as you notice them.

• Spray, beginning when leaves appear, with a mixture of 1 tablespoon baking soda, 2 tablespoons horticultural oil, and 1 gallon water. Repeat every seven days. This mixture will not completely protect from disease, but it will delay disease onset.

• Neem oil has shown some promise as a fungicide and may also be used.

• Replace the mulch under your rose every spring.

Chemical strategies for black spot control:

• Spray, beginning when leaves appear, with chlorothalonil, or triforine or myclobutanil. Repeat the spray every two weeks.

• Every month, change the chemical you use. This reduces the possibility of the fungus developing resistance to a single chemical.

Annual weeds can be controlled by applying a weed-preventer to your rose beds now.

## PRUNING

**"Tree" roses** have been pruned and trained to grow into a tight head of leaves and blooms topping a single straight stem (the standard). To keep the head compact, prune it back by half, leaving as many forks and short branches as possible. After pruning, retie the standard to its support structure if one is present.

# APRIL
## ROSES

### PLANNING

Roses do not serve well as foundation plants near a home. They may be covered with blooms and leaves during the warm season, but they are leafless in winter. There are several ways to use them as part of a landscape:

- Use roses in a mass planting in front of a hedge or in a shrub border.
- Train **trailing roses** to cover a fence.
- Plant **climbing roses** on either side of an arbor.
- Install **miniature roses** in a bed of perennial flowers.

### PLANTING

Roses make good container plants outside on your patio. You can enjoy them when blooms are present, and move them back to a less conspicuous spot when the show is over. Select **roses** that grow medium-sized or smaller.

- To keep the plants upright, use a 24-inch-wide or larger pot, except when planting miniature-sized rose plants. Clay pots or wooden containers "breathe" better than do plastic pots.

- Purchase a good-quality potting soil. It should be light and fluffy, not heavy and smelly.
- Place the rose in the sunniest spot possible.
- Check soil moisture every day. Plan to water daily during the heat of summer.

### CARE

If you want large, exhibition-quality flowers, you can encourage their formation on **hybrid tea** roses by disbudding several individual stems. Select a stem that has a small but healthy-looking bud at the tip. Cut off any side buds below it.

This directs the plant's energy into producing a large bloom on that stem instead of a few smaller flowers.

### WATERING

Check on roses that you planted earlier this spring.

- Pull back the mulch underneath the plant.
- Make sure the top of the rootball is still at (or slightly below) the surrounding soil surface. If not, pull mulch away completely and add soil to the proper height.
- Replace mulch and water.

Disbudding individual stems on a hybrid tea, such as this 'Peace' rose, help develop large, stunning blooms.

### FERTILIZING

Fertilize each plant at mid-month with 10-10-10 or water-soluble fertilizer (see March). It is not necessary to remove the mulch before fertilizing; irrigation and rainfall will take the nutrients to the roots.

# PROBLEMS

Look for aphids clustered at the tips of fast-growing branches.

• Blast them off with a water hose, and give a ground-dwelling spider a hearty meal.

• Examine nearby leaves for ladybugs. Do not use insecticides if you see them: ladybugs (and their orange, alligator-like offspring) consume aphids voraciously.

• Tiny, light-brown pods on the backsides of leaves signify you have been joined by another garden friend: tiny, harmless wasps that parasitize and kill aphids. The pods are the parasitized, dying aphids.

• If you are using a fungicide, continue spraying every two weeks (see March).

Were the edges of your rose petals brown when they opened last year? See May, Problems, for a description of thrips.

Now, before buds open, apply a systemic rose insecticide containing disulfoton, dimethoate, or imidacloprid) to control thrips.

## HELPFUL HINTS

Do not allow winter weeds like chickweed or henbit to grow beneath your roses. Pull them out and sprinkle more mulch in their place to inhibit any sprouts you left behind.

# PRUNING

Many rose plants are produced by grafting a desirable rose onto the stem of a vigorous, but possibly unattractive, rose (the rootstock). The area where the two join is called the graft union. It looks like a swollen knob a few inches above ground level. Don't leave stubs on the graft union when pruning. A fine-toothed saw blade or sharp knife makes clean cuts and permits you to get close to the graft.

Roses that have been grafted onto a rootstock may produce thin sprouts (suckers) arising from the ground around the trunk, or below the graft union. The flowers produced on these suckers will not be the same as those on the grafted rose above. Prune away all suckers back to the root or stem from which they come.

Do not simply cut flush with the ground—follow the sucker back to the origination point on the main plant to make your cut.

If the rose is growing on its own roots, flowers on the suckers will be identical to those on the parent.

You may choose to leave these suckers, in order to have a bigger plant, or to remove them.

"Own-root" roses are those that have been propagated by rooting a cutting rather than grafting.

Some rose fanciers believe that own-root roses are more vigorous, more long-lived, and, if the top is frozen, able to sprout back true to the original variety.

# MAY

## ROSES

 PLANNING

As the first flowers on your **shrub roses** fade, remove them regularly. This will allow new flowers to form.

Notice that roses have compound leaves composed of three to seven small leaflets. Whether cutting roses for display indoors or just to remove old flowers, make your cut just above a "five-leaflet" leaf. Buds growing at the base of "five-leaflet" leaves will produce long stems and healthy flowers. Buds growing at the base of "three-leaflet" leaves are more likely to produce weak stems and flowers. If you prune down to a "seven-leaflet" leaf, you will remove too much of the plant.

Make cuts just above a five-leaflet leaf.

 PLANTING

Container-grown roses have been in your local nursery for months by this time. When you remove one from the pot prior to planting, you may find a thick mat of encircling roots.

• Use pruners to cut off any thick roots on the rootball surface. (You could choose to untangle them instead, but this would be time-consuming.)

• Shake the rootball vigorously to loosen roots and remove potting soil from the surface. Roots will now be more likely to explore the surrounding soil when you plant.

• Spread the roots in the planting hole as much as possible before filling with native soil.

• Water thoroughly. Check back the next day and add soil if the earth has settled too much.

 CARE

When tying a rose to a supporting structure, the attachment should be strong enough to hold the rose in place but not so tight that the stem is damaged. Many rosarians use a "figure-eight" knot. Use biodegradable jute twine or special green rose tape sold for this purpose.

1. Cut a length sufficient to go around the support once and still have 12 inches left over.

2. Tie the material around the support, using a square knot. Two 6-inch lengths should dangle next to the rose stem.

3. Pull the cane gently to the support, and tie another square knot around it. Don't strangle the stem. The tie should be loose enough to allow the cane to slip freely within it.

4. Clip off any excess tying material.

 WATERING

**Rose standards** (those trained to have a single upright stem topped by foliage and flowers) are sometimes used as potted patio plants. Check the soil's moisture in the pots daily until you have a good feel for how often they need to be watered. When the top inch of soil is dry, water until the water runs from the bottom of the pot.

If the soil is dry every day, the container is too small. Repot the rose into a container that is double the size of the present one.

Check on roses you planted within the last six months. They will not yet have enough roots to easily survive the summer. Water them deeply each week. Use a trowel to check how far the water penetrates (6 inches is a good depth). Two gallons of water are usually sufficient.

## FERTILIZING

Fertilize each rose plant in mid-month with 10-10-10 or water-soluble fertilizer (see March).

Roses growing in containers need more frequent feeding that those growing outdoors (constant watering leaches fertilizer out of the potting soil). Use a slow-release granular fertilizer that dispenses fertilizer each time the plant is watered, or use a liquid fertilizer: cut the recommended dosage in half, but use it twice as often as the label indicates.

## PROBLEMS

Powdery mildew is a leaf disease whose name perfectly describes its appearance: white powder covering individual leaves and flower buds. It is common in spring and fall when days are warm and humid and nights are cool. Roses that have been planted too close together or where the air remains still are easy victims.

## HELPFUL HINTS

Fragrance varies widely among roses. The smell will be strongest on a warm and humid afternoon and weakest on a rainy morning. See November for a list of fragrant roses.

• Plant roses where they have plenty of room between adjacent plants.

• Do not plant roses close to a wall or solid fence.

• If you have had a powdery mildew problem before, select resistant varieties for planting.

• A fungicide spray can be used to control the disease.

The fungi that cause rose diseases can become resistant to a chemical if it is used over and over. To prevent resistance, change to a different fungicide chemical each month (see March).

Read the product label to make sure you are purchasing a different chemical, not just a different brand.

Rose thrips are tiny yellowish insects that damage rose petals by scraping the cells with their mouth parts in order to suck plant juice. Though they are barely visible to the naked eye, their damage is easy to see: brown edges on rose flower petals. If you suspect thrips are present, cut a damaged rose

bloom and slap it against a page of white paper. You'll be able to see the thrips scurrying for cover. Many beneficial insects (lacewings, ladybugs, etc.) feed on thrips. Avoid using contact insecticide sprays. They not only harm the beneficials, but do a poor job of killing thrips.

Pick off and discard infested blooms. Make a thrips trap by coating a bright-yellow card with sticky oil (see Edibles, August). If the problem is severe, use a systemic insecticide.

## PRUNING

Do not let faded blossoms remain on your roses. Remove and discard them regularly, unless you want rose hips (seedpods) to develop. These are often quite attractive.

# JUNE
## ROSES

## PLANNING

There are many kinds of structures onto which **climbing roses** can be trained. The size of the structure should be in keeping with the eventual size of your rose. Roses do not twine around a support; they must be trained to it. This can be done by tying the canes in place or by resting the canes on supportive parts of the structure. Don't weave the canes in and out of narrow spaces on a trellis. They will be impossible to remove when you prune. When training a rose up a pillar, curve it around the post, barber-pole fashion.

You may notice that your **climbing roses** tend to bloom only at the tips. See January for ideas on how to correct this.

## PLANTING

Roses that remain unsold at nurseries are often put on sale in June. Use extreme caution when purchasing sale roses.

• Do not buy a plant with light-yellow foliage—it may be weak from lack of fertilizer.

• Examine each leaf for black spot disease. If found, do not purchase.

Train climbing roses by tying them to supports; it doesn't have to be fancy.

• Pull the rose from its pot and examine the roots. If they are brown, smelly, or non-existent, do not bring the plant into your garden.

## CARE

Perhaps you have a particularly beautiful rose that all your friends admire. Now is a fine time to propagate your rose from cuttings in order to have a nice gift for your friends next spring. Examine stems in mid-June to find those that began growing in April and have now begun to turn from green to brown. A good cutting for rooting is 8 inches long and has brown bark at the base. The stem should not be limber, but should be hard enough to snap when bent.

1. Fill a 6-inch pot with a 50:50 mixture of perlite and peat moss that has been soaked and allowed to completely drain.

2. Dip the severed end of a cutting into a powdered rooting hormone such as Rootone™.

3. Poke a 3-inch-deep hole in the perlite:peat moss mixture with a pencil.

4. Insert the base of the cutting 3 inches into the hole. Firm the soil around it.

5. Insert a pencil or wooden chopstick beside the cutting. The top of the stick should be 2 inches taller than the leaves of the cutting.

6. Slip a clear plastic bag over the pot and cutting. The plastic should touch the leaves minimally. Adjust the wooden stake to keep the plastic from touching the leaves.

7. Place the pot, cutting, and bag in a bright but shady spot. Check the soil every three days to make sure it is moist.

The cutting should be well rooted in six weeks. It can be transplanted to a gallon pot for further growth during the summer.

## WATERING

Regularly water any roses planted in the last nine months. Avoid wetting the foliage when you water. A water wand is very handy. It causes a shower of water to cascade over the mulch at the base of the plant without dislodging it.

Check your soaker hoses to make sure they are working properly before the summer heat sets in.

## FERTILIZING

Follow the fertilization schedule described in March.

## PROBLEMS

Japanese beetles love no plant better than rose leaves and flowers. Nothing is more disheartening than seeing the backsides of a half-dozen beetles merrily feeding on a beautiful blossom. If not controlled, rose leaves will be lace, and the flowers will be disfigured.

### Non-Chemical Control
• In early morning, grab an empty soup can and pour an inch of soapy water in the bottom.

## HELPFUL HINTS

Never put Japanese beetle traps near roses. The scent in the product will attract more beetles than it traps. If you choose to use them, place the traps at the far corners of your property. Experienced gardeners have found that traps attract more pests than they destroy.

• Quietly approach your plants and observe where the cold, slow-moving creatures are resting.
• Gently place the can under a leaf and tap the leaf.
• The beetles will fall off the leaf into the water, and will drown.
• Repeat every morning until the population is decreased.
• Spray leaves with an anti-feedant containing Neem oil. Neem is not 100 percent effective, but beetles seem to avoid eating leaves where it has been applied.

Make a note to apply milky spore disease powder to your lawn in spring. The disease is deadly to Japanese beetle grubs but harmless to animals and birds.

### Chemical Control
• Spray leaves thoroughly with a contact insecticide every three to four days.

• Do not worry if the insects don't immediately fall from the plant—if they come in contact with the insecticide, they will die in a few hours.

Grub-control granules for your lawn are rarely effective in reducing beetle numbers. Japanese beetles can fly from neighboring untreated lawns, and the poison will be for naught.

## PRUNING

In general, **climbing roses** produce most of their blooms in early summer, though some may bloom off-and-on during the season. After they bloom is a good time to prune **climbers** to make them healthier.

• Cut away any old, weak, or woody canes.
• Examine the canes that are left. Depending on the size and vigor of your plant, you should leave three to seven strong and vigorous canes.

# JULY
## ROSES

### PLANNING

Most hybrid roses produce a single flush of blooms in spring or early summer. Some may bloom again in fall. Some species of rose are able to bloom throughout the growing season. Some good repeat bloomers are:

- 'Nearly Wild'
- 'Old Blush'
- 'Archduke Charles'
- Butterfly rose 'Knockout'

### PLANTING

There is no shame in admitting to yourself that a rose has died despite your best efforts. Healthy roses are still available in containers at large nurseries and can be planted now to replace those that fell by the wayside.

- Take extra care when digging a new hole for the rose. If the soil is not rich and moist, add plenty of compost or manure.
- Untangle the roots in the container and spread them outwards in the hole.
- Fill the hole with soil while keeping the roots spread.
- Water deeply, and cancel any long vacations you've planned—this new bloomer will need regular weekly watering between now and October.

Butterfly rose

### CARE

Roses that have limber stems can be propagated by soil layering. Like any plant propagated from a cutting, the new plant will be a genetic duplicate of the rose from which it came. Follow these steps for soil layering:

1. Bend a stem down until it touches the earth. Use a dull knife to gently scrape the bark from the stem in a 1-inch-wide area at the point where it touches the soil.

2. Dust the wounded stem with Rootone™.

3. Use a trowel to scoop a shallow depression in the soil under the scraped area.

4. Lay the stem in the depression. Cover it with damp soil and place a brick on top to hold it in place. In four months, roots will form underground. You can clip the stem that goes back to the mother plant but do not dig up your new plant.

5. Water the rooted plant regularly until it loses its leaves.

The new, well-rooted plant can be moved next spring.

Brown jute twine makes a good material for tying rose canes to an arbor. Unlike nylon, the twine will rot after one season and will not harm plant stems.

## WATERING

Give roses that were planted last spring at least 2 gallons of water per week.

Check the depth of the mulch under your plants. It should be at least 2 inches thick.

If mulch is touching the stem, pull it back a few inches from the stem of the rose.

## FERTILIZING

Halve your fertilization rate during the hot months of summer. Fertilizer will force a rose to produce new leaves, which will demand water that may be scarce (see March).

## PROBLEMS

Spider mites are tiny members of the arthropod family that suck sap from rose leaves. They are not insects, because they have eight legs, like spiders. Most insecticides do not control them; instead, the insecticide kills the beneficial insects which can keep a small mite invasion in check. To identify spider mites, look for creatures that are about the size of a grain of salt and may be red, yellow, or orange. Damage such as bronzed or stippled yellow leaves may be the first indication they are active; tiny webs between the base of a leaf and the stem of a plant may be present. To control spider mites:

• Examine leaves weekly during the hot and dry days of summer. If mites are found early, use a stiff spray of water daily to wash them off.

• Spray leaves thoroughly with horticultural oil.

• A miticide can be used if the population is widespread.

• Avoid planting **verbena** and **foxglove** (they're spider mite magnets!) near your roses.

Rose slugs are not true slugs but the larvae of small sawflies. They feed from underneath a leaf, consuming the soft tissue between the veins. The damage appears similar to the damage caused by Japanese beetles feeding, but rose slugs eventually chew large holes in leaves rather than leaving them skeletonized.

Hit the underside of leaves with a stiff spray of water. Insecticidal soap is very effective on rose slugs.

## PRUNING

Look for extremely weak or dead limbs every time you walk through your rose garden.

Use a sharp pair of pruners to remove any you find.

The broad blades of common handpruners are sometimes too big to fit easily into tight spots on a rosebush. Look for special rose pruners, such as Felco #6, to make pruning easier—its handles are also smaller and more comfortable for female operators.

It is a good idea to occasionally sterilize your pruners, even if you are not aware of any diseases that are present. Sterilize them with 1 part bleach mixed with 9 parts water.

---

**HELPFUL HINTS**

If you are forced to dig a hole for a post for a rose arbor this month, first let your water hose trickle moisture into the spot all night long. The water will soften the soil from its concrete-like state. You might have to stop digging after the first foot and allow another night's trickling to soften the soil even deeper.

# AUGUST

## ROSES

### PLANNING

Some roses have been developed to spread across the ground, becoming a garden groundcover rather than a **shrub** or a **climber.** The blooms may not be huge, but several **groundcover roses** are very resistant to diseases and insects. Use shears or a lawn mower raised to its highest setting in spring and fall to keep **groundcover roses** neat and at a uniform height.

### PLANTING

If you move from one home to another in August, you might want to carry your favorite roses with you. Although transplanting in the heat of summer is not recommended, it can be done successfully:

1. Prune roses to a manageable size one week before you intend to dig them. Water thoroughly.

2. Collect a sturdy cardboard box for each plant. Line the inside with a plastic garbage bag. Poke drainage holes in the plastic.

3. Dig each rose carefully, remembering that the roots must fit in the box.

4. When the plant is in the box, cover the roots with moist soil. Insert a label with the rose name or description. Place the boxes in the shade near an outdoor faucet at your new home.

5. Inspect the plants daily, water when needed, and plant within two weeks of moving. Although you might have only bare stems left, healthy roses can usually recover their form in a year or two.

### CARE

Part of the enjoyment of roses is to recognize different ones by name. If you grow more than one or two roses, it can be difficult to remember which roses you have. Make it a practice to label each as it is planted, using a permanent label.

• White plastic stakes are inexpensive, but they become brittle, breaking easily after one year.

• Metal labels that stand atop two thick wire legs are durable but can be lost or pulled by accident.

• Thin metal tags that are attached to a rose stem by loose

'Red Meidiland' is a well-known groundcover rose.

wire aren't likely to be lost but are difficult to read without risking contact with the rose thorns.

See the Helpful Hint to learn how to make your own rose tags.

## WATERING

Sometimes rose leaves begin to wilt even though you are watering regularly. Wilting can be caused by too much water (which causes root rot) as well as too little.

• Pull mulch back from the base of the plant before you water. Scrape the soil with a trowel.

• If the soil is moist down to 2 inches deep, no water is needed. Wait until the soil is barely damp at the 2-inch level before watering again.

• If the plant continues to wilt, dig it up and examine the roots to determine if they are healthy. Healthy roots feel firm, not mushy, when squeezed between your fingers. The soil should smell "musty" but not "stinky." If the roots do seem rotted, remove them, replant the rose, and correct your watering practices.

## FERTILIZING

Fertilize roses with 1 to 2 tablespoons of 10-10-10 per foot of height now, accompanied by the pruning noted below.

---

## HELPFUL HINT

Make your own rose tags:

1. Purchase a package of thin aluminum cookie sheets at the grocery store.

2. Use scissors (not your best ones!) to cut rectangular tags 1 inch wide by 3 inches long.

3. Using a ballpoint pen, print the name of the rose on the aluminum. The metal is so thin that it will be embossed by the lettering.

4. Punch a hole near the end of the tag with a hammer and small nail. Thread 6 inches of thin wire (ask the neighborhood handyperson for some) halfway through the hole. Give the two "legs" of wire a twist or two.

5. Attach the tag to a low limb with the wire.

---

For a quick pick-me-up, spray rose leaves directly with a diluted liquid fertilizer (Miracle-Gro®, etc.). Dilute the fertilizer to $1/4$ the rate recommended for soil application. A tablespoon of Epsom salts (magnesium sulfate) per gallon of liquid fertilizer adds magnesium to the soil.

## PROBLEMS

If you read much about roses, you may see mentions of fungicide products with which you are not familiar. If the chemical name is mentioned, write it down exactly so you can take it to your local nursery. If they have never heard of it, call your County Extension office for their expertise—it is possible that the fungicide is only available to professional rose growers or that

it is so expensive that the average gardener could not afford it.

## PRUNING

Rose blooms are borne on new growth. If you are able to water your roses regularly during this hot season, they can be cut back to stimulate new twigs that will bear flowers in September

• In the southern half of Georgia, cut back **bush roses** by $1/2$.

• In the northern half of the state, cut back **bush roses** by $1/3$.

• **Ever-blooming roses** such as 'Nearly Wild' and 'Knockout' rose benefit from a good shearing now, even though they have many flowers.

# SEPTEMBER

## ROSES

### PLANNING

If you have an informal garden, you might consider incorporating roses into your perennial flower garden. **Clematis** and roses make happy companions. Vigorous free-flowering **clematis** vines can be easily trained to grow through a rose plant. Attach the stems to the canes with jute or string. The rose acts as a living trellis. Plant the **clematis** at least 2 feet away from the rose, and lead the stems of the **clematis** to the rose with strings or thin bamboo cane.

They can be fertilized together since they are heavy feeders.

**Other Rose Companions**

• Try some herbs: **oregano, rosemary,** and **thyme.**

• *Erigeron* 'Profusion' has white to pink small daisy flowers throughout the summer; this spreading plant grows to about 10 inches high.

• *Geranium macrorrhizum* has magenta flowers in spring and good fall color; it is easy to grow.

• *Geranium sanguineum* var. *striatum* has light-pink flowers with crimson veins.

• *Geranium* 'Johnson's Blue' is a **hardy geranium** that produces a profusion of blue flowers in spring.

Roses need not always be planted in formal beds; they can be used as hedges or as part of a border. Though they aren't dense enough to make an opaque screen, like a **holly,** they can obstruct rambunctious children and pets without being un-neighborly. Be sure to check plant labels for height, width, and appropriate spacing when buying roses for hedges or privacy. You might want to try 'Cecile Brunner', 'Nearly Wild', 'Archduke Charles', and 'Carefree Beauty'.

### PLANTING

You may someday find an old, possibly **heirloom**, rose that has been completely covered by vines or adjacent shrubbery. It is too weak to move now but could be strong enough by spring if it is uncovered and pampered:

• Prune away the vine or shrub covering the rose. Try not to break rose stems or pull off leaves. Prune nearby trees and shrubs, if possible, to allow more light to reach the rose.

• Fertilize the rose with houseplant fertilizer diluted to half strength.

• Move the rose in early spring to a "nurse bed." Note the flower color when it blooms and observe whether it seems prone to black spot or powdery mildew. If it is not vigorous and healthy after one year, toss it on the compost pile. Don't struggle to grow a loser.

• If the rose performs well, add it to your permanent collection and try to find out its real name from local rosarians!

### CARE

Continue to remove faded flowers from **ever-blooming roses**. Prune out dead stems. Pull weeds as they appear. Edge your beds using a hand- or motorized edger.

### WATERING

The usual lawn sprinkler system is fine for your turf but bad for roses; wet leaves lead to diseases that are almost impossible to control. Try a drip system or use black rubber soaker hoses instead.

• Drip systems come in kits containing all the parts to water several plants.

• Soaker hoses can be snaked near each plant under the mulch. The soaker hose is attached directly to your water hose (see Helpful Hint).

## FERTILIZING

Fertilize each plant in mid-month with 1 to 3 tablespoons of 10-10-10 per foot of plant height, or use a water-soluble fertilizer like Miracle-Gro®.

Some rose growers swear by the magical powers of alfalfa pellets (sold at seed and feed stores as animal food). Alfalfa tea is a great fall potion that doesn't interfere with normal rose growth.

1. Add 10 to 12 cups of alfalfa meal or pellets to a 32-gallon plastic garbage can that has a lid.

2. Add water, stir, and steep for four or five days, stirring occasionally; you may also add 2 cups of Epsom salts.

3. The tea will start to smell in about three days, so keep the lid on. Schedule the opening of the barrel for when the rest of the family is away.

### HELPFUL HINT

Black rubber soaker hoses are sold wrapped in a tight circle that is almost impossible to untangle and lay out without help. You can do it single-handedly by slightly pressurizing the hose with water.

• Choose a hot day; wear old clothes and tennis shoes.

• Lay out the soaker hose near your plants.

• Connect the soaker to your water hose. Turn on the water at full flow for a moment.

• Cut the water flow to a trickle, just enough for a bit of water to weep from the soaker.

• Pull back mulch, put the soaker in place, and re-cover with mulch.

• An inexpensive water timer attached at the faucet makes watering your roses a breeze.

4. Use a gallon of brown "tea" on large rosebushes to make strong canes and green leaves late in the growing season.

## PROBLEMS

Caterpillars are not typically a major rose pest, but September is the month you'll notice them, if at all. Caterpillar damage is usually in the form of irregular holes chewed at leaf edges. Small leaves may have more than half of the leaf consumed. The disease spore *Bacillus thuringiensis*, commonly called B.t., is an excellent caterpillar control. B.t. is not harmful to birds or humans or other mammals. Apply the spray or dust thoroughly to cover your rose leaves.

B.t. is deactivated within a few days, so repeat applications may be necessary.

Replace all the mulch under your roses. This will prevent diseases on next year's leaves.

## PRUNING

Prune **hybrid tea** and **grandiflora** roses to remove dead limbs and to shape them for winter.

# OCTOBER

## ROSES

### PLANNING

One of the best ways to succeed with roses is to grow varieties recommended by experts. When you have proven that roses are easy to grow in your landscape, you can branch out to grow varieties about which you know nothing but that intrigue you.

### PLANTING

This is an excellent time to transplant roses (see March). As plants lose their leaves, less water is demanded from the roots; the soil is still warm, and root growth can occur in the new bed before winter.

Rose growers can be divided into three classes: lackadaisical, committed, and fanatic. Those in the first class dig a small planting hole, shove the rose in place, and hope it survives. Committed rose growers rototill their soil and add organic amendments. Fanatic rose growers develop their very own special rose soil and use it whenever they plant. If you are one of the fanatical rose growers, you can take the advice of Pat Henry, the owner of Roses Unlimited (see January list). She digs a hole 18 inches deep and wide, fills the hole halfway with the following soil mixture, then packs more around her rose roots as she plants it. Pat swears by the results!

**Pat Henry's Special Rose Soil**

In a wheelbarrow, mix enough of the following ingredients, in the proportions indicated, to fill the hole:

- 1 part compost
- 1 part peat moss
- 1 part good topsoil
- 1 part red clay

Add and mix thoroughly:

- 1 cup 0-46-0 (superphosphate)
- 1 cup dolomitic lime
- 2 cups alfalfa meal or pellets
- 1 cup gypsum

### CARE

- Tip back long canes that are in the way as you walk through the garden.
- Re-tie the canes of **climbing roses** to their support structure. It is easier to do this now than when icy winds are howling through your garden.
- Pull weeds from underneath your plants.

**Miniature rose** plants are often a temptation when seen at a garden center or on the floral aisle of a grocery store. The plants are small enough to keep indoors and enjoy through the coming winter. Unfortunately, **miniature roses** kept indoors never seem to prosper. They are susceptible to spider mites, root rot, leaf diseases, and low humidity. To maximize your chances for success, heed the following tips:

- Place **miniatures** near a very bright window but never touching the glass. Plan to turn the pot halfway around each week to keep the plant symmetrical.
- If you don't have a well-lit window, build a light stand (see Annuals, February).
- Water only if the soil seems dry to the touch. Do not overwater.
- Keep a sharp eye out for spider mites or mealybugs on the leaves. Control them at once with an insecticide labeled for indoor use.
- Though the blooms are small, a **miniature rose** planted outdoors will eventually rival in size of some of the larger-blooming types.

### WATERING

One way to minimize watering and weeds at the same time is to use landscape fabric under your roses. Landscape fabric is a porous plastic material that allows water and fertilizer to come through but does not allow weeds to grow up through it.

1. Spread the fabric over your well-tilled rose bed before planting.

2. Cut an "X" with a razor knife where you wish to plant a rose.

3. Plant through the fabric. Tuck the fabric around the stem when finished. (If you decide to use the fabric after your roses are established, cut the fabric into strips that can be placed between and alongside individual plants. Avoid arranging the fabric more than two layers thick.)

4. Cover the landscape fabric with mulch.

5. Remove and renew the mulch every two years. As it decomposes, weed seeds will sprout in it, which is the situation you're trying to avoid.

## FERTILIZING

Do not fertilize now. The nitrogen in the fertilizer could cause your roses to be less cold-tolerant.

## HELPFUL HINTS

Several rose societies meet regularly in Georgia. To find the group nearest you, write the American Rose Society:

The American Rose Society
P.O. Box 30,000
Shreveport, LA 71130

The society's Web site (**www.ars.org**) offers a huge amount of information on rose culture, expert advice, and rose society contacts.

## PROBLEMS

Rose mosaic virus is a common rose disease that seems to do little harm. It appears as a bright-yellow mottling on individual rose leaves or small branches. The disease is not fatal to plants, but it may reduce flowering and cause early autumn leaf drop. The disease is not spread by insects, by water splash, or by pruning tools. Amateur rosarians simply prune off the affected leaves.

Professionals seek out roses from reputable growers who can guarantee that their plants are disease-free. These roses will remain healthy unless accidentally infected.

## PRUNING

Take time to examine each rose plant individually. Prune out any dead branches or weak limbs.

1/50"

Spider Mite

185

# NOVEMBER

## ROSES

 PLANNING

More than a few gardeners avoid roses because of their thorns. Though most roses have thorns of varying ferocity, some are known to be quite amiable. See the list on page 288.

 PLANTING

Roses can still be planted or transplanted in the southern part of the state.

 CARE

Here's some good news for gardeners who have grown roses in the colder parts of the United States. Temperatures in Georgia do not usually drop low enough to permanently harm roses. While a late spring frost can eliminate rose blooms for the season, cold rarely kills Georgia roses. You can put away your rose hoops, bales of straw, and snow shelters.

Tie down the canes of **climbing roses** so they can't whip against their arbor in the wind.

### HELPFUL HINTS

Though your roses have faded, you can still remember their fragrance by making potpourri. Use ingredients you find at a craft shop for your first experiments. Next year you can collect fragrant rose petals and fragrant leaves, blooms, and colorful berries from other plants. A typical potpourri consists of:
- Flower buds, blooms, or petals
- Differing textures added by leaves, peels, or berries
- A fixative to hold the scent of the various components
- Essential oils to add strong scents (such as cinnamon or citrus) to the mix

Once you have gained confidence making potpourri, you can spend next November making personalized mixtures as gifts for your friends during the upcoming holidays.

 WATERING

Roses need at least twelve months to establish or to reestablish a root system.

Water regularly any roses that have been planted or transplanted in the last six months.

 FERTILIZING

Do not fertilize roses during their dormant season.

Organic fertilizers such as cottonseed meal, bloodmeal, or bonemeal that have been stored for the winter are attractive food for opossums, rats, and raccoons.

Store organic products such as these in a metal trash can that has a tightly fitting lid.

 PROBLEMS

Thoroughly clean your garden sprayer (see Edibles, November), and allow it to dry before storing for the winter.

 PRUNING

Prune out any dead branches or "in-the-way" limbs.

# DECEMBER

## ROSES

### PLANNING

Some gardeners plan their rose beds so they will be as attractive when the blooms are absent as when the plants are covered with blossoms. Rose hips are the fruit (seed container) of a rose bloom. As they age in fall, the hips turn vivid shades of yellow, orange, and red. They are edible and are an excellent source of vitamin C. Do not remove flowers after they fade or the hips will not form. Roses with attractive hips are:

- 'Dortmund'
- 'Frau Dagmar Hartopp'
- 'Old Blush'
- *Rosa rugosa* 'Alba'
- *Rosa rugosa* 'Rubra'

### PLANTING

Roses need not always be planted in the ground. They grow quite nicely in containers if given the sunshine, water, and shade they need.

#### Container Growing Pros

- You can determine the exact flower color before planting in a permanent location.
- You can evaluate if the rose will grow in a semi-shaded spot.

- The rose does not have to compete with its neighbors for sun, moisture, and nutrients.
- There are no worries about soil problems if you use a premium potting soil.
- Maintenance (pruning, fertilizing, spraying, etc.) is easier.

#### Container Growing Cons

- Water management is imperative throughout the year.
- Large containers (at least 5-gallon-size or larger) will be needed for large plants.
- A rose plant must grow in a new container for at least a year before it can be moved to a bed.
- Containers may overheat (see Watering).

### CARE

Roses growing in pots may need protection if winter temperatures threaten to go lower than 20 degrees Fahrenheit. Here's how to keep them safe:

- Move the pot close to the house, preferably against a north- or east-facing wall.
- Wrap the entire plant and pot with burlap or an old sheet. Remove when temperatures warm up.

### WATERING

Summer sunshine in Georgia can heat the soil in black plastic containers enough to kill plant roots. If you choose plastic pots, use the clay-colored type rather than the dark green or black. Group plants close enough so that each shades the other. Use potted foliage perennials to screen the outermost pots. Place a 1-inch layer of small pine nuggets on top of the soil to insulate it.

### FERTILIZING

Do not fertilize this month.

### PROBLEMS

Make sure all your pesticides are stored in a relatively inaccessible spot, preferably a locked cabinet.

If you have pesticides that have lost their label, contact the Georgia Department of Natural Resources at (888)-373-5947, Environmental Protection Division for disposal options. While you clean and straighten your pesticide storage area, take time to reread the label on each product. Note the Caution, Warning, or Danger signal word, and doublecheck your application practices.

# SHRUBS

While trees help create the framework for a garden, shrubs act as the middle ground between trees and the herbaceous layer of perennials and annuals. Both native and exotic, shrubs come in all sizes and shapes and perform myriad functions. Depending on the particular selection, a shrub can play many roles. It can provide screening, privacy, or windbreaks; direct foot traffic; create a source of shelter and food for birds; add color and beauty to the landscape with fragrant and showy flowers; and, in winter, can serve as an evergreen anchor or bright accent with showy stems and bark. Evergreen shrubs, including anise,

boxwood, holly, and cherry laurel, are ideal plants for creating privacy, defining areas of your lawn, making effective hedges, or serving as a backdrop for your perennial garden. Deciduous shrubs like chokeberry, beautyberry, and deciduous hollies provide food and shelter for birds, and they make handsome ornamentals with their colorful displays of berries in fall and winter. Some shrubs, such as butterfly bush, glory bower, and summersweet, attract butterflies and bloom for weeks during the hot summer months.

When you select a shrub, be sure to choose the right plant for your specific environment. Learn about what cultural conditions it requires, such as full sun, part shade, acid soil, or lots of water. This will help you select a plant that will thrive in your garden. It is also useful to know how large a particular shrub will be at maturity. This knowledge will help you site a shrub. For example, if you choose a large holly as a foundation plant in front of windows, it will require constant pruning to keep it in bounds. Refer to the planting charts for information about the cultural requirements and mature size of individual shrubs.

If you have a garden that receives full sun but the soil stays wet, choose plants like *Itea virginica* that will thrive under these conditions. While many native azaleas will flourish in full sun or part shade, many hybrid azaleas will languish if you plant them in full sun. When choosing shrubs for your foundation planting, think beyond broad-leaved evergreens like hollies or camellias. Consider using a mixture of evergreen and deciduous shrubs, including those with brightly colored spring blooms, colorful fall foliage, and fragrant flowers in winter. With this approach you will be more likely to have a garden that offers year-round beauty. If the spot gets sun in the morning and shade in the afternoon, try combining *Fothergilla gardenii* with boxwood and a few of the smaller lace-cap hydrangeas like *Hydrangea serrata* 'Blue Billow'.

With shrubs there is a bit more flexibility than with trees. If you plant a shrub and decide next year that it is in the wrong place, you can move it to another location more easily than you can move a large tree. Still, it is best to do some research before you plant so you won't make costly mistakes.

## PLANTING SHRUBS

Most shrubs available for purchase are grown in containers. In certain cases, large specimens may be offered balled and burlapped. Shrubs grown in containers can be planted throughout the growing season, provided the ground is not frozen, although early spring and fall are best. Follow these steps when you plant your shrubs.

1. Take a soil test before you plant. The results will determine how much lime and other nutrients you need to add. Add soil amendments and rototill to a depth of 8 to 12 inches. This is also a good time to add any lime to the soil (see Perennials, February, Planning).

2. Dig a hole as deep as the container the plant is growing in and twice as wide.

3. Remove the plant from the container. Use a shovel to hit the sides of the container; this will loosen the rootball and make it easier to slide out of the pot.

4. Use a sharp pair of handpruners to make two or three cuts into the bottom of the rootball. This will encourage roots to sprout and establish more quickly.

5. Place the rootball in the hole, and fill in with soil. The top of the rootball should be covered only slightly with soil—piling on lots of extra soil can suffocate surface roots.

6. Water the shrub well (refer to the following Watering section for tips on watering). Soak the rootball and the surrounding soil.

7. Apply a 2-inch layer of mulch around newly planted shrubs. Be sure to keep the mulch away from the main trunk or stems. This will reduce the chances of certain disease and insect problems (see the following Fertilizing section for fertilizer recommendations).

If you have heavy clay soil, plant your shrub high, so that the top third of the rootball is out of the ground. Mound plenty of soil around the rootball, then apply a good layer of mulch. This technique will ensure that your plant doesn't dry out too quickly, and that the roots won't stand in wet soil.

## WATERING

Water your shrubs as soon as you plant or transplant them. Place the hose at the base of a shrub and let a slow stream saturate the area. A good rule of thumb is to apply 1 to 2 gallons per foot of plant height. Water once a week for the first six months unless there is a good rain (one or more inches per week is a good rain).

• When watering by hand, apply 5 gallons of water per 10 square feet. This is approximately the amount of water delivered by a garden hose operating one minute at medium pressure.

• Soaker hoses are effective, too. They can water a swath one foot wide on either side of a hose. Depending on the water pressure, a 50-foot-long soaker hose can water 100 square feet of landscape bed in two or more hours.

• Apply 50 gallons of water per 100 square feet when plants show signs of water stress, such as wilting or leaves that turn blue/gray. In coastal areas where soils are sandy, shrubs may need watering more frequently. Dig down 2 to 3 inches. If the soil is dry at that depth, water.

• During periods of extended drought when it doesn't rain for a month or longer, your shrubs will benefit from supplemental watering.

## FERTILIZING

If your shrubs are vigorous and they put on new growth each season, you probably don't need to fertilize. If fifty percent of the leaves are pale and yellow and the plant lacks overall vigor, you can fertilize three times a year. Fertilize once in early spring, once in early summer, and then once in the fall. If you fertilize with a slow-release granular product like Nursery Special in early winter when shrubs are dormant, this will replace the spring-time application of fertilizer. When you plant new shrubs, you can use a starter fertilizer. These products have a high percentage of phosphorus to help establish roots quickly. A fertilizer with a ratio like 5-20-10 is fine. If you don't use a starter fertilizer, you can use a balanced fertilizer like 10-10-10, but you need only to apply one or the other. Read the label carefully before applying any fertilizers.

## PRUNING

Gardeners are often confused about why and when to prune their shrubs. While it's true that your shrubs will grow and bloom even if you don't prune them, a certain amount of pruning, depending on the type of shrub, can help keep a shrub vigorous, increase flower production, and improve overall appearance.

There is no ideal shape or form for shrubs, but there are some useful guidelines for pruning.

• Pruning to remove dead or diseased wood on a regular basis helps to keep shrubs vigorous and can be done during any season.

• Drastic pruning (reducing a shrub by $1/3$ to $1/2$, perhaps to renovate an old shrub that is overgrown and has stopped blooming) should be done in early spring right before the shrub begins to put out new growth (see March for details on renovating overgrown shrubs).

• When deciduous shrubs are dormant, it is easier to see their natural growth habit, which will help guide you when you prune.

• Selecting the right shrub for the right spot can reduce the amount of pruning. For example, forsythia is a large shrub that when left unpruned forms a graceful fountain of foliage. For this reason it is best sited in a spot where it won't have to be hacked back because it covers a window or crowds other plants.

• In general, it is best to prune flowering shrubs as soon as they finish blooming. This way you will avoid the problem of cutting off next year's flowerbuds.

## CHAPTER SEVEN

• Become familiar with the growth habit of your shrub. Some hydrangeas, like *Hydrangea macrophylla,* bloom on second-year wood. This means that flowerbuds form on stems that were produced last year or prior to that. In the case of this hydrangea and other shrubs that bloom on old wood, pruning right after they flower keeps you from removing branches that will have blooms next year. *Hydrangea paniculata,* on the other hand, produces bloom on new growth, so you can prune back the old growth in early spring just before the shrub begins actively growing.

## PEST CONTROL

The best way to keep pests at a minimum is to start with healthy plants and make sure they get plenty of water, good air circulation, and the proper amount of light. Practice Integrated Pest Management (IPM). Examine your plants on a regular basis for signs of insect or disease problems. If only 1/3 of the plant is affected by a pest problem, try using an organic control method before you resort to chemicals. If fifty percent or more of a particular shrub is infested with a pest problem, you may need to resort to a chemical control.

## Shrubs for Georgia

| Botanical Name / Common Name | Height / Spread | Culture | Comments |
|---|---|---|---|
| *Abelia chinensis* **Chinese Abelia** | 5 to 7 feet / 5 to 7 feet | Full sun to part shade in a well-drained soil. | White flowers tinged with pink from summer to fall. |
| *Aesculus parviflora* **Bottlebrush Buckeye** | 8 to 10 feet / 8 to 12 feet | Full sun to half shade in a moist, well-drained soil. | White flowers in summer and yellow foliage in fall. |
| *Buddleia davidii* **Butterfly Bush** | 5 to 10 feet / 5 to 8 feet | Full sun and a well-drained soil. | Fragrant flowers in shades of pink, purple, yellow, and white. |
| *Callicarpa americana* **American Beautyberry** | 3 to 8 feet / 3 to 8 feet | Full sun or shade with a well-drained soil. Tolerates coastal conditions. | Large clusters of magenta fruits in fall. |
| *Callicarpa dichotoma* **Purple Beautyberry** | 3 to 5 feet / 3 to 6 feet | Full sun or half shade with a well-drained soil. | Violet-purple fruits in fall. |
| *Calycanthus floridus* **Carolina Allspice Sweetshrub** | 5 to 15 feet / 5 to 8 feet | Full sun or half shade in a well-drained soil. | Dark-maroon, spicy, pungent flowers in spring. |
| *Camellia* spp. | 6 to 5 feet / 4 to 6 feet | Partial shade with a moist, well-drained soil is best. | Many selections, including thoser that flower in spring or fall. |
| *Cephalotaxus harringtonia* 'Duke Gardens' **Spreading Plum Yew** | 2 to 3 feet / 4 to 5 feet | Shade is best, but this plant will tolerate full sun. | Glossy needles look good all year. |
| *Chimonanthus praecox* 'Concolor' **Fragrant Wintersweet** | 10 to 15 feet / 8 to 12 feet | Full sun or partial shade in a well-drained soil. | Frangrant flowers in winter. |
| *Clethra alnifolia* **Summersweet** | 4 to 8 feet / 4 to 6 feet | Full sun or shade. Tolerates a range of soil types including wet soils. | Fragrant spikes of flowers in summer attract bees and humans alike. |

# CHAPTER SEVEN

## Shrubs for Georgia

| Botanical Name / Common Name | Height / Spread | Culture | Comments |
|---|---|---|---|
| *Cotinus coggygria* **Smokebush** | 8 to 12 feet / 8 to 12 feet | Full sun is best. Adapts to a wide range of soil types. | Purple-leaved selections stand out in the landscape. |
| *Daphne odora* **Winter Daphne** | 2 to 4 feet / 2 to 4 feet | Partial shade is best. Requires a well-drained soil. | Fragrant flowers in winter make this a winner. |
| *Fothergilla gardenii* 'Mt. Airy' **Dwarf Fothergilla** | 3 to 5 feet / 3 to 4 feet | Full sun to half shade with a well-drained soil. | Tiny bottlebrush-like flowers in spring. Leaf color in fall can be red, orange, or yellow. |
| *Gardenia jasminoides* **Cape Jasmine** | 4 to 6 feet / 4 to 6 feet | Full sun to half shade with a moist acid soil. | Frangrant flowers in spring and summer. |
| *Hamamelis x intermedia* **Witchhazel** | 15 to 20 feet / 10 to 15 feet | Full sun to half shade with a moist acid soil. | Fragrant flowers in shades of yellow, orange, and red that look like spiders in late winter. |
| *Hibiscus syriacus* **Rose of Sharon** | 8 to 12 feet / 6 to 10 feet | Full sun, tolerates most types of soil provided they are well drained. | Flowers from summer to fall. Selections come in shades of pink, lavender, and white. |
| *Hydrangea arborescens* **'Annabelle' Hydrangea** | 4 to 6 feet / 4 to 6 feet | Partial shade is best, but will tolerate full sun if there is plenty of moisture. | Flowers in early summer. Large white balls provide a long season of interest. |
| *Hydrangea macrophylla* **Bigleaf Hydrangea** | 3 to 8 feet / 3 to 10 feet | Full sun to partial shade in a moist, well-drained soil. Acid soils produce bluest flowers. | Depending on the selection, flowers appear in summer in shades of blue, white, maroon, and purple. |
| *Hydrangea paniculata* 'Tardiva' **Panicle Hydrangea** | 10 to 15 feet / 10 to 20 feet | Tolerates full sun better than most types of hydrangeas. Prefers well-drained soil. | One of the latest of the hydrangeas to flower. Cones of white in early fall. |
| *Hydrangea quercifolia* **Oakleaf Hydrangea** | 4 to 8 feet / 4 to 10 feet | Sun to half shade with a moist, well-drained soil. | White flowers appear in late spring to early summer and are effective for months. |
| *Ilex cornuta* **Chinese Holly** | 8 to 20 feet / 8 to 15 feet | Full sun and a well-drained soil. This holly is heat- and drought-tolerant. | The glossy green foliage looks good all year. The cultivar 'Burfordii' is a heavy fruiter. |
| *Ilex crenata* **Japanese Holly** | 3 to 15 feet / 2 to 10 feet | Grows in full sun or shade but likes a well-drained soil. | Small evergreen foliage. |
| *Ilex glabra* **Inkberry Holly** | 4 to 8 feet / 8 to 10 feet | Full sun to shade with a moist soil. | The olive green foliage looks good all year. 'Nigra' has purplish foliage. |

# CHAPTER SEVEN

## Shrubs for Georgia

| Botanical Name<br>Common Name | Height /<br>Spread | Culture | Comments |
|---|---|---|---|
| *Ilex verticillata*<br>**Winterberry Holly** | 6 to 10 feet /<br>6 to 8 feet | Full sun to partial shade. Tolerates soils that are wet or dry. | The colorful red fruits on bare stems stand out in the winter landscape. |
| *Illicium* spp.<br>**Anise** | 6 to 10 feet /<br>5 to 10 feet | Most types prefer partial to full shade with a moist, well-drained soil. | The foliage is evergreen and, depending on the species, ranges from olive to dark green with tinges of red. |
| *Itea virginica*<br>'Henry's Garnet'<br>**Virginia Sweetspire** | 3 to 8 feet /<br>4 to 8 feet | Full sun to half shade. This plant will grow in swampy conditions as well as dry soil. | White pendulous flowers in summer and fall foliage in shades of red, burgundy, and orange. |
| *Loropetalum chinense*<br>**Loropetalum** | 6 to 10 feet /<br>6 to 10 feet | Full sun to half shade. | Many selections available. Most have burgundy-colored foliage and pink flowers. |
| *Rhapidophyllum hystrix*<br>**Needle Palm** | 6 to 8 feet /<br>6 to 8 feet | Grows in full sun to shade in a wide range of soil types. | Native to the coastal plains, this palm is hardy in most parts of Georgia. |
| *Rhododendron catawbiense*<br>**Catawba Rhododendron** | 6 to 10 feet /<br>5 to 8 feet | Partial to half shade in a well-drained soil. | Lilac-purple flowers in spring. There are many selections with a variety of flower colors. |
| *Rhododendron prunifolium*<br>**Plumleaf Azalea** | 7 to 10 feet /<br>6 to 8 feet | Full sun to half shade. Likes well-drained soils. | Orange to red-orange flowers in late summer. |
| *Rhododendron* spp.<br>**Azaleas** | 2 to 8 feet /<br>4 to 10 feet | Partial shade with a moist, well-drained soil is best. | Spring-flowering selections come in a wide range of colors. |
| *Trachycarpus fortunei*<br>**Windmill Palm** | 20 to 30 feet /<br>10 to 15 feet | Full sun to part shade in a well-drianed soil. | A good choice for coastal gardens, this palm is hardy to 10 degrees F. |
| *Spiraea* spp.<br>**Spirea** | 2 to 9 feet /<br>2 to 8 feet | Full sun to partial shade in well-drained soil. | Many types of this old-fashioned favorite. |
| *Viburnum dilatatum*<br>**Linden Viburnum** | 8 to 10 feet /<br>4 to 8 feet | Will tolerate full sun, but partial shade is best, with a moist soil. | The cultivar 'Iroquois' has large clusters of scarlet fruit in fall. |
| *Viburnum x pragense*<br>**Prague Viburnum** | 8 to 12 feet /<br>8 to 10 feet | Full sun to half shade with a well-drained soil. | The glossy evergreen foliage is this plant's main attribute. |
| *Viburnum setigerum*<br>**Tea Viburnum** | 8 to 12 feet /<br>4 to 6 feet | Full sun or partial shade with a moist, well-drained soil. | The fall fruits in shades of red to orange are the best reason to grow this viburnum |

# JANUARY

## SHRUBS

### PLANNING

Take a good look at your landscape and think about what you would like to add or change. The best gardens happen not by accident but by careful planning (as well as by a good bit of trial and error!). Come up with an overall plan and you will be able to refer to it as you develop your garden over time. Ask yourself some basic questions before hiring a designer or before you design your own garden.

• How do I like to use my garden? During what seasons is it most important to me?

• Which of my existing plants are thriving and which ones are not performing well?

• How will my garden look in spring, summer, fall, and winter?

• Am I planning to include plants with attractive foliage as well as those with beautiful flowers?

• Which types of plants do I like to feature in my garden? For example, do I like spiky flowers, delicate foliage, pleasing scents, other features . . . ?

Follow these steps if you are drawing your own garden plan:

1. Use a piece of graph paper. Your drawing doesn't have to be exactly to scale, but include a rough sketch of your house to use as a reference when deciding where to locate plants.

2. Indicate the major trees, shrubs, and lawn areas on your plan.

3. Indicate where you have full shade, full sun, or a mixture of shade and sun.

4. Mark areas where there are extreme soil conditions such as soils that stay constantly wet or soils that have a high percentage of sand.

5. A North arrow will help you determine the direction light comes from and how to site future plants.

Once you have your basic visual information you can begin to decide where you want to place additional plants. Start with trees and shrubs—later you will add perennials, annuals, vines, and bulbs. Begin a garden journal so you can keep track of what happens in your garden as it develops. You should note changes to your original plan as well as make comments on the weather and take notes on how your plantings develop. Photograph your garden now so you will be able to compare how it looks in winter with how it looks during other seasons.

Now is the time to take a look at your garden. Some shrubs may have outgrown their allotted space, or they may not be thriving because

conditions have changed. Where you once had full sun may be shady now because a large tree has matured. Perhaps a natural disaster turned a shade garden into a virtual desert. Whatever the reason for the changes in your garden, you can take action in response to them:

• In south Georgia, shrubs can be moved to a better spot now.

• Plan to replace shrubs that are not thriving with those better suited to your environment.

• Make a list of possible replacement plants with notes on their cultural requirements, ultimate size, and other features. Collect color photographs from catalogs and develop your own reference guide.

• Locate plant sources. When possible, purchase plants from a local or regional nursery—this will help ensure that they will be best adapted to grow in your Georgia garden. Contact the Georgia Green Industry Association (see Resources, p. 290) for a list of nurseries in your area.

### PLANTING

As long as the ground is not frozen or saturated with water, you can plant shrubs during mild spells at this time of year.

## WATERING

Water new plantings.

If there is no rain during mild spells, water evergreen shrubs. Don't let them get to the stage where the leaves or needles begin to look crisp and fall off.

Don't allow large shrubs in containers to dry out. When the top 2 inches of the soil in a container is dry to the touch, water until water rushes out the bottom of the container. If the soil has shrunk away from the sides of the pot you may have to apply water several times, allowing it to soak in after each dousing.

## FERTILIZING

Topdress shrub beds with 1 to 2 inches of organic amendments such as mushroom compost, cottonseed meal, or cow manure. As the organic material continues to break down, it will be a good source of food for your plants when the roots begin to grow in spring. Be sure you don't pile it up around the stems or trunks of plants.

Apply a 2-inch layer of mulch around new plantings. Use pine straw, bark nuggets, shredded bark, leaves, peanut hulls, or cocoa shells.

## HELPFUL HINTS FOR CUT FLOWERS

Cut branches of **winter honeysuckle** *Lonicera fragrantissima* to bring into the house to force into bloom.

Snip a few stems of **Japanese flowering apricot** *Prunus mume* when it is in bud. The sweet-scented flowers will perfume a room and lift your spirits.

Cut **camellias** when they are still in bud but beginning to show color. You will enjoy blooms for a week or more, and the foliage can last for a month if the stems are kept in water.

## PROBLEMS

Remove debris and dead leaves from planting beds to reduce future insect and disease problems.

Depending on the variety, **camellias** bloom at various times from November through April. Check them for signs of petal blight, which is caused by a fungus—the flowers may have brown spots that are irregular in shape, or the buds may turn brown before opening, or the blooms may have a netted appearance. Remove and destroy any flowers or buds that show signs of this blight. The first spots appear on expanding petals; then they spread until the flower is brown and dead. Collecting the fallen flowers will help reduce the spread of this fungus. If more than 50 percent of the flowers appear infected, you may want to use a fungicide to control the problem.

## PRUNING

Remove any dead or damaged wood from existing shrubs. Dead wood is dry and brittle—if you are not sure if a branch is dead, scratch it with your fingernail. If the inside is green, then there is still hope, and you can wait until spring to if any buds form.

Renovate overgrown shrubs by removing one-third of the oldest branches from the base of the plant. The oldest branches are usually the thickest. Remember that many spring-flowering shrubs bloom on old wood (branches that grew the previous season), so you will want to wait until after they flower to do any drastic pruning.

# FEBRUARY

## SHRUBS

### PLANNING

Visit public gardens and make a list of shrubs that provide interest in the winter with blooms, bark, or berries. Note the cultural requirements for these plants. Some shrubs that have fragrant flowers in winter are:

- *Chimonanthus praecox* **Wintersweet**
- *Daphne odora* **Winter daphne**
- *Hamamelis mollis* **Chinese witchhazel**
- *Hamamelis × intermedia* **Witchhazel** selections
- *Mahonia bealei* **Leatherleaf mahonia**
- *Prunus mume* **Japanese flowering apricot** (a large shrub or small tree)

Make notes in your garden journal about the weather, changes in light, and how your plants perform. Photograph your garden at least once a month to help you keep up with changes.

Plan to add at least one shrub with winter blooms or berries to your garden this spring. Winter wonders include **winter honeysuckle, evergreen hollies,** and **deciduous hollies.** When you select **hollies** for your garden, keep in mind that you will need a male plant for pollination in order to guarantee the best fruit

production. The female selections display fruit in season, while the male does not. For example, the **American holly,** *Ilex opaca* 'Merry Christmas', needs one male selection of the same species or hybrid; the same is true of **deciduous hollies.** Some nurseries sell male selections with the females; one male is sufficient to pollinate a group of females.

### PLANTING

Prepare the soil for planting in the spring.

1. Add soil amendments and rototill to a depth of 8 to 12 inches. You have many choices when it comes to soil amendments for your garden. Although peat moss is an option, it is expensive, breaks down quickly, and causes soil to be more acidic. It is better to use a soil amendment like chicken manure, horse manure, or mushroom compost, or a product like Nature's Helper™ or Clay Cutter™.

2. Test your soil (see Horticultural Practices, p. 7). You can purchase a kit from your local garden center and do it yourself, or send a sample to your local Extension Service (see Resources, p. 289). Contact your Extension Service for information on how to take a soil sample. The Exten-

sion Service charges a nominal fee and will send you a detailed analysis of your soil, including information about what you need to add in the way of nutrients and lime.

3. Add lime if recommended by your soil test.

Continue planting shrubs as long as the ground is not frozen. Plant container-grown, bare-root, or balled- and-burlapped shrubs. Remove plants from containers.

If you have a balled-and-burlapped shrub and the burlap is a synthetic material, place the plant in the hole and gently pull out the material from around the rootball. This will cause the least amount of stress to the roots.

Dig holes as deep as the size of the container the plant is growing in. For bare-root or balled-and-burlapped shrubs, the hole should be as deep as the roots are long. The width of the hole should be at least twice the width of the container.

This is an ideal time to plant a **winter daphne** *Daphne odora*, an evergreen that should be in full bloom at nurseries now. One whiff of the powerfully fragrant flowers and you'll be hooked. A hardy evergreen shrub, it grows happily in a large pot, or in the garden if the soil is slightly moist and extremely well drained.

## PRUNING

Continue to prune deciduous shrubs to remove dead wood, rejuvenate them, or keep them from getting too big for the space in which they are growing (as when they block the view from windows or spread out into a pathway). One way to avoid the need to prune constantly is to select the right plant for the right place. Do some research before you plant!

If shrubs have outgrown their original location or have become straggly and spindly in appearance, prune them back severely while they are dormant. Prune back **azaleas, spiraea, privet,** and *Abelia × grandiflora* to a height of about 12 inches.

You may choose to stretch out the pruning over a period of years. Remove $1/3$ of the oldest wood in the first year; in the second year, take out $1/2$ of the remaining oldest stems and cut back long shoots that grew from the previous season; in the third year, prune out whatever old wood (the oldest wood has the thickest stems) is remaining, and prune new shoots just enough for a pleasing effect.

## A RECIPE FOR AMENDING CLAY SOIL

$1/3$ coarse sand (builders sand, not play sand—almost like a very small gravel)

$1/3$ organic material (compost, Nature's Helper™, or other bagged products)

$1/3$ existing topsoil (some clay is beneficial but if you have one hundred percent clay, remove it and replace it with a quality topsoil)

Prune **camellias** once they finish flowering. Remove faded blooms and snip back the tips of branches for an overall pleasing effect.

A fungal disease that affects the flowers of *Camellia japonica* and other varieties is spread by spores. Good cultural practices are the best way to control this disease. Refer to the discussion of petal blight in January.

Prune evergreen shrubs like **boxwood, holly, anise, leucothoe,** and others before new growth begins. Remove dead wood and tip back branches to a desired height.

## WATERING

Keep new plantings well watered (new plantings are those that have been planted in the last six months). Water once a week if you get no rain.

## PROBLEMS

Reapply weed-preventers (see September) to prevent any future crops of chickweed from being established. A pre-emergent will prevent weed seeds from germinating.

Pull weeds when they are young, before they set seed. This will reduce future populations of weeds.

Use a hand cultivator to scratch out weeds around shrubs. Apply a fresh layer of mulch to help kill weeds and retain moisture in the soil.

To kill insects that overwinter such as scales, lace bugs, and mites, spray horticultural oil. Scale insects are particularly difficult to control. Closely related to mealybugs and aphids, they have a waxy shell-like covering, either hard or soft, that protects them from natural enemies and insecticides.

# MARCH

## SHRUBS

 PLANNING

Try not to be an impulsive shopper. Before you head out to the nursery or garden center, make sure you have a list with specific information such as the height, flower color, foliage, cultural requirements, and botanical names of the plants you want. Knowing the botanical names (see Horticultural Practices, p. 11) will help ensure that you get the plants you want. A good example of the confusion that can be caused by plant names is the common name **wild honeysuckle.** This name is used for many different types of **native azaleas.** If you want a specific type of **native azalea,** it is good to know, for example, that *Rhododendron austrinum* is different from *Rhododendron alabamense.* Have alternatives in mind if you can't find a specific variety.

When you purchase your shrubs, consider which perennials, annuals, and bulbs will make happy companions for them.

**Companions for Shade**
- **Azalea** and **woodland phlox** or **foam flower**
- **Camellias** and **hellebores**
- **Oakleaf hydrangea** and ferns like the **autumn fern**

If soil sticks together when you squeeze it, it's probably still too wet to work.

**Companions for Sun**
- **Butterfly bush** and **lantana**
- **Boxwood** and **ivy** or **mondo grass**
- **Slender deutzia** and *Scabiosa* 'Butterfly Blue'

Keep up with changes in your garden by recording them in your garden journal.

 PLANTING

This is an ideal time to plant shrubs, provided the ground is not too wet. The soil should hold some moisture. Try the squeeze test:

Take a handful of soil and squeeze it. If it forms a hard ball, than it is probably too wet for planting. If it sticks together momentarily but crumbles easily, it is just right.

Remove plants from their containers. (Refer to February for instructions on how to do this.)

If you have heavy clay soils, plant high so the top third of the rootball is out of the ground. This is especially true for shrubs like evergreen **rhododendrons,** which resent soils that are not well drained. Mound plenty of soil around the rootball and then apply a good layer of mulch, making sure to keep it away from the main trunk. This will ensure that your plant doesn't dry out too quickly, but the roots won't sit in wet soil.

When you plant, fill in with soil around the rootball and tamp it down with your shoes or a shovel handle. This will remove air pockets and prevent soil from settling.

 WATERING

Water new plantings "long and slow"—if you use the hose, a pencil-size trickle is good. Any plants that you have added to your garden within the past six to twelve months will benefit from some extra tender loving care. Depending on the size of the rootball, it may take anywhere from 15 minutes to an hour, with the hose at slow trickle, to water an individual shrub.

## FERTILIZING

Use a balanced granular fertilizer (10-10-10) around shrubs. Determine amounts according to the size of plants. As a rule of thumb, use 1 tablespoon of 10-10-10 per foot of shrub height. Refer to the product label for specific usage directions.

Mulch new plantings 2 to 3 inches deep, being sure to keep mulch away from the trunk or stems.

## PROBLEMS

Inspect **azaleas** for signs of lace bugs: the leaves will have tiny yellow speckles. You will treat for these pests in April or May before adults lay eggs.

Use horticultural oil and insecticidal soap to control insects like aphids, scale, and mites. Read the label carefully. The best time to spray your plants is on a clear day when rain is unlikely for at least six hours—this will give the spray enough time to dry completely. It is best to spray early in the morning when temperatures are coolest. Avoid spraying on windy days when the spray can easily drift to other plants.

## TIPS FOR GROWING BOXWOOD

According to Walt Harrison, formerly of Habersham Gardens in Atlanta, the secret to growing **boxwood** in Georgia is having the right soil pH. **Boxwoods** are happiest in a soil that is neutral to slightly basic, a pH around 7 to 8. This allows for better uptake of iron, which prevents the chlorosis (yellowing of leaves) that **boxwoods** often exhibit.

Certain plants like **boxwood** are sensitive to heat and drought stress. To prevent problems, keep the shrubs watered throughout the growing season.

Many gardeners have good success with their **boxwoods** when they mulch with a 1-inch layer of cottonseed meal.

## PRUNING

Some evergreen shrubs get overgrown or leggy over time. Now is a good time to renovate **boxwoods** and other broadleaf evergreens like **hollies:**

• Prune them back hard, reducing the overall size of the plant by one third.

• Prune back shrubs drastically to a height of 12 inches if they are straggly and have leaves only at the tips of the branches.

Pruning now will give shrubs time to put out new growth that will harden off before hot weather sets in. Pruning tips:

• If you use electric hedge trimmers to prune your evergreens, follow up with a pair of handpruners. Use handpruners to remove stems down to where a branch forks. This will open up the plant and allow light to get in, which will encourage new growth. The result will be fuller, healthier plants.

• In coastal parts of the state, prune spring-flowering shrubs like **azaleas** and **camellias** after they finish flowering. If your **hybrid azaleas** (many ornamental **azaleas** are hybrids) are getting overgrown or leggy, prune them back to about 12 inches tall. If you keep them watered and fertilized, they should recover and develop into fully leafed plants.

• **Native azaleas** require little or no pruning unless they are too large for the space in which you have planted them. They should never be sheared (which means cut back to an even height with electric hedge trimmers or hand shears), but should be pruned to enhance their natural form. It should be noted that some **native azaleas** can reach heights of 10 feet or more.

# APRIL

## SHRUBS

 PLANNING

This is a great time to add shrubs to your garden or to transplant existing shrubs. Make sure you have selected varieties that are suited to the growing conditions in your garden. The advantage of purchasing plants in bloom is that you will know the color of the flowers and will be able to give them your own personal sniff test to determine whether or not they are fragrant.

Photograph your garden as it begins to bloom. In your garden journal, keep track of how long your shrubs bloom, noting perennials that bloom at the same time. This will help you plan pleasing combinations like **beautybush**, *Kolkwitzia amabilis,* underplanted with *Scabiosa* 'Butterfly Blue'.

 PLANTING

Soak bare-root plants in a bucket of water before planting, and prune off any dead or badly damaged roots, such as those that are cracked or broken.

You can plant container-grown shrubs all month long, following these steps:

1. Dig a hole that is as deep as the container and twice as wide.

Dig a planting hole that's as deep as the container and twice as wide.

Depth of Hole

Width of Hole

2. Use a shovel to hit the sides of the container. This will make it easier to slide out the whole rootball.

3. Use a sharp pair of hand pruners to make two or three cuts into the rootball, spacing the distance between cuts equally. This will encourage new roots to sprout and establish more quickly.

4. Trim off any dead top-growth.

5. Place the rootball in the hole and fill in the soil around it. Don't pile lots of extra soil on top of the top layer of soil—this will suffocate surface roots.

6. Water the shrub well.

7. Apply a 2-inch layer of mulch around newly planted shrubs.

When you are transplanting shrubs, dig as large a rootball as possible. The more roots you get, the better success you'll have moving your shrubs. If your shrub is 3 feet across, you should measure 3 feet out from the main stem, all the way around the plant. At this point, take your spade and cut into the roots. Some shrubs, like **azaleas,** have lots of shallow roots that spread out in every direction, so it is necessary to dig a rootball that is wider than it is deep, looking almost like a thin, wide pancake.

Prepare the new location ahead of time. The less time a plant stays out of the ground, the fewer roots will dry out and die. Sometimes a piece of burlap or 4 mil plastic is a useful tool to help drag the rootball to its new home. Place the rootball on the burlap and pull it to where it will be planted.

After planting, tamp down the soil around the roots to remove any air pockets. Fill up the hole halfway with soil, add water, let it settle, and then fill in the remaining soil. Apply a 2-inch layer of mulch, keeping it away from the main trunk. Mulching helps keep the soil cool or warm, depending on the season, and reduces infestations of weeds.

## WATERING

Water newly planted and transplanted shrubs after you plant them and then once a week (unless there is a good rain) for the first month. Place the hose at the base of the shrub and let a slow stream saturate the area. A good rule of thumb is to apply 1 to 2 gallons per foot of plant height. Soaker hoses also work well.

In coastal areas where soils are sandy, shrubs may need watering more frequently. Dig into the top 2 to 3 inches of the soil to determine if it is dry. Established plantings will also benefit from supplemental watering during periods of drought.

## FERTILIZING

You can fertilize established shrubs in spring. A balanced fertilizer like 10-10-10 is good. Follow label directions for proper application. Too little is better than too much.

As an alternative to chemical fertilizers, you can topdress your shrubs with compost or an organic soil amendment, either store-bought such as bagged cow manure, or homemade compost. Apply a good 1 to 2 inches over the soil surrounding your shrubs. As this material breaks down, it provides welcome nutrients for the soil, resulting in healthier roots and overall increased vigor for the plant.

## PROBLEMS

Check for signs of insect activity or damage. Aphids, scale, or chewing insects may be visible. Try using insecticidal soaps or a strong blast from the hose to control aphids before you resort to using chemical controls. If you notice that **azalea** leaves are bleached out (silvery and speckled), you may have lace bugs.

Spray with insecticidal soap or an insecticide to treat lace bugs.

Handpull any weeds, or use a cultivator to scratch them out. Once an area is free of weeds, apply a pre-emergent and a layer of mulch. This practice will greatly reduce weed infestations.

Some gardeners put down weed fabrics to control weed problems, but newspaper will also work. Apply a layer of newspaper at least three sheets thick and then cover it with mulch. (This technique may not be practical for formal gardens.)

## PRUNING

Prune flowering shrubs like **forsythia, flowering quince,** early-blooming **spireas** (*Spiraea nipponica* 'Snowmound', *S. thunbergii*), and **azaleas** as soon as they finish blooming. If shrubs are overgrown and lacking vigor, with very few blooms, pruning can help rejuvenate them. Remove one-third of the oldest wood completely, and cut the remaining stems to a height of 12 inches. Follow this practice for the next few years, and you will create a healthy, vigorous plant.

# MAY

## SHRUBS

PLANNING

Now that spring is in full bloom, it is a good time to evaluate individual shrubs and decide if you have the right plants in the right places. Pick a bouquet of flowers from your favorite shrubs. Arrange the flowers in a vase and note the various color combinations. This can help you decide on which colors to add to your garden.

**Shrubs for Spring Blooms**
- *Deutzia gracilis* (white flowers)
- *Kolkwitzia amabilis* (pink flowers)
- *Philadelphus coronarius* (white flowers)
- *Rhododendron* species and hybrids (many colors)
- *Spiraea* (many species and colors)
- *Viburnum* (many cultivars and hybrids)

PLANTING

Continue adding shrubs to your garden. Container-grown plants can be planted throughout the year as long as you water properly after planting.

If you transplant a shrub while it is in bloom, cutting it back by one-third will reduce the transplant shock, and the plant will recover more quickly. In the warm coastal parts of the state you will have better success if you transplant shrubs during the cooler months of March or November.

WATERING

Water all new plantings once a week unless you have regular long, soaking rains (more than a quick thunderstorm). Keep this practice up until plants are well established, or at least for the first growing season. If you use a sprinkler to water a shrub bed, make sure that all parts of the bed receive good coverage.

One way to measure water application is to use shallow cans like tuna fish cans, placing them in several different areas. When they average $3/4$ inch full, you have probably watered a shrub area long enough for that week.

FERTILIZING

It's still not too late to fertilize your shrubs for the spring if you haven't already done so. Your plants still have time to use fertilizer while they are actively growing. Once it gets hot, growth slows down and plants don't require as much fertilizer. Use a complete balanced fertilizer like 10-10-10. As a general rule, apply 1 tablespoon per foot of plant height. Refer to the product label for detailed information.

PROBLEMS

Leaves on **azaleas** or **camellias** may become distorted and pale green; as they thicken, they turn brown, then white. These are symptoms of leaf gall. While the disease doesn't kill the plant, they are unsightly. Handpick the galls and destroy them before they turn white.

Continue to examine shrubs for signs of damage from insects or diseases. Spider mites and aphids will be more active as the weather gets warmer.

If the leaves on your **crapemyrtle** have a grayish coating, you probably have powdery mildew. Cool nights followed by warm days, poor air circulation, and not enough sun all contribute to an environment that favors powdery mildew. This fungus can affect **crapemyrtle, lilac, hydrangea,** and other plants. For severe infestations, use a fungicide. For an organic alternative to a synthetic fungicide, try spraying a mixture of 4 teaspoons baking soda in 1 gallon of water on the plants. Apply this spray once a week. Be sure to cover the tops and bottoms of the leaves with whatever spray you use.

Spot-spray weeds in shrub beds with a nonselective herbicide. Use extreme caution: do not apply on windy days, since nonselective herbicides kill everything they touch. You can hold a piece of cardboard in front of a shrub to protect it from damage while you spray the surrounding weeds with the herbicide. If the weeds are close to stems or foliage on shrubs, dip a small paintbrush in the diluted chemical and carefully "paint" the chemical on the weeds. Another, similar method is to don two rubber gloves—to ensure safety—on one hand. Dip that hand in the herbicide and swipe the foliage with the chemical. Discard the paintbrush or gloves after use.

## SOIL LAYERING

A simple method for propagating **hydrangeas** and certain other shrubs is by soil-layering, a method that can be used from April through autumn.

1. Choose a limb close to the ground. Press it downward until the stem touches the ground.

2. At the point where the branch touches the ground, scratch the stem (wound it) to expose the inner bark. This is where the roots will develop. You will get even better results if the point of contact also has a node (the part of the stem where shoots, leaves, or buds emerge).

3. Cover the wound (not the entire limb) with soil—the richer the soil, the better results you can expect.

4. Place a brick or rock on top to hold the branch in place. At least 6 inches of branch tip and leaves should be showing beyond the brick.

5. Keep it watered—don't let it dry out.

6. In two months, tug gently to see if roots have formed. If there are substantial roots, cut the new plant from the mother plant. If there are only a few roots, recover with soil and check again in another month.

Cut out the bottom of a plastic jug to use when you spot-spray weeds in beds.

 PRUNING

Prune shrubs like **viburnum, rhododendron,** and **mock orange** after they finish flowering.

Remove spent blossoms before they set seed on evergreen **rhododendrons** and **mountain laurel.** This helps with overall vigor. The plant will be able to put its energy into forming next year's flower buds and new growth instead of seeds.

# JUNE

## SHRUBS

### PLANNING

Now is a great time to add some summer-blooming shrubs to your garden.

**Summer-Blooming Shrubs**

- *Aesculus parviflora* **Bottlebrush buckeye**
- *Buddleia davidii* and selections **Butterfly bush**
- *Clerodendrum trichotomum* **Harlequin glory bower**
- *Clethra alnifolia* **Summersweet**
- *Gardenia jasminoides,* many cultivars ('Klein's Hardy' is hardy to 0 degrees Fahrenheit)
- *Hibiscus syriacus* 'Diana' **Rose of Sharon,** white-flowered selection
- *Hydrangea paniculata* 'Tardiva' **Panicle hydrangea**
- *Hydrangea quercifolia* **Oakleaf hydrangea**
- *Hypericum frondosum* 'Sunburst' **Golden St. John's wort**
- *Lantana camara* 'Miss Huff' (really a hardy perennial, it acts like a small shrub in coastal areas and can grow to 6 feet or more tall)
- *Vitex agnus-castus* **Chaste tree**

Think about having a variety of shrubs in your garden so it will have something of interest— like flowers, foliage, or fruit— during every season. Record your observations in your garden journal, keeping track of what's in bloom, which plants are thriving, and which plants may need to be replaced. Take photos of your garden in summer; they will help you remember what blooms when and the color of different flowers. If you have a videocamera, you can produce a tour of your garden, which may help you decide what to add or subtract in the future.

### PLANTING

Add container-grown plants to your garden as long as the temperatures are not too hot. If temperatures are in the 90-degree F. range, the plants will be slow to put out roots.

Rototill and add soil amendments to areas in which you will plant shrubs in the future.

If you have time, handdigging is another option. You can work on one area at a time, making sure to mix in organic materials to a depth of 12 to 18 inches.

Mulch new plantings with a 2- to 3-inch layer. Keep mulch away from the main stems; when it is piled up around stems, it can create an environment that is attractive to insects and pests.

### WATERING

Summer can arrive quickly. Keep new plantings well watered. Don't wait until plants look wilted before you water; check them once a week. If the top 2 to 3 inches of soil is dry to the touch, it is time to water. When you water, do so thoroughly once or twice a week rather than a little every day. This will help your shrubs develop strong, deep roots. If you use a hose, place it near the center of the shrub and let a small stream of water soak in for at least a half hour. If you use a sprinkler, place some shallow tuna fish or cat food cans around the plants, and water until the cans are 3/4 inch full.

Established shrubs will benefit from supplemental water during periods of drought. Place the hose at soil level near the center of the plant, and saturate the root area.

### FERTILIZING

If you haven't fertilized shrubs yet, apply some 10-10-10. A granular slow-release fertilizer persists longer than a liquid feed, but both are effective. As a general rule, when using granular fertilizers, apply 1 tablespoon per foot of plant height.

## PROBLEMS

Good cultural practices will help reduce pest and disease problems:

• Clean up any leaf litter that accumulates under or around shrubs.

• Destroy infected leaves to prevent the spread of diseases.

• Keep shrubs watered and mulched.

• Keep weeds out of shrub beds.

• You can add ground covers under your shrubs and trees to help keep roots cool as well as add interest to the garden.

Examine your shrubs for signs of damage by insects or disease. If you have Japanese beetles in small numbers, try handpicking them and drowning them in soapy water. This is best done in the early morning when they are less active. If infestations are severe, you may want to consider using an insecticide (see Roses, June).

Check shrubs for signs of aphids or spider mites. Use insecticidal soaps to control these pest problems before resorting to chemical controls. Spray early in the day before temperatures are too hot. When you spray, be sure to cover both the tops and undersides of the leaves and the stems; spray to the point where it drips off the plant.

## PRUNING

Shear hedges when they look untidy and branches are uneven. Prune them so they are slightly wider at the bottom than they are at the top. This will result in fuller, healthier plants.

• Conifers like **hemlocks** should be sheared before midsummer or when dormant in winter.

• **Privet, barberry,** and other rapid-growing shrubs can be sheared several times during the growing season.

Use electric or hand shears to prune the top and the sides of a hedge. Follow up with a pair of handpruners to even out rough spots or clip any stems that were missed. This will result in a more symmetrical hedge over time.

• Prune *Abelia grandiflora* to shape it up. Cut back long shoots. If the shrub is overgrown and straggly, remove one-third of the oldest wood from the base of the plant and then remove another third next year.

Prune spring-blooming shrubs that flower on old wood once they finish flowering. Most shrubs will not require extensive pruning, but if there are long wild shoots or you want to shape the plant, now is a good time to prune so new growth will have time to harden off, and there will be less chance the pruning will affect next year's bloom.

### Shrubs to Prune Selectively

• *Kolkwitzia amabilis* **beauty bush**

• *Viburnum × burkwoodii*

• *Viburnum × carlcephalum*

• *Viburnum carlesii*

• *Viburnum macrocephalum*

Prune any late-flowering varieties of **azaleas** and **rhododendrons** after they stop blooming. If you wait until later in the season, you'll prune off potential flower buds for next year. Deadhead **rhododendron** blossoms once they finish flowering. This will result in many more blooms next spring.

**HELPFUL HINT**

Invest in a good pair of pruning shears. You will have them for years to come, and if you purchase a high-quality type, you'll never have to replace them. Many gardeners swear by their Felco #2 pruners.

# JULY

## SHRUBS

### PLANNING

Evaluate the shrubs in your garden. Do they look attractive even when they are not fruiting or in bloom? Do they provide a background or complement for your perennials and annuals? Do you have a mix of evergreen and deciduous shrubs, including those with colorful flowers, foliage, and fruits?

There may be gaps in your garden where shrubs would help fill the void. Think about which shrubs you would like to add or eliminate so you can develop a plan for the fall. Make notes in

Shrubs are an important part of landscape design even if they serve only as a backdrop for annuals and perennials.

your garden journal about which plants still look good during the hot summer months.

### PLANTING

This month is generally too hot to add new plants to the garden, as the soil and air temperatures are not ideal for encouraging root growth . . . but if this is the only time you have to plant, get out the shovel! Many of the shrubs that nurseries offer are grown in containers that stay outside all year long. This means that unless the ground is frozen or saturated, plants can be added to your garden throughout the year. This is not true for bare-root plants, which must be dormant when you plant them.

**Growing Shrubs in Decorative Containers:** Even when the weather is hot, you can add instant color to your garden with containers of shrubs, trees, annuals, and perennials. Mixing colorful perennials with shrubs can create a pleasing effect. Shrubs like **boxwood** grow happily year-round in containers and can add a touch of formality to the garden. When growing shrubs in containers, make sure you use a soil mix that includes organic amendments, coarse sand, and even a small amount of clay. The clay will help the soil hold moisture. Soilless mixes dry

out quickly and offer little in the way of nutrients.

### WATERING

This is an important time to check shrubs regularly and make sure they are getting enough water. Any shrubs in large containers will probably need watering at least once a day or more. When you water containers, whether shrubs, trees, annuals, or perennials, water until it rushes out the holes in the bottom of the pot. If the soil has shrunk away from the sides of the pot, water, let it soak in, and then water again.

When watering shrubs in the ground, too much water can be as harmful as too little. If you're not sure whether to water or not, check the rootball—don't base your watering decisions solely on the time of year.

New plantings should be watered once a week. Saturate the rootball. If you use the hose, place it near the center of the shrub and leave it on a slow trickle for 15 minutes or more, depending on rootball size.

If you have a problem spot in your garden where the soil stays moist all or most of the time, it's best not to fight it but to select plants that will not only survive but thrive in such an environment. Shrubs that tolerate soils that are constantly moist include:

- *Clethra alnifolia*
  **Sweet pepperbush**
- *Ilex verticillata*
  **Winterberry holly**
- *Itea virginica*
  **Virginia sweetspire**

## FERTILIZING

Wait until fall to fertilize shrubs.

## PROBLEMS

Hot weather seems to encourage pests like spider mites and aphids. Examine shrubs regularly for signs of damage; use insecticidal soaps to control these problems before resorting to a chemical pesticide. Sometimes even a blast of cold water from the hose can eradicate a problem like aphids.

Spot-spray weeds around shrubs with a nonselective herbicide. Protect stems and foliage from coming into contact with spray.

If any of your shrubs suffer from powdery mildew, black spot, or insect problems, make sure to collect and destroy infected leaves as soon as they hit the ground. This will help reduce the spread of diseases and insects.

A good time to handweed is the day after a long, gentle rain. Scratching the soil with a cultivator around and between shrubs when weeds are small, and before they set seed, is a good practice to prevent serious infestations of weeds. This is also a good time to apply a light layer of mulch around shrubs. Mulch can reduce weeds and help keep the soil cool.

Check leaves of **rhododendrons** and large-leaved **azaleas** for notches. This symptom is characteristic of the black vine weevil, which feeds at night and hides underneath the shrub by day. Use contact insecticide granules or spray under your shrubs.

You may notice a black mold on the leaves of your **crapemyrtle.** Called sooty mold, this fungus occurs when insects such as aphids and scale secrete a substance called honeydew—the mold grows on top of the honeydew. Simply wash off the leaves and treat the insects with insecticidal soap or insecticide.

## PRUNING

Remove dead branches or blossoms on shrubs once they finish flowering.

Prune hedges of fast-growing species such as **privet, glossy abelia,** *Abelia grandiflora,* **cherry laurel,** and even **holly.** The new growth they put out will still have time to harden off before winter.

Deadheading (removing the dead flower blossoms) your **butterfly bushes** will encourage more blooms, and if you are lucky, the shrubs will flower until frost.

### HELPFUL HINTS

- Practice Integrated Pest Management (IPM). This approach to pest control is based on the idea of managing insect populations rather than eliminating them. By choosing the right plants for your growing conditions and using good cultural practices, you can minimize potential pest problems.
- Examine your shrubs and other plants on a regular basis. If less than fifty percent of a plant is affected with a pest, use a physical or biological control before you resort to a chemical control. Physical controls include traps and barriers like copper strips to keep away slugs and snails. Biological controls include the use of beneficial insects like ladybugs that eat aphids and the use of *Bacillus thuringiensis*, a bacterium that kills caterpillars.

# AUGUST

## SHRUBS

### PLANNING

Larger shrubs provide welcome shade for some annuals and perennials, especially during the dog days of summer. Consider underplanting your shrubs with perennial ground covers. Fall is a good time to add plants to the garden. Not only will these ground covers add interest to the garden scene, they will help keep the roots of shrubs cool.

While **ivy** is a popular ground cover, there are other plants that perform equally well, making good ground covers or companions to plant under shrubs:

• *Acorus gramineus* 'Pusillus' **Dwarf sweet flag** is a diminutive grass that makes a good partner for **Virginia sweetspire.**

• *Ajuga reptans* **Carpet bugleweed** has numerous cultivars with colorful foliage.

• *Chrysogonum virginianum* **Green and gold** offers yellow flowers in spring and fall.

• *Helleborus orientalis* **Lenten rose** is a great companion for **rhododendrons** and **azaleas** or **witchhazels.**

• *Vinca minor* **Common periwinkle** is another good choice for ground cover.

**Hydrangea** flowers are great to collect and dry for projects in the fall:

1. Collect blooms when they are dry, or they will rot. A good time of day to collect is after 10 a.m. and before noon.

2. If the bloom feels crisp to the touch, it is ready to cut and dry. If it feels soft to the touch, then it is still too early to harvest for drying.

3. Once you cut the flowers, strip all the leaves and remove any brown or damaged parts of the flower.

4. The best place to store the flowers is in a dark, dry, and warm place. Penny McHenry, founder of the American Hydrangea Society, once used the trunk of her car to dry **hydrangea** flowers. Other methods are to store them in a vase without water or to hang them upside down.

Dried **hydrangea** blooms will last for months or years, but the colors will fade over time.

### PLANTING

It is generally too hot to plant shrubs now, but you can prepare the soil for planting in the fall. If you plant container-grown shrubs, be sure to keep them well watered during the summer.

### WATERING

Water shrubs planted in the last six months weekly, providing 2 to 3 gallons of water per plant. Water plants growing in pots every day. Water containers until the water rushes out the holes in the bottom and sides of the pot.

### FERTILIZING

Hold off on any fertilizing until early fall.

### PROBLEMS

Continue examining plants for insect and disease problems. Sometimes a good blast of water will take care of minor insect pest problems.

If needed, spray insecticidal soap to control aphids, spider mites, or whiteflies. You can spray insecticidal soap three to four times a week. Always spray in the early part of the day before temperatures get too hot.

Whether you are using an organic or a chemical spray, good coverage is essential. Spray the tops and undersides of leaves as well as the stems, covering completely, until the spray begins to drip off the plant. When you mix your sprays, never use more than the recommended amounts of product, whether organic or synthetic. More is not better. In fact, you can damage or kill plants by using too much chemical in one application.

Spot-spray weeds in shrub beds with a nonselective herbicide. Spray early in the morning when there are no winds and temperatures are coolest.

Use a yellow sticky trap to control whiteflies on **gardenia.** (See Edibles, August for directions on making a sticky trap.)

## PRUNING

Finish any pruning or shearing now so there will be enough time for new growth to harden off before winter arrives.

# SHRUBS FOR COASTAL GARDENERS

Coastal gardeners must often consider salt tolerance and drought resistance when selecting plants for their gardens. Here is a list of shrubs that tolerate salt spray and coastal conditions:

- *Baccharis halimifolia* **Groundsel-bush**
- *Hippophae rhamnoides* **Sea buckthorn**
- *Hydrangea macrophylla* **Bigleaf hydrangea**
- *Ilex glabra* **Inkberry holly**
- *Ilex vomitoria* **Yaupon holly**
- *Juniperus conferta* **Shore juniper**
- *Myrica cerifera* **Wax myrtle**
- *Nerium oleander* **Oleander**
- *Pittosporum tobira* **Japanese pittosporum** (winter hardy only in the most southern parts of the state)
- *Rosa rugosa* **Rugosa rose**

Bigleaf hydrangea is a good candidate for coastal areas.

# SEPTEMBER

## SHRUBS

### PLANNING

Fall is an ideal time to plant in the South. Determine now which shrubs you will add to your garden once the temperatures cool off and we get some rain. Make a list before you head out to the nursery. This way you will have an idea of what you want and won't be overwhelmed by all the choices. Plan to include some plants with colorful fall foliage and fruit.

If you haven't taken a soil test in two years, now is the time to do it. Not only will the results provide information about what you need to add to your soil in the way of Nitrogen, Phosphorous, and Potassium (N-P-K), it will give you a reading of the pH. You could have a soil that is rich in nutrients, but if the pH (acidity or alkalinity of the soil) is too low, plants won't absorb the necessary nutrients they require for healthy growth.

Soil pH can range anywhere from 4.0 to 9.0. Most plants are happiest in a soil that has a pH between 6 and 7. Certain plants, however, have particular pH requirements. Knowing what your plants like before you plant will help you determine what to add to your soil.

Fall is a good time to amend your soil, too. Organic soil amendments include mushroom compost, cow manure, chicken manure, and cottonseed meal, to name a few. Make sure you mix in plenty of amendments. Spread a 3- to 4-inch layer over the top of the soil before you rototill. Till the soil so that it is mixed in to a depth of 12 to 18 inches. If your soil has a high clay content, mixing in a layer of coarse sand 1 inch thick will help improve drainage.

Record what is happening in the garden in your garden journal. Take photographs of the garden in fall.

If you don't have a compost pile, begin one now. Start with all the leaves that you rake up this fall. Chop up these leaves and other materials—this will lead to compost faster than if you leave the leaves whole. Add your grass clippings and kitchen scraps (minus any meats, bones, or animal fats).

To make compost, you need oxygen and moisture. Stir the pile with a garden fork every two weeks and spray it with water. Depending on the weather, you could have "black gold" in as little as six months.

### PLANTING

Plant container-grown and balled-and-burlapped shrubs.

1. Dig a hole that is at least three times as wide as the rootball. When planting balled-and-burlapped plants, it is important to loosen the burlap and any twine that is surrounding the trunk. If the material that surrounds the rootball is artificial burlap, carefully place the plant in the hole and carefully remove as much of the material as possible without disturbing the roots.

2. Apply a 2- to 3-inch layer of mulch around all new plantings, making sure to keep it away from the main stems or trunks. This way you won't create a damp, moist environment that is conducive to potential pest and disease problems.

3. Water all new plantings once a week unless there is adequate rainfall (1 inch a week). Water thoroughly, making sure the root area is saturated. This could take anywhere from $1/2$ to 1 hour, placing the hose at the center of the plant and allowing a pencil-size trickle.

Look for selections of *Camellia sasanqua*, which bloom early fall into winter. **Camellias** need a well-drained soil that is rich in organic material. Be sure not to plant them too deep (don't pile up soil around the trunk). Apply a 2-inch layer of mulch over an area extending at least 3 feet from the trunk. Although they will tolerate full sun, partial shade is best.

With its lustrous evergreen foliage and handsome flowers, *Camellia sasanqua* is popular to train as an espalier, in a hedge, for screening, or in a pot. The flowers—single, double, and semidouble—come in shades of red, white, pink, or rose.

## FERTILIZING

Removing diseased leaves from around shrubs will reduce insect and disease problems next year.

If deer are a problem, the best solution is to build a fence. Often this is not possible and gardeners must resort to other tactics. Deer Off® is an organic product reputed to repel deer and discourage other browsing animals because of its taste and smell.

If you have problems with whiteflies on **gardenia,** try blasting them with a jet of water from the hose.

Spray with insecticidal soaps to control aphids and spider mites. Be sure to get good coverage—spray until it drips off the plant.

---

# SHRUBS WITH COLORFUL FALL FOLIAGE OR FRUITS

F = colorful foliage      FR = colorful fruits
- *Aesculus parviflora* **Bottlebrush buckeye** F
- *Aronia arbutifolia* 'Brilliantissima' **Chokeberry** FR
- *Callicarpa americana* **American beautyberry** FR
- *Callicarpa dichotoma* **Beautyberry** FR
- *Calycanthus floridus* **Sweetshrub** F
- *Clethra alnifolia* **Sweet pepperbush** F
- *Fothergilla gardenii* 'Mt. Airy' **Fothergilla** F
- *Hydrangea quercifolia* **Oakleaf hydrangea** F
- *Ilex serrata* **Finetooth holly** FR
- *Ilex verticillata* **Winterberry holly** FR
- *Lagerstroemia* many cultivars **Crapemyrtle** F
- *Viburnum dilatatum* 'Iroquois' FR
- *Viburnum setigerum* 'Aurantiacum' FR

---

To prevent unwanted crops of chickweed in established shrub beds, apply a granular weed preventer. Read labels carefully before using any pesticide.

If you have a weedy area where you want to plant shrubs in the spring, you can use newspaper to smother the weeds. Put down a layer of newspaper, about three to four sheets thick, and then cover it with mulch. Come spring you can rototill the area, add soil amendments, and plant.

One of the advantages of not using chemical sprays to control insect and disease problems in your garden is that beneficial insects that can help control pest problems will not be killed. For example, ladybugs are known to feed on aphids, mites, scale, and many insect eggs. Praying mantises feed on a wide range of insects.

## PRUNING

Prune only dead, damaged, or diseased branches during this season.

# OCTOBER

## SHRUBS

### PLANNING

Fall leaf color is usually at its best during this month. Make notes on your favorite shrubs for fall. When you think about what to add to your garden, consider plants with colorful flowers, persistent fruits, and showy bark for fall and winter. Visit public gardens and discover the joys of the fall garden. Keep track of which plants have notable fall color in your garden journal.

### PLANTING

Both soil and air temperatures are cooler now, and with any luck we have had some rain. Plants and people are less stressed now than they were during the hot months of summer when keeping hydrated takes precedence over planting. Now is an ideal time to add new shrubs to your garden or move existing shrubs. Prepare the new location ahead of time so that the rootball will stay out of the ground for the least amount of time. The size of the rootball will be determined in part by the size of the shrub. When transplanting shrubs, be sure to dig a rootball large enough to ensure there are plenty of roots. If you can manage lifting a large rootball, remember that bigger is better.

Transplanting
• If your shrub is 2 feet tall and wide, start digging out about 12 to 18 inches from the center of the plant.
• Dig at this distance all the way around, loosening the roots as you go.
• Then dig under as far as you can and cut the roots so the rootball is free from the hole.

With two people and two spades, you have the advantage of working on opposite sides.
• Once the rootball is free, take a piece of burlap and slide it under the rootball. This will make it easier to move to its new home.
• When you plant your shrub in its new spot, make the planting area a bit higher than the surrounding soil. Plant the shrub so that the top of the rootball is at the same level as the soil surface in the planting area. This is the best way to provide excellent drainage for the roots.
• Fill in with soil and water in.

• Apply a 2- to 3-inch layer of mulch.

If you have an area that you want to plant next spring, you can prepare the soil now. Spreading 2 to 3 inches of composted manure on top of the soil and tilling it in immediately will result in a soil that is rich in nitrogen and ready to plant in spring.

If possible, perform a soil test (see Horticultural Practices, p. 7) before you begin planting this fall. When you plant, you may want to add a cup of garden lime and fertilizer, which can be mixed into the individual planting hole. If you use an organic product like animal manure, make sure it is well composted so it won't burn the roots of plants.

Mulch all new plantings with 2 to 3 inches of mulch.

This is also a good time to topdress your shrubs with homemade compost or other materials such as mushroom compost, cot-

Periodically perform a soil test to pinpoint the amendments needed.

tonseed meal, cow manure, or horse manure. Apply 1 or 2 inches of the selected material on top of the soil around the shrub, keeping it away from the main trunk. (Prior to doing this you should have removed old mulch.) Apply a new layer of mulch and water well.

Make sure any homemade compost or manure is well rotted (this usually takes about six months) before you use it in the garden. By following this practice you will avoid burning tender young growth with ammonia. While most shrubs are not likely to put on new growth in the fall, tender growth in the spring can burn if compost is too fresh.

## SHRUBS FOR FALL AND WINTER INTEREST

E = evergreen      D = deciduous

• *Euonymous alatus* **Burning bush** D (leaves turn fiery red in fall)

• *Fothergilla gardenii* **Fothergilla** D (exhibits red, orange, and yellow foliage in fall)

• *Ilex glabra* **Inkberry holly** E (olive-green leaves)

• *Kalmia latifolia* **Mountain laurel** E (glossy green leaves all year)

• *Leucothoe fontanesiana* **Drooping leucothoe** E (dark-green leaves turn purplish-bronze in winter)

• *Nandina domestica* **Heavenly bamboo** E (many selections, some with leaves in intense shades of red)

• *Rhododendron catawbiense* **Catawba rhododendron** E (large green leaves)

• *Sarcococca hookerana humilis* **Himalayan sweet box** E (glossy dark-green foliage)

• *Skimmia japonica* **Skimmia** E (evergreen leaves and brilliant berries)

• *Viburnum × pragense* **Prague viburnum** E (glossy green foliage)

## WATERING

Keep all new plantings well watered. Check them weekly and water as needed if there has not been a good rain (1 to 2 inches is a good rain). Don't let the cooler weather fool you. Wind can also cause plants to dry out more quickly.

## FERTILIZING

You can use a starter fertilizer when planting your new shrubs. Starter fertilizers have a high percentage of phosphorous to help plants establish roots quickly. A 10-52-17 ratio is fine. You can also fertilize shrubs with a balanced fertilizer such as 10-10-10. Read the label carefully before applying any fertilizers.

## PROBLEMS

There should be fewer insect problems as the weather cools off, but continue to check for signs of damage. Use an Integrated Pest Management (IPM) approach. This includes selecting varieties of plants that are best suited to grow in your environment and eliminating those that have proved to be in constant need of spraying just to keep them healthy. Check **euonymous** for scale, **azaleas** for lace bug, and **rhododendron** for black vine weevil (refer to July for recommended treatment).

## PRUNING

Prune dead or diseased wood from established shrubs. If there are any wild shoots or suckers, you can also remove them. (Suckers are shoots that arise from roots or underground stems.)

# NOVEMBER

## SHRUBS

### PLANNING

Once leaves fall, examine the structure of your shrubs and determine if they need pruning. Wait until they are dormant in winter or early spring before you do any drastic pruning. If two branches are rubbing or crossing, remove one of them.

### PLANTING

This is an ideal time to plant balled-and-burlapped and container-grown shrubs. The sooner you get them into the ground, the better. This will give them time to acclimate before the weather turns cold. Guidelines for planting shrubs:

1. Dig a hole that is at least twice as wide as the container the plant is growing in or the width of the rootball.

2. The depth of the hole should be no deeper than the depth of the container or the rootball.

3. Use the soil you dug out of the hole and fill in around the rootball, tamping it down to minimize air pockets.

4. Water well and apply a 2- to 3-inch layer of mulch.

Propagate **azaleas, hollies,** and other broad-leafed evergreens from cuttings. Here is

Walter's preferred method for propagating favorite shrubs:

1. Fill a plastic shoebox halfway (6 to 8 inches deep) with a 50:50 mix of peat moss and perlite. Make sure the mix is barely moist.

2. Take your cuttings. They should be 4 to 6 inches long. Strip off most of the leaves except for the top three or four.

3. Dip the end of the cutting in a rooting hormone like Rotone™, and insert it into the rooting medium.

4. Label each variety. Cover the box with clear plastic wrap and place in a sunny window. Check on weekly to make sure the medium has not dried out.

5. In one month, tug gently to see if any roots have developed. If the cutting does not resist, press it back into the mix and

check again in a few weeks. You should have roots in six to eight weeks.

6. Once you have roots, pot up the cuttings in small pots. Overwinter them indoors or in a cold frame until spring, when you can plant them outside.

### WATERING

Water all new plantings as well as existing plantings so that they are well prepared to go into winter.

### FERTILIZING

You can apply fertilizer lightly once shrubs are dormant. Use a balanced fertilizer like 10-10-10, applying $1/2$ pound per 100 square feet of shrub bed.

---

## MOLES AND VOLES

Moles may be mistakenly blamed for eating the roots of plants, but it is more likely that voles are the problem. Moles prefer insects. They tunnel through the soil, causing havoc as they go when plants are uprooted. Trapping is the most effective control for moles. Voles burrow under mulch and eat roots and stems as they go. To discourage them, try these techniques:

1. Pull leaves and mulch away from trunks and stems of plants (voles).

2. Put a shovelful of sharp gravel or expanded shale (Permatil™) in the planting hole (moles).

3. Use some castor oil in each planting hole (voles). For small plants a tablespoon should be adequate; for larger plants, use several tablespoons.

The fertilizer will be available to plants in early spring once they start actively growing again. As a general rule when using a granular 10-10-10, apply ¹/₂ tablespoon of fertilizer per foot of shrub height.

## PROBLEMS

Remove leaf litter that may harbor overwintering insects or diseases from the ground around shrubs.

## PRUNING

Limit your pruning to dead or damaged wood. If you want to prune evergreens, wait until they are dormant, usually in December, January, and February.

Here is a list of shrubs that bloom on old wood. Wait until after they flower to prune these shrubs:

- *Chaenomeles japonica*
- *Forsythia* species and cultivars
- *Fothergilla gardenii*
- *Hydrangea macrophylla*
- *Hydrangea quercifolia*
- *Philadelphus coronarius*
- *Rhododendron calendulaceum*
- *Rhododendron catawbiense*
- *Rhododendron maximum*
- *Spiraea prunifolia*
- *Viburnum* (most species and cultivars)

## CAMELLIAS

**Camellias** are a staple for many Southern gardens. By growing a range of types you can have blooms from early fall through spring. Mulch them with 2 to 3 inches of mulch. The mulch is especially important to conserve moisture and keep the camellia roots cool since they are close to the surface of the soil. Plants do not thrive in soils with a high pH. Water regularly for at least the first two years.

*Camellia japonica.* This is the **camellia** that most people think of when they refer to **camellias**. They grow 10 to 15 feet tall and 6 to 10 feet wide.

*Camellia sasanqua.* This species is more refined with smaller leaves and flowers. It may grow 6 to 10 feet tall. This species flowers from September into December. Many selections will tolerate full sun and drought but the better the growing conditions, the better the performance of your shrubs in general.

A camellia such as 'Guilio Nuccio' can be stunning in the garden.

# December

## SHRUBS

### PLANNING

Make notes in your garden journal about shrubs that look good in the winter. Don't limit yourself to evergreens. Deciduous shrubs with colorful berries, beautiful bark, or fragrant flowers also look good in winter. Plan to add some of these to your garden in the spring, or even now, provided the ground is not frozen.

Evergreen shrubs effective for screening or hedging in the shade:

- *Abelia grandiflora* **Glossy abelia** (5 to 7 feet)
- *Ilex glabra* **Inkberry holly** (8 to 10 feet)
- *Illicium* spp. **Anise** (6 to 10 feet, fragrant foliage)
- *Leucothoe populifolia* [*Agarista populifolia*] **Leucothoe** (8 to 12 feet)
- *Osmanthus heterophyllus* **Holly tea olive** (10 to 20 feet)
- *Viburnum* × *pragense* **Prague viburnum** (10 feet)

### PLANTING

If the ground is not frozen, continue to plant both container-grown and balled-and-burlapped shrubs. Wait until spring to plant bare-root shrubs.

### WATERING

Unless there is at least 1 inch of rainfall, water new plantings weekly and check to make sure evergreens don't dry out. If their needles are beginning to drop or to become dry and brittle, the plants may be dried out, a condition that can be avoided by timely watering.

### FERTILIZING

If you didn't topdress your shrub beds earlier in the fall, go ahead and do it now. Apply a 1- to 2-inch layer of organic material such as mushroom compost, cow manure, cottonseed meal, or horse manure around your shrubs. Don't pile it up around branches or stems where insect or disease problems could develop.

### PROBLEMS

Keep removing dead and diseased leaves from shrub beds. This will reduce the chances of insect and disease problems in the spring.

### PRUNING

You can do a little selective pruning of evergreens like **hollies, nandinas,** and **camellias** if you want to use them for holiday decorations, but wait until early spring, just before they begin to actively grow, to do any substantial pruning.

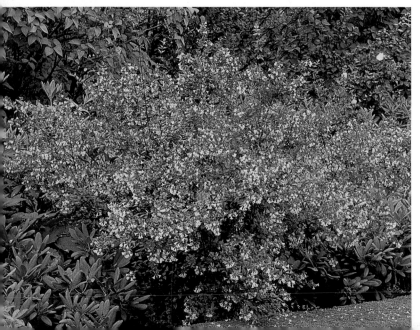

Glossy abelia is an old-fashioned favorite for a reason; it makes a terrific hedge for screening.

# TREES

Trees provide a framework for a garden, acting like a picture frame for the garden scene. They help create scale, and they set the tone for a particular garden type or style.

Whether deciduous, evergreen, weeping, upright, or columnar, trees come in all sizes, shapes, and forms. Depending on the variety, a tree can provide flowers in spring, shade in summer, and colorful foliage in fall. Trees help to define space, create privacy, provide windbreaks, and reduce the amount of energy needed to cool your home. In addition, they add curb appeal and increase property values. Evergreen trees provide screening or a backdrop for shrubs, perennials, and bulbs. Some trees, like paperbark maple with its glistening cinnamon-colored bark, brighten the winter landscape.

When it comes to choosing a tree for your own garden, be sure you know what the ultimate size of the particular tree will be. This information will help you determine where to site an individual specimen so it won't outgrow its allotted space in a short time or require constant pruning to keep it contained. When you design your garden, site your trees before you choose their companion shrubs and herbaceous plants. Where you locate your trees and the types you select can determine the feel of your landscape. Evergreens are often used in more formal gardens, while deciduous trees can be either formal or informal.

Planting a tree is an investment in the future. Choose your trees carefully, and you will reap the rewards for years to come.

## PLANTING TREES

Trees are sold as balled-and-burlapped, bare-root, or container- grown. Bare-root trees are available for purchase when they are dormant (not actively growing). The best time to plant bare-root trees is as soon as they are dug, or as soon as you receive them.

With balled-and-burlapped and container-grown trees there is more flexibility about what time of year you can plant. Provided the ground is not frozen, container-grown trees can be planted almost anytime, although during the hottest months the trees will sit and wait until soil temperatures cool off before they begin to put out roots.

Balled-and-burlapped trees are dug when trees are dormant, but they may be available from your local nursery throughout the growing season. This means they might have been dug a year ago and have had a chance to recover from any root loss they suffered during the digging process.

When you plant a tree, dig a hole that is wider than it is deep. As a rule of thumb, the planting hole should be at least twice as wide as the root-ball. While there may be some controversy about the best way to plant trees, as a general practice it is not necessary to amend the soil in the hole in which the tree will be growing. The sooner the tree adapts to unamended soil, the faster it will become established. If you amend it, you are creating an artificial environment for the tree. It is important, however, that the soil is loose and soft to help root growth.

It is also important to make sure the site where you plant drains easily. If it does not, dig out some of the existing soil and add organic amendments to help improve the texture and drainage.

After you plant, apply a 2- to 3-inch layer of mulch such as pine bark nuggets or pine straw to help keep tree roots cool and conserve moisture.

## WATERING

Water your trees as soon as you plant them; for the first six months, apply 1 gallon per foot of tree height per week unless there is one inch or more of rain weekly.

Once they are established, you should have to apply supplemental water only during periods of drought. If there has been no rain for a month or longer, get out the hose. Water is not free, but the money you spend to irrigate a mature tree may save it, which is especially desirable when the tree is a hundred-year old oak.

To supply a tree's minimum needs during times of drought, apply 15 gallons of water per inch of trunk diameter once per week. Example: a tree whose trunk is 12 inches thick, 4 feet from the ground, needs 180 gallons of water per week. Attach an inexpensive water timer to your soaker hose and set it to 180 gallons. It will shut off once 180 gallons has soaked out of the hose. Depending on the length of the hose, this could take two to three hours; for this amount of water, the cost will be just a few dollars.

For optimum tree health, apply the amount calculated twice each week during times of drought.

## FERTILIZING

A starter fertilizer may be the answer if you want to give a newly planted tree a jump-start. Some starter fertilizers come in a liquid form and can be mixed with water and applied at planting (refer to the product label for detailed information). In general, trees need little in the way of supplemental fertilizer unless you want to accelerate their growth, in which case you should apply fertilizer once in March and once in June. (Extra fertilizer tends to cause problems for mature trees and should be applied only if recommended by a professional arborist.)

## STAKING

Not all new trees need to be staked. If you have planted your tree in a windy location with very soft soil, staking will help keep the tree upright. To avoid girdling of the trunk or restricting growth, it is important not to pull the cords that attach to the stakes too tight. There should be a little give so the tree can sway naturally and develop a strong trunk. Remove stakes from small trees after the first year, and from large trees after the second year.

## PRUNING

When you plant trees, prune off dead or diseased roots or branches. Let the tree get established over a period of one year before you remove any large branches. Limit your pruning for all newly planted trees, including those that are balled-and-burlapped or container-grown; restrict your pruning to removing branches that cross or rub and those that are growing back into the crown of the tree.

Once your trees are established, they should require only a minimum amount of pruning to enhance their natural shape. If you want to train a tree in a formal shape or use it for espalier, more rigorous pruning or shearing may be appropriate.

Using the right tools is one of the keys to proper pruning. Use handpruners for branches 1/2 inch or less in diameter, loppers for branches 1/2 to 2 inches, and a pruning saw for branches larger than 2 inches. Pole pruners are best for trimming branches high up in a tree. If you need a ladder to reach branches, it's time to call a professional.

Timing is also important when it comes to pruning. If you're not certain of the best time to prune a particular tree, follow these guidelines: prune spring-flowering trees as soon as they finish blooming, and summer-flowering types in late winter or early spring. Doing so will reduce the chances that you will cut off next year's flower buds. Restrict your pruning in late summer and early autumn to grooming: removing dead twigs, spent blossoms, or seedpods.

Hiring a professional arborist is the best way to care for large trees. As your shade trees mature, you may want to put them on a pruning schedule. You can have a certain number of trees pruned each year, rotating so that mature trees are checked and/or pruned once every three years to remove dead or diseased wood. Regular pruning will help keep your trees vigorous, which makes them better able to ward off pest and disease infestations. If your trees need to be sprayed for any insect or disease problems, the arborist can do this, too.

# WHAT TO PLANT?

Gardeners are often overwhelmed with plant selections. Growers and garden designers who have many years of experience growing plants in our Georgia climate can help. Garden designer Jane Bath is the owner of Land Arts Nursery in Monroe, Georgia, a retail nursery that offers an extensive selection of ornamental plants. Here is a list of small to medium-sized trees that Jane finds outstanding for Georgia gardens:

- *Acer buergeranum* **Trident maple**
- *Acer palmatum* **Japanese maple** (many selections)
- *Chionanthus retusus* **Chinese fringe tree**
- *Cladrastis kentukea* **American yellowwood**
- *Cornus florida* **Flowering dogwood** (many selections)
- *Lagerstroemia indica* 'Natchez' **Crapemyrtle** (white)
- *Magnolia* 'Elizabeth'
- *Malus* 'Callaway' **Callaway crabapple**
- *Oxydendrum arboreum* **Sourwood**
- *Vitex agnus-castus* **Chaste tree**

## Trees for Georgia

| Botanical Name<br>Common Name | Height /<br>Width | Culture | Comments |
|---|---|---|---|
| *Acer barbatum*<br>**Florida Maple** | 25 to 30 feet /<br>10 to 15 feet | Full sun to light shade. | More adaptable than **sugar maple** for coastal gardens. |
| *Acer buergeranum*<br>**Trident Maple** | 20 to 25 feet /<br>10 to 15 feet | Full sun to light shade. | A good choice for small garden. |
| *Acer griseum*<br>**Paperbark Maple** | 15 to 30 feet /<br>10 to 20 feet | Full sun to half shade, with a moist, well-drained soil. | Outstanding cinnamon bark, leaves often exhibit good fall color. |
| *Acer palmatum*<br>**Japanese Maple** | 2 to 25 feet /<br>4 to 20 feet | Morning sun or light shade is best. | Many cultivars with colorful foliage and showy bark. |
| *Cercis canadensis*<br>**Eastern Redbud** | 20 to 30 feet /<br>25 to 35 feet | Full sun to half shade, average well-drained soil. | A wonderful native tree. 'Alba' has white flowers, and 'Forest Pansy' has purple leaves in spring that turn to green as they mature. |
| *Chionanthus retusus*<br>**Chinese Fringe Tree** | 15 to 25 feet /<br>15 to 20 feet | Full sun or part shade, a moist, well-drained soil. | A cousin to the native **fringe tree**, this species has glossy foliage and handsome bark. |
| *Cladrastis kentukea*<br>**American Yellowwood** | 30 to 40 feet /<br>40 to 50 feet | Full sun or part shade, a moist, well-drained soil. | Smooth gray bark, fragrant white flowers in late spring. Tolerates alkaline soils. |
| *Cornus florida*<br>**Flowering Dogwood** | 20 to 30 feet /<br>20 to 30 feet | Full sun to half shade; moist, well-drained soil. | Great tree for four seasons of interest. |

# CHAPTER EIGHT

## Trees for Georgia

| Botanical Name<br>Common Name | Height /<br>Width | Culture | Comments |
|---|---|---|---|
| *Crataegus viridis* 'Winter King'<br>**Winter King Green Hawthorn** | 20 to 25 feet /<br>20 to 30 feet | Full sun, well-drained soil. | Outstanding persistent red fruit and handsome peeling bark make this tree a winner. |
| *Cryptomeria japonica*<br>**Japanese Cryptomeria** | 40 to 60 feet /<br>20 to 30 feet | Full sun to part shade; moist, well-drained soil. | An elegant conifer for screening or a specimen. Look for the cultivar 'Yoshino'. |
| *Magnolia* 'Elizabeth'<br>**Elizabeth Magnolia** | 20 to 30 feet /<br>20 to 30 feet | Full sun to part shade; moist, well-drained soil. | Deciduous **magnolia** with creamy yellow flowers in early spring. |
| *Magnolia grandiflora*<br>**Southern Magnolia** | 40 to 60 feet /<br>30 to 40 feet | Full sun; moist, well-drained soil. | Use as a specimen tree or for evergreen screening. |
| *Magnolia virginiana* var. *australis*<br>**Sweet Bay Magnolia** | 40 to 50 feet /<br>15 to 20 feet | Full sun, tolerates wet soils. | Lemon-scented flowers, green leaves with silver undersides. This native is very adaptable. |
| *Malus* 'Callaway'<br>**Crabapple** | 20 to 25 feet /<br>20 to 25 feet | Full sun; moist, well-drained soil. | Pink buds open to white flowers. |
| *Oxydendron arboreum*<br>**Sourwood** | 25 to 30 feet /<br>15 to 20 feet | Full sun to part shade; well-drained soil. | White flowers in summer; red fall foliage. |
| *Prunus x yedoensis*<br>**Yoshino Cherry** | 30 to 40 feet /<br>25 to 40 feet | Full sun to part shade; well-drained soil. | Pink buds open to white flowers in spring; great specimen tree with a graceful habit. |
| *Quercus* spp.<br>**Oaks** | 40 to 80 feet /<br>50 to 90 feet | Full sun to part shade; well-drained soil. | Many species are suited for street trees or good for locations where a large specimen is needed. |
| *Tsuga canadensis*<br>**Canadian Hemlock** | 40 to 70 feet /<br>25 to 35 feet | A woodland with well-drained soil is ideal. | Effective as an evergreen screen, hedge, or specimen. |
| *Ulmus parvifolia*<br>**Lacebark Elm** | 40 to 50 feet /<br>40 to 50 feet | Full sun, well-drained soil. | Look for selections Athena and Allee. A choice tree for both urban and suburban landscapes, it provides interest in every season. |

# JANUARY
## TREES

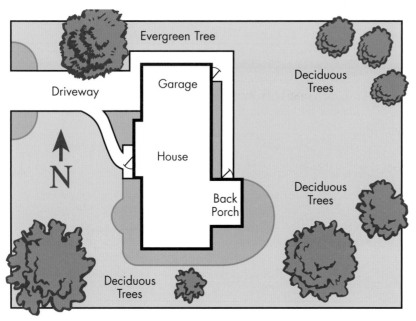

Sketch a simple layout of your property before planting trees.

## PLANNING

Make an inventory of existing trees, and draw a sketch of where they are located in your garden. Use your house as a point of reference, and indicate which direction is North. How do the shadows of the trees fall? Where are the densest shadows? Sketch where the shadows fall and how far they extend. This will help you determine where you have the most sun or shade and where you need to add trees.

Consider the type of soil you have as well as how well it holds moisture. This will help you decide what type of tree to plant.

Plan a mix of evergreen and deciduous trees to create maximum interest in your garden all year long. Evergreens planted in groups make an effective backdrop for deciduous trees. Mixing individual evergreens with a planting of deciduous trees will create interest throughout the year.

## PLANTING

This is a good time to plant trees, especially in the most southern parts of the state where winters are mild and the ground is never frozen. Plant balled-and-burlapped, container-grown, or bare-root trees. Before you plant,

remove all turfgrass and weeds from the soil surface. A flat shovel works well for this.

Bare-root trees are less expensive and easier to handle, and you can order them through the mail. A bare-root tree is usually up to 10 feet tall with a trunk less than 2 inches in diameter. When you purchase a bare-root tree, you are investing in its root system. If the tree has lots of branches but very few roots, it will take a long time to become established.

1. Make sure roots are healthy. Prune off any broken or dried-up roots. With clean cuts, the roots will heal quickly and there will be less chance of root-disease problems. This should be done when trees are dormant and temperatures are cold or cool (30 to 40 degrees Fahrenheit is ideal—slightly warmer is acceptable).

2. Keep tree roots moist until you plant. If the roots are dry when you receive the tree, soak them in a bucket of cool water for up to eight hours.

3. If you can't plant within a day or two, dig a temporary pit for the tree roots. Water the roots and fill in around them with a mixture of mulch and soil. This will cause the least amount of

stress for the tree and help reduce air pockets.

4. When you dig the hole to plant a tree, set the soil aside and use it to fill in around the roots. This way the tree roots will adapt quickly to their soil environment. If needed, adjust the pH by adding lime to your planting hole. It is best to have your soil tested (see Horticultural Practices, p. 7) before you plant.

Do not add fertilizer to the planting hole—it could burn the roots, and it's not necessary until the tree is established. If you use a root stimulator, follow directions carefully.

Although it is not necessary to amend the soil before you plant trees, it is important to be sure the soil is well drained. If the spot stays damp, select varieties that will thrive in wet soils, such as the **sweet bay magnolia** or **bald cypress.**

To help improve drainage, add soil amendments like ground pine bark or gritty all-purpose sand, both available at your local home improvement store. If you purchase a product labeled as builder's sand, make sure it contains only sand.

## HELPFUL HINT

Choose trees that offer more than one season of interest, like **dogwoods**, which have flowers in spring and red berries in fall, or **paperbark maple**, which has deep-green foliage in summer and peeling cinnamon-colored bark in winter.

If the existing soil is infertile clay subsoil, you should remove it and replace it with soil that has been amended with organic materials.

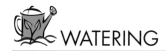

## WATERING

Water trees immediately after you plant them, and then once a week unless the ground is frozen. Apply 1 gallon per foot of tree height per week.

## FERTILIZING

In a natural forest, trees are the ultimate recyclers. They depend on the breakdown of the leaves that they lose each year for food. In general, trees need little in the way of supplemental fertilizer unless you want to accelerate their growth. Extra fertilizer tends to cause problems for mature trees and should be avoided.

## PROBLEMS

Inspect your trees for pest and disease problems. If you find scale (see Shrubs, March, Problems) on the bark or in the crotches (where the branches meet the trunk), spray with horticultural oils. Scale is common on **Bradford pear** trees. Be sure to get good coverage, spraying the branches, trunk, and crotches.

## PRUNING

Prune bare-root trees when you plant them. *Thin* branches that are closely spaced. This will allow better light and air circulation, resulting in better overall growth. *Prune* any broken roots.

When you prune, make your cut on a slant, just above a bud. On the side branches, make your cut just beyond a bud pointed towards the outside.

# FEBRUARY

## TREES

 PLANNING

Trees are classed as overstory and understory types. Overstory trees like **oak, pine,** and **hickory** form the upper canopy layer in a forest that has more than one layer. Understory trees like **red-bud, dogwood,** and **blackgum** grow beneath the overstory trees. For the most diverse and interesting landscape, plant a mixture of these two types of trees, as well as evergreen species for year-round interest.

 PLANTING

In the central and upper parts of the state, plant bare-root trees while they are still dormant. In southern and coastal areas, this is a good time to plant balled-and-burlapped or container-grown trees.

Because the soil in the planting hole settles a bit, plant so the top of the rootball is slightly higher than the ground level. This also helps correct a poorly drained soil situation.

 WATERING

Water new plantings weekly (new plantings are those that have been in the ground for less than six months). Apply 1 gallon per foot of tree height per week.

 FERTILIZING

Wait until early spring, just as new growth begins, to fertilize.

 PROBLEMS

As the weather warms, you might notice small holes in the bark of your **maple, pecan, pear,** or **magnolia** trees. The holes are characteristically $1/4$ inch in diameter and occur in rings around the trunk; often there are several rings in close proximity. The damage is not caused by borers, but by a bird: the yellow-bellied sapsucker. This member of the woodpecker family pecks holes in the bark and licks the sap that oozes out.

Control is nearly impossible. Fortunately, trees are not injured by the annual springtime visit. Hole-pecking will cease for the summer but may briefly recur in late fall.

 PRUNING

This is a good month to prune deciduous trees. Because there are no leaves, you can see the form of the tree and determine where you need to prune. When pruning to remove a large limb, do so in stages so the branch doesn't tear and split back to the tree, peeling off a section of the bark. Do not make a flush cut. Prune back to where the swollen part of the branch comes out from the tree. This is called the branch collar.

Sharp, good-quality tools are best; regular maintenance will ensure they last for a long time.

• Handpruners are ideal for heading and thinning stems up to $1 1/2$ inches in diameter.

• Loppers are ideal for selective pruning of larger branches.

• Saws are useful for branches that are more than 2 inches thick.

Some saw blades can be sharpened, but others should be replaced periodically. Check the product label for specific information about your blades.

Tips for pruning your newly planted trees:

1. Remove dead or diseased branches.

2. Remove broken branches below the point of injury back to a healthy branch.

3. Prune to remove branches that are crossing or rubbing. Wounds can develop where branches rub, creating an environment conducive to pest and disease problems.

4. Remove branches that form narrow V-shaped crotches with the main trunk. These crotches are weak and may break in the future. To minimize this problem, select improved varieties of trees with strong branching habits.

## CONIFERS FOR THE GEORGIA GARDEN

Both needled evergreens and broadleaf evergreens like **hollies** and **magnolias** take center stage in the winter garden. Needled evergreens come in shades of blue, green, golden, and silver (examples are **pines, cedars,** and **hemlocks**). They range in size from the dwarf to the majestic and are useful as hedges, screening trees, windbreaks, or specimens. It is true that **Leyland cypress** is fast-growing, but there are many other choices when it comes to conifers for your Georgia garden:

• *Cephalotaxus harringtonia* **Japanese plum yew** tolerates part shade, and deer consume it only as a last resort. There are both upright and prostrate forms. Depending on the cultivar, they range in size from 5 feet to 20 feet at maturity.

• *Chamaecyparis obtusa* **Hinoki falsecypress**—there are many different cultivars and sizes of this conifer. It prefers a moist, well-drained soil and full sun.

• *Chamaecyparis nootkatensis* **Alaska cedar**—growing 20 to 40 feet in the garden, it likes full sun or light shade.

• *Chamaecyparis pisifera* 'Filifera Aurea' is a golden form of the **Japanese falsecypress**.

• *Cryptomeria japonica* **Japanese cedar**—there are a number of cultivars available, including the popular 'Yoshino', which can reach 50 feet at maturity.

Limb Removal

Branch Collar
(Do not cut here)

February is a good month for maintenance pruning because you can easily see what needs to be pruned.

# MARCH
## TREES

### PLANNING

Plan to add at least one tree to your garden this spring. Visit your local botanical garden to get an idea of how large a particular variety will be when it matures (see Resources, p. 288).

**Sweet gum** trees have distinctive fall foliage, but the seedpods they drop ("sweet gum balls") can be a tremendous nuisance. There are sprays that cause the flowers to abort so there will be no seedpods, but these are expensive and impractical, as the tree must be sprayed completely every year.

A better solution is to plant the selection known as 'Rotundiloba', which does not form fruit.

### PLANTING

Plant balled-and-burlapped or container-grown trees; refer to February for planting directions.

### WATERING

Water newly planted trees once a week (unless you get 1 inch of rain) for at least the first six months and up to a year after they are planted. After they are established, check them monthly, and plan to water if there is a drought.

Winter winds can dry out established conifers. Check the soil (feel down several inches), and water if it is dry.

### FERTILIZING

Fertilize trees once they leaf out, with a slow-release fertilizer such as Nursery Special™. Read product label directions carefully before applying any fertilizers.

For mature trees, use the following guidelines when applying a granular fertilizer:

1. Estimate the canopy spread of an individual tree in square feet. Apply $3/4$ pound ($1^1/2$ cups) of 16-4-8 or 12-4-8 (or a fertilizer with a similar ratio) for each 100 square feet of canopy spread.

Reduce the rate applied by half when fertilizing conifers such as **pines, hemlocks,** and **junipers,** or when trees are growing in a lawn that receives regular applications of fertilizer.

2. Apply by broadcasting the fertilizer evenly under the tree, as far as the canopy extends and slightly beyond.

3. Water-in the fertilizer—this will wash it off any grass blades and help the fertilizer get to the tree roots more quickly.

4. Repeat this fertilizer application in July.

### PROBLEMS

If you see webs in the crotches of your **crabapple** or **ornamental cherry** trees, the trees probably have tent caterpillars. The caterpillars leave their nests during the day to feed and can defoliate your tree in no time. Wait until early evening, then remove each nest by piercing it with a

Prepare a good-sized hole—as deep as and about twice as large as the rootball—and add amendments if needed.

long stick and winding the web around the end.

For severe infestations, spray inside the web with a product containing B.t. Remember that even complete defoliation of a limb will not hurt a healthy tree; it will have plenty of time to grow new leaves after the caterpillars disappear in May.

 PRUNING

Prune to remove dead, broken, or diseased branches, and prune out branches that are rubbing or crossing. Both young trees and established mature trees respond to this type of pruning. Pruning large mature trees helps keep them vigorous; such pruning is best done by a professional arborist.

Remove water sprouts (clusters of branches that grow straight up, often from an old pruning wound) on a regular basis. Water sprouts can weaken a tree and can be difficult to get rid of later.

## HELPFUL HINT

**Pines** send out new growth called "candles." This new growth is soft and pliable and usually a bright, fresh green. To encourage a **pine** to produce dense foliage, wait until the candles are 2 to 4 inches long, then pinch or clip off the tips. If you want to prevent the **pine** from growing larger, wait until the candles are about 1 inch long, then shear them off from both the sides and the top of the tree.

Grafted trees (several weeping forms are grafted) may send out suckers from the underground rootstock. Prune off these suckers so your tree can use its energy efficiently to produce the desired healthy leaves, branches, and blooms of the cultivar you selected.

Don't prune **maples** or **river birch** now. They bleed (produce excess sap) if pruned in late spring.

Although anxiety-producing for the gardener, bleeding does not harm the tree.

Sometimes mature trees create too much shade—even shade-loving plants need light to grow. If your shaded **rhododendrons** and **azaleas** are not blooming and lack vigor, they may not be getting enough sunlight. Selectively prune to remove branches; this will open up your tree and allow more light to reach the plants below.

It will also improve air circulation and reduce the potential for disease problems like powdery mildew.

Prune needled evergreens such as **pines, cedars, hemlocks, and junipers.**

Shearing means that every branch is clipped to an even height at the surface, as with hedges or topiary. The best time to shear needled evergreens is just after they begin to put out new growth in early spring, a time that brings warmer soil and air temperatures.

Pruning now will stimulate dormant buds to begin growing, resulting in a fuller tree.

# APRIL

## TREES

### PLANNING

When you consider what happened to the **American elm**, you can see why you should avoid monoculture, even in your own garden. (Monoculture is planting many plants of only one species in an area.) Years ago, the **American elm,** *Ulmus americana*, was planted in great numbers throughout the United States; when used as an avenue tree, its graceful vase shape created a dramatic effect. Then the trees were attacked by a fungus known as Dutch elm disease, a fatal disease carried by **elm** bark beetles that bore into elm limbs. The disease spread from tree to tree very quickly, with devastating effects: whole neighborhoods were denuded.

Fortunately for gardeners today, there are a number of disease-resistant selections of the **American elm.** Look for 'American Liberty' **elms,** a series of six selections introduced by the Elm Research Institute. Other resistant selections are 'Delaware #2', 'New Harmony', 'Washington', and, 'Valley Forge'. Another **elm** species that exhibits resistance to the Dutch elm disease (but not the elm leaf beetle) is the **Chinese** or **lacebark elm,**

*Chinese elm makes a great substitute for the American elm.*

228

*Ulmus parvifolia.* The cultivar Allee® ('Emer II') has an upright spreading habit and gray to orange-brown peeling bark; Athena® ('Emer I') is a broad-spreading tree with shiny green leaves, some yellow fall color, and colorful bark in shades of gray, green, and orange-brown—both of these are fast-growing and adapt to a range of growing conditions.

Even if you choose these disease-resistant selections, it is still important to plant a diversity of trees in your garden.

### PLANTING

This is a good time to add container-grown or balled-and-burlapped trees to your garden. Be sure to water them regularly during the first year while they become established.

### WATERING

Keep watering new plantings. Apply 1 gallon per foot of tree height per week.

### FERTILIZING

Fertilize trees once they leaf out. Use a slow-release fertilizer such as Nursery Special™.

**Palms** like a fertilizer that is rich in micronutrients, especially magnesium and manganese. Use a slow-release fertilizer that includes micronutrients (refer to the label). A nutrient ratio of 3:1:2 such as 12-4-8 is best.

### PROBLEMS

Dogwood anthracnose (an-THRAK-nose), a fungus, has been attacking **dogwoods** throughout forests in the Eastern United States. The symptoms of this disease, also called *discula*, usually show up in lower limbs first and may spread to the whole tree if not controlled. The disease affects **dogwood** trees whose leaves do not dry off during the day. Leaves will exhibit spots with tan or brown blotches, bordered in purple, and the leaves will become severely distorted. Infected leaves cling to the tree, even after other leaves drop normally in the fall, and cankers form on the main trunk at the junction of each stem. (Cankers are swollen protrusions that can surround a twig or stem, girdling it and causing the branch to die). Trees in a weakened condition are more susceptible to discula—a healthy tree is the best defense against disease and insect problems. Most home landscape **dogwoods** have plenty of air circulation around them, which protects the leaves from infection. *Discula* is not expected to cause problems for Georgia **dogwoods,** except those growing in cool mountain valleys. To help prevent **dogwood** diseases:

• Plant **dogwoods** in moist, fertile soil, in light shade or full sun.

• Remove and destroy any leaves infected with fungus as soon as you notice them. Rake up leaves as soon as they fall, and burn them or dispose of them. Do not add them to your compost pile.

## DISEASE-RESISTANT CRABAPPLES

The best way to avoid problems with any plant is to keep it healthy. By choosing varieties that are disease-resistant, you are a step ahead of the game. Many **crabapple** are susceptible to scab, fireblight, cedar-apple rust, and powdery mildew. Some **crabapple** selections have been hybridized for disease resistance.

• 'Centurion' grows to 25 feet high and wide at maturity. Red buds open to rose-red flowers.

• 'Donald Wyman' grows to 25 feet high, with a large rounded habit. It has white flowers and persistent red fruits in winter.

• 'Harvest Gold' offers flowers that are pink in bud and white in flower. Its habit is upright and spreading, growing 25 feet high and 25 feet wide. Its golden fruits look good well into December.

• 'Indian Summer' has rose-red flowers and red fruit. It grows to 18 feet high and 19 feet wide.

• 'Jewelberry' is a small tree, growing 8 to 12 feet high. Pink buds open to white flowers and are followed by masses of glossy red fruits.

• Prune out any dead twigs or branches. Prune only during dry weather since fungus problems are usually worse in wet weather.

• Spray trees that you place a high value on with a fungicide in early spring.

• Keep trees watered during periods of drought.

• Plant disease-resistant **dogwood** hybrids such as 'Aurora', 'Galaxy', and 'Constellation'.

*Cornus kousa* **Kousa dogwood** blooms later and is also less susceptible to diseases than *Cornus florida*. Its flowers appear on the tops of the branches above the foliage and are more starlike in appearance. The large, red, strawberry-like fruits hang down and put on a show in late summer to fall. In winter, the colorful peeling bark adds color to the landscape.

 PRUNING

There is still time to prune or shear candles on evergreens. Restrict your pruning of deciduous trees to removing dead or diseased branches—wait until winter to do any extreme corrective pruning or to remove any large branches.

# MAY

## TREES

### PLANNING

Take notes in your garden journal on spring-blooming trees. Record the color of their flowers and how long they bloom, the trees' overall appearance, any pest or disease problems, and whether faded blossoms persist or if they drop off and disappear. Use this information to help guide you in your decisions about adding or deleting trees to your garden.

Keep track of varieties that are successful. Knowing the scientific name is the best way to assure that you get the plant you want.

### PLANTING

Plant container-grown trees. Apply 2 to 3 inches of mulch, making sure to keep it away from the trunk. (You can also grow trees in containers on a permanent basis. **Japanese maple**s make lovely specimens when planted in a decorative pot.)

Before you purchase a container-grown tree (or shrub), make sure the plant has healthy roots.

1. One way to check the roots is to lift up the plant by gently tugging on the trunk. If it pulls easily away from the soil, then the plant may have root rot. If it

holds firm, it probably has enough healthy roots.

2. Another way to check the health of the whole root system is to gently ease the rootball out of the container. If the upper half of the rootball has lots of healthy roots, you can remove any roots on the lower half that look unhealthy, and your tree should thrive.

### WATERING

Water all new plantings. Thereafter, if there is not adequate rainfall (1 inch per week), apply 1 gallon per foot of tree height per week. Check established trees (trees that have been in the ground for a full year or longer) once a month to make sure they are getting enough water.

### FERTILIZING

When you plant new trees, mix some root stimulator into the existing soil. This will help plants get established more quickly.

If you want to give new trees (those you planted during the past six months) an extra boost, fertilize them with a complete slow-release fertilizer that has a ratio like 10-10-10. This should only be done twice a year—

March and July are recommended. (See March for more information and application suggestions.)

Generally, established trees don't need to be fertilized.

### PROBLEMS

A bagworm is a wingless moth that forms a protective mass of brown twigs in a cocoon around its body. From a distance the bagworms look almost like tiny cones hanging from a tree. The moths consume great numbers of needles from evergreen plants like **juniper, arborvitae,** and **Leyland cypress.** Pick off and destroy the bags whenever you find them. Be sure to wear gloves to protect your fingers from the tree needles.

If you choose to use a contact insecticide, April and May are the months when the moths are most susceptible.

If you notice that the leaves on your **sycamore** tree have irregular brown dead spots and leaf stems are black at the base, you may have sycamore anthracnose. This leaf blight is caused by several fungi. The fungus first appears on the leaves, then spreads through the veins and down into the stem and branch. The spores that spread the fungus overwinter in the cankers on the branches and in diseased leaves. A lack of overall vigor, heavy rainfall, and low temperatures exacerbate the effects of this disease, which can include total defoliation. Fungicides are effective only if they are applied before the disease appears in the spring. To control the disease:

• Prune out any dead or infected leaves, twigs, and branches.

• Rake up and burn infected leaves, to reduce infections in the future.

• Fertilize in spring to increase tree vigor.

• Water trees during a prolonged dry spell (a month or longer without rain).

You may notice that leaves on your **red maple, oak, hickory,** or **pecan** are disfigured and deformed—by small growths—bumplike swellings—that cover the leaves. In the worst cases, leaves turn yellow and drop prematurely. These are leaf galls, which are caused when insects like mites, midges, and tiny wasps lay their eggs on tree leaves. These curiosities of nature will not go away even if the larvae in the leaves are killed. There are two approaches to dealing with galls:

## WEEPING TREES

No matter what the season, trees with a weeping habit make a dramatic statement in the landscape, whether planted in a container or in the ground. The following trees have a weeping growth habit or arching branches.

- *Acer palmatum* var. *dissectum* **Japanese maple**
- *Cercidiphyllum magnificum* 'Pendulum' **weeping katsura**
- *Cercis canadensis* 'Covey' (also known as 'Lavender Twist') **weeping redbud**
- *Cercis canadensis* ssp. 'Traveller' **weeping redbud**
- *Cedrus atlantica* 'Glauca Pendula' **weeping blue Atlas cedar**
- *Cornus florida* 'Pendula' **weeping Florida dogwood**
- *Fagus sylvatica* 'Pendula' **weeping European beech**
- *Malus* 'Red Jade' **weeping crabapple**
- *Prunus subhirtella* 'Pendula' **weeping Higan cherry**
- *Styrax japonicus* 'Pink Cascade' **weeping Japanese pink snowbell**
- *Ulmus alata* 'Lace Parasol' **weeping winged elm**

1. Learn to live with this oddity.
2. Rake and dispose of the leaves each fall to reduce insect populations.

## PRUNING

Remove dead or diseased leaves and limbs on trees. Don't put them in your compost pile or they may introduce problems into your garden in the future.

Prune **Leyland cypress** to control seridium canker. The symptoms: older foliage, especially the interior foliage, turns yellow and then brown; branches and twigs die; sunken reddish, dark brown, or purple areas (the cankers) form on the bark; and sap oozes. The sunken areas are the cankers. Often the infection starts on the lower branches of the tree and moves up.

Prune out diseased limbs, being sure to cut 6 inches below where the infection occurs. This will ensure that you prune where healthy wood is growing. Prune branches that are broken or torn from the main trunk. Sterilize your pruner between each cut with a 1:10 bleach: water mixture.

## TREES

## PLANNING

If you only have trees that bloom in the spring, now is the time to think about planting some that offer blooms in summer. Many of the southeastern natives offer beautiful blooms and interesting forms. Some consider the **southern magnolia** *Magnolia grandiflora* the quintessential southern landscape plant, with its large, white, delicious lemon-scented flowers and glossy evergreen leaves. In recent years, a number of meritorious hybrids have been introduced into cultivation.

• 'Bracken's Brown Beauty' is a selection with a dense, compact habit. It grows to 30 feet high.

• 'Edith Bogue' is a cultivar that has a pyramidal habit and leaves that are narrower than those of the species, often with wavy margins.

• 'Hasse' is a selection that offers an upright growth habit and small, very glossy leaves.

• 'Little Gem' is a cultivar that flowers when it is young, and the undersides of the small leaves are rust-colored. It reaches only 15 to 20 feet at maturity. Great for a container or small garden, it flowers most of the summer.

If you see attractive summer-blooming trees that you like, make notes so you will be ready to purchase and plant them in the fall or next spring.

## PLANTING

Plant container-grown trees, and be sure to keep them watered regularly. Mulch the area around a tree immediately after planting.

## WATERING

The summer months can be stressful for plants and people. If you don't have an irrigation system, soaker hoses are one way to water your plants thoroughly. Sprinklers are also an option, but make sure you get uniform coverage. Water newly planted trees once a week unless you get 1 or more inches of rain.

**Japanese maples** with finely divided leaves are quite susceptible to moisture stress during the heat of the summer. The first sign of stress is browning and scorching of the leaves. When planting, consider that **Japanese maples** prefer a location where they will receive light shade during the hottest part of the day. Spread a 2-inch layer of pine bark mulch under **Japanese maple** trees to help conserve moisture. Water trees weekly, allowing the soil to dry slightly between waterings.

## FERTILIZING

Trees do not need to be fertilized until July.

## PROBLEMS

**Ornamental cherry** trees are affected by a disease called bacterial canker, which causes gum to ooze from the trunk of the tree. It can be distinguished from borer damage because there is no sawdust mixed with the gum. Bacterial canker most often infects weak trees, particularly those that have been planted in heavy clay soil or a place where water stands after a rain.

Transplant the tree if it is small, or redirect the water flow.

Trees are also weakened by a low soil pH. Raise the pH quickly by dissolving 1 pound of hydrated lime in 5 gallons of water. Sprinkle on the soil under the tree branches.

Maintain the pH by scattering 1 pound of garden lime per inch of trunk diameter evenly under the branches of the tree. Wait one year, then have the soil tested to determine if additional lime is needed.

Handpull weeds that are right next to tree trunks. A nonselective weedkiller can be used under and around trees if you make sure not to spray it on foliage, bark, or exposed roots.

Most diseases are detected with your eyes. **Oak** trees, however, sometimes contract a disease that is perceived with your nose. Sap dripping down the trunk of an **oak,** a few feet from the ground, may indicate a slime flux infection. Also called "wet wood," slime flux is caused by fermentation of the sap under the tree's bark. The oozing sap may smell like vinegar or beer. Wasps, bees, and butterflies are drawn to the smell.

Wash the ooze and slime off the trunk to prevent bark damage. Water the tree regularly during the summer to help it internally fight off the infection.

A silvery sheen on **dogwood** leaves usually signifies the presence of a fungus called powdery mildew. The fungus sucks moisture from the leaves and causes them to yellow and fall prematurely. It can be prevented by spraying leaves with a fungicide in early May and continuing through mid-June. Fungicide applied now will not cure the infected leaves. Once you see the fungus on the leaves, all that can be done is to protect new leaves.

## SUMMER BLOOMING TREES

- *Clerodendrum trichotomum* **Harlequin glory bower**
- *Franklinia alatamaha* **Franklin tree**
- *Koelreuteria paniculata* **Goldenrain tree**
- *Lagerstroemia indica* **Crapemyrtle**
- *Magnolia grandiflora* **Southern magnolia**
- *Magnolia virginiana* **Sweet bay**
- *Sophora japonica* **Scholar tree**
- *Stewartia* spp. **Stewartia**
- *Vitex agnus-castus* **Chaste tree**

If the infection is severe, the **dogwood** may lose up to half its leaves in July. Water infected trees regularly to help them withstand moisture stress.

**Crapemyrtle** leaves may be covered with grayish-white powder, which indicates they are affected by powdery mildew. Spray leaves with a synthetic fungicide before plants bloom. Neem oil may be helpful in minimizing symptoms. The National Arboretum developed mildew-resistant hybrid **crapemyrtles** by crossing *Lagerstroemia indica* with *L. fauriei* (native to Japan, *L. fauriei* has beautiful bark, is cold hardy, and exhibits a high resistance to powdery mildew). The following hybrids are mildew-resistant:

- 'Acoma' (white flowers)
- 'Biloxi' (light pink flowers)
- 'Comanche' (coral pink flowers)
- 'Hopi' (orange-red to dark-red flowers)
- 'Lipan' (medium-lavender flowers)
- 'Miami' (medium-pink flowers)
- 'Muskogee' (light-lavender flowers)
- 'Natchez' (white flowers)
- 'Osage' (clear, light-pink flowers)
- 'Sioux' (bright pink, fragrant flowers)
- 'Tuskegee' (deep-pink to red flowers)
- 'Yuma' (medium-lavender flowers)
- 'Zuni' (medium-lavender flowers)

 PRUNING

Prune back spring-flowering trees once they finish blooming. Remove seedpods.

# JULY

## TREES

### PLANNING

It is tempting to transplant small **dogwood** or **magnolia** trees from the woods into your landscape, but this is usually not a good idea. The roots may be tangled with the larger roots of nearby trees, making transplant shock likely. Only small seedlings can be transplanted successfully—a tree taller than 4 feet is not likely to survive. Because the parentage of the tree isn't known, the seedling may never produce the number of flowers you anticipate. Named, improved selections of trees are more robust, easier to plant, and more likely to bloom regularly.

Make notations in your garden journal about how trees are performing. Are there places in your garden where trees can be added? Think about what type of tree would best suit your needs. A medium to large deciduous shade tree can help keep your house cool in the summer and warm in the winter when sunlight is more welcome. When it comes to selecting shade trees, there are many choices. Here is a list of medium to large trees well suited to provide shade:

- *Acer rubrum* **Red maple** (there are many selections)
- *Betula nigra* 'Heritage' **Heritage birch**
- *Cladrastis kentukea* **Yellowwood**
- *Fagus grandifolia* **American beech** (there are many selections)
- *Ginkgo biloba* **Ginkgo**
- *Nyssa sylvatica* **Black tupelo**
- *Prunus × yedoensis* **Yoshino cherry**
- *Quercus virginiana* **Live oak**
- *Robinia pseudoacacia* **Black locust** (there are many selections)
- *Ulmus parvifolia* **Lacebark elm**

### PLANTING

Wait until fall to plant trees. They won't put out many roots or much branch growth when planted in hot weather.

Gardeners that live on the coast are challenged to find plants that will tolerate constant winds, salt spray, and sandy soils. Here is a list of trees for coastal gardens.

- *Cryptomeria japonica* **Japanese cryptomeria**
- *Magnolia grandiflora* **Southern magnolia**
- *Ilex opaca* **American holly**
- *Pinus thunbergiana* **Japanese black pine**
- *Quercus virginiana* **Live oak**
- *Thuja occidentalis* **American arborvitae**
- *Ulmus parvifolia* **Lacebark elm**

### WATERING

Keep newly planted trees watered. Water once a week unless you get 1 or more weekly inches of rain. Drought stress can make your trees more susceptible to insect and disease problems.

### FERTILIZING

Refer to March for fertilizing guidelines.

### PROBLEMS

Pick off and destroy bagworms whenever you find them (see May). If you choose to use a contact insecticide, April and May are the months when the moths are most susceptible.

### PRUNING

There is still time to prune trees that bloomed in the spring. Cut off seedpods and prune lightly to shape the trees. Prune summer-flowering trees as soon as they finish blooming, if pruning is needed. There are a couple of ways to prune trees.

**Heading:** Selectively remove the tips of branches at their growing points rather than shearing them back. This selective pruning will leave behind a dormant bud which will eventually grow and fill in empty spaces.

Before
Heading

## HELPFUL HINTS

Fresh tree stumps are a nuisance in the landscape. Chemical removal is totally ineffective. There are two methods for removing stumps.

1. Naturally is the slow, inexpensive method. Eventually, Mother Nature will prevail and the stump will rot away. You can speed up the process by drilling several large, deep holes in the top of the stump. Pack the holes with topsoil gathered from under a nearby tree. Thoroughly soak the soil and stump with water. Cover the stump with clear plastic, and let the sun's heat accelerate the decomposition process.

2. Mechanically is the fast method. Rent a stump grinder, or hire a company to grind your stump below the soil surface. Collect the chips, and use them for mulch under shrubs and nearby trees. Avoid mixing the chips into the soil—during decomposition, they will rob nutrients from the grass or plants you use to replace the tree.

2. Cut off the stub just outside the branch collar (this is the swollen part that comes out from the tree where the branch attaches). The branch collar will gradually close over the wound.

After
Heading

Before
Thinning

After
Thinning

**Thinning:** This type of pruning removes the branch or stem at its origin. Be sure not to make a flush cut—leave a branch collar. When removing large limbs, remove a large section first. A section about a foot long should remain; this will make it easier to finish pruning correctly.

1. Cut upward partway through the branch, and then downward, slightly away from the first cut.

# AUGUST

## TREES

 PLANNING

Are your existing trees healthy? Begin to make a list of trees to add to your garden this fall. Now is a good time to observe trees and make notes on which ones have survived the summer intact, without any damage from insect or disease problems. Examine the foliage and bark for signs of damage.

• If the bark is cracked and loose around the tree, inspect it for signs of insect problems, and treat as needed.

• If more than 50 percent of the leaves have brown spots or rings around spots, examine them more closely. Your tree may have a fungus that can be identified and treated, if necessary.

• If the edges of the leaves are scorched, make sure your tree is being watered on a regular basis to protect it during periods of drought. Even established trees that have been in the ground for a year or longer benefit from watering if there is no rain for a month.

 PLANTING

Wait until the weather cools off a bit before you plant any trees.

 WATERING

Keep newly planted trees watered. Check them weekly. If you are growing trees in containers, they will need watering more frequently than those planted in the ground.

Trees need watering in summer as do lawns, flowers, and shrubs. A drought-stressed tree is more likely to suffer damage from insects and disease.

• A soaker hose laid under the drip line of the tree and an inexpensive water timer are the best tools.

• Apply 15 gallons of water per inch of trunk diameter once per week to supply a tree's minimum needs during drought. Example: a tree whose trunk is 12 inches thick, 4 feet from the ground, needs 180 gallons of water per week. Attach the water timer to the soaker hose and set it to 180 gallons; it will shut off once 180 gallons has soaked out of the hose. Depending on the length of the hose, this could take two to three hours. For this amount of water the cost is just a few dollars.

• Apply the amount calculated twice each week for optimum tree health.

*A rain guage, soaker hose, and mulch will help in the struggle against drought.*

 FERTILIZING

Wait until spring to fertilize trees.

 PROBLEMS

If you have a wooded lot, chances are you have poison ivy. Identifying poison ivy is not always easy, but as a rule, avoid "vines with three leaves." Sometimes **Virginia creeper,** a desirable vine that has five leaflets, is mistaken for poison ivy. If in doubt, leave it alone! Purchase an inexpensive guide to plants that includes color photographs of poison ivy.

As a young vine, poison ivy crawls along the ground and eventually climbs nearby trees. If left untended, these small vines can climb up the trunks of mature trees and develop into huge vines. As a vine matures, the leaves also get larger and in the fall may turn beautiful shades of red, orange, and yellow. Don't be fooled by its autumnal beauty; this vine causes severe allergic reactions in many people. Do not use burning as a method to control poison ivy. Breathing in the fumes can cause a severe reaction in some people. There are several ways to control it. Whichever way you select, be sure to wash your clothes, gloves, and body immediately after contact with the plant.

1. If you decide to be brave and handpull poison ivy, be sure to wear heavy-duty gloves and a long-sleeved shirt.

2. You can also use the plastic newspaper bag method to avoid touching the plant. Slip the bag over your hand and arm. Pull the poison ivy, then carefully pull off the bag so it encloses the plant.

3. Spray the mature leaves on the tops, bottoms, and stems with a nonselective weedkiller.

If the foliage on your **hemlocks, junipers,** or **hollies** is speckled with brown or red spots, they may have spider mites, tiny sap-sucking creatures that are kin to the spider. Tap a branch over a piece of white paper, and circle any spots. If they move, you will know mites are present and active. To control, first use the hose to blast these critters off the foliage. If this doesn't work, try using insecticidal soap or a miticide. Wait ten to fourteen days after you spray, then try the white-paper test again.

You may need to repeat applications of miticide for effective control.

You may notice the leaves on your mature **tulip poplar** trees turning yellow and dropping prematurely. Premature leaf drop, leaf scorch, and many other dieback problems are often caused by environmental stresses like pollution, or lack of moisture during hot, dry summers. The best control is to keep established trees watered and stress-free during the hot summer months.

Each week, apply at least 15 gallons of water per inch of trunk diameter.

## PRUNING

After a major thunderstorm, you are probably tempted to get out the saw and clean up! Before you prune, here are some things to think about.

• You may need to hire a professional arborist or tree-removal company if large limbs are hanging or broken and require a chain saw, or if damage to the trees is up so high that an extension ladder is required to reach it.

• Always follow safety precautions. Be aware of any power lines that may be hanging in the tree. Don't touch any wires that may be on the ground.

• Remove broken branches that are still attached to the tree. Remove hanging branches, and smooth ragged edges with a sharp knife; this will encourage wounds to heal faster and reduce the number of places for insects to hide.

• Damaged smaller branches should be pruned back to where they join a larger branch.

• Don't top your trees. Cutting the main trunk back to stubs will reduce the vigor of the tree. New growth from the stubs tends to be spindly and susceptible to future storm damage.

# September

## TREES

### PLANNING

With fall approaching, it's a good time to start shopping for trees. Here is a list of deciduous trees that display flowers or colorful foliage in the autumn.

- *Acer palmatum* (many selections exhibit leaves of red, yellow, orange)
- *Acer rubrum* (many selections with colorful leaves of red, yellow, and orange)
- *Amelanchier* spp. (leaves of red, yellow, and orange)
- *Cornus florida* (red fruits and red to purple leaves)
- *Ginkgo biloba* (yellow leaves)
- *Hamamelis virginiana* (fragrant yellow flowers)
- *Hamamelis × intermedia* 'Diane' (leaves turn gold)
- *Nyssa sylvatica* (leaves of red, yellow, and orange)
- *Parrotia persica* (leaves in shades of red, yellow, and orange)
- *Stewartia* spp. (orange and red leaves)

### PLANTING

Plant container-grown trees this month, but wait until cooler weather to plant balled-and-burlapped trees (refer to February for guidelines on planting).

*Acer rubrum* Red maple

### WATERING

Continue to check newly planted trees on a weekly basis, and water them if you don't get at least 1 inch of rain per week.

### FERTILIZING

Wait until spring to fertilize newly planted trees. As long as they are thriving, established or mature trees don't need to be fertilized. However, if you want to topdress your trees with an organic material such as mushroom compost or horse or chicken manure, now is the time to do so. Topdressing breaks down over time and feeds the soil. This is also a good time to apply a fresh layer of mulch around trees. Scrape away old mulch, and apply 1 to 2 inches of topdressing and 2 to 3 inches of fresh mulch.

### PROBLEMS

Fall webworm attacks certain deciduous trees including **birch, maple, cherry, linden, willow, honeylocust,** and **crabapple.**

- Unlike the eastern tent caterpillar, which builds its nest in the spring, the fall webworm is not noticeable until late summer or early fall when the nests appear at the end of the branches.

• Since defoliation is minimal and occurs late in the season, at a time when trees naturally begin to drop their leaves, there is generally no cause for alarm.

• Destroy any nests that can be easily reached by pruning them out (if possible, burn the infested branch once you have removed it from the tree), and don't worry about those you can't reach.

Rake up fallen leaves, and add them to an existing compost pile or use them to start a compost pile. One way to speed up the process of leaf decomposition is to mow with a mulcher mower. The chopped leaves will turn into compost more quickly.

**Bamboo** is an attractive plant for screening, but it is extremely hard to control. It spreads by aboveground rhizomes and belowground roots. A clump can expand more than 20 feet in just a few years. To control **bamboo** as it is planted:

• Transplant small clumps in spring, just before growth begins.

• Identify where you want the plant to grow—and where you don't want it. Dig a trench 18 inches deep around the area. A powered ditching machine is a great help in this endeavor.

• Insert 24-inch-wide aluminum roof flashing edgewise in the trench, leaving 2 inches showing above the soil surface.

Lap the ends of the flashing at least 18 inches over each other.

To control **bamboo** once it has escaped, chop down every cane in the area where you do not wish it to grow.

**Bamboo** shoots will continue to arise each spring where the canes were chopped down. Inspect the spot weekly, and knock down the shoots as they arise. The **bamboo** roots will eventually starve if you are diligent about removing the shoots.

 PRUNING

Remove any dead or diseased branches, but wait until trees are dormant to do any severe pruning. Trees that are pruned now before they are completely dormant could experience cold damage. This damage occurs when new young growth sprouts during mild spells and doesn't have time to harden off before winter sets in (see July).

If the scale-like leaves on your **cryptomeria** are turning yellow and brown and the plant looks wilted, you may have phytophthora root rot, a secondary problem that occurs in soils that are poorly drained or wet.

The best way to avoid this problem in the future is to select the right plant for the right place. If your soil is poorly drained,

select tree species that will thrive in this environment.

You may notice caterpillars with spines and barbed horns chewing on the leaves of your **oaks, hickories,** or **maple** trees. If you do, you are being visited by the orange striped oakworm, whose eggs were laid on the branch by a moth in June. These caterpillars are about 2 inches long with eight yellow stripes and a row of large yellow spots. It is disturbing to see an entire branch stripped of its foliage, but the damage done by the caterpillar is not serious (the tree is about to lose its leaves anyway this season). Handpicking is an option; be sure to wear gloves. If the tree is small or newly planted, spray the leaves with *Bacillus thuringiensis.*

It is not likely that the caterpillars will return next year, even if you do nothing about them.

If your tree has a long dark line running from the top of a branch all the way to the ground and its bark is split open and peeling back from the trunk and branches, you probably have lightning damage. Prune back exploded bark to a healthy strong attachment. Water the tree regularly. Do not fertilize.

Only time will tell if the tree will survive.

# OCTOBER

## TREES

### PLANNING

This is a great month to plant both evergreen and deciduous trees in Georgia. In the more northern parts of the state they will still have time to establish roots before winter, and in the southern parts of the state, soils will be cooler and less stressful for new plants.

Although it is tempting to transplant small **dogwood** or **magnolia** trees from the woods into your landscape, this is usually not a good idea (see July, Planning).

### PLANTING

*Ginkgo biloba* is a handsome large tree whose leaves turn golden in the fall. Its only disadvantage is the messy and offensive-smelling fruit that the female tree produces. To avoid this problem, plant only male cultivars purchased from a reliable source. Male selections grafted or grown from cuttings of other males include 'Autumn Gold', 'Fairmount', and 'Princeton Sentry'.

As trees begin to drop their colorful fall foliage and prepare for winter dormancy, nurseries will begin to dig trees for fall planting. These balled-and-burlapped trees should be planted

as soon as you purchase them, to ensure the roots acclimate as quickly as possible. Before planting, loosen the burlap around the main trunks of balled-and-burlapped trees, and take container-grown trees from their containers. To plant a balled-and-burlapped tree:

1. Dig a hole that is at least twice as wide as the rootball and no deeper than the rootball.

2. Cut holes in or remove the burlap that surrounds the rootball. This allows better penetration of water for the roots and helps the tree to become established more quickly.

3. After planting, water thoroughly (water the tree weekly for the first year).

4. Mulch with a good 2- to 3-inch layer of compost, shredded pine bark, pine straw, or other similar materials, being sure to keep it from direct contact with the main trunk. (When the mulch is thick and comes into contact

Follow the directions in this section to ensure successful planting. Remove the burlap—often of synthetic material—as much as possible.

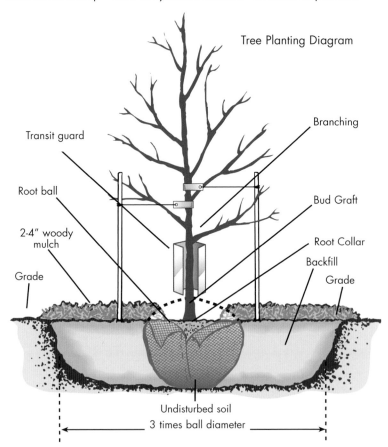

Tree Planting Diagram

Transit guard

Root ball

2-4" woody mulch

Grade

Branching

Bud Graft

Root Collar

Backfill

Grade

Undisturbed soil

3 times ball diameter

with tree bark, and we have lots of rain, the tree is bound to have insect and disease problems.)

5. Water the tree weekly for the first year.

## WATERING

Keep newly planted deciduous trees or conifers well-watered (newly planted trees are those planted within the past six months). Conifers will survive the winter much better if their needles or scales are filled with water when they go into winter dormancy—they will be less likely to dry out from winter winds.

## FERTILIZING

If your trees are growing well, there's no reason to fertilize. If you decide to fertilize, first get a soil test—it will help you determine which nutrients you need to add in the spring.

## PROBLEMS

Rake up any diseased leaves, and dispose of them separately from the compost pile. This will cut down on the possibilities for spreading pest and disease problems in the future.

## STAKING TREES

Wind, humans, and animals can sometimes uproot newly planted trees.

• For small trees, two stakes hammered into the ground near the trunk are adequate. Use a soft rope or cord. Loop a figure eight around the trunk, and tie it to the stake.

• For larger trees, use three stakes placed at equal distances around the tree, outside the root system. Use cord or wire, covered in rubber hose to protect the trunk. Loop the wire around the trunk, and attach it to the stake. Allow for some slack in the cord or wire. The trunk should be able to move a little as it grows so it will develop strength.

• Stake small trees for one year and larger trees for two years.

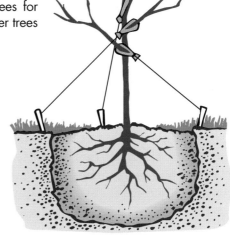

Stake newly planted trees to help prevent high winds from uprooting them.

## PRUNING

Prune out any dead or diseased wood from newly planted trees.

# NOVEMBER

## TREES

### PLANNING

This is an ideal month to plant trees in Georgia, provided the ground is not too wet. To determine the ground's wetness, dig up a shovelful of soil. If you can form a loose, crumbly ball that holds together briefly but still breaks apart easily, then the soil is just moist enough for planting. If you can't get the shovel out of the ground easily, then it is too wet.

Evergreen trees provide interest in the landscape all year long, serving as focal points, wind barriers, screening, and hedges, while large deciduous trees provide much welcome shade in the summer. Once you have large key trees sited, it is a good time to think about adding understory trees that will grow happily under the canopy of the larger trees such as **oak, hickories,** and **ash.** Some good understory trees are:

- *Acer barbatum* **Southern sugar maple** (25 to 30 feet, good choice for wet coastal areas)
- *Acer buergeranum* **Trident maple** (20 to 25 feet, colorful fall foliage, handsome bark)
- *Acer leucoderme* **Chalk maple** (25 to 30 feet)
- *Amelanchier arborea* **Juneberry** (20 to 30 feet, flowers in spring, berries in summer)

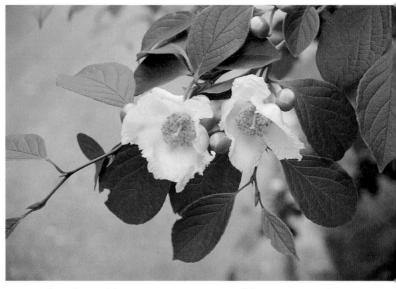

Imagine how beautiful a Japanese stewartia will be in your garden next spring.

- *Cercis canadensis* **Eastern redbud** (20 to 30 feet, pink flowers in spring, flowers appear before leaves)
- *Chionanthus retusus* **Chinese fringe tree** (20 feet, white flowers in spring)
- *Chionanthus virginicus* **Grancy graybeard** (20 to 30 feet, white flowers in spring)
- *Franklinia alatamaha* **Franklin tree** (20 to 30 feet, white flowers in summer)
- *Halesia carolina* **Carolina silverbell** (30 to 40 feet, white bell-shaped flowers in spring)
- *Stewartia monadelpha* **Tall stewartia** (20 to 30 feet, white flowers in summer)
- *Stewartia pseudocamellia*

**Japanese stewartia** (20 to 40 feet, white flowers in spring/summer)
- *Styrax japonicus* **Japanese snowbell** (20 to 30 feet, white bell-shaped flowers in spring)
- *Styrax obassia* **Fragrant snowbell** (20 to 30 feet, fragrant white bell-shaped flowers in spring)

### PLANTING

If you have cracked and heaved sidewalks, the common culprits are tree roots. The damage occurs when a root grows under the concrete and then swells to a much greater diameter as the years pass.

• Avoid planting trees within 15 feet of a sidewalk or drive.

• If the cracking has just begun, you might find relief by trenching beside the sidewalk and removing the offending root. Next, install 12-inch-wide aluminum flashing edgewise in the trench to prevent other roots from growing under the concrete.

Tree roots depend on a network of soil organisms, called mycorrhizae, to do much of the work involved to absorb water and nutrients. Research has shown that in poor soils, adding mycorrhizae to the soil when a tree is planted can help it become established faster.

Although any tree can be valuable in some situations, a few seem to have so many problems that they are rarely appropriate for a home landscape.

• **Silver maples** are prone to weak limbs, which crash down unexpectedly in windstorms. The roots often swell aboveground, making lawn mowing a hazardous experience.

• **Lombardy poplar** trees are sold for quick screening. They grow tall quickly, but they typically survive only a few years in the Georgia climate.

## HELPFUL HINT

Older trees often develop hollows in the trunk due to damage from previous years. It is not recommended that you fill these hollows. Concrete, foam, or other materials will eventually crack, making an excellent hiding place for borers and disease fungi.

• **Norway maple** has invasive roots and is usually short-lived in our summer heat.

## WATERING

Conifers can dry out quickly in winter winds. Be sure to keep them watered even during the colder months, unless the ground is frozen.

## FERTILIZING

Fertilize in the spring.

## PROBLEMS

**English ivy** is an attractive and hardy ground cover that spreads rapidly, but when the **ivy** climbs up trees, it is damaging. As it grows into the treetop, the **ivy** foliage shades lower branches. In addition, the **ivy** collects additional ice and rain, and the tree may be damaged by the additional weight. **English ivy** is not a parasite—its aerial roots simply

cling to the tree bark for support. Here's how to get rid of it:

• Use a heavy screwdriver to pull the vine from the bark so your pruners can grip the vine enough to clip it in two.

• Pull the vine from the tree trunk as high as you can reach.

• Remove the **ivy** from an area 6 feet from the tree trunk in all directions.

• The **ivy** in the tree will gradually wither over the next year.

Protect newly planted young trees from damage caused by rodents and lawnmowers.

Build a simple wire cylinder. Use 1/4-inch hardware cloth that is 18 to 24 inches high. Wrap it very loosely around the tree trunk.

Trees purchased from a nursery may have tree wrap covering the lower trunk. Tree wrap makes a great hiding place for boring insects. The string or wire used to attach a stake to the tree will eventually girdle the trunk.

Remove the wrap and any stakes attached to the trunk soon after planting.

# DECEMBER

## TREES

### PLANNING

Deciduous trees in the winter landscape become studies in shape and form. Some display striking bark or interesting flowers. Visit botanical gardens and arboreta, and take note of the trees that stand out in the winter garden.

Evergreens serve a multitude of roles as specimen plants, hedges, screens, and windbreaks. **Hemlocks, pines, holly,** and **arborvitae** withstand pruning and can be maintained as large hedges. **Pines** for Georgia vary in their rate of growth, habit, and ultimate size; they thrive with little or no fertilizer and can survive a good bit of drought. Most **pines** develop a large taproot; therefore, with the exception of small seedlings, they are best purchased as balled-and-burlapped or container-grown plants. Consider these **pines:**

- *Pinus rigida* **Pitch pine** (40 to 60 feet in height by 30 to 50 feet)
- *Pinus strobus* **White pine**
- *Pinus taeda* **Loblolly pine** (60 to 90 feet tall)
- *Pinus thunbergiana* **Japanese black pine** (20 to 80 feet by 20 to 40 feet; tolerates salt spray)
- *Pinus virginiana* **Virginia pine** (15 to 40 feet by 10 to 30 feet)

### PLANTING

In the southernmost parts of the state where the ground does not freeze, you can plant container-grown trees.

1. Remove the tree from the container. Examine the roots to be sure they are healthy.

2. Use a hand cultivator to loosen the roots. If roots are wrapped around the rootball many times, use a sharp spade or pair of pruners and make four vertical cuts, evenly spaced around the rootball. Gently tease the roots at the bottom of the rootball so that they spread out. Make sure there are no large roots at the top of the rootball that could girdle the trunk.

3. Place the tree in the hole on top of a solid mound of soil. Fill in the hole around the tree, about halfway, using your shovel handle or foot to firm the soil and eliminate air pockets. Water the tree and add the rest of the soil, being careful not to compact it.

4. Mulch the area around the tree with a 2- to 3-inch layer of material, keeping it away from the trunk of the tree (mulch piled up against the trunk of the tree can cause it to rot).

5. Once it is planted, water the tree thoroughly. Thereafter, water the tree regularly, weekly for the first six months or so, and then once a month for the next year, if there is not adequate rainfall.

### WATERING

Keep new plantings watered.

---

## CHOOSING A "CUT-YOUR-OWN" CHRISTMAS TREE

- Call the Georgia Farmers and Consumers Market Bulletin (404-656-3682) in early November and ask for their yearly Christmas tree farm issue.
- To investigate other farms, visit the Georgia Christmas Tree Growers Association (**www.gachristmastree.com**).
- Plan to bring the whole family on the outing. Many farms have wagon rides, a petting zoo, or other activities.
- Bring a big piece of plastic to use to cover the tree on the way back. Otherwise, the tree needles will be as dry as toast after a frigid and windy ride on top of your car.

## FERTILIZING

Hold off on fertilizing until early spring.

## PROBLEMS

Rake up any leaf litter that you missed in the autumn; this will reduce the number of places for insects to overwinter.

## PRUNING

Prune out any dead, diseased, or broken branches from trees planted in the past six months.

If you have deciduous trees that require major pruning, schedule the work to be done in the next few months while trees are still dormant. Be sure you hire or consult with an arborist if you are not sure which branches are alive and which are dead.

# HELPFUL HINTS
## Choosing a Cut Christmas Tree from a Lot

• Good varieties are **Fraser fir, Scots pine, Noble fir, white pine, Virginia pine,** and **Leyland cypress**.

• Shake the tree or pull your fingers lightly down a branch—few needles should drop out.

• Remember to cut at least $1/2$ inch off the base of the tree before standing it in water.

## Caring for a Live Christmas Tree

• Good varieties are **cryptomeria, hemlock, Hinoki cypress, umbrella pine, arborvitae, Leyland cypress,** and **Virginia pine**. Not recommended: **Colorado blue spruce, Alberta spruce,** and **white pine**.

• Plan to have the tree indoors for no more than seven days so it will have a better chance of surviving when you plant it outside.

• Keep the rootball moist. Ice cubes wrapped in a cloth and placed on top of the ball will slowly trickle water to the roots.

• If you cannot plant the tree on your property, offer to plant the tree at a local school, church, or synagogue.

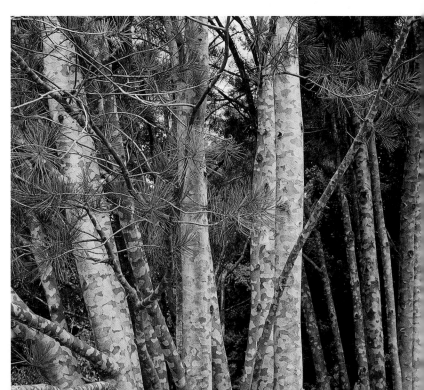

A lacebark pine's beautiful bark is an added bonus in the winter landscape.

# VINES & GROUND COVERS

Much as rooms are more complete with window treatments and floor coverings, gardens have a more finished look when they are enhanced with vines and ground covers. Both groups of plants play important roles in the landscape and extend the possibilities for adding color and interest to your garden all year long. Vines add verticality and help make maximum use of your growing space; ground covers provide a carpet beneath shrubs and trees, offer an alternative to lawns, and help conserve soil moisture.

## VINES AND HOW TO USE THEM

There are many selections of vines for Georgia gardeners, both annual and perennial, including types grown for brightly colored flowers, attractive seedpods, dramatic foliage, and distinctive bark. Whether you train them to grow up a masonry wall, fence, or arbor, vines require a structure or surface to grab, cling to, twine around, or drape over. The types and styles of available supports are as diverse as the many varieties of vines that grow and thrive in Georgia. The size and durability of the structure you use to support your vines should be determined by the characteristics of the particular vine you are growing. Large woody ornamental vines such as wisteria require substantial support, perhaps a large solid arbor. Other vines, such as Carolina jessamine, can be trained to cover a fence.

# CHAPTER NINE

What makes a plant as a vine? This depends on the individual plant. Some plants, like certain types of cotoneaster or old-fashioned shrub roses, are not true climbing plants but simply have a lax habit—you can train them to grow up a structure or against a wall by tying branches and stems in place. Certain other roses require little or no encouragement before they threaten to take down a building. To keep them in check you must prune them two or three times a year. Still other plants bloom in the same spot year after year without requiring constant care.

Vines enhance the garden scene and complement other blooms: Roses and clematis are a classic combination, often blooming at the same time. Some vines, like Carolina jessamine and English ivy, can be left to sprawl on the ground, making effective ground covers. Vines come in all forms, from the cultivated climbing 'New Dawn' rose to the cross-vine *Bignonia capreolata,* a native vine in our woods.

Vines and shrubs can live as happy companions in the garden. There are vines with fantastic foliage, colorful flowers, and interesting fruits, helping to provide year-round interest. When you use a shrub as a living trellis for a clematis, you can have blooms in more than one season. For example, if you train a summer-blooming hybrid clematis to grow up through an azalea that blooms in spring, you will have flowers in the same spot at two different times of year. To maintain this combination, simply cut back the clematis after it flowers (see March for more information about pruning clematis).

## HOW VINES CLIMB

The popular English ivy attaches itself to trees, walls, and other surfaces with short, clinging adventitious roots. In a similar fashion, climbing hydrangea and Boston ivy, also true clinging vines, attach themselves with rootlike holdfasts. Honeysuckle, akebia, wisteria, and star jasmine twine their stems around supports. Porcelain berry and climbing types of clematis attach themselves by twisting, using a leaf petiole as a tendril to cling to a support. There are also vines like climbing roses, which have no means of attachment and require tying to hold them to a support.

## GROUND COVERS AND HOW TO USE THEM

Any plant that effectively covers the ground might be considered a ground cover. Turf or lawn is perhaps the most popular ground cover, but in this chapter we will focus on alternatives to turf. Ground covers serve a number of functions. As a living mulch, they not only help conserve soil moisture, but they keep roots of trees and shrubs cool in the summer and warm in the winter. Some ground covers, like periwinkle, offer handsome evergreen foliage. Others, like green and gold, display attractive flowers in spring, and handsome foliage throughout the growing season. On a steep bank where turf is impractical, ground covers like monkey grass can be invaluable for controlling erosion.

## AREA COVERED BY 100 GROUND COVER PLANTS

The following chart (reprinted with permission) comes from the publication "Spacing Plant Material: Groundcovers" produced by The University of Georgia Cooperative Extension Service. It predicts the area that will be covered if you use 100 plants at various planting distances.

| Planting Distance (inches) | Area Covered (sq. ft.) |
|---|---|
| 6 | 25 |
| 12 | 100 |
| 18 | 225 |

# CHAPTER NINE

This information is especially useful when you are trying to figure out how many plants you will need for covering large areas with ground covers. Remember that starting with small, well-rooted plants is not only easier but more cost-efficient. The chart is intended as a guide, not absolute instructions. In certain places where you want an immediate effect, such as on a steep bank where erosion is a problem, you may want to space plants closer together. Or you may be planting a fast-growing spreader like English ivy, and you can space plants farther apart if you have time before you need the spot to look filled in.

## PLANNING

Before you purchase vines and ground covers to add to your garden, take stock of where you will use these plants. If you are planting a vine like wisteria, make sure you provide a structure that is strong enough to support this tenacious climber. It twists its stems around a support and can get very large, both in height and in the diameter of its woody stem (4 inches in no time)—the bigger the arbor, trellis, or gazebo, the better. Other vines, like many of the hybrid clematis, will be happy to twine around a piece of clear nylon line and won't threaten to take down your two-car garage.

When it comes to ground covers, some, like mondo grass, are well suited as a substitute for lawns while others, like green and gold, are better for creating a patch of color in a woodland garden. It pays to do some research before you begin to plant. Choose the right plant for the right place, and you will have greater success.

## SOIL PREPARATION

Whether you are planting vines or ground covers, soil preparation is important. If you are trying to cover a large area of ground, there are two methods you can use for preparing the soil.

1. Prepare the entire area before you plant.

2. Prepare individual holes, mixing a shovelful of organic material with the existing soil in the hole.

The second technique may be faster and is all that is needed for certain plants that have many stoloniferous roots, or for plants that root easily from their stems and leaf nodes (Ornamental raspberry puts out roots wherever it touches the soil). Another approach for covering a large area with a ground cover is to prepare the planting area, put down 1 to 2 inches of mulch, and then plant through the mulch.

## FERTILIZING

Vines and ground covers can be treated like perennials and shrubs when fertilizing. If you mix a slow-release granular fertilizer into the soil when you plant, you will not need to fertilize as often as you would if you use 10-10-10 or 8-8-8. As a general rule, you can apply fertilizer twice a year, once in March and once in June. If you have a large area of ground covers in place of a lawn, you can broadcast the fertilizer. If you plant vines in combination with shrubs or trees, they won't need to be fertilized separately but will get enough fertilizer when you fertilize their companions.

## PEST CONTROL

Vines and ground covers are subject to many of the same pest and disease problems that affect other ornamental plants, like aphids, spider mites, scale, and fungus. To help keep damage to a minimum, select varieties that are suited for the environment in which you will plant them. Practice Integrated Pest Management, or IPM. Keeping plants watered and mulched will help them ward off problems, too.

## PRUNING

Once established, most ground covers require only a minimum of pruning. English ivy and periwinkle can be pruned if they are getting out of

## CHAPTER NINE

bounds or if you want them to fill in and become more bushy in growth. Other ground covers, like green and gold, bugleweed, and mazus, do not require regular pruning but may need to be divided if clumps get too large and begin to lose vigor. Monkey grass will benefit from annual pruning or shearing in early spring to a height of 2 to 3 inches. This can be easily accomplished with a lawn mower. Within weeks new growth will cover any sign of pruning.

Perennial vines should be pruned selectively, depending on when they flower. To avoid cutting off flowerbuds, it is important to learn whether a particular vine blooms on old or new growth. Certain perennial vines like Carolina jessamine can be pruned back to a height of 1 foot if they are straggly and lack vigor. Annual vines don't require pruning; they can be left until they are killed by a frost. At this point you can easily clean up and remove the dead vines.

## Perennial Vines for Georgia

| Botanical Name<br>Common Name | Size and Habit | Culture | Comments |
|---|---|---|---|
| *Akebia quinata*<br>**Five-leaf Akebia**<br>Raisin Vine | Grows 20 to 40 feet long. An evergreen climber, the leaves emerge with purple tinges and turn blue-green as they mature. | This tough vine tolerates a wide range of soil types and grows in sun or part shade. | There are curious chocolate-purple flowers and showy dark-purple fruits. |
| *Ampelopsis brevipedunculata*<br>**Porcelain Berry** | A deciduous climber with twining tendrils. Grows to 20 feet or higher and needs a strong support. | Plant this vine in full sun or part shade in a well-drained soil. | Grow this vine for its colorful fruits, which appear in late summer in shades of lavender-blue and purple. Aggressive. |
| *Bignonia capreolata*<br>**Crossvine** | Grows to 30 feet or higher. Produces 2-inch brownish-orange, trumpet-shaped flowers in spring. | Plant this semi-evergreen (except in the most northern and coastal areas, where it is evergreen) vine in full sun or part shade in a soil that is moist, but well-drained. | 'Tangerine Beauty' has bright apricot-orange flowers that last for weeks. |
| *Clematis* spp. and cvs.<br>**Clematis** | Depending on the type, clematis vary greatly in height from less than 1 foot to over 40 feet high. The flowers on the species are often tiny, but the hybrids can have flowers up to 10 inches across. | **Clematis** like sun and a soil that is moist, but well-drained. Mulching is especially helpful to retain moisture. | The climbing types are not self-clinging, but twist for support, clinging with a petiole. If you don't provide a structure (even string will do), **clematis** will sprawl on the ground. |
| *Decumaria barbara*<br>**Climbing Hydrangea** | Grows to 30 feet high or higher with glossy green leaves that are 2 to 4 inches long and 1 to 2 inches wide. | A native vine that likes shady woodland situations with a moist soil, it will also tolerate dry soils. | This deciduous vine bears clusters of fragrant white flowers in May or June. |

# CHAPTER NINE

## Perennial Vines for Georgia

| Botanical Name<br>Common Name | Size and Habit | Culture | Comments |
|---|---|---|---|
| *Gelsemium sempervirens*<br>**Carolina Jessamine** | This hardy evergreen vine grows 10 to 20 feet high and spreads out with equal vigor if given a support to grow on. | Grows best in full sun, but tolerates shade. Plant in a moist, well-drained soil. | Fragrant yellow flowers appear any time from February to April. |
| *Hydrangea anomala petiolaris*<br>**Climbing Hydrangea** | A true clinging vine that attaches itself with rootlike holdfasts. Grows 60 to 80 feet. | Plant this woody vine in full sun or shade in a moist, well-drained soil. | Slow to get established—once it does, this is a four-season plant. White flowers in midsummer, fresh green leaves all summer. Foliage turns buttercup yellow in fall. |
| *Lonicera* x *heckrottii*<br>**Goldflame Honeysuckle** | Grows 10 to 20 feet high but is not invasive like many **honeysuckles**. From spring until frost, produces flowers that are carmine in bud with yellow insides. | Grows in full sun or half shade. Plant this vine in a soil that is moist, but well-drained. | A deciduous vine except in the lower and coastal parts of Georgia, where it is semi-evergreen. |
| *Parthenocissus quinquefolia*<br>**Virginia Creeper** | This vigorous vine grows 30 to 50 feet high and clings to the ground, fences, and walls. | Grow this deciduous vine in full sun or shade, in moist soil types. | In the autumn the leaves turn shades of purple, red, and crimson. |
| *Passiflora* spp. and cvs.<br>**Passionflower** | These vines climb by tendrils, reaching 20 to 30 feet or higher. There are evergreen, semi-evergreen, and deciduous types. | Plant this vine in full sun in a well-drained soil. Has beautiful flowers; some have edible fruit. | A favorite larval food of the Gulf fritillary butterfly. |
| *Polygonum aubertii*<br>**Silver Lace Vine** | A fast-growing deciduous vine, it can cover 100 square feet in a season. It becomes a mass of creamy-white flowers in spring. | Great for quick cover on a fence, arbor, or hillside. Plant in full sun. This aggressive grower is drought-tolerant. | To delay flowering, cut this vine back to the ground in early spring. A good candidate for seashore gardens. |
| *Schizophragma hydrangeoides*<br>**Japanese Hydrangea Vine** | This woody vine climbs by holdfasts to 30 feet or higher. | Train this vine to cover masonry walls or trees, in a shade garden. | The selection 'Moonlight' has blue-green foliage that has a silvery cast. |
| *Trachelospermum jasminoides*<br>**Confederate Jasmine** | With support, this evergreen vine will grow to 20 feet high. Fragrant white flowers, shaped like pinwheels, appear in spring and summer. | Plant in sun or shade in moist, well-drained soil. | Foliage starts out a glossy light green and turns darker as it matures. Great for training on walls, pergolas, and arbors. |

## CHAPTER NINE

## Perennial Vines for Georgia

| Botanical Name<br>Common Name | Size and Habit | Culture | Comments |
|---|---|---|---|
| *Wisteria floribunda*<br>**Japanese Wisteria** | The leaves are 12 to 16 inches long, divided into fifteen to nineteen leaflets. Clusters of violet flowers are 1½ feet long. This vine will grow to heights of 40 feet or more. | Plant this aggressive vine in a well-drained soil in full sun. | Prune after it stops flowering and then again in summer. Stop pruning by the end of June so that you won't prune off next year's flowerbuds. |
| *Wisteria frutescens*<br>**American Wisteria** | The leaflets are 7 to 12 inches long, and the compressed clusters of flowers are 4 to 6 inches long. | Plant in full sun in a well-drained soil. | Overall, the **American wisteria** is less aggressive than the Asiatic types. |

## Ground Covers for Georgia

| Botanical Name<br>Common Name | Size and Habit | Culture | Comments |
|---|---|---|---|
| *Ajuga reptans*<br>**Bugleweed** | Depending on the cultivar, it can grow 4 to 10 inches tall and spread 18 inches or more. | Grow in moist, well-drained soil in part shade. | There are many selections with dark-purple foliage. This ground cover can be invasive. |
| *Chrysogonum virginianum*<br>**Green and Gold** | Grows 6 to 9 inches tall and 12 inches wide. There are 1-inch-wide yellow daisy flowers in spring, followed by sporadic flowers in autumn. | Plants thrive in shade in a moist, well-drained soil. If planted in full sun, they must have soil that is constantly moist. | A great woodland ground cover. 'Eco Lacquered Spider' has gray-green foliage and long stolons. It spreads much more rapidly than the species. |
| *Fragaria* 'Pink Panda' | Each plant grows 4 to 6 inches tall and spreads out 12 to 18 inches in one season. | Plants are happiest in full sun to partial shade in a soil that is well-drained. | This ground cover has beautiful foliage and pink flowers in early spring. |
| *Juniperus conferta*<br>**Shore Juniper** | Grows 1 to 2 feet high and 6 to 8 feet wide. | Plant in full sun in a well-drained soil. Great for coastal gardens. | There are numerous prostrate selections of **juniper** that make good ground covers for full-sun situations. |
| *Lamium maculatum*<br>**Spotted Nettle** | Grows 8 to 12 inches high and 18 inches wide. Stoloniferous and creeping, this plant makes a good variegated ground cover. | Part shade is ideal for this ground cover. A moist, well-drained soil is best. | There are many improved selections with handsome foliage. |

## CHAPTER NINE

# Ground Covers for Georgia

| Botanical Name<br>Common Name | Size and Habit | Culture | Comments |
|---|---|---|---|
| *Liriope muscari*<br>**Monkey Grass** | Grows 12 to 18 inches tall and 12 inches wide. Forms large clumps but does not spread by underground stems. Produces spikes of lilac-purple flowers in August. | Grows in heavy shade or full sun. This tough evergreen will tolerate heat and drought better than most. | **Monkey grass** can be used as a substitute for turf. Mow clumps to the ground in late winter, and plants will put out a flush of new growth as spring arrives. |
| *Liriope spicata*<br>**Creeping Liriope** | Spreads by under-ground stems to form large clumps. Grows 8 to 9 inches high. | Grows in sun or shade. | Can be very invasive. Effective for holding soil on banks. |
| *Mazus reptans*<br>**Mazus** | Grows 2 to 4 inches tall and 12 inches wide. This mat-forming ground cover is useful between stepping stones, in a woodland, or in a rock garden. In the spring it produces purplish-blue or white flowers. | Plant this aggressive spreader in a moist but well-drained soil in partial shade or full sun. Protect it from hot afternoon sun. | The tiny flowers, purple and yellow, look like miniature snapdragon-like blooms. There is also a white-flowered form. |
| *Ophiopogon japonicus*<br>**Mondo Grass** | Grows 3 to 12 inches tall and spreads 9 to 12 inches wide. The pale-lilac flowers that appear in summer are often hidden by leaves. | Grow in a moist, well-drained soil in part shade, although it will tolerate full sun. | Great for an evergreen ground cover or edging plant. **Black mondo grass** grows to 6 inches high and has almost black foliage. |
| *Pachysandra terminalis*<br>**Pachysandra** | Grows 9 to 12 inches tall and 18 inches across. A rapid spreader, it roots wherever its stems touch soil. | Plant this evergreen under trees or in other shady locations. Prefers a moist, well-drained soil. | There is also a variegated selection 'Silver Edge', with creamy-edged foliage. |
| *Rubus calycinoides*<br>**Ornamental Creeping Raspberry** | Grows 6 to 12 inches tall. A rapid spreader, it roots wherever its stems touch soil. | Plant this tough creeper in full sun or partial shade in a well-drained soil. | Fast-growing and ever-green, this ground cover adapts to a wide range of landscape situations. |
| *Saxifraga stolonifera*<br>**Strawberry Begonia** | Grows 4 to 6 inches tall and 12 inches across. Spreads to cover an area with long stoloniferous runners. Produces white flowers in summer. | Plant this handsome ground cover in the shade in well-drained soil. | The **strawberry begonia** is also used for handing baskets and in pots. |
| *Vinca minor*<br>**Periwinkle** | Grows 6 to 12 inches high and spreads out in every direction. The glossy evergreen foliage looks good all year. | This species prefers shade and moist areas. | **Vinca** can be used for erosion control on banks. |

# FLOWERING AND FRUITING GROUND COVERS

*Ceratostigma plumbaginoides*
**Dwarf plumbago**
6 to 12 inches high
This hardy perennial may be semi-evergreen in the mildest parts of the state but even where it is deciduous, the indigo-blue phlox-like flowers in late summer to early autumn are reason enough to grow this plant. The foliage is bronzy to dark green and then in autumn it gets tinges of red. Plant this bloomer in full sun or part shade.

*Cotoneaster* spp. and cvs.
**Cotoneaster**
Many different types exist from the very low-growing ground huggers to those with long trailing branches. Many are effective for bank plantings with colorful fruit in shades of red and orange. Some begin to color in summer and provide interest through the winter. **Cotoneasters** prefer full sun or part shade.

*Galax urceolata*
**Galax**
6 to 9 inches high
The foliage is 6 to 9 inches high with spikes of white flowers 2$^1$/$_2$ feet tall. This native perennial grows in tufts and is a slow grower, but in a woodland garden it makes an elegant evergreen ground cover. Up to 5 inches across, the shiny heart-shaped leaves take on shades of bronze in the autumn.

*Galium odoratum*
**Sweet woodruff**, 6 to 12 inches high
Long grown for the fragrant flowers and foliage used to make May wine. Great for the shade or part shade, this perennial likes a moist, well-drained soil. Be warned: this plant is an aggressive spreader. Give this plant full shade in the most southern part of the state.

*Hemerocallis* spp. and cvs.
**Daylily**
1 to 6 feet tall
**Daylilies** make a trouble-free flowering ground cover on a bank, or as part of a mixed planting. The dwarf varieties are well suited for mass plantings. Plant daylilies in full sun or part shade.

*Hypericum calycinum*
**Creeping St. Johnswort**
1 foot tall
This evergreen to semi-evergreen plant is a survivor that can grow and compete with tree roots, tolerate poor soil, or help control erosion on a steep bank. Bright yellow flowers, 3 inches across, occur throughout the summer. If the plant gets overgrown, use the lawn mower or prune it back hard when it is dormant. *Hypericum* prefers full sun or part shade.

*Mitchella repens*
**Partridgeberry**
3 to 6 inches tall
This creeping native is perfect for the woodland garden with **ferns**, **mosses**, and other shade loving plants. The roundish evergreen leaves are less than 1 inch long. Tiny white flowers appear in late spring to early summer and are followed by bright red berries, less than $^1$/$_4$ inch wide.

*Sarcococca hookerana humilis*
**Himalayan sweet box**
1 to 2 feet high
This ground cover spreads very slowly by underground runners. The glossy evergreen leaves, 1 to 3 inches long, hide the tiny but powerfully fragrant flowers when they perfume the air in early spring. The flowers are followed by small black fruits. A great ground cover for the shade garden.

# JANUARY
## VINES & GROUND COVERS

### PLANNING

This is a good month to begin planning what you will add or take away from your garden. Identify areas where you want to add vines or ground covers. If your garden looks flat or one-dimensional, vines might be the answer, as they provide instant verticality. If you are running out of space to grow plants, remember that vines grow upwards, and some require only a wall or fence to grab onto and a narrow space to put down some roots. Many vines will also grow happily in large containers, trailing over the edge or climbing up onto a trellis.

Add a structure such as an arbor, trellis, pergola, or gazebo. Gather information and ideas about the best structure for your garden; it should be functional and attractive. Peruse garden magazines and books for ideas, or consult with a garden designer about which type of structure will work best for your garden style. In addition to providing a place for your vines to climb, cling to, or twine on, arbors and other garden structures can serve as key elements in the design of your garden. Placement of the structure is very important. An arbor can lead a visitor from one point to another, invite you to approach, or direct your attention toward a

particular view. Positioning an arbor at the end of a path, with a bench placed beneath the arbor, makes a stronger statement than placing one in the middle of your garden.

If you are growing perennial ornamental vines, think about what they will look like throughout the year. What does the foliage look like in autumn? If there are flowers, are they fragrant? Does a particular vine offer attractive bark in winter?

Hire a professional to draw up landscape design plans, or refer to plans in a book. Take time to make sure the scale of whatever structure you build or have built fits into your garden and relates to your house and garden. As a rule of thumb, bigger is usually better. What looks like a massive structure on paper is often just right once it is constructed and standing in the garden. If you don't feel confident about getting the proportions right, and hiring a professional is too expensive, invest in some bamboo poles and construct a temporary arbor. Observe it for a week to determine if the size is appropriate. This is an inexpensive way to learn about scale before you build a permanent structure.

If you have an area of lawn that is thin and patchy because it is beneath large shade trees, think about replacing the lawn with ground covers. Measure the

Liriope is a great ground cover replacement for grass.

area so you will know how many plants to purchase in the spring (see Area Covered by 100 Ground Cover Plants, p. 247). **Mondo grass** or **liriope** are alternatives to turf, and both thrive in the shade.

Visit your local botanical garden or arboretum, and make notes about ground covers or vines that offer interesting foliage and flowers.

### PLANTING

Unless you live in the most southern part of the state, wait until the weather is a bit milder and the ground is not frozen or soggy before you begin to plant.

## WATERING

If you have areas of ground covers that have been planted in the past six months, they should be watered weekly (at least 1 inch per week) if there is no rain and if the ground is not frozen. Use a sprinkler, and set out small cans, such as tuna fish cans, to measure how much water the plants receive. Water until the tuna fish can is approximately $3/4$ full, which should equal about an inch of water.

## FERTILIZING

Wait until early spring to fertilize vines or ground covers.

## PROBLEMS

In South Georgia, check evergreen ground covers like **vinca** and **euonymus** for insect infestations such as scale or spider mites. Scale looks like white and brown specks firmly attached to stems and leaves. The scale, sucking insects that cause leaves to turn yellow and drop, also causes branches to die back. Spray with horticultural oil to control. Read and follow label instructions.

## HELPFUL HINTS

If you love **wisteria** and have planted one but still have no blooms after many years, here are a few things to consider:

• Budded, grafted, or cutting-grown plants bloom much sooner than seed-grown plants. If you have grafted plants, be sure to remove any suckers that sprout below the graft so they won't overpower the upper part of the vine. If you purchase a named selection of **wisteria,** chances are it is a grafted plant. Look for a swollen area, almost like a collar, that surrounds the main trunk. This is a good indicator of a grafted plant.

• **Wisteria** does not need fertilizer on a regular basis. If your vine is healthy and producing lots of vegetative growth but not blooming, withhold all nitrogen fertilizer for an entire growing season. If it still doesn't flower, try pruning the roots in spring, after the time when it would normally bloom. Make vertical cuts through the roots with a spade, 1 foot from the main trunk.

## PRUNING

If you have annual vines that are still clinging to walls, fences, arbors, or other supports, it should be easy to pull or prune them off and clean up the surfaces now that they have died. Save any seeds that you missed collecting in the fall. They make easy and inexpensive presents for your gardening friends. Once they drop their leaves, it is easier to see where you want to prune your vines, especially if you want to train them as an espalier (see May).

• Prune to remove dead or damaged stems and twigs from woody vines.

• Prune **wisteria** vines to reduce or thin side shoots from the main stems. These shoots produce flower-producing spurs. For the best blooms, shorten these shoots back to two or three buds. Because it is such an aggressive grower, **wisteria** needs to be pruned on a regular basis, sometimes two or three times a year.

If you have large areas of evergreen ground covers like **English ivy** or **vinca,** wait until early spring to prune them back close to the ground, and do so only if they need it. Established beds of **English ivy** or **vinca** can go for years without being pruned, but if they become overgrown and straggly or start to spread beyond where you want them to, prune away.

# FEBRUARY
## VINES & GROUND COVERS

 PLANNING

This month it's time to peruse catalogs and think about which annual vines you might like to add to the garden in spring. Many are easy to grow from seed that can be started indoors in March (see Annuals, February). Think about adding some with colorful flowers or interesting fruits. Below is a list of annual vines with a brief description of each. All of these vines are happiest if they receive full sun and are planted in well-drained soil.

• *Clitoria* spp. **Butterfly pea vine** produces striking blue flowers.

• *Cobaea scandens* **Cup-and-saucer vine** is a vigorous grower to 25 feet with bell-shaped flowers that open yellow-green and then turn to purple. There is also a white form.

• *Cucurbita* spp. **Gourd vines** come in many different sizes and shapes.

• *Dolichos lablab* **Hyacinth bean** has purple flowers followed by purple pealike pods; it is a perennial in the coastal South.

• *Ipomoea alba* **Moon vine** is known for its fragrant white flowers. Measuring 6 inches across or larger, the flowers open in late afternoon and wither the following morning.

• *Ipomoea batatas* **Ornamental sweet potato vine** is grown for its colorful foliage. There are selections with nearly-black foliage and others with leaves that are chartreuse.

• *Ipomoea purpurea* **Common morning glory** is a twining climber with heart-shaped leaves. The funnel-shaped flowers range in color from deep purple to bluish-purple or reddish flowers with white throats.

• *Ipomoea quamoclit* **Cypress vine** is a twining vine with delicate ferny foliage and striking scarlet flowers. It's a hummingbird magnet.

• *Mandevilla* 'Alice du Pont' is a tropical vine that may be root-hardy in the Coastal South but should be grown as an annual farther North. This vine is best purchased as a small plant.

Black-eyed Susan vine

• *Mina lobata* **Firecracker vine** has flowers that are scarlet, yellow, and orange. A vigorous climbing vine, it blooms in fall.

• *Podranea ricasoliana* **Pink trumpet vine** is really for coastal gardeners but can be treated as an annual in other parts of the state. It has glossy green foliage and 2- to 3-inch-wide flowers shaped like pink trumpets marked with red veins. You may want to purchase a plant instead of growing it from seed, since it is a slow grower.

• *Thunbergia alata* **Black-eyed Susan vine** may survive as a perennial in the coastal parts of Georgia but is an annual in the rest of the state. A twining plant, the flowers are orange, yellow, or white with a purple-black throat.

• *Tropaeolum* spp. **Climbing nasturtium** has flowers that range from orange to yellow to cream. Slightly fragrant, the flowers are also edible.

**Ground Covers:** If you have a bank where grass won't grow, plant ground covers to control erosion. One way to get started is to use erosion-control burlap. Put down a layer of pine straw, then put down the burlap. You can use metal stakes to hold it in place. Plant the ground covers in the open areas of the burlap netting. Small, 4-inch pots or plugs are easy to plant, and if the plants are well rooted, they should establish quickly. The burlap will decompose as the ground covers grow. Some people put down the mulch before they plant and then dig small holes into the mulch for each plant. Whether you mulch before or after you plant, be sure to water afterwards. See the facing page for a list of ground covers to use for erosion control.

## PLANTING

In the southern parts of the state, this is a good time to plant ground covers and perennial vines. Wait until soil and air temperatures warm up to plant annual vines.

## WATERING

Water ground cover plantings that have been planted within the past six months. A sprinkler is a good way to cover a large area of ground covers. Place several small cans around the area (tuna fish or cat food cans work well). When the cans are about 3/4 full, the ground covers are probably watered well enough for the week.

## FERTILIZING

Wait until March to fertilize vines and ground covers.

# PLANTS THAT HELP CONTROL EROSION

Evergreen ground covers can help control erosion. The following list of erosion-control plants includes vines that are also effective ground covers.

- **Carolina jessamine** (a vine)
- **Creeping liriope**
- **English ivy** (a vine)
- **Monkey grass**
- **Ornamental raspberry**
- **Pachysandra**
- **Periwinkle**
- **Shore juniper**

## PROBLEMS

**English ivy** is a popular ground cover for shade, and with good reason. Mostly undemanding, it is only occasionally affected by a bacterial leaf spot that causes leaves and stems to blacken and shrivel. Such leaves have brown or black spots that are surrounded by yellow halos. Environmental conditions like overhead watering and frequent rain contribute to the spread of this disease. The best control is to remove and destroy infected leaves and stems. It is also good to avoid using sprinklers at night when the foliage will stay wet for a long period of time. Spray diseased foliage with Mancozeb.

**Periwinkle** (*Vinca minor*) can develop a root fungus if it is planted in soils that are not well drained. Leaves and stems wilt and die, making it easy to pull them out of the ground. This soilborne fungus enters through the roots, especially in soils that are poorly drained. The best solution is to remove and destroy infected plants, and to improve soil drainage or eliminate water flowing through the area.

## PRUNING

This is a good month to get out the lawn mower and cut back your tattered or winter-damaged **monkey grass.** By cutting it back now there will be a reduced chance of cutting off new growth. Set the mower at the highest setting and mow down the foliage. The grass should be about 3 inches high when you finish. If you have only a small patch of **monkey grass,** you can cut it back with a pair of sharp shears. Once spring arrives, fresh dark-green leaves will quickly cover up the ragged edges.

# MARCH
## VINES & GROUND COVERS

 PLANNING

Start annual vine seeds indoors under lights (see Annuals, March). Read seed packages carefully to determine how long it will take until they are ready to plant outdoors. Some require a cold treatment before they will germinate, and others require mechanical abrasion such as nicking the seed coat.

If you have an area of turf that you want to change to ground covers, be sure to prepare the soil before you plant. If there is any grass left, spray it with a nonselective weedkiller. After the grass is dead, rototill to a depth of 8 to 12 inches, adding soil amendments as you go.

 PLANTING

Plant perennial vines and ground covers that have been grown in containers and are now available at garden centers.

This is a good time to divide overgrown plantings of **monkey grass, creeping liriope,** or **English ivy**. Use a large spading fork and dig up clumps. If you have a large bare area you want to cover, you can divide the clumps into small sections and plant them 12 to 18 inches apart. Make sure each division

has an equal ratio of roots to foliage or shoots. Replant the divisions, apply a 2-inch layer of mulch, and water.

Transplant **clematis** vines before new growth begins. Dig as large a rootball as possible—the more roots, the better. Prepare the new site ahead of time so that the roots are out of the ground for the shortest amount of time. This way fewer will dry out. It is often said that **clematis** like a hot top (foliage) and cold feet (roots). It is more accurate to say that **clematis** prefer full sun and plenty of soil moisture. Mulching is very important in conserving soil moisture.

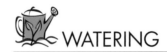 WATERING

Water any new plantings of vines and ground covers as well as existing plantings if there has not been rain (at least 1 inch a week is best).

 FERTILIZING

If ground covers are planted under trees that are on a regular fertilizing program, they will get plenty of nutrients when the trees are fed. It is not absolutely necessary that you fertilize your ground covers, but if you think they need it, apply 1 pound (2 cups) of 8-8-8 or 10-10-10 per

Be cautious about allowing English ivy to use a tree as support.

100 square feet. Use a broadcast-type spreader to get even distribution over the area. Wash any fertilizer off the foliage when you finish. If you do fertilize, twice a year is adequate, once in March and once in June.

 PROBLEMS

If your **pachysandra** has leaves that are light brown or tan on

top, it has leaf scorch. Transplant your **pachysandra** to a shadier location.

Use a granular weed-preventer twice each year, once now and once in September. An application this month will help cut down on infestations of summer annual weeds. Look for products formulated specifically for ground covers.

**English ivy** can be a blessing or a curse . . . it can become a pest. A rapid spreader, sometimes it leaps from the planting bed and climbs up into the trees. Shading lower branches and collecting litter, rain, or ice, **ivy** can cause damage to tree limbs. For information on controlling **English ivy,** see Trees, November.

 PRUNING

Prune back vines that are overgrown, including **wisteria, ivy, trumpet creeper,** and **climbing hydrangea.** Wait to prune spring-flowering vines like **Carolina jessamine** until after they bloom.

Prune back late-flowering **clematis** to a height of about 2 to 3 feet. Such **clematis** flower on current-season's growth, which is the last 2 to 3 feet. Plants in this group include *Clematis viticella, C. flammula, C. tangutica, C. x jackmanii, C. maximoiczziana, C.* 'Perle d'Azur', *C.* 'Duchess of

Albany', and others.

Prune back large-flowered **hybrid clematis** such as 'Nelly Moser', 'Duchess of Edinburgh', and 'Marie Boisselot'. These hybrids bloom in mid-June on short stems from the previous season's growth. Prune to remove dead or weak stems, and cut back remaining stems to the first pair of healthy green buds. You can plant other plants under the **clematis** in this group to conceal the bare stems that develop at

the base of the plant as it matures. Perennials like **hardy geraniums** or small evergreen shrubs make happy companions for **clematis.**

Wait until after they flower before pruning early-flowering **clematis** such as *Clematis alpina, C. macropetala, C. armandii, C. montana,* and *C. chrysocoma.*

## HELPFUL HINTS

The main reason to prune **clematis** is to encourage plants to produce a maximum amount of blooms. The question of when to prune is determined by whether the particular **clematis** blooms on second-year wood (growth from the previous season) or on new growth, and if it blooms early or late. Even without pruning, your **clematis** will grow and bloom, but perhaps not as profusely. Try to purchase named varieties; this will make it easier to determine what the plant requires in terms of its environment and pruning. Here are some simple tips to guide you when pruning your clematis.

• If you are growing **early-blooming clematis**, both the large-flowered types and the small-flowered types, prune lightly in early spring so as not to destroy the growth that has the flowerbuds.

• Late-blooming clematis, large-flowered and small-flowered types, should be pruned hard in early spring so the plant can produce strong growth on which blooms will later develop.

• If early-blooming large-flowered types develop into a tangled mess, cut them down below the tangle. Close to the ground is fine, but don't cut into the larger woody stems. Your **clematis** should recover by the end of the growing season and produce good blooms the following season.

• If you want early-blooming large-flowered types to bloom later, prune them back hard in the spring, and they will bloom in the summer.

# APRIL
## VINES & GROUND COVERS

 PLANNING

Now that spring is here, **daffodils** are in bloom. Think about adding some ground covers to help mask **daffodil** foliage once the bulbs finish blooming. Remember that you should leave foliage on **daffodils,** as it is storing energy for next year's flowers. **Hellebores** and **hosta** are both well suited as ground covers for **daffodils, hyacinth, Dutch iris,** and **summer snowflake.**

**Clematis** vines make great companions for **roses.** You can choose **clematis** that bloom around the same time that a **rose** does so that the two flowers will complement each other, or select a **clematis** that will bloom after the **rose** is finished. For a winning combination, train *Clematis viticella* 'Etoile Violette', which has purple blooms with yellow stamens, to grow up and through *Rosa* 'New Dawn'. Vigorous and free-flowering, this **clematis** blooms from midsummer to early autumn, so that even when the **rose** has finished blooming, you will still have flowers. When you choose a **clematis** to grow with a **rose,** select species or hybrids that bloom on current-season's growth so that if you need to prune back the vine early in the spring you will still get blooms that season.

If you have an infestation of **Japanese honeysuckle** or **English ivy** that you want to eradicate, this is a good time to get started. Digging out plants, especially the roots, will be easier if you recognize the plants early. Learn to identify the foliage. You can also cut **ivy** and **honeysuckle** back to the ground, let them put out new growth, and then spray with a nonselective weedkiller. It may take this twofold approach to get rid of **ivy** or **honeysuckle,** as both are tenacious plants.

 PLANTING

Direct-sow seeds of annual vines in spots where you want them to grow. Some vines like the **moon flower** are easier to establish if you start the seed in peat pots and then, once the seed has germinated, transplant the peat pot directly into the garden.

Plant ground covers and perennial vines in your garden.

Transplant annual vine seedlings you started indoors under lights to small pots outside. Place the pots in an area that gets lots of bright light but no hot sun. Keep them in this location for a week to ten days before moving them to a spot where they receive full sun.

If there is a threat of frost, move the plants to a garage or a protected area. Wait until the frost-free date arrives before planting your new vines in the garden. Check with your local Extension Service about the date of the last frost in your region.

 WATERING

Water newly planted vines or ground covers, and water the areas where you sow annual seed. Use a sprinkler to get gentle, even coverage. Keep vines in containers watered, too. Let the soil get dry to the touch, then water thoroughly, letting the water run out of the bottom of the pot.

 FERTILIZING

To help them get established, fertilize ground covers that were planted within the last six months. Use 1/2 pound or 1 cup of 8-8-8 or 10-10-10 per 100 square feet (this is half the recommended rate for established ground covers).

Fertilize vines only if they need it. If they are healthy and robust, there is no need to fertilize.

Applying a fresh layer of well-composted manure around the base of your vines will provide them with nutrients over a long period of time. Use caution to keep the manure from touching the main stem.

## PROBLEMS

Beware of the vine with "leaves of three." Many people are allergic to the toxic oil from poison ivy leaves and vines (for control, see Trees, August).

Handweed ground cover areas. Scrape away old mulch, and apply a fresh layer of mulch approximately 2 to 3 inches deep. This will cut down on weed problems and help conserve moisture.

Aphids are tiny, soft-bodied, pear-shaped, and mostly wingless insects, coming in many colors, including green, yellow, tan, and black. They can attack the new growth of **clematis** and other vines, sucking plant juices and disfiguring the buds and leaves. Try using a strong blast of water from the hose to get rid of them.

## PRUNING

If they need to be tidied up or are getting too rampant for the space they are growing in, prune spring-flowering vines like **Carolina jessamine** as soon as they finish blooming.

## HELPFUL HINTS

Clematis wilt is caused by a fungus. Present in the soil and on the plant, the spores become active when a specific combination of temperature and humidity occurs. The stems appear to wilt suddenly, often just when the flowers are beginning to open, and the leaves and stems are discolored. The fungus works itself around the stem of the clematis, cutting off the flow of sap. As soon as you notice that a stem is wilted, prune it off until you reach healthy tissue. Sometimes this means you will have to prune a stem to below ground level. Discard all prunings and dead material. Do not add them to your compost pile.

• **Clematis** are usually more susceptible to attacks by fungus during the first two years of growth. Once they develop woody stems the fungus has a harder time penetrating the bark.

• Pinch back your **clematis** to encourage side shoots on a regular basis during the first two years. This reduces foliage and therefore the stress on the roots.

• Plant **clematis** deeply. If a shoot is killed to ground level, new shoots may appear from a node below the soil surface.

Clematis and roses are a classic combination.

# MAY
## VINES & GROUND COVERS

### PLANNING

Ground covers can help you solve problems in the garden. For example, the area between steppingstones is the perfect place to use ground covers instead of turf. If the site is sunny, try some of the **creeping thymes** or *Laurentia*, which has beautiful, tiny blue flowers. For shade, **dwarf mondo grass, ajuga, or** *Vinca minor* provide evergreen foliage all year long and require a minimum of upkeep.

In addition to training vines to grow on arbors and pergolas, you may find they are great for covering concrete walls and chain-link fences or framing doors, windows, or garages. Selecting the right vine for the right location will help ensure success.

Self-clinging vines such as **English ivy, Virginia creeper, cross-vine,** and **trumpet creeper** are ideal for a concrete wall. You may have to help them get started by tying up a few vines and attaching them to the wall until they take hold.

### PLANTING

Plant ground covers and vines throughout the month.

There is still time to direct-sow seeds of annual vines like **purple hyacinth bean, moon vine,** and others in spots where you want them to grow. Check seed packages for more information about how long specific varieties of vines take to germinate.

### WATERING

Water new plantings of ground covers and vines.

### FERTILIZING

Fertilize annual vines with half the recommended rate (on the label) of a complete liquid fertilizer with a ratio like 20-20-20.

Fertilize newly planted ground covers (planted within the last six months) to help them get established at a rate of $1/2$ pound or 1 cup of 8-8-8 or 10-10-10 per 100 square feet. This is half the recommended rate for established ground covers. Remember, you need only fertilize your ground covers twice a year. The recommended times are March and June.

If you add organic material to the soil when you plant, you won't have to fertilize your vines, but topdressing with composted manure will give them extra nutrients.

### PROBLEMS

New growth on some of your vines may look puckered and may be covered with tiny lime green bugs. Aphids voraciously feed on new growth of vines like **clematis** and **honeysuckles.** Try blasting them off with a jet of cold water from the hose. If this doesn't do the trick, use an insecticidal soap.

### PRUNING

Make sure vines are tied in place, firmly but not tightly, where you want them to be. If they are woody vines like **akebia,** make sure the stems are not girdled by the wire or cord you used to tie them to a trellis, arbor, or fence. **Wisteria** is an aggressive vine. After it blooms, cut back long twining new growth before it forms a tangled mess with the main vine. Save those stems that you want to use to extend the height or width of the vine. Tie them to supports. Use plastic tape so you won't girdle the stems. Many **wisteria** are grafted and have a swollen area, the graft union. Prune to remove any suckers that occur below this union, as they will not produce the strong growth that the grafted plant does.

# ESPALIER

Developed by gardeners in Europe during the 16th and 17th centuries, the term espalier was applied to fruit trees that were trained in the open, either as a permanent feature or in preparation for placing them on walls or against a trellis. Although they were trained in many shapes, the most common was a tier of horizontal branches on either side of the main stem. When trained on posts and wires, they were not only productive in a small space, they screened views and acted as walls between one section of garden and another. Today, espalier is also practiced to train plants for pure ornament, in both traditional and irregular patterns, depending on the growth habit of the individual plant.

When you grow vines on a wall, there are several approaches. You can attach panels of lattice to an existing wall and then train the vines on the lattice. This forms a flat trellis. To give the trellis more depth, attach the lattice to the wall on top of 2×4 spacers. Use 1×4 boards to cover up where two sections of lattice join. Plantings at the base of the lattice will help cover up the fact that the trellis is not attached at ground level.

On wooden fences or walls, you can create a framework using screw eyes threaded with galvanized wire (12 to 14 gauge). The wires should be about 1 1/2 feet apart.

For masonry walls, use anchors with screws or lag screws, threaded rod, nuts, and washers.

The goal is to provide firm support, good air circulation for the plants, and an appealing design. Be patient—it will take a few years of pruning and training to achieve a desired design. For formal designs, any branches that obscure the design can be pruned away. For informal designs, let the natural growth habit of the plant determine where you prune. Here is a list of perennial vines for espalier that produce showy flowers and/or fruit:

- *Akebia quinata* has clusters of purple flowers in spring that are often followed by 2- to 4-inch-long, purple, sausage-type fruits in summer to fall.
- *Bougainvillea* cultivars offer a long season of bright color for coastal gardens. The colorful parts that surrounds the tiny flowers are actually bracts.
- *Clematis armandii* is an evergreen species that has masses of tiny white fragrant flowers in early spring.
- *Pyracantha* hybrids produce red, orange, or red-orange fruit in late summer. The fruit last well into winter.
- *Rosa banksiae* is an evergreen climber that produces masses of yellow or white flowers in early spring.
- *Wisteria* spp. is an aggressive vine that has beautiful clusters of violet to violet-blue flowers in April to May.

To provide firm support, a pyracantha is espaliered against this rock wall.

# JUNE
## VINES & GROUND COVERS

### PLANNING

Make notes in your garden journal about the performance of vines and ground covers in your landscape. Which ones are thriving, and which ones have pest or disease problems? If an area of ground cover is not successful, think about which plants you will use to replace them. Visit your local botanical garden and see what's blooming.

If you have an area that's infested with poison ivy or **English ivy** that you want to eradicate, spray with a nonselective weedkiller, and then come back in two to four weeks and spray again, or dig out the roots. (Use extreme caution when working around poison ivy if you are allergic to it.) When fall arrives, you can amend the soil and plant something new!

### PLANTING

You can still add vines and ground covers to your garden. Annual vines like the **cypress vine, mandevilla,** and **passionflower** add a tropical flair to the summer garden. They can be trained on a structure or a trellis, or combined with lots of colorful annuals in a large decorative pot. When you add a **clematis** to your garden, apply 2 inches of mulch over the soil, keeping it away from the main stem. This will help retain soil moisture. As an alternative, you can plant ground covers or herbaceous perennials over the root area of the **clematis** and then lightly mulch the ground covers. *Vinca minor* plants or some of the **hardy geraniums** make good ground covers for **clematis.**

### WATERING

With the arrival of warmer weather, plants dry out more quickly. Be sure to check new plantings of vines and ground covers weekly to see if they need water. If the soil feels dry to the touch when you push your finger into it 2 inches, it's time to water. **Clematis** vines like plenty of moisture, so be sure to check them on a regular basis. Plants growing in pots will need to be checked on a daily basis.

### FERTILIZING

To help them get established, fertilize new plantings of vines and ground covers that have been planted in the last six months.

If ground covers are not planted under trees or shrubs that are fertilized on a regular basis, apply 1 pound (2 cups) of 8-8-8 or 10-10-10 per 100 square feet. Use a broadcast-type spreader to get even distribution over the area. Wash any fertilizer off the foliage when you finish.

During the growing season, **clematis** vines will benefit from monthly feeding with a complete liquid fertilizer (a ratio like 20-20-20) at half the recommended rate on the label.

### PROBLEMS

Pull weeds in ground cover beds.

If leaves and buds on your **clematis** vines are disfigured and have a dusty grayish-white coat-

Powdery mildew affects many plants in our humid summer weather.

ing and the flowerbuds don't open, your vine has a fungal disease called powdery mildew. Poor air circulation can contribute to this problem. If possible, move the vine to a more favorable location. You can try to improve air circulation in the area where your **clematis** is growing by removing or pruning nearby shrubs that are crowding your vine, but it may be more practical to relocate the vine. As soon as you notice signs of this disease, spray with a fungicide.

Look for signs of spider mites. Infested leaves will be spotted with yellow or black specks. Pests like aphids typically cluster around the new growth; where they feed, buds and shoots look distorted. If less than 50 percent of a plant or group of plants is affected with a particular insect pest, then use insecticidal soap to try to eradicate the problem. If more than 50 percent of the plant is affected, you may want to use a synthetic contact insecticide.

If the lower leaves on your **bugleweed** are yellow and the plants are mushy and die (they pull up easily and have no roots), the problem is crown rot. Fortunately, the problem is environmental—usually poorly draining soil. Once you improve

soil drainage by adding coarse sand or small coarse gravel, you will eliminate the problem, and the area can be replanted.

The problem is scale if clusters of hard white and brown specks cover the stems and leaves of your **euonymus** ground cover, and the leaves turn yellow and branches die. Spray with horticultural oil or a systemic insecticide.

## HELPFUL HINTS

**Clematis** can be propagated by stem cuttings.

1. Take cuttings in May or June from the semi-hard shoots produced in the current season. This means that they will probably be taken from the middle of a long stem.

2. Find a section of stem that has a node (a joint on a stem, the point of origin for a leaf or a bud; sometimes swollen or with a distinctive scar) with leaves.

3. Cut between this node and the node below. You should end up with a section that has only a node at the top end of the cutting. The cutting should be 1 to 2 inches in length.

4. Dip the cutting in water and then in rooting hormone like Rootone™.

5. Stick the cutting in a mix of two parts sand or perlite and one part peat moss.

6. Supply high humidity, warmth, and bright light. The cuttings should root in four to six weeks.

7. If the cuttings root by early August, plant them in your garden. If rooting occurs in late August or September, overwinter the plants in pots in a protected spot, and plant them out in the spring.

 PRUNING

Prune any wild suckers or shoots of your **wisteria** for one last time this season. Next year's flowerbuds will begin to form in midsummer.

There is still time (wait no later than July) to prune spring-flowering **clematis**, including *Clematis alpina, C. macropetala, C. armandii, C. montana*, and *C. chrysocoma*. Prune to reduce their size or train them to fit a certain framework or trellis.

# JULY
## VINES & GROUND COVERS

### PLANNING

**Monkey grass, English ivy**, and **mondo grass** are familiar evergreen ground covers for shade. There are even some ground covers that bloom in shade. Below is a list of those that bloom in shade. Think about adding some of these to your garden this fall. They will brighten up the woodland and add interest under a shrub. You can also plant these ground covers as a carpet for spring bulbs, like some of the early-blooming miniature **daffodils** or **giant crocus**. Plant the ground covers in fall at the same time you plant your bulbs. This way you'll know where your bulbs are, even when they're not blooming.

• **Bugleweed** has 4- to 5-inch spikes of blue flowers in spring to early summer.

• **Green and gold** has yellow flowers in spring, some in summer, and then a few in fall.

• **Mazus** has purplish-blue **snapdragon**-like flowers with yellow markings in spring and early summer

• **Partridgeberry**, *Mitchella repens*, has tiny white flowers in late spring or early summer followed by bright-red berries less than $1/4$ inch wide. It is not a good choice for coastal gardens.

• **Periwinkle** has five-petaled lavender-blue, purple, or white flowers in spring.

### PLANTING

You can plant ground covers or vines now, but don't expect much growth while the air and soil temperatures are hot. The roots will wait until soil temperatures begin to cool off in the fall before they put on any significant growth.

### WATERING

Keep any new plantings well watered. Check containers daily and plants in the ground weekly (see June for more details on watering). Apply 1 to 2 inches of mulch to new plantings. This will help reduce weed infestations, keep soil temperatures cool, and conserve moisture.

### FERTILIZING

Fertilize annual vines with half the recommended rate of a complete liquid fertilizer with a ratio like 20-20-20. With any luck, many of your vines will bloom until frost. There's no need to fertilize perennial vines or ground covers now.

### PROBLEMS

Look for signs of aphids, spider mites, or other insects. Try washing them off with a blast of water from the hose or using an insecticidal soap before you resort to using a stronger pesticide.

Pull weeds in ground cover beds.

You may see young branch tips on your ground cover **junipers** turn red or brown, then gray. Once they die, tiny black spots, which are the fruiting bodies of the fungus, may appear on the dead needles and stems. These symptoms mean your **juniper** suffers from twig blight, a fungus that can enter the plant through both healthy and wounded tissue. Young plants are more susceptible than mature plants. Prune out and destroy infected twigs and branches as soon as you notice them. Spray plants with a fungicide at two-week intervals in the spring, when plants begin to put out new growth. Here are some prevention tips:

1. Plant **junipers** in sites where they will get plenty of sunlight and good air circulation.

# HELPFUL HINTS

You may inherit a garden that has been neglected for a long period of time, and has aggressive vines like **wisteria** may be running rampantly through it. Here are some suggestions for controlling or eliminating **wisteria**:

1. Spray the vine when it has lots of foliage with a nonselective weedkiller like glyphosate. Spray the foliage on the top and undersides until it drips off the plant.

2. Wait ten days to two weeks. Cut off any remaining green foliage.

3. Wait another two weeks, and when a new batch of foliage flushes out, spray it with the weedkiller again. Repeat this until the **wisteria** goes dormant in winter.

Another method is to cut the **wisteria** vine down to the ground, and paint the cut surface with a weedkiller containing triclopyr. These techniques can also be used to eliminate **English ivy**, **bittersweet**, and **grapevines**.

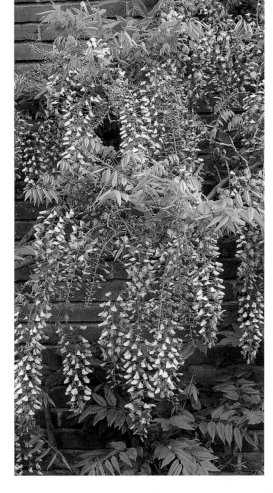

Although beautiful, wisteria can overrun a garden.

2. Avoid overhead watering or watering at night when foliage will stay wet for several hours.

3. Don't overfertilize, and avoid wounding the plant; prune during winter if possible.

 PRUNING

If you have **English ivy** or **Virginia creeper** growing on a wall around doors or windows and it threatens to cover the windows, cut it back now. You can root the **ivy** clippings by sticking them in a soilless mix or wet sand. In four to five weeks you should have rooted cuttings that you can plant directly in the ground.

# AUGUST
## VINES & GROUND COVERS

### PLANNING

It's too hot to do much in the garden this month, so plan ahead for fall. If you have areas of ground covers that need renovating, you can spray with a non-selective weedkiller, and then wait until fall to amend the soil and plant.

### PLANTING

Wait until fall to add vines and ground covers to your garden.

### WATERING

Keep new plantings watered. Check them on a weekly basis. Water if the soil is dry when you dig down 2 inches with your finger.

### FERTILIZING

Wait until spring to fertilize your vines and ground covers.

### PROBLEMS

Your **junipers** may have spider mites if tiny yellow spots appear on the needles and some needles are brown and covered with tiny webs. To test for mites, hold a blank sheet of white paper under a branch and tap lightly. Circle some of the specks (no bigger than a pinhead) that fall onto the paper. If the specks move, you have spider mites, which are most active during hot, dry weather. Inspect plants on a regular basis. To control the mites, spray your **junipers** with a blast of cold water from the hose. For severe infestations (when 50 percent or more of the needles are damaged), spray with insecticidal soap, horticultural oil, or a synthetic miticide. You may have to use two or three applications, spaced at weekly intervals, to eradicate the problem.

**Bougainvillea** normally blooms in the spring and fall, and it is hardy for coastal gardeners. For gardeners in the rest of the state, it can be grown in a container and kept in a greenhouse or sun porch over the winter.

Check ground cover junipers periodically for spider mite infestation.

## HELPFUL HINTS

Kudzu, although not native to the South, spreads as if it has always lived here. This woody vine is native to China and Japan. Here in Georgia, an established vine can grow to reach 60 feet in one season, with leaves up to 12 inches wide and long. This hardy pest climbs and covers buildings and trees, shades their leaves, and strangles them until they die. If left untended, it keeps growing. Here are some tips for control:

• The key to success is to attack the entire area covered in kudzu at one time. Kudzu plants put out roots all along the vine, and when one section of the vine is killed, this tough plant has the ability to segment itself so that the rest of the vine can keep growing. By the end of August, kudzu plants are exhausted from vigorous summer growth and have expended most of their reserves.

• One approach to eradication is to mow all the foliage before the plant goes dormant each winter and again in spring and summer.

• Another approach is to spray the entire plant with a broadleaf herbicide containing triclopyr or glyphosate. Apply the spray until it drips off the leaves. Since the plants have no reserves, they will not have the energy to sprout many new leaves in spring.

• Watch for signs of growth in early spring. An established kudzu vine can send up sprouts for years before it is substantially weakened. Spray new growth when leaves have expanded but before the plant has a chance to harden-off and spread.

• Kudzu is also vulnerable when it flowers, usually in September. The long pendulous purple flowers are fragrant and attractive for such a pesky vine. Spray the flowers and the foliage with triclopyr or glyphosate. It is quickly translocated to the roots where it kills the plant.

• Some people take advantage of these woody vines to make baskets. Collect the vines in winter, and you will have less kudzu to kill in the spring!

---

Sometimes **bougainvillea** doesn't bloom in spring, and there may be no indication that it will bloom in fall. The "no bloom" syndrome is the result of not enough sunshine. Follow these steps to a remedy:

1. **Bougainvillea** should be planted in a spot where it gets full sun—this means four to six hours of direct sun each day.

2. **Bougainvillea** produces more blooms when potbound, so plant it in a confined pot or planting bed.

3. Apply a water-soluble fertilizer such as 20-20-20 every three to four weeks in the spring or summer.

4. Let the soil get slightly dry between thorough waterings. Plants will go dormant in the winter. Begin to reduce watering in November to once every three to four weeks. Wait until spring to resume regular watering and feeding.

 PRUNING

Remove and dispose of any dead or diseased stems or twigs of vines and ground covers. It is best to discard diseased plant material away from your compost pile. Check vines on your arbor or pergola to make sure they are not being girdled, which means the tie cuts into the stem, restricting the flow of water and nutrients. Tie up shoots that you want to train as part of an espalier.

# SEPTEMBER
## VINES & GROUND COVERS

### PLANNING

Fall is a great season to add vines and ground covers to your garden. Plan to plant as soon as the weather cools off a bit. Make notes in your garden journal on how annual vines performed this year and which ones you'd like to add to the garden next year. Think about combinations of vines, both annual and perennial. Take a soil test (see Horticultural Practices, p. 7). The results will tell you the quantities of nutrients and lime you need to add to the soil. Prepare the soil (see Horticultural Practices), add soil amendments, and rototill the areas where you will add ground covers later this fall or next spring.

### PLANTING

Add container-grown ground covers and vines to your garden. This is a good time to add **clematis.** Whether you are planting or transplanting **clematis,** experts recommend that you dig a hole 18 inches wide and 24 inches deep, mixing in 1 part good topsoil and 1 part composted manure. **Clematis** is known to put out roots to a depth of 18 to 24 inches—this is the reason for preparing such a deep hole.

Divide established ground covers if they are crowded, or you want to move some to another area.

• Dig up large clumps of **liriope** or **mondo grass** with a digging fork or shovel.

• Use a digging spade or straightedge shovel, and chop straight through the clump to break off sections. Shake off loose soil, but remember, the more roots, the better. Make sure each division has roots and shoots.

• Dig up individual pieces or small sections of **ornamental raspberry** and **English ivy**. They put out roots all along their stems, just about anywhere they touch soil. With these particular vines there is no need to dig a deep bed, as the roots are close to the soil surface.

• Have the new planting area prepared ahead of time so that roots won't dry out.

• Water and mulch transplants.

Clematis is such a spectacular vine; it deserves a spot in your garden.

## WATERING

Even as the weather starts to cool off a bit, don't forget to water new plantings. Any ground covers or vines that have been planted in the last six months should be checked on a weekly basis to see if they need water.

## FERTILIZING

Wait until spring to fertilize perennial vines and ground covers. If you want to topdress areas where you have vines planted, use mushroom compost or well-rotted horse or cow manures. This will provide good organic material, which will provide nutrients as it breaks down over the winter and next spring.

## PROBLEMS

Check vines and ground covers for signs of dieback or root rot, such as black stems or a group of leaves that are partially black and wilted. If a section of ground cover is suffering because of poor drainage, dig up the plants and add coarse sand (builder's sand or small crushed stone) to the soil. Replant only the healthy portions, and discard those with unhealthy roots or foliage. Sometimes starting over com-

pletely with new plants is the most cost-effective control.

Check for insect problems like aphids or mites The more insects you eradicate this fall, the fewer will overwinter and cause problems next spring. If you notice only a few pests, use a blast of cold water from the hose to control them. If there is a severe infestation, use an insecticidal soap or a synthetic pesticide.

Use a granular weed-preventer in established ground cover beds to prevent winter weeds like chickweed and hairy bittercress.

## PRUNING

Limit your pruning to dead or diseased leaves, stems, and twigs on vines.

Prune off dead or diseased leaves on ground covers, but don't cut them back severely now—wait until they are dormant.

Cut off seedpods as they ripen from annual vines like the **purple hyacinth bean, moon vine,** and others. Do this on a cool, dry day. Remove the seeds from the pods as soon as possible, carefully cutting away the seedpod. Keep seeds cool and dry until you sow them next spring (see Annuals, September). If you store them in plastic baggies, like sandwich bags, be sure to include a label with the name of the seed in the bag. Seeds from your garden make great gifts for the holidays.

## HELPFUL HINTS

For gardeners who like edible ornamentals beyond **grapes,** there are a number of uncommon ornamental vines that also produce tasty fruits.

- *Actinidia arguta* **Hardy kiwi** is a heavy bearer of greenish-purple edible skinned fruits the size of grapes.
- *Momordica charantia* **Bitter melon** or **balsam pear** has light-green lobed and puckered leaves and bright-orange fruits that split open to reveal red interiors.
- *Passiflora incarnata* **Maypop** or **passionflower** fruit is prized for its juice.
- *Passiflora* 'Incense' **Passionflower** has egg-shaped fruits.
- *Rubus laciniatus* **Fern-leaved blackberry** produces slightly tart berries.
- *Schisandra chinensis* has fragrant white flowers and bright-red edible fruits.

# OCTOBER
## VINES & GROUND COVERS

### PLANNING

Looking at plant combinations in nature is often the best teacher of what can work in your own garden. Deciduous trees provide the perfect living trellis for many vines. The key is selecting those vines that will make good companions for particular trees. A chosen vine should never be so vigorous that it suffocates the tree, and the tree should not be so strong as to overshade the vine.

When planting, keep in mind that the soil near the tree roots may be on the dry side. For this reason it is best to apply a good 2 inches of mulch around the roots of the vine, using caution to keep it away from the main stems. If you start with a small vine, in a 1-gallon pot, it will be easier to dig a hole large enough to accommodate the vine. Self-clinging vines like *Hydrangea anomala petiolaris* and **Virginia creeper** are well-suited for training on trees, but those that climb by tendrils also make happy companions for many trees. Train vines like **English ivy, wisteria, trumpet creeper,** and **akebia** to grow up dead but sturdy small trees. In this way their aggressive nature becomes an asset.

Because the soil near tree roots is often exhausted and shady, certain vines like **clematis** should be planted a good distance from a mature tree (4 feet).

1. Plant on the sunny side of the tree so the **clematis** will get a good start.

2. Use bamboo canes or strings to guide the vine into the tree.

3. Once the **clematis** reaches the tree, it will decide where it wants to grow.

Here is a list of vine-and-tree combinations to consider:

- *Bignonia capreolata* /**oak** trees, **black gum, maple** trees
- *Clematis* 'Jackmanii'/ *Robinia pseudoacacia* 'Frisia'
- *Hydrangea anomala petiolaris* /**oak** trees or **loblolly pine**
- *Lonicera* × *heckrottii* /**oak, maple,** or **pine** trees
- *Schizophragma hydrangeoides* 'Moonlight'/ **oak** trees, **loblolly pine, black gum**

### PLANTING

Plant container-grown vines and ground covers this month. When planting **clematis,** a 2-foot-deep planting hole is recommended, filled with equal parts of soil and compost. Set the crown at least 1 inch deep (some experts suggest 3 to 4 inches deep). Water generously, and apply 2 inches of an organic mulch. To encourage better branching as well as an abundance of larger flowers, cut the **clematis** back by half at the time of planting.

If you are growing **ornamental sweet potato** vines (*Ipomoea batatas*), you can dig the tubers and overwinter them now. They are also edible, but stringy. Some have handsome foliage,

---

## HARVESTING AND CURING GOURDS

L.H. Bailey, the famous botanist, wrote the following definition of **gourds**: "hard-shelled durable fruit grown for ornament, utensils, and general interest." **Gourds** grow on vines. Here are some tips for harvesting and curing ornamental **gourds**:

- **Gourds** must reach maturity on the vine.
- Once stems turn brown and dry, it is safe to cut and remove **gourds**.
- To preserve their colors, store **gourds** in a cool, dry place.
- The American Gourd Society recommends the following recipe to preserve **gourds**:

Mix 1 cup of Twenty Mule® Team Borax into 3 cups of hot water. Stir until dissolved. Let the mixture cool to lukewarm. Bring another pot of water to boil. Dip the **gourd** into the boiling water briefly, then soak it in the borax solution for 15 minutes. Do not rinse. Hang **gourds** in a cool place to dry for several weeks. Provide the best air circulation possible. **Gourds** can be waxed with a good-quality floor wax when dry.

like 'Blackie', which has leaves of dark purple brown; 'Margarita', which has chartreuse foliage; and 'Tricolor', which has leaves of pink, white, and green.

## WATERING

Water plants that have been planted within the last six months, unless they receive at least 1 inch per week of rainwater. Check weekly to see if they need water.

## FERTILIZING

There is no need to fertilize ground covers or vines now, but it is a good idea to prepare the soil in new beds, adding organic material before you plant, whether you will plant later this fall or next spring.

## PROBLEMS

During mild weather, certain insects may still be active. Check for evidence of aphids or scale. Signs may include distorted leaves or shoots, or brown hard spots on the undersides of leaves. If there is a mild infestation, spray with insecticidal soap or horticultural oil.

Rake up leaves that cover your ground covers. The better the

## HELPFUL HINTS

There are a number of vines that exhibit colorful leaves or leaves with interesting textures. Below is a list of both annual and perennial types that are noted for their foliage.

- *Humulus japonicus* 'Variegatus', **Variegated Japanese hop vine** (annual) has handsome variegated leaves that brighten the garden all summer until frost.
- *Hydrangea anomala petiolaris* **Climbing hydrangea** (perennial) has leaves that turn buttercup yellow in fall.
- *Lygopodium palmatum* **Climbing fern** (perennial) has delicate lacy foliage until frost.
- *Parthenocissus quinquefolia* **Virginia creeper** (perennial) has leaves that turn shades of purple, red, and crimson in fall.
- *Wisteria frutescens* **American wisteria** (perennial) leaves turn yellow in autumn.

light and air circulation, the happier they will be. Add these leaves to your compost pile, or use the lawn mower to chop them up. Finely chopped leaves can be put back on your flower beds as mulch.

## PRUNING

Limit your pruning to removing dead or diseased wood of vines.

Dig up ornamental sweet potato vines in October if you plan to overwinter the tubers.

# NOVEMBER
## VINES & GROUND COVERS

## PLANNING

This is a good month to look at the garden and see where you can use vines and ground covers to help solve problems. If you have a chain-link fence in an area that is mostly shady and want to cover it quickly, vines like **Carolina jessamine** or **English ivy** are ideal. Both are evergreen and easy to train. You can tuck new growth up and through the links of the fence. The yellow flowers of **Carolina jessamine** in spring are an added bonus. If you want to have late-season color in the garden with vines, the **climbing aster** *Aster caroliniamus* produces masses of lavender daisies in November. It has a lax habit, and the long stems must be tied up. An open brick wall is ideal, because you can weave the stems in and out of the openings.

Sometimes an area where a patch of lawn is required is simply too shady to grow turf with any success. In all but the northern parts of the state, there is an alternative: **Dwarf mondo grass** can make a rich green carpet that looks good all year long and requires only a minimum of care. It will thrive even with a moderate amount of foot traffic. The ultimate height of **dwarf mondo grass** is 3 to 4 inches. When

## HELPFUL HINTS

Color in the winter garden comes from foliage, fruits, flowers, and bark. Below is a list of ground covers and vines that hold their own in the winter garden:

- *Acorus gramineus* 'Ogon' (ground cover)
- *Asarum shuttleworthii* 'Callaway' (ground cover)
- *Cyclamen hederifolium* (ground cover)
- *Gelsemium sempervirens* (vine)
- *Hedera colchia* 'Sulphur Heart' (vine)
- *Hedera helix* cultivars (vine or ground cover)
- *Helleborus* hybrids and cultivars (ground cover)
- *Juniperus* species and cultivars (ground cover)
- *Liriope muscari* (ground cover)
- *Ophiopogon japonicus* (ground cover)
- *Rubus calycinoides* (ground cover)
- *Vinca minor* (ground cover)

planting, you will probably want to space individual plants 6 to 8 inches apart to get a thick covering in a short amount of time. Once your new lawn is established you can use a broom to sweep off leaves that accumulate. The more air, light, and moisture your **mondo** lawn receives, the happier it will be.

## PLANTING

Plant container-grown vines and ground covers as long as the ground is not frozen.

## WATERING

Keep up with watering new plantings on a weekly basis if

there is no regular rainfall, at least 1 inch per week. Fall weather may be cooler, but it can also be dry.

## FERTILIZING

There is no need to fertilize established vines and ground covers now. If you plant a large area of ground covers and use small rooted plugs, prepare the soil before you plant, being sure to incorporate generous amounts of organic material. When the soil is friable and rich in organic materials, it will be easier for roots to establish.

## PROBLEMS

Once there has been a hard freeze, pull down annual vines and dispose of them. This will help reduce the number of places in which insects can over-winter. Rake up leaves in ground cover beds, and add them to the compost pile.

Weed ground cover beds. Whenever possible, pull weeds before they flower and set seed. This will reduce future infestations of weeds.

Check vines and ground covers for insects like scale, aphids, or spider mites. Spray with horticultural oils.

## PRUNING

Before or when you pull up annual vines that were killed by frost, collect any remaining seed-pods, and save the seed for next year. Prune to remove any dead, diseased, or broken branches of vines. Cut away and dispose of any leaves or stems on ground covers that are damaged by insects or fungus. You can usually recognize fungus because the leaves and stems are black and look rotten.

A compost pile is an invaluable addition to the garden.

## HELPFUL HINTS

The ancient art of topiary is defined as the practice of training shrubs and small trees into ornamental or fantastic shapes such as animals, letters, and geometric forms. One way to create topiary is to train vines on forms. Usually metal, these forms can be placed in the ground or in a large decorative pot. Many types of **English ivy** and **Asian star jasmine** are easy to train on topiary forms.

1. Start with many small plants (in 2- to 4-inch pots) that have long trailing stems.

2. Tuck the stems up and through the form, covering as much area as possible.

3. Clip new growth on a regular basis to encourage stems to branch.

4. Tuck stems as they develop, and clip as needed to define the shape of the topiary. (This can be as often as once every two weeks during the growing season.)

275

# DECEMBER
## VINES & GROUND COVERS

 **PLANNING**

As winter approaches, take time to review the gardening year and examine your successes and failures. If you tried certain vines for the first time, did you grow them in the best manner? While many vines make good garden companions for **roses**, shrubs, or trees, some are best grown alone. Take, for example, the **moon vine.** This aggressive vine will quickly cover a structure or plant. If paired with another aggressive grower like the 'New Dawn' **rose**, it can create a maintenance headache. When the **moon vine** dies at the end of the growing season, it is nearly impossible to extricate it from amongst the canes of a **rose** without incurring bodily harm. For this reason, **moon vine** and other aggressive annual vines like **morning glories** are best grown on their own structures where they won't damage other plants.

 **PLANTING**

Plant container vines and ground covers before the ground freezes.

 **WATERING**

Keep new plantings well watered. Check them once a week.

 **FERTILIZING**

There's no need to fertilize vines or ground covers this month. Their growth is slowing down, as they enter the dormant season.

 **PROBLEMS**

Pull weeds out of ground cover beds and from the base of vines. If you see signs of scale or spider mites, treat plants with horticultural oil.

 **PRUNING**

Once vines are dormant, you can prune to shape them, but be sure not to prune off flowerbuds for next spring.

If your **luffa gourds** have turned brown on the stem, you may think it is too late to harvest them—but it's not. **Luffa gourds** should be left on the vine until the stem is completely dry and the **gourd** is beginning to turn brown at both ends or the **gourd** is completely dry. Once they are harvested, they can be peeled. If the shell has dried completely, you can peel it away bit by bit. You can also soak the **gourd** for 15 minutes to 2 hours, softening the shell and making it easier to peel. The interior sponge will have 40 to 80 seeds.

Soak the sponge in warm water, and then hang to dry. Adding a small amount of bleach to the water will make for a bright **luffa** sponge. Save any seeds from desirable **luffa** sponges for next year's crop. **Luffa** sponges make good gifts.

To avoid damaging other plants, it is best to grow moon vine and other aggressive annual vines on their own supports.

# USING CHEMICALS IN YOUR GARDEN

In a perfect world, insects and diseases might attack other people's gardens . . . but **never** yours! In a perfect world, diseases and insects would be easy to control with little forethought. Unfortunately, Georgia gardeners do not live in a perfect world. Not even close!

Our long, hot, humid summers provide an excellent breeding ground for insects and diseases. Although these pests serve nature's overall purpose, that is little consolation when we find disfigured flowers and vanishing leaves.

Some gardeners avoid using chemical pesticides in their garden. Some prefer to use chemicals only sparingly. Others use chemicals, where appropriate, to solve many of their garden pest problems.

We do not take sides in the organic versus synthetic pesticide debate. We realize that some pesticides that are considered to be organic can still be dangerous if used improperly, and we know that some synthetic chemicals have a very good environmental safety record when used according to label directions.

Our preference is that landscape and vegetable garden plants be grown in the healthiest manner possible. Healthy plants are better prepared to fight against pests and usually thrive in spite of them, without the use of pesticides of any kind.

Even healthy plants, though, may suffer so much damage that they become unsightly, and diseases or insects can cause a weak plant to die. In such situations, gardeners may want to resort to pesticides.

## WHAT IS A PESTICIDE?
A pesticide is a chemical that is used to kill or control a pest. The chemical can come from organic sources and be called an organic pesticide, or it can come from a chemical manufacturer and be called a synthetic pesticide. In either case, it is still a pesticide.

Pesticides can be classified according to the pests they affect. An insecticide kills insects. A fungicide kills fungi. A herbicide kills plants. Miticides, bactericides, and molluscicides are also used in the garden or landscape, to control mites, bacteria, and slugs and snails.

## ORGANIC PESTICIDES
Organic pesticides usually come from plant, animal, or mineral sources. *Pyrethrin* is an insecticide that comes from chrysanthemum flowers—*pyrethroids* are insecticides similar to pyrethrin that have been synthesized in a laboratory. *Bacillus thuringiensis* (B.t.) is a disease spore that is an excellent control for caterpillars. Diatomaceous earth is a mineral that kills crawling insects by drying out their protective body coating. Many organic pesticides are used by commercial farmers and landscapers because they offer superior efficacy or safety.

## SYNTHETIC PESTICIDES
A synthetic pesticide is manufactured in a laboratory or chemical plant. Synthetic chemistry allows great amounts of a chemical to be manufactured at low cost.

## WHICH ONE IS SAFER?
Most of the synthetic and organic pesticides available to gardeners have been tested and studied at length by scientists to make sure they do not present a great risk to the user or to the environment.

Neither organic nor synthetic pesticides can be considered safe in all circumstances. Just because it comes from a laboratory does not mean a synthetic pesticide is more dangerous than an organic one. Before any product may be sold as a pesticide, it must pass extensive tests devised by researchers and the government. The tests help make sure the pesticide is effective and, when used properly, is unlikely to harm humans, animals, other organisms, or unintended targets.

It is important to treat *all* pesticides with caution and to use them properly.

## HOW DO PESTICIDES WORK?

Whether synthetic or organic, most pesticides work by interfering with a chemical process in the pest. The synthetic insecticide *permethrin* interferes with nerve transmission in an insect. Organic insecticidal soap dissolves pest cell walls so they dry out. If you want to know more about how a pesticide works, visit ExToxNet (http://extoxnet. orst.edu/) on the Web.

Some pesticides are *systemic* and some are *contact* pesticides. A systemic insecticide, like the chemical *imidacloprid*, is drawn into a plant's leaves and is spread throughout the plant's tissue. An insect feeding on any part of the plant is affected by the chemical. A contact insecticide, like horticultural oil, must touch the insect directly in order to affect it.

## READ THE LABEL!

The best way to learn how to use a pesticide safely is to read its label. Government rules mandate that specific information must be included on the label. Signal words such as WARNING, CAUTION, and DANGER must be clearly visible. Usage instructions must be plainly written. The active ingredients must be listed (although the tongue-tangling names of some chemicals are intimidating to all but scientists!). Do not use a pesticide until you have read the label completely and understand how to use the product.

## PESTICIDE SAFETY

Any chemical, whether vinegar from the kitchen, bleach from the laundry, or soap from the bath, can be harmful if it touches the wrong part of your body. Garden chemicals can harm your body as well. When applying pesticides, take special note of whether you are required to wear long pants, gloves, or eye protection. Follow the recommendations *exactly* each time . . . even if you have used the chemical dozens of times before. Wash your hands after using garden chemicals. If a pesticide is sprayed on your sleeve or pants leg, wash the clothing separately from the rest of your family's clothing.

## STORING PESTICIDES

In general, dry fertilizers and pesticides need to be kept dry, and liquid fertilizers and pesticides should be kept from freezing. Dry chemicals need to be protected from humidity as well as rain. A lockable cabinet is the safest place to store pesticides. Failing that, store yours in a large plastic sealable tub. Label the tub and place it where children and pets cannot get to it.

Labels on pesticide containers tend to become tattered over time. Use a rubber band around the bottle to keep the accordion-style directions neat. If the label comes off a container completely, dispose of the chemical according to the directions below.

## DISPOSING OF PESTICIDES

It is hard to estimate how much of a pesticide you'll need for some jobs. When spraying dormant oil on an apple tree, will it take a quart or a gallon? When spot-spraying weeds, should you mix a pint or a sprayerful? Sometimes you'll have pesticide left over when you are finished with a job, and what should be done with the excess?

# USING CHEMICALS IN YOUR GARDEN

Often the best answer is to save the mixture for a few days and use up what's left. Most pesticides do not deteriorate rapidly and will remain effective for at least a week. If the job at hand doesn't need another application, look for another site. Does a neighbor need the pesticide on his or her lawn? It is not a good idea to simply dump the surplus in one spot; that could lead to surface water contamination.

Most homeowner pesticide products are not manufactured in such a concentrated form that a single accident would pose great harm to the environment. Call your county government for specific directions. Small containers of pesticide concentrate can be disposed of by pouring the liquid into a gallon container of kitty litter, wrapping the container several times with newspaper, and putting it out with your garbage. Municipal landfills are designed to keep chemical contaminants out of the environment.

## BENEFICIAL INSECTS

Most gardeners use insecticides with reluctance, knowing that beneficial or harmless insects perish alongside harmful ones. You can minimize the need for insecticides by encouraging beneficial insects to make their home in your garden.

Remember that it takes a few days or weeks for beneficial insects to build their populations enough to control pest insects. One reason we consistently recommend using water to wash aphids from plants is that water does not harm the tiny beneficial wasps that parasitize aphids naturally. Initially allowing a bit of damage to your plants often permits natural controls to strengthen. Common beneficial insects include the following:

• Ladybugs (both adults and larvae) are voracious aphid eaters.

• Green lacewings have larvae that eat spider mites, aphids, and other small insects.

• Ground beetles consume many insects that hide in mulch at night.

• Garden spiders catch whiteflies, ants, beetles, and leafhoppers in their webs.

• Hornets, paper wasps, and yellow jackets may be pests at times, but these insects love to eat leaf-feeding caterpillars.

• Parasitic wasps are tiny insects that are non-threatening to humans. They lay their eggs on aphids and caterpillars, parasitizing and killing them.

The following are some ways to encourage beneficial insects:

• In out-of-the-way corners, plant bronze fennel, queen anne's lace, dill, lemon balm, and parsley. Do not remove their flowers, since these provide nectar for adult beneficial insects.

• Plant attractive annual flowers such as alyssum, candytuft, marigolds, and salvias, which are also alluring to beneficial insects.

• Learn to identify beneficial insects and their immature life stages. A lady beetle larva looks like an orange-and-black alligator. You might think it a pest unless you have learned to recognize it.

• Emphasize ant control in your garden or landscape. Ants tend aphids, scales, and mealybugs, and they interfere with the natural enemies of these pests.

• Use low-impact insecticides such as insecticidal soap, horticultural oil, and B.t. before reaching for synthetic contact insecticides.

Some gardeners feel they can achieve control of pests by releasing purchased beneficial insects in their landscapes. Researchers caution that it probably doesn't pay to make a mass release. Most will disperse and fly to other yards some distance away. It is usually best to *attract* beneficials rather than *import* them.

# SMALL GARDEN PLAN

## Small Garden Plan for Georgia
### Garden Size: 25 feet wide, 50 feet long

| | |
|---|---|
| 2 ft. | Asparagus [1] |
| 2½ ft. | Cabbage + lettuce [2] |
| 2½ ft. | Onion sets [3] |
| 2½ ft. | Parsley or turnips + radishes + carrots + beets [4] |
| 2½ ft. | Garden peas + cabbage [5] |
| 2½ ft. | Bush green beans + broccoli [6] |
| 2½ ft. | Southern peas + cauliflower [7] |
| 2½ ft. | Staked tomatoes + bell peppers + eggplant [8] |
| 3½ ft. | Staked cucumbers + pole beans [9] |
| 2 ft. | Potatoes [10] |

Planting dates are for middle Georgia. South Georgia can plant 10 to 14 days earlier in spring. North Georgia should plant two weeks later in spring.

[1] Set crowns in March. Buy one-year-old crowns. Do not harvest the first year.
[2] Set cabbage and lettuce March 1. Set leaf lettuce between cabbage plants.
[3] Set March 10–20. Set thick; then thin and eat as needed.
[4] Around March 20. Set parsley or turnips thick; mix radish seed sparingly with carrots.
[5] Early and late February for peas. Sow peas as early as the ground can be prepared. Cabbage plants will need to be grown, because they will not be available from commercial sources at this time of year.
[6] Beans April 1; broccoli July 10.
[7] Peas April 1; cauliflower July 10. Cauliflower plants will need to be grown from seed.
[8] After frost danger. Prune tomatoes to one stem.
[9] After frost danger. Stake and prune cucumbers and train to climb string or stakes.
[10] Late February.

| Vegetable | Recommended Cultivar | Vegetable | Recommended Cultivar |
|---|---|---|---|
| Asparagus | Jersey Gem | Lettuce | Bibb |
| Bush green bean | Tendergreen | Onion set | Granex 33 |
| Pole bean | Kentucky Wonder 191 | Parsley | Extra Curled Dwarf |
| Beets | Detroit Dark Red | Garden pea | Little Marvel |
| Broccoli | Green Comet | Southern pea | Pinkeye Purple Hull |
| Cabbage | Early Round Dutch | Bell pepper | Yolo Wonder L |
| Carrots | Scarlet Nantes | Radish | Cherry Belle |
| Cauliflower | Snowball Y Improved | Staked tomato | Better Boy |
| Staked cucumber | Dasher II | Turnip | Purple Top |
| Eggplant | Black Beauty | Potato | Red Pontiac, Kennebec |

Courtesy of Wayne J. McLaurin, Extension Horticulturist, University of Georgia College of Agricultural and Environmental Sciences.

# FRUIT ZONE MAP

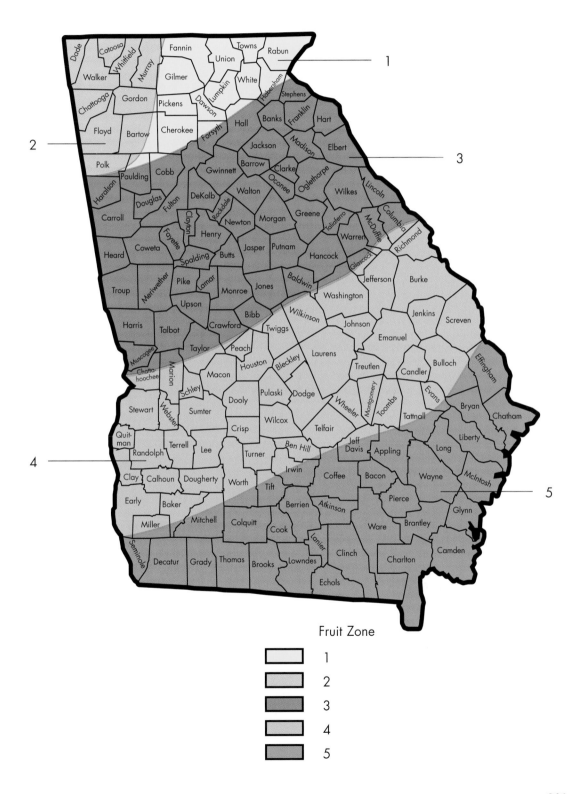

Fruit Zone

- 1
- 2
- 3
- 4
- 5

# Apple Varieties Recommended for Home Use for the Different Zones in Georgia

| Variety[1] | Zone[2] | Characteristics[3] | Pollination Code[4] |
|---|---|---|---|
| 'Anna' | 5 | Excellent shaped fruit with blush of red. Ripens mid-June to early July. Very early crisp yellow apple of excellent quality. | A |
| 'Ginger Gold' | 1-2-3 | Good for fresh eating, sauce, and pies. Ripens late July to early August. Excellent-quality apple. | B |
| 'Gala' | 1-2-3 | Good for fresh eating or salads. Ripens early August. | B |
| 'Mollie's Delicious' | 1-2-3-4 | A versatile apple. Good for fresh eating, pies, and sauce. Ripens late July to early August. | B |
| 'Ozark Gold' | 1-2-3 | Matures in early August. Yellow, russet-free apple of excellent quality. | B |
| 'Red Delicious' | 1-2-3-4 | Early fall variety ripening in late August to early September. Large, firm, crisp, sweet. Good for fresh eating or salads. | B |
| 'Jonagold' | 1-2-3 | Ripens early September. Very large, yellow apple with red blush. Very high-quality, sweet, juicy apple. | C |
| 'Golden Delicious' | 1-2-3-4 | Ripens one or two weeks after 'Red Delicious'. Good producer. Fruit good for sauce, fresh eating, and pies. | C |
| 'Fuji' | 1-2-3 | Fall variety ripening in early October. Does not color well, but quality is superb. Good for cooking, eating, and baking. | B |
| 'Mutzu' | 1-2-3 | Ripens early October. Yellow apple of exceptional quality. Crisp and juicy. Slightly tart. All-purpose. | B |
| 'Rome Beauty' | 1-2 | Ripens early October. Red apple that is primarily grown for baking. | C |
| 'Stayman' | 1-2 | Ripens early October. Rusty red finish. Superb-quality all-purpose apple that is tart. Fruit cracking a problem when dry period followed by rainy period. | C |
| 'Yates' | 1-2-3-4 | Late fall variety ripening in late October. Small, dark dark red. Juicy, mellow, sub-acid. Best keeper. | B |
| 'Granny Smith' | 1-2-3-4 | Matures in late October to early November. Yellow-green apple of excellent quality. Good all-purpose variety. | B |

[1] Listed in order of ripening.
[2] See Fruit Zone Map, p. 281.
[3] Ripening dates for all varieties except 'Anna' are based on averages from Athens, Georgia. Ripening dates for 'Anna' are based on averages from Monticello, Florida.
[4] Varieties followed by a common letter bloom at approximately the same time. Since most apple varieties are self-unfruitful (require pollen from another variety to set fruit), plant two or more varieties that have the same letter so fruit set will result. 'Stayman', 'Mutzu', and 'Jonagold' have sterile pollen and should not be used as a pollen source for other varieties; therefore, plant at least two other varieties with any or all of these varieties.

# FRUIT VARIETIES

## Pear Varieties Recommended for Home Use for the Different Zones in Georgia

| Variety / Hybrids | Zone[1] | Characteristics | Pollination Code[2] |
|---|---|---|---|
| 'Orient' | 1-2-3-4-5 | An excellent pear for most of the state. Resistant to blight. Flesh white; a good keeper. Very large fruit. | B,C |
| 'Carrick' | 1-2-3 | Excellent for preserving. Trees resistant to blight. | B |
| 'Waite' | 1-2-3 | An excellent pear for the northern half of the state. Resistant to blight. Pollen sterile. Plant with 'Orient'. | C |
| 'Kieffer' | 1-2-3 | Large; skin yellow. Poor quality. Subject to blight in wet years. Good for preserves. | A,B |
| 'Baldwin' | 4-5 | An excellent pear for the southern half of the state. Resistant to blight. | A |
| 'Magness' | 1-2-3-4 | Pollen sterile. Plant with 'Orient'. Fruit excellent quality but not very productive. | C |
| 'Moonglow' | 1-2-3-4 | Vigorous tree that produces fair to good-quality fruit. Nearly free of grit cells. | C |
| 'Starking Delicious'[3] | 1-2-3-4 | An excellent pear for the northern half of the state. Fruit excellent quality. Moderately vigorous. | C |
| 'Dawn' | 1-2-3-4 | Good-quality fruit. Almost entirely free of grit cells. Moderately vigorous tree. | C |
| 'Warren' | 3-4-5 | Very high-quality fruit. Resistant to blight. | B,C |

[1] See Fruit Zone Map, p. 281.
[2] Plant two or more varieties followed by a common letter. Multiple letters by some varieties indicate that they will pollinate other varieties followed by either letter.
[3] 'Starking Delicious' is considered by many experts to be the same as 'Maxine'.

## Peach Varieties Recommended for Home Use for the Different Zones in Georgia

| Variety | Zone[1] | Flesh Color | Stone Freeness | Harvest[2] |
|---|---|---|---|---|
| 'Junegold' | 4,5 | Yellow | Cling | 47 |
| 'Surecrop' | 1,2,3 | Yellow | Semi-free | 43 |
| 'Juneprince' | 4,5 | Yellow | Semi-free | 35 |
| 'Gala' | 3,4 | Yellow | Semi-free | 33 |
| 'Redhaven' | 1,2,3 | Yellow | Semi-free | 28 |
| 'Suwanee' | 4,5 | Yellow | Free | 22 |
| 'Nectar' | 1,2,3 | White | Free | 22 |
| 'Harvester' | 3,4 | Yellow | Free | 21 |
| 'Redglobe' | 1,2,3,4 | Yellow | Free | 13 |

(Continued on the next page)

# FRUIT VARIETIES

## Peach Varieties Recommended for Home Use for the Different Zones in Georgia

| Variety | Zone[1] | Flesh Color | Stone Freeness | Harvest[2] |
|---|---|---|---|---|
| 'Georgia Belle' | 1,2,3 | White | Free | 3 |
| 'Cresthaven' | 1,2,3 | Yellow | Free | 3 |
| 'Redskin' | 1,2,3,4,5 | Yellow | Free | 2 |
| 'Jefferson' | 1,2,3 | Yellow | Free | -3 |

[1] See Fruit Zone Map, p. 281.
[2] Days ripening before or after (-) 'Elberta' at Byron, Georgia. The average ripening date for 'Elberta' at Byron is July 20, but the actual date will vary slightly from season to season. North Georgia (Zones 1, 2, and upper part of 3) is 7 to 10 days later, while Zone 5 to 7 is 7 to 10 days earlier.

## Plum Varieties Recommended for Home Use for the Different Areas in Georgia

| Variety | Zone[1] | Characteristics | Peak Harvest[2] |
|---|---|---|---|
| 'A.U. Amber' | 1-2-3-4-5 | Medium size, excellent flavor for season. Red-purple skin with yellow flesh. Partially self-fruitful. | May 31 |
| 'Methley' | 1-2-3-4-5 | Medium size, excellent quality. Dark purple skin; deep red flesh. One of the best varieties. Partially self-fruitful. | June 3 |
| 'Rubysweet' | 1-2-3-4 | Large firm red-fleshed fruit with greenish-red skin; excellent flavor. | June 12 |
| 'A.U. Rubrum' | 1-2-3-4-5 | Red flesh. Fruit medium to large. Maroon skin color. | June 15 |
| 'Morris' | 1-2-3-4 | Fruit medium to large. Reddish-black skin and red flesh. Firm and crisp with good flavor. | June 16 |
| 'A.U. Homeside' | 1-2-3-4-5 | Red skin, amber flesh. Large size. Soft. | June 18 |
| 'A.U. Roadside' | 1-2-3-4-5 | Red flesh. Medium to large fruit size. Very good quality. | June 19 |
| 'A.U. Producer' | 1-2-3-4-5 | Dark red skin with red flesh. Good quality. | June 20 |
| 'Byrongold' | 1-2-3-4 | Medium to large round fruit. Mild to slightly tart flavor. Yellow skin with occasional blush. Firm and keeps well. Good quality. | June 29 |
| 'Black Ruby' | 1-2-3-4-5 | Purple-black with yellow flesh. Upright tree. Good quality. | June 29 |

[1] See Fruit Zone Map, p. 281.
[2] Average date at Byron, Georgia. (Courtesy Jim Thompson, USDA)

# FRUIT VARIETIES

## Rabbiteye Blueberries

The most important things to remember about starting rabbiteye blueberries is to plant more than one variety for cross-pollination. Cross-pollination is necessary for fruit set.

| Early Season | Mid-Season | Late Season |
|---|---|---|
| 'Austin' | 'Bluebelle' | 'Baldwin' |
| 'Brightwell' | 'Briteblue' | 'Centurion' |
| 'Climax' | 'Chaucer' | 'Choice' |
| 'Premier' | 'Powderblue' | 'Delite' |
| 'Woodard' | 'Tifblue' | |

'Climax', 'Chaucer', 'Choice', and 'Woodard' are not suggested for mountain areas because they bloom early. 'Austin', 'Climax', and 'Premier' are the earliest ripening rabbiteye varieties. To lengthen your harvest season, select one or more of these varieties, and one or more of the other varieties. 'Baldwin', 'Centurion', and 'Delite' are the latest maturing rabbiteye varieties. With early, mid-season, and late varieties, you should enjoy fresh blueberries for six weeks.

'Woodard' is a good berry for fresh eating but develops a tough skin when frozen. 'Brightwell', 'Centurion', 'Tifblue', and 'Powderblue' are generally the most resistant to spring freeze.

## Strawberry Varieties by Season and Areas of Adaptability

| Variety | Early | Mid-Season | Late |
|---|---|---|---|
| 'Fla 90' | S[1] | | |
| 'Sunrise' | M,N | | |
| 'Earliglow' | M,N | | |
| 'Cardinal' | | M,N | |
| 'Surecrop' | | M,N | |
| 'Tioga' | | M | |
| 'Apollo'[2] | | M,N | |
| 'Albritton' | | | M |
| 'Delite' | | | M,N |

[1] S = South Georgia, M = Middle Georgia, N = Piedmont and North Georgia.
[2] 'Apollo' should be planted with another variety to ensure fruit set. Other varieties can be planted alone.

## Recommended Raspberry Varieties

- 'Heritage' (for northern third of Georgia)
- 'Redwing' (for northern third of Georgia)
- 'Dormanred' (a trailing variety; good for entire state)

## Recommended Blackberry Varieties

- Navaho (erect)
- Cherokee (erect)
- Cheyenne (erect)
- Gem (trailing)
- Black Satin (trailing)
- Kiowa (trailing)

# FRUIT VARIETIES

## Fig Varieties for Georgia

| Variety | Color of Fruit | Size | Quality of Fruit For Fresh Use | For Preserving |
|---|---|---|---|---|
| 'Brown Turkey' | Bronze | Medium | Good | Excellent |
| 'Celeste' | Lt. brown to violet | Small | Very good | Excellent |
| 'Hunt' | Bronze with white specks | Small to medium | Good | Excellent |
| 'Kadota' | Bright greenish yellow | Small to medium | Fair | Excellent |
| 'LSU Purple' | Reddish to dark purple | Medium | Good | New variety–unknown |
| 'Magnolia' | Bronze with white flecks | Medium | Fair | Excellent |

## Pecan Varieties for Homegrowers

| Variety | Size | Kernel Quality | Scab Resistance | Productivity |
|---|---|---|---|---|
| 'Stuart' | Large | Excellent | Resistant | Very good |
| 'Elliott' | Small | Good | Very resistant | Very good |
| 'Curtis' | Small | Excellent | Very resistant | Very good |
| 'Gloria Grande' | Large | Excellent | Resistant | Very good |
| 'Sumner' | Large | Excellent | Resistant | Very good |

## Bunch Grape Varieties for the Upper Piedmont and Mountains in Approximate Order of Ripening

| Variety | Area of Georgia | Red Wine | White Wine | Juice, Jelly | Fresh Eating | Comments |
|---|---|---|---|---|---|---|
| 'Aurora' | 1 | | X | | X | Good wine and fresh eating |
| 'Cascade' | 1 and 2 | X | | | X | Performed well in Georgia test |
| 'Ontario' | 1 | | | | X | Green to amber |
| 'Fredonia'[1] | 1 and 2 | | | X | X | Blue fruit |
| 'Delaware'[1] | 1 and 2 | X | | X | X | Reddish fruit, small but sweet, good red wine[2] |
| 'Venus' | 1 and 2 | | | X | X | Seedless, blue-black fruit |
| 'Mars' | 1 and 2 | | | | X | Seedless, blue fruit |
| 'Reliance'[1] | 1 and 2 | | | | X | Seedless, red fruit |
| 'Buffalo' | 1 and 2 | | | X | X | Good yields |
| 'Niagara' | 1 and 2 | | | X | X | Golden fruit[2] |
| 'Cayuga White' | 1 and 2 | X | | | | Vigorous vine |
| 'Concord' | 1 | X | | X | X | Blue fruit ripens unevenly, not recommended |

[1] Most outstanding varieties.
[2] Should be grafted on 'Dog Ridge' or similar rootstock for best results.

# FRUIT VARIETIES

## Bunch Grape Varieties for Middle and South Georgia in Approximate Order of Ripening

Several hybrid bunch grape varieties have recently been developed which are worthy of trial plantings in middle and south Georgia. All of these have good resistance to Pierce's Disease, the primary limiting factor to bunch grape culture in the middle and southern portion of Georgia. The following table lists suggested varieties for home plantings.

| Variety | Red Wine | White Wine | Juice, Jelly | Fresh Eating | Comments |
|---|---|---|---|---|---|
| 'Blanc Dubois' | | X | | X | Good white wine |
| 'Orlando Seedless' | | | | X | Small, greenish-yellow fruit |
| 'Suwanee'[1] | | X | | X | Good fresh and as wine |
| 'Blue Lake' | | | X | | Purple fruit |
| 'Conquistador'[1] | X | | X | X | Very good, similar to 'Concord'[2] |
| 'Lake Emerald' | | X | | X | Greenish fruit |
| 'Black Spanish' ('Lenoir') | X | | | | Dark purple fruit |
| 'Daytona' | | | | X | Low yield but good eating, pink fruit[2] |

[1] Most outstanding varieties.
[2] Graft on 'Tampa', 'Lake Emerald', 'Florilush', or 'Dog Ridge' rootstock.

## Muscadine Varieties Recommended for Home Use for the Different Zones in Georgia

| Variety | Flower Type[2] | Size | Color | Main Uses | Comments |
|---|---|---|---|---|---|
| 'Carlos'[1] | P.F. | Medium | Bronze | Juice, wine | Productive |
| 'Cowart' | P.F. | Large | Black | Fresh eating | Good flavor |
| 'Dixie' | P.F. | Medium | Bronze | Juice, wine | Good cold tolerance |
| 'Fry'[1] | F. | V. large | Bronze | Fresh eating | Fruit rot and winter injury a problem; excellent flavor |
| 'Higgins' | F. | Large | Bronze-pink | Fresh eating | Mild flavor; late season |
| 'Jumbo' | F. | V. large | Black | Fresh eating | Low sugar content |
| 'Loomis'[1] | F. | Med-large | Black | Fresh eating | Excellent flavor |
| 'Magnolia' | P.F. | Medium | Bronze | Juice, wine | Good flavor; winter hardy |
| 'Nesbitt'[1] | P.F. | V. large | Black | Fresh eating | Good cold tolerance |
| 'Noble'[1] | P.F. | Small | Black | Juice, wine | Productive |
| 'Scuppernong' | F. | Medium | Bronze | Wine, fresh eating | Very old variety; low yields |
| 'Summit'[1] | F. | Large | Bronze-pink | Fresh eating | Winter hardy; more disease-resistant than 'Fry' |
| 'Tara'[1] | P.F. | Large | Bronze | Fresh eating | Fairly good flavor |
| 'Triumph'[1] | P.F. | Med-large | Bronze-pink | Fresh eating | Early season |

[1] Most outstanding varieties
[2] P.F. = Perfect flowered (produces pollen and fruit)  F. = Female flowered (produces fruit only)

# RECOMMENDED ROSES FOR GEORGIA

Although we don't have perfect growing conditions for all roses, there are many roses that do very well in Southern gardens. Sandy coastal soil and high levels of sunshine and heat are challenges. EarthKind™ roses are designated (E). Roses recommended specifically for coastal or sandy environments are designated (C).

## FLORIBUNDA ROSES
- 'Apricot Nectar' (apricot with pink)
- 'Europeana' (deep crimson)
- 'First Edition' (orange-blend)
- 'Iceberg' (white)
- 'Livin' Easy' (apricot/orange)
- 'Nearly Wild' (E) (rose pink)
- 'Pinocchio' (C) (orange-pink)
- 'Sunsprite' (deep yellow)

## SHRUB ROSES
- 'Sea Foam' (E) (creamy white
- 'Carefree Beauty' (rosy-pink)
- 'Katy Road Pink' (E) (medium pink)
- 'Dortmund' (bright red)
- 'Belinda's Dream' (E) (C) (light pink)
- 'Knockout' (E) (cherry red)

## HYBRID TEA ROSES
- 'Alabama' (rose-pink)
- 'Brigadoon' (Cream with coral/pink)
- 'Chicago Peace' (Hot pink/yellow rev)
- 'Chrysler Imperial' (deep red/crimson)
- 'Duchesse de Brabant' (C) (light pink)
- 'Garden Party' (creamy white)
- 'Gemini' (pink/cream)
- 'Ganada' (red/orange/yellow mix)
- 'Lady Hillingdon' (C) (yellow blend)
- 'Marie van Houtte' (C) (pink blend)
- 'Midas Touch' (neon yellow)
- 'Mr. Lincoln' (velvety red)
- 'Pascali' (white)
- 'Peace' (yellow with pink)
- 'Pristine' (ivory with pink)
- 'The McCartney Rose' (medium pink)

- 'White Masterpiece' (white)
- 'Yankee Doodle' (yellow blend)

## GRANDIFLORA ROSES
- 'Love' (scarlet red)
- 'Montezuma' (orange-pink blend)
- 'Queen Elizabeth' (medium pink)

## POLYANTHA ROSES
- 'Marie Daly' (E) (medium pink)
- 'Else Poulsen' (E) (mediun pink)
- 'The Fairy' (light pink)
- 'Marie Pavié' (white)
- 'La Marne' (pink blend)
- 'Caldwell Pink' (E) (lilac-pink)
- 'Perle d'Or' (C) (yellow-pink)

## CLIMBING ROSES
(The Cl. abbreviation means it is a climbing form of a bush-type rose.)
- 'Altissimo' (blood red)
- 'America' (pink with salmon/coral)
- 'Cecile Brunner' (C) (light pink)
- 'Champney's Pink Cluster' (C) (light pink)
- Cl. 'Clotilde Soupert' (C) (near white)
- Cl. 'Cramoisi Superieur' (C) (medium red)
- Cl. 'Souvenir de la Malmaison' (C) (light pink)
- 'Crepuscule' (C) (apricot blend)
- 'Don Juan' (deep red)
- 'Fourth of July' (red/white stripes)
- 'New Dawn' (soft pink)
- 'Pinkie' (medium pink)
- 'Sombreuil' (C) (near white)

# USDA COLD HARDINESS ZONES

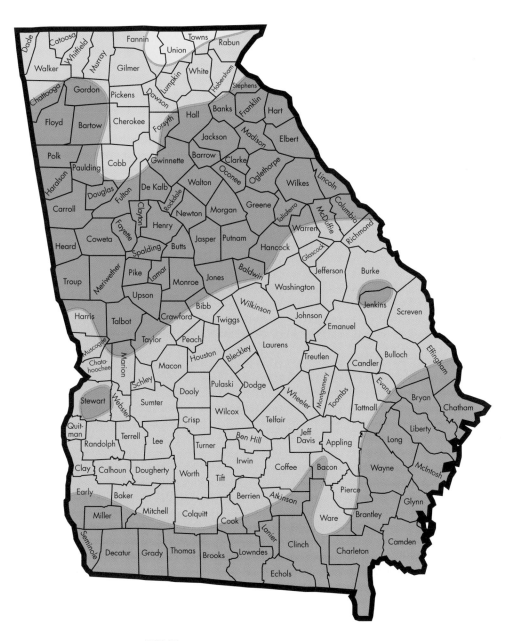

| ZONE | Average Annual Min. Temperature (°F) |
|------|--------------------------------------|
| 6b | 0 to -5 |
| 7a | 5 to 0 |
| 7b | 10 to 5 |
| 8a | 15 to 10 |
| 8b | 20 to 15 |

## BOTANICAL GARDENS

### Atlanta Botanical Garden

Piedmont Park at The Prado
Atlanta, Georgia 30357
(404) 876-5859
http://www.atlantabotanicalgarden.org

The Atlanta Botanical Garden is a lush oasis in the heart of Midtown Atlanta. The ABG features fifteen acres of landscaped gardens, a conservatory that houses endangered tropical and desert plants from around the world, and a fifteen-acre hardwood forest with walking trails. This is an easily accessible gardening resource in the midst of urban Atlanta.

### Atlanta History Center

130 West Paces Ferry Road, NW
Atlanta, Georgia 30305
(404) 814-4000
http://www.atlhist.org

On the grounds of the Atlanta History Center, visitors can experience thirty-two acres of gardens, woodlands, and nature trails that show the horticultural history of the Atlanta region. Seven distinct gardens feature a variety of gardening styles from native plantings to formal landscaping with boxwoods and classical statuary. A Garden for Peace has been installed as part of an international effort to promote world peace.

### Callaway Gardens

P.O. Box 2000
Pine Mountain, Georgia 31822-2000
(800) 225-5292
http://www.callawaygardens.com

Located seventy miles southwest of Atlanta and thirty miles north of Columbus, Callaway Gardens is a manmade landscape in a unique natural setting. It was conceived by its creators Cason Callaway and his wife Virginia as a place for visitors to discover natural beauty. Today, Callaway Gardens features the largest glass-enclosed butterfly conservatory in North America, and Mr. Cason's Vegetable Garden showcases Southern vegetables and annual flower trial gardens. In addition, the Sibley Horticulture Center showcases a year-round floral display that integrates indoor and outdoor plant settings. More than a million people visit the 1500 acres of Callaway Gardens each year.

### Fernbank Museum of Natural History

767 Clifton Road, NE
Atlanta, Georgia 30307
(404) 929-6300
http://www.fernbank.edu/museum

### Fernbank Science Center

156 Heaton Park Drive, NE
Atlanta, Georgia 30307-1398
(404) 378-4311
http://fsc.fernbank.edu

The grounds of the Fernbank Museum of Natural History and Fernbank Science Center feature two distinct garden areas. Adjacent to the Fernbank Science Center is the Fernbank Forest. For many years visitors have walked through the sixty-five-acre woodland, a primeval Piedmont forest containing one-and-a-half miles of paved trail lined with signs identifying various specimens. The grounds of the Fernbank Museum of Natural History feature the Stanton Rose Garden. Visitors there will see 1300 roses, including All-America Rose Selections test plants.

### Georgia Southern Botanical Garden

Georgia Southern University
1211 Fair Road (State Highway 67)
Statesboro, Georgia 30460
(912) 871-1114
http://www2.gasou.edu/garden

The Georgia Southern Botanical Garden is a ten-acre site located two blocks from the campus of Georgia Southern University. The garden features native plants of Georgia, particularly those of the Coastal Plain. Various gardens include a Magnolia/Holly allee, a butterfly border, and an arboretum. Also within the botanical garden are a children's vegetable garden, nature trails, and seven original farm structures.

### Massee Lane Gardens
One Massee Lane
Fort Valley, Georgia 31030
(912) 967-2358
http://www.peach.public.lib.ga.us/ACS
Beginning with the planting of one Camellia plant in 1936, Massee Lane Gardens now serves as the headquarters for the American Camellia Society. Located on the site of a former peach farm dating from the early 1900s, the garden also features an education museum, a rose garden, and a Japanese garden.

### Perimeter College Botanical Garden
3251 Panthersville Road
Decatur, Georgia 30034
(404) 244-5090
http://www.gpc.peachnet.edu/~ddonald/botgard/george3.htm
The Perimeter College Botanical Garden focuses exclusively on Georgia native plants, and includes the largest collection of native plants in the state. Dozens of native ferns are featured along a shaded forest path. Approximately 1500 sun- and shade-loving native plants can be seen at the Perimeter College South Campus.

### Southeastern Flower Show
(404) 888-5638
http//www.flowershow.org
The Southeastern Flower Show benefits the Atlanta Botanical Garden as well as amateur and expert gardeners throughout the South. Held in the later part of February every year, the show features dozens of gardens presented by top garden designers, judged horticultural classes, and an extensive vendors market. Seminars and workshops by gardening experts make this a must-go event for Georgia gardeners.

### State Botanical Garden of Georgia
2450 South Milledge Avenue
Athens, Georgia 30602
(706) 542-1244
http://www.uga.edu/~botgarden
The State Botanical Garden of Georgia is a 313-acre preserve under the direction of The University of Georgia. The garden has five miles of nature trails, an International Garden, and a three-story tropical conservatory. The State Botanical Garden holds educational programs all year long and has a growing and active patrons organization.

## EDUCATIONAL AND PROFESSIONAL ORGANIZATIONS

### Extension Service
www.gaurbanag.org
Local phone numbers can be found under your county government phone listings. The University of Georgia Cooperative Extension Service is an educational organization sponsored by the University of Georgia and local county governments. All Extension Service offices have staff members who specialize in agriculture/horticulture, home environment, and youth development. Offices offer free educational pamphlets and advice, and many publications are available for download at the Extension Service Web site.

### The Garden Club of Georgia
(706) 227-5369
http://www.uga.edu/gardenclub
A statewide organization of gardeners dedicated to inspiring beautification, conservation, and gardening education in Georgia.

# GARDENING RESOURCES IN GEORGIA

**Georgia Environmental Monitoring Network**
http://www.georgiaweather.net
This unit of The University of Georgia maintains dozens of weather monitoring sites scattered throughout the state. Data from each site is uploaded daily to the Internet, where visitors can track historical and current rainfall amounts, soil temperatures, air temperatures, and other climatic conditions. Very handy for settling arguments about how "bad" the weather was in the past.

**Georgia Forestry Commission**
(800) GA-TREES
http://www.gfc.state.gas.us
Educates citizens about the importance of Georgia timber and forests. Supplies tree seedlings in bulk at low cost to citizens.

**Georgia Green Industry Association**
(888) GET-GGIA
http://www.ggia.org
A statewide organization of landscape and nursery companies that promotes professionalism in the industry. Sponsor of the Georgia Certified Landscape Professional and Georgia Certified Nursery Professional programs.

**Georgia Native Plant Society**
(770) 343-6000
http://www.gnps.org
An organization of gardeners interested in learning more about the care and culture of native plants. Monthly meetings are free and open to the public.

**Georgia Organics**
(770) 621-GOGA
http://www.georgiaorganics.org
An organization of gardeners interested in learning more about gardening organically.

**Georgia Perennial Plant Association**
(404) 237-8071
http://www.georgiaperennial.org
An organization of gardeners interested in learning more about the care and culture of perennial plants. Monthly meetings are free and open to the public.

**Metro Atlanta Landscape & Turf Association**
(770) 732-9832
http://www.malta-inc.org
An organization of Atlanta landscape companies and associated professionals. Publishes "The Landscape Source," a free booklet listing members and their areas of expertise.

# BIBLIOGRAPHY

Ajilvsgi, Geyata. *Butterfly Gardening for the South.* Dallas, TX: Taylor Publishing, 1991.

Armitage, Allan. *Armitage's Garden Annuals: A Color Encyclopedia.* Portland, OR: Timber Press, 2004.

Armitage, Allan. *Armitage's Garden Perennials.* Portland, OR: Timber Press, 2000.

Armitage, Allan. *Herbaceous Perennial Plants.* 2nd edition. Champaign, IL: Stipes Publishing, 1997.

Armitage, Allan, and Asha Kays, and Chris Johnson. *Armitage's Manual of Annuals, Biennials, and Half-Hardy Perennials.* Portland, OR: Timber Press, 2001.

Bender, Steve, and Felder Rushing. *Passalong Plants.* Chapel Hill, NC: The University of North Carolina Press, 1993.

Bender, Steve, et al. *The Southern Living Garden Book.* Birmingham, AL: Oxmoor House, 1998.

Brown, Claude, and L. Katherine Kirkman. *Trees of Georgia and Adjacent States.* Portland, OR: Timber Press, 2000.

Cutler, Karan, ed. *Starting from Seed.* Brooklyn, NY: Brooklyn Botanic Garden, 1998.

Greenlee, John. *The Encyclopedia of Ornamental Grasses.* Emmaus, PA: Rodale Press, 1992.

Dirr, Michael. *Dirr's Hardy Trees and Shrubs.* Portland, OR: Timber Press, 1997.

Dirr, Michael. *Manual of Woody Landscape Plants.* Champaign, IL: Stipes Publishing, 1998.

Gardiner, J.M. *Magnolias.* Chester, CT: Globe Pequot Press, 1989.

Gates, Galen, et al. *Shrubs and Vines.* New York: Pantheon Books, 1994.

Halfacre, R. Gordon, and Anne R. Shawcroft. *Landscape Plants of the Southeast.* Raleigh, NC: Sparks Press, 1979.

Harper, Pamela. *Time-Tested Plants.* Portland, OR: Timber Press, 2000.

Hastings, Don. *Gardening in the South: Flowers, Vines, and Houseplants.* Dallas, TX: Taylor Publishing, 1991.

Hastings, Don. *Gardening in the South: Trees, Shrubs and Lawns.* Dallas, TX: Taylor Publishing, 1987.

Hastings, Don. *Gardening in the South with Don Hastings: Vegetables and Fruits.* Dallas, TX: Taylor Publishing, 1987.

Heath, Brent, and Becky Heath. *Daffodils for American Gardens.* Washington, DC: Elliott & Clark Publishing, 1995.

Hipps, Carol Bishop. *In a Southern Garden.* New York, NY: Macmillan Publishing, 1995.

Howells, John. *A Guide to Clematis.* London: Bookmark Ltd., 1990.

Jones, Samuel, and Leonard Foote. *Gardening with Native Wild Flowers.* Portland, OR: Timber Press, 1997.

Lawrence, Elizabeth. *A Southern Garden.* Chapel Hill, NC: University of North Carolina Press, 1991.

Lawson-Hall, Toni, and Brian Rothera. *Hydrangeas.* Portland, OR: Timber Press, 1995.

Loewer, Peter. *Tough Plants for Tough Places.* Emmaus, PA: Rodale Press, 1996.

McLaurin, Wayne, and Sylvia McLaurin. *Herbs for Southern Gardens.* Available from the University of Georgia Agricultural Business office (706-542-8999), 1999.

Mickel, John. *Ferns for American Gardens.* New York, NY: Macmillan Publishing, 1997.

Murphy, Tim, et al. *Weeds of Southern Turfgrasses.* Available from the University of Georgia Agricultural Business office (706-542-8999), 1993.

Ogden, Scott. *Garden Bulbs for the South.* Dallas, TX: Taylor Publishing, 1994.

Olkowski, William, and Sheila Daar. *Common Sense Pest Control.* Newtown, CT: Taunton Press, 1991.

Overy, Angela. *Sex in Your Garden.* Golden, CO: Fulcrum Publishing, 1997..

Still, Steven. *Manual of Herbaceous Ornamental Plants.* Champaign, IL: Stipes Publishing, 1993.

Swenson, Allan. *Fruit Trees for the Home Gardener.* New York, NY: Lyons & Burford, 1994.

Tekulsky, Matthew. *The Butterfly Garden.* Boston, MA: Harvard Common Press, 1986.

Tripp, Kim, and J.C. Raulston. *The Year in Trees.* Portland, OR: Timber Press, 1995.

Vertrees, J.D. *Japanese Maples.* Portland, OR: Timber Press, 2001.

Wasowski, Sally. *Gardening with Native Plants of the South.* Dallas, TX: Taylor Publishing, 1994.

Welch, William C. *Antique Roses for the South.* Dallas, TX: Taylor Publishing, 1990.

Welch, William C., and Greg Grant. *The Southern Heirloom Garden.* Dallas, TX: Taylor Publishing, 1995.

Wilson, Jim, *Bulletproof Flowers for the South.* Dallas, TX: Taylor Publishing, 1999.

# BOTANICAL NAME INDEX

# BOTANICAL NAME INDEX

# BOTANICAL NAME INDEX

# COMMON NAME INDEX

# COMMON NAME INDEX

# COMMON NAME INDEX

# COMMON NAME INDEX

# COMMON NAME INDEX

# COMMON NAME INDEX

# COMMON NAME INDEX

# MEET ERICA GLASENER & WALTER REEVES

**Erica Glasener** is a horticulturist and garden designer living in Atlanta, Georgia. She is the award-winning host of "A Gardener's Diary" on HGTV. Glasener is the former director of education for the Scott Arboretum of Swarthmore College in Swarthmore, Pennsylvania. In addition, she writes a bi-weekly column on garden design for *The Atlanta Journal-Constitution.* She has written numerous articles for *The New York Times, The Farmer's Almanac, Fine Gardening*, and *Atlantic* magazine. Erica is the co-author of the *Georgia Gardener's Guide* (original and revised editions) and *My Georgia Garden: A Gardener's Journal,* both published by Cool Springs Press.

**Walter Reeves** is a former DeKalb County Extension Agent living in Atlanta, Georgia. Best known to Atlanta-area listeners as the radio host of "The Lawn and Garden Show with Walter Reeves," he also reaches gardeners through his weekly columns in *The Atlanta Journal-Constitution.* Walter helps gardeners throughout the state as the host of "Gardening in Georgia," shown weekly on Georgia Public Television. When answering gardeners' questions, the Fayette County native often draws upon his years of gardening experience acquired while growing up on his family's farm. Walter is the co-author of the *Georgia Gardener's Guide* (original and revised editions) and *My Georgia Garden: A Gardener's Journal,* both published by Cool Springs Press.

# ENJOY THESE OTHER HELPFUL BOOKS FROM COOL SPRINGS PRESS

Cool Springs Press is devoted to state and regional gardening and offers
a selection of books to help you enjoy gardening wherever you live.
Choose Cool Springs Press books with confidence.

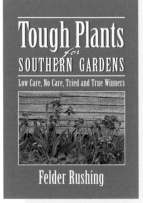

Tough Plants for Southern Gardens
ISBN# 1-59186-002-4 • $24.99

The Landscape Design Answer Book
ISBN# 1-59186-250-7 • $29.99

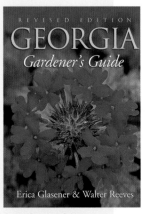

Georgia Gardener's Guide:
Revised Edition
ISBN# 1-59186-044-X • $24.99

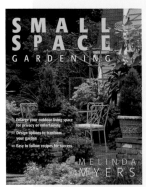

Can't Miss Small Space Gardening
ISBN# 1-59186-185-3 • $18.99

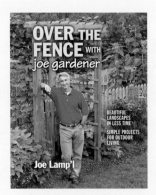

Over the Fence with Joe Gardener
ISBN# 1-59186-262-0 • $24.99

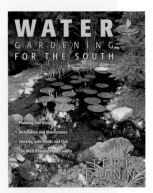

Can't Miss Water Gardening
for the South
ISBN# 1-59186-150-0 • $18.99

COOL SPRINGS PRESS

www.coolspringspress.net

See your garden center, bookseller, or home improvement center for these
Cool Springs Press titles. Also, for more great titles from Cool Springs Press
be sure to visit www.coolspringspress.net.